Violence, Spectacle, and the American Action Movie

Revised and Expanded Edition

Action Speaks Louder

Wesleyan Film

A series from Wesleyan University Press

Edited by Jeanine Basinger

The new WESLEYAN FILM series takes a back-to-basics approach to the art of cinema. Books in the series will deal with the formal, the historical, and the cultural—putting a premium on visual analysis, close readings, and an understanding of the history of Hollywood and international cinema, both artistically and industrially. The volumes will be rigorous, critical, and accessible both to academics and to lay readers with a serious interest in film.

Series editor Jeanine Basinger, Corwin-Fuller Professor of Film Studies at Wesleyan University and Founder/Curator of the Wesleyan Cinema Archives, is the author of such landmark books as *The World War II Combat Film: Anatomy of a Genre*, *A Woman's View: How Hollywood Spoke to Women, 1930–1960*, and *Silent Stars*.

Anthony Mann
by Jeanine Basinger

Physical Evidence
Selected Film Criticism
by Kent Jones

Action Speaks Louder
Violence, Spectacle, and the American Action Movie
Revised and Expanded Edition
by Eric Lichtenfeld

Eric Lichtenfeld

Action Speaks Louder

WESLEYAN UNIVERSITY PRESS Middletown, Connecticut

Published by Wesleyan University Press,
Middletown, CT 06459

© 2007 by Eric Lichtenfeld

All rights reserved

Printed in United States of America

5 4 3 2 1

Originally *Action Speaks Louder: Violence, Spectacle, and the American Action Movie* by Eric Lichtenfeld, published by Praeger, an imprint of Greenwood Press. Copyright © 2004 by Eric Lichtenfeld. Published in an edited paperback by arrangement with Greenwood Publishing Group, Inc., Westport, CT. All rights reserved.

Library of Congress Cataloging-in-Publication Data
Lichtenfeld, Eric.
Action speaks louder : violence, spectacle, and the American action movie / Eric Lichtenfeld.
    p.   cm. — (Wesleyan film)
Includes bibliographical references and index.
ISBN-13: 978–0–8195–6801–4 (pbk. : alk. paper)
ISBN-10: 0–8195–6801–5 (pbk. : alk. paper)
1. Adventure films—United States—History and criticism.
I. Title.
PN1995.9.A3L48 2007
791.43'655—dc22   2006038725

FOR MY NEPHEW JULIAN

who one day, when he grows up,

may find this useful.

AND FOR MARLOWE

who has added the most by far.

"America is vain about its violence."

—Stanley Kauffmann, film critic

"Ooooh, guns, guns, *guns.*"

—Clarence Boddicker (Kurtwood Smith)

  in *Robocop* (1987)

Contents

Foreword

BY RICHARD SLOTKIN

Olin Professor of American Studies, Wesleyan University

The study of film genres is critical to our understanding of the way the movie and television industries work and to our comprehension of our own national culture.

Since the consolidation of the movie business in the studio system of the 1930s, one of the hallmarks of the industry had been the development of distinct families or genres of similarly structured films. Initially, genres developed by hit or miss, as studios sought to capitalize on successful films by copying their plots, settings, visual styles, and characterizations. From 1927 through the 1950s, the studios developed what, in critical retrospect, looks like a canon of standard genres: the Western, the musical, the gangster or crime film, the woman's picture, the horror film, and so on. Film historians and critics took note of the highly conventionalized forms these genres had developed over thirty-odd years and produced exacting analyses of their formal qualities: narrative structure, editing rhythms, pacing, point-of-view, iconography, and the like.

But formal analysis of this kind suggested that film genres were like the idealized tropes of comedy, tragedy, romance, and chronicle that classically defined the different forms of literature. In fact, the formal structures of the original canon of film genres were not developments of any pre-existing Aristotelian formula; they were improvisations governed by the resources and economics of studio production, by the pressures of the historical moment, and by the complex relationship between the producers and their audiences. There was more to that relationship than is expressed in market demographics. In the twentieth century, movies became the most important of the mass media for the creation of public myths: the body of stories and symbols—part fiction, part history—through which Americans defined themselves as a national culture.

Film genres were not only categories of production; they also roughly corresponded to key strains or elements in public myth. Myth is a way of thinking about and understanding the historical moment in which one lives—not an analytic but a symbolic or poetic way of thinking, in which the telling of a story or fable provides an effective way of looking at things. Thus the studio-era

Western addressed the beliefs and concerns arising from the nation's obsession with growth, progress, the conquest of nature, and the necessity of violence. The 1930s gangster film spoke to the dark side of the success ethic and to the Depression-era mood of disillusionment and cynicism. The combat film allowed the public to imaginatively enter and explore the meaning of the World War that had disrupted and transformed their lives. The horror movie addressed a more fundamental set of fears and anxieties. Although each genre was responsive to the concerns of the era that produced it, as those concerns changed the genres were also adapted. And these modifications of genre corresponded to changes in public myth. Thus the post-1960 Western and combat film reflected national self-doubt in a generally jaundiced view of "progress" and warfare, while horror movies found more terror in the children of "normal" families (The Omen, Rosemary's Baby, It Lives), the countryside (The Texas Chainsaw Massacre), and good neighborhoods (The Exorcist, Halloween) than in Dr. Frankenstein's lab or Dracula's castle. So to understand the ways in which film genres develop and change is to open a window on the forces that shape America's national ideology—our way of looking at the world.

Eric Lichtenfeld's Action Speaks Louder does just that, by combining careful historical analysis with a brilliant and well-informed analysis of individual films. He first demonstrates that the process of genre-improvisation did not come to an end with the studio system. The "New Hollywood" of the 1970s would develop its own distinctive variations on the canonical genres, and it would also go beyond the canon to develop its own distinctive categories of film production. Among these there is no genre more significant than the "action film." It is, first of all, an extrapolation of the most essential narrative elements from all of the pre-existing action-oriented genres: Western, combat film, horror movie, crime film, science fiction. This study of its development therefore sheds light on the processes by which filmmakers draw on and transform the language and properties of their artistic tradition. By looking into the production process itself—interviewing filmmakers and examining production records—Lichtenfeld shows just how this improvisation played out historically. The close analysis of individual films demonstrates that this process of adaptation and innovation did, in the end, produce a new genre, with its own distinct conventions of setting, narrative, and cinematic form.

He also looks beyond the industry to consider the ways in which the action film draws on American national mythology, in particular the "vigilante" tradition that is so deeply woven into our national culture. He shows how that tradition is taken up by the action film; and he also shows how the action film aggrandizes that tradition, reinforces it, and thus helps to shape the culture that it also reflects. This makes *Action Speaks Louder* a valuable contribution not only to the study of film and culture, but also to our self-knowledge as Americans.

Acknowledgments

It is only fitting that these acknowledgments begin with Eric Levy, an excellent editor and friend, who put out fires when necessary and started ones when needed and, most remarkably of all, signed up for a second go-around. His efforts to turn concept into written word and written word into printed page were heroic. Maybe not shooting-mad-snipers heroic, but heroic.

Next, I would like to thank professors Jeanine Basinger and Richard Slotkin, who remain my models and my standards—as film scholars and moviegoers both. Thanks also to Wesleyan University's Lisa Dombrowski for her enthusiasm and Scott Higgins, an early adopter, sounding board, and compatriot.

Thanks also to friends and colleagues from UCLA, including Nick Browne, Brian Clark, Layla Danley, Jennifer Holt, Lisa Kernan, and Jordan Lucoff, and to the staff of the Academy of Motion Picture Arts and Sciences' Margaret Herrick Library for answering my many research questions (or more accurately, for answering my one or two research questions many times).

I am especially grateful to those film industry professionals, some of whom I am proud to say are friends, who generously gave me their time, insight, interviews, contacts, resources, meals, drinks, and in two cases, houses. For this and more I'd like to thank Oren Aviv, Larry Baldauf, Terry Curtin, Steven E. de Souza, Jack DeGovia, Richard Francis-Bruce, Robert Fried, Mark Goldblatt, Bob Israel, Joanna Johnston, Gloria La Mont, Graham Leggat, Lynda Miller, Craig Murray and his associates, John Muto, Basil Poledouris, Nick Redman, Sandy Reisenbach, John Rogers, Don Rosenberg, William Sandell, Peter Schindler, Mark Trugman, and Mary Vogt.

Then there are the civilians: Jeremy Arnold, Aimee Barille, Peter Bracke, Jennie Edes-Pierotti, Daniel Goldwasser, Eric Greene, Ian Haufrect, Jason Lee, Ross D. Levi, Tonia Lopez-Fresquet, Louie and Liesbeth Maggiotto, Amanda Marks, Pam Postrel, Owen Renfroe, Matt and Stacey Wein, and Amanda Winn-Lee. All are good friends who have shown much support and spent many more hours discussing these films with me than they were obligated to (though less time actually watching them than they promised they would). I would also like to thank Meghan McCarron for her research assistance. In particular, I would like to single out Jeremy Bernstein and Rafael Ruiz, who made significant contributions to the completion of this book, and who braved many double- and even triple-features. In the words of John Milius, they will never have to prove their courage in any other way.

My family has provided much support. Thanks to my father, Edwin, who raised me on many of the movies studied here; my mother, Barbara, who did not; my brother, Marc; and sister-in-law, Holly.

And lastly, but chiefly, there is Marlowe, my wife. Acknowledgment, gratitude, thanks—none of these do justice to what she is owed. Completing this edition would not have been possible without her love, her enthusiasm, her help, and frankly, her indulgence.

As ever, I also wish to acknowledge the memories of my grandparents, Frances and Julius Lichtenfeld and William Stern. And Hilda Stern, who lived to see much, including the first edition of this book. I am thankful for what she saw and for what she instilled, and while my choice of subject may not have been her cup of tea, I hope what follows does justice to how she valued the life of the mind.

Action Speaks Louder

Introduction
A Little Violence
Never Hurt Anyone

I really hate to see people killing each other.
—John Woo

When bounty hunter Nick Randall (Rutger Hauer) leads Islamic terrorist Malak al Rahim (Gene Simmons) out of a chemical factory with a grenade in his mouth, parades him past an army of police officers, and pulls the pin, he brings to a violent close the violent business of the 1987 film *Wanted Dead or Alive*. Though a grisly climax, it is also strangely comforting. By 1987, such violence, character types, and even locations would have long been familiar to spectators of the action movie, a genre central to modern American cinema.

The action genre, like any other, is a concoction of elements—some a matter of plot, some mythological, some purely cinematic—that creates for the audience a sense of ritual and a host of expectations. To that end, *Wanted Dead or Alive* is nearly a catalogue of the action genre's raw materials, including a loner hero; his battles for justice, if not the law; his slain best friend (also co-combatant); a murdered love interest; vengeance; a past he is trying to live down; a burden he must live *with*, the burden of being "the best;" a governmental bureaucracy willing to betray and sacrifice him; industrial settings; brutal beatings; visually exotic killings; an array of impressive weapons; explosions; one-liners; chases and crashes; and a depraved enemy. So, when al Rahim caresses a little girl's face before blowing up the movie theater she and her idealized nuclear family have just entered (a theater playing *Rambo: First Blood Part II*, as it happens), or when Randall's CIA contact tells him, "This is a flashpoint situation, Nick. We need the best," most viewers recognize these moments—on some level—as components of a well-known formula.

Such conventions and others are featured in a number of films from 1987 alone, a roster that also includes (but is not limited to) *Assassination*, *Beverly Hills Cop II*, *Cold Steel*, *Death Before Dishonor*, *Death Wish 4: The Crackdown*, *Lethal Weapon*, *Predator*, *Robocop*, *Steel Dawn*, *Steele Justice*, and *The Running Man*. While all of these films are generic in some way, several actually transcend their genre and represent a lasting influence on the action film, a lasting memory in our popu-

Facing page: Hollywood Theatrics: *Heroism, violence, weaponry, spectatorship, self-parody, and Arnold Schwarzenegger—the stuff of John McTiernan's* Last Action Hero *(1993). (From the author's collection.)*

lar culture, or both. Most, however, are more forgettable. But even these ephemera—*Wanted Dead or Alive* included—serve a purpose. Lacking the imagination that might differentiate these movies from their generic mold, these films offer snapshots of the connective tissue that has given the genre its form, its power. They reveal the fundamentals. They stand for the whole.

And yet, for all of the plot devices and visual cues that place *Wanted Dead or Alive* within the fold of the action genre, some critics detected the influence of other genres at work. "Randall's interrogation techniques are right out of a Mike Hammer textbook," the *Los Angeles Times* remarked, also noting how the filmmakers give Los Angeles "a moody, '80s *film-noir* look. They paint the town in cold, gray brush strokes . . . while shooting scenes either through windows or with a telephoto lens, as if to emphasize the voyeuristic quality of the chase."[1] Similarly, *The Hollywood Reporter* noted how *Wanted Dead or Alive* braids "a Romantic attitude of the Old West with a modern-day terrorist storyline."[2] More pointedly, the film implies—and its publicity outright states—that Nick Randall is a direct descendant of Josh Randall, the bounty hunter played by Steve McQueen in the 1958–1961 Western television series, *Wanted: Dead or Alive.*[3]

It is no accident that facets of these earlier genres are embedded in *Wanted Dead or Alive.* America has had a longstanding infatuation with its warriors, and as the action genre began taking form in the early 1970s, it liberated the warrior heroes of American cinema from the foreign battlefields of combat films and the long-gone frontier of the Western. While no longer the sheriffs of the Old West, these characters continued to embody its ethos as the new sheriffs of New York, Los Angeles, and other modern cities—locales that were more typically the domain of such genres as *film noir*, the police procedural, and the gangster film.

Combining conventions of the Western with conventions of *film noir*, the developing action film reconciled two genres that might otherwise seem starkly opposed. As the most fundamentally American movie genre, the Western had been a force in the film industry for nearly as long as there had been one. The genre is set in a distant time and place obsessed with progress, is populated by vigorous heroes straddling the border between the law and the lawless, and stereotypically (which is not to say always) pits these heroes against Indians whose very blood defines them as *other*. All of this constitutes the rich mythic stuff one senses beneath the white hats, black hats, Indian headdresses, and horseshoes. *Film noir*, on the other hand, is more recent, a phenomenon of World War II America. *Noir* stories tend to be contemporary, though use flashbacks and other devices to look to the past. In *noir*, cities are both grim and alluring, sexuality can be abnormal at best and lethal at worst, and the male antihero is less active than acted upon—especially when on the receiving end of a sadistic beating. He is also unstable, as is noir's border between past and present (after all, no other genre is as closely identified with the flashback and the voiceover). But noir's most recognizable convention may be its expressionistic visuals: dramatic camera angles, atmospheric lighting, shadows that pool, shadows that slash, and smoke.

The Western and film noir are also dissimilar as industrial forces. While both are derived from American literary traditions (the Western can be traced back to the writings of James Fenimore Cooper and others, while noir owes a debt to the crime fiction of Raymond Chandler, Dashell Hammett, and their ilk), "Western" was always a classification used by the film studios themselves in the allocation of resources, in production, and in marketing. Film noir, on the other hand, is a designation invented by critics—and not even American ones at that. The French, importing these films in a glut after the easing of World War II trade restrictions, applied the term to a body of movies long after the individual films were made and shown on American screens. Only after French critics viewed the films en masse and saw their stylistic consistencies was the category "film noir" invented and then adopted by Americans. But prior to this, in the 1940s, filmmakers were not making "film noir." They were making "crime pictures," "thrillers," etc.—often as the cheap bottom halves of double-bills. Moreover, while the critical community widely agrees on the Western's status as a fundamentally American genre, the role it has played in American film history, and how it has evolved, the same community is deeply divided over whether film noir is a "genre" at all. Some scholars insist it is a "cycle," and others a "style," while author James Naremore (More Than Night: Film Noir and its Contexts) claims it is "an idea."

The Western and film noir may indeed be the positive/negative images of each other, but the action film reconciles them, as we will see. This makes for a potent generic mix, one that is completed with a dash of one other genre's influence: that of the police procedural. It is ironic though, that the action film draws only from the police procedural's outermost trappings, as this last genre would seem to be the action film's most immediate progenitor. The genre does just what its name suggests: offer viewers a look into the procedures of criminal investigation. For that reason, police procedurals are not limited to stories about the police; rather, stories about all law enforcement agencies may be counted, so long as their narratives detail the investigative process.

Like the Western, the police procedural had been popular as far back as the silent era and also on television. The genre enjoyed a heyday that roughly spanned the 1930s through the 1950s. Thriving during the years of the Motion Picture Production Code, police procedurals usually depicted law enforcement positively. Also because of the Production Code, the genre became detached from its more violent roots seen by audiences during the silent years and in the sound era prior to the Code. In these earlier incarnations, many police procedurals displayed a flair for vigilantism that predicted the violent mavericks of law enforcement movies in the late 1960s and 1970s. What distinguishes the police procedural from its successor, the action film, is that while the former is concerned with the investigation of crime, the latter makes only token use of the investigative process. In the action film, investigative procedure is second to the genre's real concern: not the investigation of crime, but rather the obliteration of criminals.

During this era, filmmakers were making the "punishment" part of their crime-and-punishment tales increasingly violent and also hitching their stories to a Western tradition, peppering them with elements of *film noir*, and codifying a new genre—knowingly or not. Of course, the heightened violence of these movies had to hang on *some* kind of frame. The mixture of Western, *film noir*, and police procedural would prove to be an effective choice: *noir's* urban, hard-bitten milieu was an appropriately cynical, disaffected stage for the pulverizing of human life, while the Western's mythos would legitimize violence as a righteous force to tame the 1970s' social wild.

This might not have occurred had it not been for a turning point in yet one more genre: the gangster movie. Amid the genre revisionism that would be a hallmark of the emerging "New Hollywood," Arthur Penn's 1967 milestone *Bonnie and Clyde* astonished audiences, critics, and the very industry that sired it, with graphic violence. Staccato editing, slow motion, overbearing sound, and gore all mesmerized, thrilled, repelled, and numbed viewers whose movies had previously shown only softer-edged brutality, but whose televisions were now showing images of the Vietnam dead.

The violence of *Bonnie and Clyde* helped end the Production Code and usher in the less restrictive Motion Picture Association of America. It also created opportunities for other filmmakers to use violence as spectacle. With *Bonnie and Clyde* as a precedent, but without its social and cinematic critiques, the new violence would be deployed more to pleasure audiences than to jar them. At first, this would be embodied not in the flamboyant cinematic technique like that of *Bonnie and Clyde*, but in more straightforward depictions of increasingly brutal acts. The importance of violence to these films would also be evident in their structure and pacing, with show-stopping sequences occurring at well-regulated intervals (in the 1980s, this would often be touted as action producer Joel Silver's "whammy theory" of featuring one major sequence per reel).[4] The action genre would pick up Penn's mantle later, especially with the hyper-stylization of such superstar directors as Michael Bay and Hong Kong émigré John Woo.

The shift in standards caused by the "New Hollywood" marks a point before which the action film as we have come to know it could not have existed. This is partly why I do not consider Westerns, swashbucklers, and other previous genres to belong to the action genre, despite the fact that they contain much action and address their audiences' appetite for physical, visceral entertainment. Obviously, the foundation for defining the action movie must be that the films showcase scenes of physical action, be they fistfights, gunfights, swordfights, fights against nature, or other derring-do. Some might go so far as to claim this to be the only criterion. Such a claim would have a certain intuitiveness to it. The problem is that this would encompass such an enormous number of disparate films that the designation "action film"—already a broad term—would become meaningless.

Though my definition of the action genre may be somewhat narrow, it is not singular. Derived from the Western, *film noir*, and the police procedural (with special guest appearances made by the disaster film and others), the action movie's evolution is actually quite analogous to that of the horror film. There is no doubt that Universal's gothic productions of the 1930s belong to this category, nor that the teen slasher films of the 1980s do either, but neither does anything suggest that these two models are more to each other than distant cousins. So it is with the action film—to a certain extent. The genre comprises different trends. As a synthesis of other genres, it has certain and few tropes one can point to as being consistent throughout its evolution. This book is an attempt to explore that synthesis, the narrative and stylistic conventions it has yielded, and the manner in which they have evolved. Thus, I have structured this study according to the trends into which the genre subdivides rather than try to chart a strict chronological history. Within that framework, I have tried to maintain the chronology as much as possible, as evolution does, of course, tend to be linear.

Dividing the genre into trends has enabled me to articulate many of its facets more clearly but also raised complications of its own. Not all of the films fit comfortably into just one category or chapter. In some cases where a film seems to belong to more than one trend, I locate it in one or the other in the interest of clarity. In other cases, I split my analysis of a movie across two chapters. For example, though I discuss *Rambo: First Blood Part II* in the context of the POW/MIA action film, the film is not exactly incidental to Sylvester Stallone's star persona or to any respectable discussion of it. At first, these decisions sometimes seemed arbitrary. But even though the genre comprises individual trends and periods, the difficulty of subdividing the action film's trajectory into manageable chapters ultimately underscores how cohesive a body of films this genre represents. So does the fact that in terms of both content and chronology, many of these trends overlap. This was an especially rewarding discovery for an author making one of his field's first attempts to verify, define, and explore a genre most critics simply take for granted and therefore approach too imprecisely.

Deciding what films qualified as belonging to the genre was sometimes easier than deciding which of these films I would study in detail in this book. Structuring each chapter as a succession of case studies has enabled me to probe each film more thoroughly but has also forced me to be more selective about which titles I would address. Some readers may ask, why is there not more on *The Exterminator?* What about *Action Jackson?* Why not discussions of John Carpenter's dystopian coasts (*Escape from New York*, *Escape from L.A.*) or Jean-Claude Van Damme's post-1990 *oeuvre?* Likewise, some readers may be distressed that there is little mention of James Bond. To that end, Bond could be (and has been) the subject of several books unto himself, and while the American action film's increasing use of spectacle and stunt work certainly evokes the Bond films, the trajectory I chart for the action genre's evolution holds up without them. The larger point is that in writing a genre study, one must often balance breadth and depth. If I was going to err, I wanted at least to err on the side of depth.

Several considerations have guided my choices: a film's significance in the history of the genre; how well the film represents a trend or set of conventions irrespective of its cinematic merits; and, only sometimes, the film's overall quality. The films chosen for that last criterion are few. Because genre filmmaking is primarily an exercise in repetition and mass-market appeal, it does not tend toward excellence. Such is the irony of heroic genres: they detail the adventures of heroes who are unique and exceptional in tales that are often, in a word, not. This does not mean the action genre contains no masterpieces. It means only that a film has not necessarily met a certain standard of quality just because six, eight, or ten pages are devoted to it. But whether good or bad, each of these films has something to reveal.

How I discuss the films does not represent any one method of approach. I do not restrict myself to say, formal analysis, or production history, or a cultural studies framework. Instead, I often use one approach to elaborate upon what I draw out with another. There may be scholars who wish I had taken a more singular approach. This might have made for a narrower book, but it would not have made for a richer one. Action filmmaking technique has received too little attention, and so I look at art direction, editing, cinematography, and sound for how they embody or further the myths on which the films are founded and also as aesthetic tools in their own right. This is a book about film, after all, and so it must engage the properties that are unique to the medium. Still, to study the style of the genre without regard for the culture with which it resonates would have too little purpose, and so I also consider some of America's cultural myths and the circumstances that surround them. I will admit here that I tend to downplay issues of race and, with a few exceptions, gender—not because the issues are unimportant, but because inasmuch as critics and scholars have considered the action film, it has been mainly in these terms.

I also integrate studio marketing, publicity, and advertising materials into my discussions of the films. To be sure, they provide a certain amount of flair; but more than that, they offer useful industrial and production histories. After all, a study that is all text and no context would not befit a genre that goes to such technical extremes as the action film does. Beyond that, however, implicit in these images and messages is the studios' or filmmakers' assumptions about what will attract us. Genre scholars such as Thomas Schatz, Rick Altman, and Steve Neale all grapple with the question of whether or not audience responsiveness to formulas represents a dialogue between the public and the film industry; I agree with Neale, who maintains that genre conventions solidify out of audience expectations, and that extra film material—trailers, posters, news features generated by film industry publicists, and the like—determines these expectations as much as anything on screen does.

In addition, I supplement my analysis with the perspectives of critics and, where appropriate, scholars. It is telling that my research yielded far more scholarship on the earlier films than on the recent ones. Compared to the Western and *noir*, little work has been done on the action genre *as* a genre, despite its prominence, despite its responsibility for being the face of the film industry Hollywood most presents to the world and for being the form that necessitates so many of the advances in film technology. Much of this material, including information on the films' production histories, I found in the production files at the Margaret Herrick Library of the Academy of Motion Picture Arts and Sciences (AMPAS).

For more than three decades, the American action film has represented potent ideas of what America is—ideas that are founded on even more fundamental myths of what America has been. My book is an attempt to articulate these ideas and these myths, the filmmaking techniques that express them, and the dialogue in which studios and filmmakers have engaged the public not only through the films, but also through advertising and publicity. It is also an attempt to engage that part of our culture that uses the movies as more than entertainment to go see, but as a place for America to look for itself.

"Teach him a lesson, Billy, but without really hurting him."
"How?"
—Jean (Delores Taylor) and Billy Jack (Tom Laughlin), in
  Billy Jack *(1971)*

Bonnie and Clyde is iconic of the output of the "New Hollywood." During this era, spanning the late 1960s and 1970s, Hollywood's young filmmakers revisited, scrutinized, and damned previously popular genres for their artifice. At least four films from 1971 drew upon previously popular film genres, often to throw their conventions into confusion and, in the process, give form to the modern urban action film. The first three set the stage for the fourth and are discussed here: Billy Jack, Shaft, and The French Connection. Billy Jack and The French Connection offer the boldest challenges to their genres: the Western and the police procedural; Shaft on the other hand uses the familiar settings and conventions of the hardboiled detective film and film noir to mythologize a new type, the black hero.

Prior to the release of Dirty Harry later that year, Billy Jack helped found a cycle of vigilante films that is one marker of 1970s American cinema. Including the blockbuster Walking Tall (1973) and its sequels (1975, 1977), this cycle represents much of the decade's newly forming action genre.[1] Set in the present but against Western-esque landscapes, Billy Jack strands itself somewhere between a Western and the modern action film. Billy Jack (classified as a "Melodrama" by Variety and a "Western melodrama" by Box Office) engages Western conventions by subverting them—or put more accurately, inverting them.[2]

As we are told by the voiceover narration that opens the film, the titular hero of Billy Jack is "a half-breed [and] a war hero who hated the war." Half Indian, half Caucasian, Billy (Tom Laughlin) protects the children of the Freedom School, a progressive school where students live as an artistic, drug-free community. The school's newest resident is Barbara (Julie Webb), a pregnant runaway and daughter of the town's vicious deputy (Kenneth Tobey). The deputy, aided by the influential and equally sinister Mr. Posner (Bert Freed) and his son Bernard (David Roya), rallies the town to force Barbara's return. Billy defends the students and Jean (Delores Taylor), the school's headmistress whom Billy loves. Matters escalate, and in the wake of Jean's rape and his favorite student's murder, Billy takes his vengeance. After killing Bernard, Billy ends his campaign in an old church, besieged by law enforcement. Ultimately, Billy surrenders, allowing the police to lead him away, past the students who stand with him in solidarity.

Billy Jack engages the most elemental and mythological tropes of the Western. As in that archetypal American genre, Billy Jack pits a representative of society against savages, expresses concern for the sexual purity of its women, and then makes these innocents the center of a scenario in which the hero must rescue them from their uncivilized captors. But Billy Jack is not merely trotting out well-worn plot devices; rather, the film reconfigures these elements and, in the process, forces the audience to reconsider them. In a classic Western such as, say, Stagecoach, white men—epitomized by John Wayne—defend themselves, their women, and their microcosm of society (in this example, the stagecoach itself) against the racially other Indians. In so doing, such characters tame this wilderness—sometimes figuratively, sometimes literally—and make it suitable for the civilization that will flourish along the trail the characters have blazed. Billy Jack preserves the basic pattern, but swaps the races of its participants. Here, the savage is white society, while the savior is Indian. More precisely, he is a half-breed, straddling two natures: warrior and pacifist.

The fact that Billy is neither racially nor ideologically "pure" intensifies the film's rendering of yet another Western convention: the hero's familiarity with the other. In Gunfighter Nation: The Myth of the Frontier in Twentieth Century America, historian Richard Slotkin calls this archetype "The Man Who Knows Indians," and describes him as an American who "must cross the border into 'Indian country' and experience a 'regression' to a more primitive and natural condition of life, so that the false values of the 'metropolis' can be purged and a new, purified social contract enacted."[3] To kill the "savage" Indian, the hero must understand the Indian and tap into a savagery all his own. Therefore, while this understanding enables him to dispatch his enemy, it also prevents him from ever fully joining the society he protects from his enemy.

As another of the Western's fundamental tropes, this character type is a prime target for inversion by the filmmakers of the New Hollywood. If The Searchers's Ethan Edwards (John Wayne), one of the genre's greatest archetypes, is "The Man Who Knows Indians," then Billy Jack's title character is "The Indian Who Knows White Men." In Billy Jack, Jean and the multiracial, multiethnic students are associated with pacifism, while white men and the town's traditional institutions are linked to unbridled violence. Billy Jack, selectively using firearms and his proficiency in hapkido, a martial art developed by Buddhist priests whose religious beliefs forbade them from wearing arms, walks the path between them.[4]

The film also manipulates the Western's concern with sexual purity, a facet of the genre's conflict between the civilized and the savage. In many classic Westerns (both on film and in literature) and in the mythology of the frontier itself, racial violence is motivated by sexual anxiety, but it is the violence that the storytellers often foreground, most likely because violence has traditionally been less censored than sex. In Billy Jack, however, the filmmakers emphasize sexuality by splitting white sexual anxiety into two spheres: in the first, Laughlin and his colleagues reassign the corruption traditionally associated with the other's touch to that of the white man's; in the second, the filmmakers link sexuality to violence not just through the white man's fear of the minority's prowess, but more notably through fear and shame of his own impotence.

The opening scene links violence and a dread of minorities' sexuality. Barbara tells her father that she is pregnant and that she has had multiple partners. When she reveals that these multiple partners have been of multiple races and that she does not know what the baby will be ("White, Indian, Mexican, Black"), he strikes her. Laughlin presents this blow in a menacing low angle that stresses the deputy's power and brutality. Echoed elsewhere in the film, this incident is significant not only for how it grounds the film in this generic fear, but also for how the scene skewers it: unlike traditional Westerns, in which this anxiety is felt by the heroes and the civilized, in Billy Jack, this fear belongs to the villains. By giving the prejudice to the characters whom we root not for, but against, the filmmakers critique this convention.

The film's most destructive villain, Bernard, is introduced soon after the opening credits, unable to shoot a Mustang on his father's orders. By contrast, his hunting buddies, men who feel none of Bernard's compunction, are presented in mythic low angles as they take up their rifles. (Hunting Mustangs is established as a crime in which the local law enforcement actively participates; it is up to Billy to protect—rather than subjugate—the landscape and its resources.) Later, Bernard's ineffectiveness resurfaces in his sexuality. He is not the seducer he claims to be, and on the occasions where he does succeed (or more accurately, pays for it), he is impotent. In fact, he cannot let loose either violent or sexual energy without unleashing them together. This is borne out in several scenes. A violent confrontation between Billy and Bernard is triggered by the humiliation Bernard suffers when one of the female students cuts low his macho bravado. Bernard later rapes Jean after Billy forces him to drive his new car into the lake with Jean watching; in fact, it is Jean who hatches the idea—a figurative emasculation. (During the rape, Bernard hisses, "For all my bragging, I've never really been able to go all the way with a girl. I get all worked up and can't finish it.") Soon after, Billy, avenging Jean's rape and a student's murder, finds Bernard in bed with a girl who tells Billy that she is thirteen. This is where Billy kills him. To underscore Bernard's depravity, it is his opposite the filmmakers have him murder: Martin (Stan Rice), the gentle Indian student who abstains from sex with Barbara because he wants her to feel that she is loved in mind and spirit.

Earlier, after Martin reveals his feelings to Barbara, he and a fellow student, Cindy (Susan Foster), are kidnapped. Cindy sacrifices her freedom to enable Martin's escape, and Billy rescues her in a violent standoff. Coming late in the film and marking an escalation of hostilities between the town and the school, this incident represents a distilled version of the captivity/rescue scenario, another of the Western's fundamental conventions, one that many scholars, including Richard Slotkin, have probed for how it has planted roots in American culture and politics, as we will see. In Billy Jack, this development does not drive the film's loose narrative; that function is reserved for the contest over Barbara's residency at the school. The school's shielding of Barbara acts as an even larger captivity scenario, but only if viewed from the perspective of the other side—that is, the town's sheriff (Clark Howat). As the film's most benign townsperson and its only sympathetic law enforcer, the sheriff believes it is his duty to bring Barbara back to town. These two captivity scenarios—the capture of the students and the shielding of Barbara—stand in opposition to each other. This robs the convention of the moral absolutism with which the Western has traditionally depicted it. With that gone, its mythic properties follow.

Billy Jack is replete with struggles: struggles over the school, over the children, over the land, over one's own duality, and over the meaning of genre conventions, the value of which had previously lain in the easy orientation they offered viewers. In the showdown that ends the film (as showdowns end almost all Westerns), all these struggles are made manifest. Now wanted for murder, Billy secures himself and Barbara inside an old church to which law enforcers lay siege. Jean enters and exposes Billy for seeking not justice, but rather, his own annihilation. With this challenge to Billy's very status as a hero, it should come as no surprise that the film ends as it does: with Billy being led away, under arrest, into a landscape that is presented in a series of aerial shots to a reprise of the film's theme song, "One Tin Soldier." The film ends precisely as it began.

The marketing of Billy Jack consolidated a similar range of conflicts into one: society against the students. In their longer forms, the print advertisements read:

YOU'VE GOT:

Due process, Mother's Day, supermarkets, air conditioning, the FBI, Medicare, AT&T, a 2-car garage, Congress, country clubs, state troopers, the Constitution, color television, and democracy.

The copy stops here to allow room for a group photo of the students and one of an angry, arrested Billy. Beneath the photos, the copy continues:

THEY'VE GOT:

Billy Jack.[5]

The copy suggests that the film's antagonist is American society itself—larger than the selected townsfolk whom we know the enemy to be—designated by a list of selected institutions. More striking, the copy aligns the viewer with that society and not Billy, nor with those he defends.

The list of what "you" (meaning "we") have is a collision of American cultural and political elements that lends a patina of consumerism even to democracy and the Constitution. The point is simple: the students of the Freedom School can no more avail themselves of the democratic process than they can make long distance telephone calls. In fact, it is likely that these amenities will be wielded *against* the students. Fortunately, their protector, while lacking serious arms (the FBI, state troopers), a social network (country clubs), technology (color television, AT&T), and authority (Congress, the Constitution), remains an equal match for everything "you" have because he is an elemental force.

On a subtler level, the copy separates Billy from traditional Western heroes. It implies that he exists in opposition to the progress America has come to enjoy—and commodify—while his counterparts in classic Westerns fought on the side of progress and civilization, even if they could not be fully integrated into them. The distinction is subtle. And as Billy serves the public good in no official capacity, the contradiction is less explicit than it will be in Dirty Harry and its successors, the heroes of which *do* represent a system that, at the same time, they violently oppose.

Billy Jack was a success when released by Warner Bros. in the spring of 1971. But it became a phenomenon two years later, when Laughlin, having bought back the rights to his film, rereleased it independently. In the press, Max Youngstein, president of the Taylor-Laughlin Distributing Company, attributes the film's newfound success to a media blitz that included television, radio, and print ads. The campaign began five days before the rerelease, and peaked just as the film opened.[6] The television advertising was fragmented, with different spots designed to appeal to different potential audiences. According to Variety, "the spots sold love angles, milked the counter-culture, appealed to action fans, karate cultists, youth, the middle-aged, and the non-filmgoers. It was, said one T-L exec, 'carefully calculated overkill.'"[7] Such a strategy would become the model for how many later—and significantly larger—action films would be marketed. What is striking here, however, is how calculated this campaign was, as Billy Jack—like 1973's vigilante-themed Walking Tall—seemed to be a populist film that drew from grassroots support: "Taylor-Laughlin offices in New York and Los Angeles are festooned with demographic maps and charts; heavy tomes profiling population density, transportation facilities, age groups, income levels, etc. are stacked everywhere."[8]

Gordon Parks's Shaft, also released in 1971, was another tremendous success. Unlike the strategy employed with Billy Jack's 1973 rerelease, however, Shaft targeted—and attracted—an overwhelmingly black audience; indeed, the film is remembered today as helping to initiate the 1970s' "blaxploitation" cycle of films. At the time, the film's plot would have been familiar enough to black and white audiences alike: a private detective is hired by one of the city's key crime figures to investigate the abduction of his daughter. In the process, the detective probes the city's underbelly and negotiates between competing criminal enterprises and the law. What separates this movie from the detective films of which it is a violent rendition is the main character, Shaft—John Shaft—played by Richard Roundtree. With this detective, Parks (a black director), and Ernest Tidyman (a white author who wrote the source novel and co-wrote the screenplay) insert into an old form a new model of black hero.

The familiarity of the story suggests that the film would have crossover appeal to multiple audiences. But while the film did enjoy patronage from white audiences, Variety reports that a full 80 percent of its audience was black.[9] This was by design. UniWorld Group, the black-owned advertising agency hired to create the film's campaign, created ad copy that UniWorld president Byron Lewis calls "a code," one that Variety claims "[came] across perfectly clear to most blacks." UniWorld hired a narrator with a "'clearly identifiable black voice;'" test-screened *Shaft* for "'every level of the black community' in a number of cities;" promoted the film to "every conceivable black newspaper and magazine;" built up stars Roundtree and Gwenn Mitchell; and stressed the participation of black talent in the film, especially Parks, editor Hugh Robertson, and composer Isaac Hayes, who would win the Academy Award for his theme song.[10]

Some have seen this as a success in terms not restricted to box-office returns. In *Black Film as Genre*, Thomas Cripps writes, "*Shaft*, the product of an interracial crew, but black-focused advertising, was close enough to white heroic models to inspire 'crossover' sequels, yet it deeply touched black urban youth with its specific references to their way of life."[11] Indeed, suggesting that *Shaft* is a meeting of generic fantasy and street authenticity, the film's publicity quotes Parks as saying that John Shaft is a detective who is "dealing with real things. In real life," and claims that the director "feels that the basic concept of the film is essentially what he's done in Harlem and other places across the country his whole life . . . [t]aking pictures with homicide squads, vice squads, and dope squads in the night."[12]

Author Mark Reid, however, sees a more insidious side to *Shaft*:

> Despite this obvious effort to attract a black popular audience by means of calculated rhetoric and images MGM [Metro-Goldwyn-Mayer], like other major studios, invested black heroes with mainstream values. In doing so, it did not create mythic black heroes. Instead, like the doll-makers who painted Barbie's face brown, MGM merely created black-skinned replicas of the white heroes of action films.[13]

Reid cites the distance Shaft places between himself and other "Harlemites" by living in Greenwich Village, having an office in midtown Manhattan, and keeping a white police detective as his closest confidant. To Reid, this suggests that Shaft has "bettered himself without forfeiting his ghetto savior faire," and that the writers—white ones, Reid emphasizes—have "created a black sufficiently knowledgeable about black street life that he can fit into it, but tore him from those roots."[14]

The film and its hero seem to offend Reid politically. But his criticism that MGM did not create a mythic black hero also betrays Reid's failure to fully appreciate the archetypal structures on which *Shaft* is founded: namely, those of *film noir*, and hardboiled detective fiction, and, to a lesser extent, the gangster film. Classic *noir* and detective fiction often feature an antihero on the margins of the law (private eye, etc.), whose past has rendered him vulnerable, psychologically unstable—an aspect of *noir* often stressed by the flashback structure, voiceover narration, and most notably, the hero's susceptibility to the *femme fatale*. The hero becomes embroiled in a case involving this cunning beauty, gangsters or other criminals, a male aesthete whose implied homosexuality is often vested with a further implication of perversity and sadism, and a bevy of minor characters, who, inseparable from the urban backdrop, provide our hero with information.[15] Throughout his investigation, the hero will cross back and forth over the different socioeconomic strata of his environment. In the process, his aplomb at dealing with each suggests that he is rarified, in contact with everyone, but connected fundamentally to no one. These environs are typically urban, and among the locations where action is staged or information revealed are diners, nightclubs, decrepit motels or tenements, and the detective's office. Complimenting the modern surroundings is the films' emphasis on contemporary music and fashion.

Author James Naremore argues that *Shaft* is grounded in the traditions of private-eye fiction, but transforms them in one crucial way: "by turning the black male into a sexually potent hero."[16] This marks two distinct departures. The first is from classic *noir* heroes. *Shaft*, like Melvin Van Peebles's *Sweet Sweetback's Baadasssss Song* (1971), refused "to depict the male hero as in any way flawed, compromised, or even vulnerable."[17] Here, the hero's rampant sexuality is the inverse of his classic-era counterpart's troubled psyche and sex life. Roundtree, along with *Sweet Sweetback*'s Van Peebles represents not only a new form of *noir* hero, but also of black protagonist. "Context is everything" writes Mike Phillips. "There had been black stars before—Sidney Poitier and Harry Belafonte were household names all over the world—but after the furor of the 60s, black people came to view them as passive, desexualized, almost impotent figures." If Phillips is generalizing, it is to establish an important shift: "In contrast, the heroes of the landmark Blaxploitation films were out of control."[18]

Shaft's carnal excesses are not limited to the detective's sexuality. In several instances, the violence is especially vigorous—most notably the fight between Shaft and two thugs dispatched by Harlem gangster Bumpy Jonas (Moses Gunn). The fight takes place in Shaft's office, and utilizes elements from the set to heighten the fight's primal quality. It also includes four direct attacks on the camera itself, three of which are launched by Shaft. Of course, the weapons of *Shaft* are not limited to fists—or the coat stand from Shaft's office: bottles, machine guns, Molotov cocktails, and a fire hose are all employed to effect the rescue of Bumpy's daughter, Marcy (Sherri Brewer). After a prolonged sequence in which black militants who have come to Shaft's aid sneak into the building where white mobsters are holding Marcy, Shaft swings through a window on a fire hose and douses his enemies. Meanwhile, Shaft's comrades open fire on gangsters elsewhere in the building. The sequence is a truncated version of ones moviegoers had seen in other rescue scenarios. Here, as in Billy Jack, the function normally served by Indians is instead served by whites, and it is the hero who is racially other.

The tone of this sequence, both climactic and cathartic, differs from that of a violent episode that takes place not long before: Shaft, in an earlier attempt to rescue Marcy, is perforated by tommy-gun fire from the mobsters. Collapsing, he is struck in the head with the butt of the weapon, and kicked. The hero is tortured, ratcheting up the film's dramatic stakes to be sure, but also aligning its hero with those of the noir and detective films that preceded him—a body of films in which the beating or torture of the hero is among the more unpleasant conventions. Such treatment draws from, and extends, a sense of the torture sequence as something ritualistic.

Still, violence punctuates Shaft's structure in spurts, rather than in the metered intervals that characterize the structures of Dirty Harry and the action films that will follow it. Instead, Tidyman and cowriter John D. F. Black keep with classic noir and hardboiled traditions and dedicate more of Shaft's narrative to the investigation, to which the hero's mobility (socially, politically, etc.) is key. Thus, Shaft's lack of roots, which Reid objects to as being socially and economically motivated, is a crucial—and conventional—aspect of the film's being, as Naremore puts it, "a straightforward entertainment, accepting of the legal establishment in the qualified manner of a typical private-eye movie."[19] Shaft must be a floater so that he can insinuate himself into any strata of the city (and its underworld); so that he can be a hero in heroism's proud loner tradition; and because, as critic Richard Combs noted at the time of Shaft's release, "Shaft's encounters with the policeman Androzzi, with other negroes of different persuasions than his own, the hoodlum, Bumpy Jonas, the young militant, Ben Buford, support the view of Shaft as a solitary and aggressively non-aligned individual."[20]

Ultimately, Shaft's cooperation, but refusal to align himself, with the police, the gangsters, and the militants secures him in relationships with both crime and law enforcement that recall "The Man Who Knows Indians." These relationships also make him larger than any one of these sectors. Inasmuch as each faction represents a slice of Parks's New York City, Shaft, then, encompasses the city as a whole. So although Reid is troubled by what he perceives as the film's socioeconomic politics, the film *does* create a "mythic black hero"—or if not that, then at the very least, a black mythic one.

In American film, a movie's mythos is often predicated on its being aligned with a genre. This accounts for *Shaft*'s borrowings from *noir* and gangster films. Critics seized upon this during the film's release, some more generously than others. *Daily Variety*, listing the film as a "Crime melodrama," recognizes *Shaft*'s key elements as being "a formula private-eye plot, update[d] with [an] all-black environment" and "Roundtree as a black Sam Spade."[21] *Playboy* singles out Moses Gunn for "playing a George Raft role better than Raft ever did" and the titular hero, who "is a soul brother to Sam Spade—no pun intended."[22] *Films and Filming*, in damning praise, calls *Shaft* "quite a lively article—a straight forward, one-to-one transformation of the elements of forties' thrillers into contemporary terms."[23] *The Hollywood Reporter*, however, sees this "one-to-one transformation" as a liability:

> But the essential problem—a deep one—remains. What Tidyman and Black, and Parks, have done is taken the conventions of a genre—the detective movie—and tried to transfer them whole to what is, in effect, an almost totally different cultural setting than the one for which they were designed.[24]

Early in the *Los Angeles Times*'s review, a line appears that is striking even today: "With no slight encouragement from the MGM publicity department, it is being said that 'Shaft' . . . recalls the Warner Brothers melodramas of the 30s and early 40s."[25] It is rare for a critic to highlight the role studios play in how critics position films to their readers or viewers. We should be glad that this one did, for scholarship tends to look at film criticism as something indicative of the public's response to a film (which, of course, it can be) to the exclusion of the studio's positioning of it. MGM does stress *Shaft*'s resemblance to these earlier films in the production notes that the studio disseminated to the press. On the initial meeting between Parks and producer Joel Freeman, which took place on the Warner Bros. lot, MGM's publicity department reports, "The Warner Brothers setting was apt, inasmuch as their film 'Shaft' is in its way a hark-back to the Bogart, Cagney, Raft films that flowed so bullet-smooth out of the Warner Brothers Studios in the thirties and early forties."[26] Innocuous enough. But the notes close on a strange, even disquieting note:

> Instead of the thirties, it's here and now. And Black. And done in a marvelously funky idiom. And from MGM.

It has a Black hero; but don't confuse that with a message. Like it was with Bogart—it's for fun.[27]

This wording borders on the bizarre, and not just because of the publicists' word choices. In a time when filmmakers were wrenching their genres to reveal some bankruptcy inherent to the form (or reached through overuse), MGM's publicity department hitched *Shaft* not to a revisionist view of its genre, but to a simple, nostalgic one—even if that view isn't the one Parks's film takes. This is not so surprising: that which is complex in a film can often be simplified in the marketing. Here, it seems that while UniWorld would help MGM by executing a campaign that pinpointed the black audience, MGM's publicity department was geared more toward a white, mainstream one. "Don't confuse that with a message" could well be a message of its own: a troublesome message when one remembers the unrest of the 1960s and wonders what preconceptions—or outright fears—about a "black" film this was meant to allay.

In retrospect, MGM's attempts to align *Shaft* with a larger, more old-fashioned tradition of detective and gangster films strains against a larger trend in genre films of the time: namely, the simultaneous drawing upon, and inversion of, generic conventions, and by extension, audience expectations. Author Todd Berliner divides such films into two categories: genre-breakers, in which the filmmakers use the conventions to attack the genre ideologically; and the lower-key genre-benders, in which the filmmakers distend their genres just enough to mislead audiences who have been prepared for a familiar, generically proscribed outcome.[28] To Berliner, *The French Connection* exemplifies genre-bending.[29]

The French Connection belongs to the police procedural, though a quick glance at the film's reviews reveals the difficulty of genre nomenclature. At the time of the film's release, *Variety* deemed *The French Connection* a "melodrama," the *New York Times* considered it both a "thriller" and "urban crime movie," the *Los Angeles Herald Examiner* called it a "crime thriller," and *Time* deemed it a "police thriller."[30] Though the late 1960s and 1970s are often viewed as a period in which filmmakers were attacking genre, it is also one in which the police procedural enjoyed a resurgence, with films including *In the Heat of the Night*, *Bullitt*, *The Detective*, and two films directed by Don Siegel: *Madigan* and *Coogan's Bluff* (all 1968).[31] Directed by William Friedkin and written by *Shaft*'s Ernest Tidyman from the book by Robin Moore, *The French Connection* is based on New

York City detective Eddie Egan's 1962 investigation of heroin being smuggled into the United States from France, an investigation that resulted in the confiscation of ninety-seven pounds of heroin.[32] Egan's filmic counterpart is Popeye Doyle (Gene Hackman), a typical—and for the coming action genre, prototypical—burnout. With his partner, "Cloudy" Russo (Roy Scheider), he tracks the elusive Charnier (Fernando Rey) and his connections throughout Brooklyn, and clashes with their police captain, Walt Simonson (played by the real Eddie Eagan) as well as with FBI agent Mulderig (Bill Hickman).

Focused on the drug hunt and on Doyle's life as a constant state of near-ruin and famous for its breakneck chase sequence, the film anticipates the action film more than Billy Jack and Shaft do. In fact, even though the film is not the archetype that Dirty Harry will be, The French Connection is widely remembered as a classic of the action genre. The reason is the chase, in which Doyle, driving a commandeered car, struggles to keep pace with an elevated subway train hijacked by one of Charnier's associates. The chase features a bevy of point-of-view and over-the-shoulder shots, which makes the action that much more immediate to the viewer, as does the frenetic pace of Gerald Greenberg's Academy Award–winning editing. Friedkin traces his inspiration for the chase to the fact that producer Philip D'Antoni had also produced the 1968 police procedural Bullitt, which is similarly remembered for a car chase—this one over the streets of San Francisco—that punctuates a plot where action is otherwise scarce. Friedkin wanted to top the earlier effort.[33]

The chase is The French Connection's most memorable scene—and certainly its most kinetic—but not its most representative. Both The French Connection and Bullitt stop the progression of the story for these excesses, unlike later urban action films, in which shorter action scenes precede extended ones like this chase, approximately once in every reel. More typical of The French Connection are the scenes that show the police at their most procedural: scenes in which Doyle and Russo perform surveillance, interrogate informants, and even dismantle Charnier's impounded car. The frequency with which these sequences occur and the detail in which they are rendered indicate that they serve the same function as do the action sequences of later action films; like action sequences in films of the later genre, they seem to direct the story itself.

The French Connection's procedural sequences are not necessarily without violence—Doyle can introduce sudden and swift brutality—but neither are they merely a pretext for it. What violence occurs tends not to drive the scene, but rather, takes place in a larger context of (and is a badge for) moral ambiguity; the violence is not intended to rouse as it is in Doyle's chase or as it is in many later action films. The distinction might be subtle, but it is key. It marks where the police procedural ends, and where the action film begins.

Admittedly, Friedkin's intent is elusive. It is apparent from the film that he, like Bullitt's star Steve McQueen and director Peter Yates, was concerned with "realism" and "authenticity" and was not interested in wielding the strong guiding hand or easy orientation of genre storytelling. Prior to directing The French Connection (for which he would win an Academy Award), Friedkin had directed thousands of hours of live television in Chicago and a dozen documentary films. He soon came to work with David Wolper, then a premier documentary producer. For Wolper, Friedkin wrote, produced, and directed three one-hour specials that aired on ABC: The Bold Men, Mayhem on a Sunday Afternoon, and The Thin Blue Line, a study of law enforcement throughout the United States.[34] Friedkin himself has spoken many times about his attempts to bring a documentary-like aesthetic to the (more or less) fictional French Connection.[35] This is realized by the film's handheld camerawork in real New York City locations, and more specifically, through the film's disinterested view of its bystanders' deaths, including those of a young mother and of teenage crash victims—an apathy, which, of course, is deliberately constructed.

"Realist" modes of filmmaking, such as the documentary, are often (and not always rightly) assumed to be more objective, partly because of their seeming spontaneity, and therefore invite viewers to make their own judgments about the material. Friedkin claims this was his goal. "[T]he whole idea behind French Connection . . . is for the audience to draw their own conclusions, whatever they may be," he claims. "I had as many people who saw The French Connection tell me it was a put-down of cops as told me it was the most accurate, realistic story of a cop. I got citations from police organizations, and I was accused of being a Fascist by the Italian press."[36]

If any genre could be successfully crossed with Friedkin's documentary aesthetic, it stands to reason that it would be the police procedural. The French Connection is the filmmakers' investigation of their subject just as it is Doyle and Russo's investigation of theirs. What's more, against the filmmakers' constant recording of New York's ruin, they craft Doyle's character as an extreme rendition of his burnt-out predecessors. (In the background of a Brooklyn bar, a radio commercial promoting sunny Florida invites the listener to "Say goodbye to air pollution, commuting, high prices, rising taxes, and cold, depressing winters" as Doyle wakes up, hung over.) In true mythic fashion, Doyle is a man with a past, one which, as alluded to by Captain Simonson and Mulderig, is relegated to offscreen space and offscreen time. The emblem of Doyle's past is a bad hunch that resulted in a police officer's death. But rather than overcome his past, Doyle repeats it with the film's ending, in which Doyle causes the death of another colleague: Mulderig. Doyle, therefore, is trapped in a cycle—a *noir* convention—just as he is trapped in space—in this case, a blasted New York City.

After Doyle accidentally kills Mulderig and then charges out of the frame in pursuit of Charnier, a gunshot is heard from offscreen. From the empty frame, Friedkin cuts to photos of the criminals and the detectives, with captions briefly detailing their fates. Still, the lack of resolution is palpable and reinforces Doyle's entrapment by preventing any transcendence, any ascension on Doyle's part. Todd Berliner focuses on this ending in his argument for *The French Connection* as a genre-bender. He claims that Doyle's virtues emerge "as character flaws," and that "Whereas all along the film has largely allied us with Doyle against his critics, the ending largely aligns us with them against Doyle[T]he detective's critics, it turns out, knew better than we did."[37]

One could argue that this ending accounts for why *The French Connection* spawned few imitators despite the film's commercial and critical success. (It earned five Academy Awards, two additional nominations, and over $26 million in domestic box office rentals—the money actually remitted to the distributor, a portion of the total gross). Such an argument would be valid, but also myopic. The ending is but the most heightened example of what has been the film's strategy all along: to draw on generic traditions only to undercut their mythic qualities with—and in the pursuit of—"realism." Realism is a style, and can be a trend, but does not have the permanence of myth; after all, standards of realism change, while for all the inversions and subversions to which filmmakers can subject a mythology, the myths endure.

The film that *would* inspire imitation soon followed *The French Connection*. It would synthesize the genres articulated in this prelude and draw from the already mythic persona of its star. It would bring a new mythos to the modern metropolis, and emerge as the prototype for a new, discrete, violent form.

1

"The Law's Crazy"
The Vigilante and Other
Myths

*Nothing's wrong with shooting. As long as the right
people get shot.*
—Harry Callahan (Clint Eastwood) in Magnum Force
(1973)

Having seen the reexamination of such signature Hollywood genres as the Western, the detective film, and the police procedural, the 1970s would now become the first (nearly) full decade of the modern action film. The most obvious marker of the genre's modernity would be the big-city backdrops that had long served *noir*, detective, and gangster pictures and against which more classically Western conflicts would now be staged. Urban warfare was about to receive the Western gunfighter, who, to bring law to the lawless, would appropriate some of the dark terrain traditionally associated with other genres. This terrain would be physical in terms of geography (cities, their shabby police precincts, their sleazy motel rooms, etc.) and in terms of the body (the kinds of violence done to it, the weapons by which it is done). In the action films of the 1970s, many of these gunfighters would be urban vigilantes. Mythologically, the filmmakers align urban vigilantism with Western heroism and individuality. Ideologically, however, the movies may ultimately affirm the hero's actions, but they are often debated and discussed with more than just token ambivalence.

Dirty Harry (1971), which marks Clint Eastwood's fourth collaboration with director Don Siegel, is the action film's first true archetype. Classified as a "Police Melodrama" by *Daily Variety*, the film draws on the persona Eastwood crafted in his Westerns—particularly Sergio Leone's "Man with No Name" trilogy of "Spaghetti Westerns."[1] Eastwood's roster of such films aside, it is still easy to see in his Inspector Harry Callahan traits of the Western hero: solitude (somehow unmitigated by the fact that he has a partner), his laconic speech, the suggestion that he is a man with a past, and the suggestion that he is a man of the past, that his methods cannot be condoned by a progressive civilization. These include his willingness to take violent action to protect the community—particularly with his iconic .44 Magnum—even though the community has no place for him afterward.

The film was originally to star Frank Sinatra under the direction of Irvin Kershner, who would later direct the 1980 blockbuster The Empire Strikes Back. While in pre-production, Dirty Harry's title was changed to Dead Right due to the original title's similarity to that of another Sinatra film, 1970's Dirty Dingus Magee. But in November 1970, a hand injury forced Sinatra to withdraw from the project. Less than a month later, Warner Bros. attached Eastwood and his Malpaso Company to take over production for Sinatra and his Bristol Productions, Inc.[2]

Sinatra's appearance would have made the film more akin to his private-eye pictures Tony Rome (1967), The Detective (1968) and Lady in Cement (1968), as did earlier versions of the script. Though ultimately credited to Harry Julian Fink, Rita M. Fink, and Dean Riesner, the original screenplay was written by John Milius. Milius's successors (particularly Riesner) were responsible for tailoring it to Eastwood's star persona—hence, Milius's story is more concerned with the investigative process in the tradition of police procedurals and more dialogue-driven than the final film. Even more unexpected is that at least one of Milius's drafts was coauthored by the reclusive artist-filmmaker, former Rhodes scholar, and philosophy professor Terrence Malick, who directed just four films between 1973 and 2005: Badlands, Days of Heaven, The Thin Red Line, and The New World. Milius, Malick, and Harry Julian Fink completed a draft of Dirty Harry as late as the day after Warner Bros. announced Sinatra's withdrawal.[3]

In the film, Harry clashes with his superiors in the police department, the district attorney's office, and even the mayor's, all in Harry's pursuit of a sniper, Scorpio (Andy Robinson), whose aim is to kill until the city pays him to stop. The triangle composed of Harry, the politicians, and Scorpio parallels the one of so many Westerns, a triangle composed of the hero, the civilized, and the savage (which in turn can include outlaws, Indians, and the wilderness itself). One point on the triangle is usually in contention with the other two. This is especially true for the hero, who as "The Man Who Knows Indians" is constantly defined against the civilized and the savage. He must be; as his nature resonates with both, he is neither wholly, but rather, is stranded between them. This is the source of his isolation, as seen in Billy Jack.

As an inspector with the San Francisco Police Department, Harry might be part of the system, but he is primarily of the streets. His methods are his own;

his spaces are not. That is, the audience never sees Harry's home, office, or, if we assume he works in a squad room, even a desk. The most we see is the car he shares with his partner, Chico (Reni Santoni)—a space that is necessarily mobile, transitory. As for the bureaucrats with whom Harry scraps, they are rooted in their offices—their state-sanctioned spaces—from which they sanction Harry for his actions. Harry and the city's officials play out their contests over power and ideology in these large (and in the case of the mayor's office, ornate) spaces.

These officials include Harry's immediate and also frustrated superior, Lieutenant. Bressler (Harry Guardino), who references the authority of the never seen "Fifth Floor," and the district attorney, who, along with an appellate court judge, tells Harry that the captured Scorpio must be released because his Constitutional rights have been violated. "It's the law," they tell Harry, who replies, "Then the law's crazy." At the top of this power structure is the mayor (John Vernon), who feels safer playing by Scorpio's rules than by Harry's. Near the end of the movie, we see that the mayor's office is marked by the words "THE MAYOR" chiseled large into the marble above the outer office's entrance. This, along with Bressler's solemn intonations of "The Fifth Floor," inflates bureaucratic authority to the level of the iconic.

Harry's methods of maintaining law and order make clear the conservative politics of Dirty Harry. Many have remarked on them. However, a counterintuitive strain of libertarianism is also at work. Author Eric Patterson argues that the individualism Harry represents defines more than just the film: "Eastwood has become and has remained the most popular movie actor in America . . . because of his persistent use of the theme of rebellion against forms of established authority which deprive the individual of autonomy," Patterson writes.[4] Harry's antiauthoritarianism recalls the Western, with its emphasis on individuality. But Patterson then argues that Eastwood's police films are ultimately "repressive rather than progressive," because they take a viewer's antiauthoritarian feelings, "which potentially could precipitate radical structural change," and channel them "in directions which will not lead to disruption of existing structures."[5]

In the end, Harry has not transformed society—at least not beyond removing its greatest cancer, Scorpio. In fact, Harry's final gesture is to throw away his badge, a show of disgust with the system that has hampered his efforts, as well as an imitation of Gary Cooper in the finale of the classic Western High Noon. Many have remarked on this connection. But in Dirty Harry's citation of High Noon, Pauline Kael sees a key distinction between the two. Kael maintains that whereas Cooper's Will Kane throws his badge into the street out of contempt for the cowards who would not join him to defend the law, Harry throws his into the water out of contempt for the law itself. Harry, Kael writes, "stands for vigilante justice."[6]

Harry also vents his frustration with the system by lobbing glib remarks at its liberal representatives. But his catharsis is saved for, and visited upon, Scorpio, whose aberration is so complete, it seems to achieve its own, albeit bent, purity. As Kael notes, "The variety of his perversions is impressive—one might say that no depravity is foreign to him. He is pure evil: sniper, rapist, kidnapper, torturer, defiler of all human values."[7] Author Richard Combs, however, is interested in a more elemental aspect of Scorpio's *otherness*. He writes, "the dissolution [Scorpio] represents is more than social and sexual, it's psychic and cellular. During the nighttime confrontation in Mt. Davidson Park [Harry and Scorpio's first meeting], he becomes animal-like and the park a jungle."[8]

Of course, Scorpio's monstrosity is a product of how the filmmakers depict him, but also of what they omit. Siegel and his screenwriters provide no context for Scorpio and only traces of disparate motives (money, racism, sexual depravity). Likewise, they give him no name but "Scorpio," recalling San Francisco's Zodiac Killer. And in the end credits, the filmmakers do not give Scorpio even that much: he is listed only as "Killer." If Harry, who, due to the workings of genre and star persona, is a man with a past, then Scorpio is a man with no past. He has no backstory, but he does have a generic referent: with his effeminate demeanor, blonde curls, and creepy linkage of eroticism and violence, Scorpio is like the sadistic, sexually ambiguous aesthetes of hardboiled fiction and film; of this *noir* character type, Scorpio is somehow both an indirect reminder and a hyperbolic version.

Patterson links Scorpio's lack of context to the type of characterizations made by Kael and Combs, and finally, to the exaggerated context of the city's authority figures:

> The movie gives us no information about the killer's history. The deliberate lack of depth in the characterization makes him seem nearly inhuman, a kind of Gothic monster more like a wild beast or a force of nature than a person. By representing him as a pure, almost abstract threat rather than as a reasoning human being, attention is focused on the conflict between Harry and his superiors over how to deal with the crisis.[9]

Patterson's first notion is interesting, but his second is flawed. Scorpio's "abstract" nature lessens the importance of his and Harry's private war in favor of

The New Sheriff: *In 1971's* Dirty Harry, *San Francisco Inspector Harry Callahan (Clint Eastwood) faces a maniacal sniper (not pictured) in the final showdown, set in a rock quarry closely resembling a Western set. (From the author's collection.)*

Harry's battle with the bureaucrats only if articulation (as opposed to abstraction) is the standard we use. But as Dirty Harry makes clear, the film's organizing principle is its violent conflicts rather than its ideological ones. The film embodies this in its very structure, with well-regulated intervals between the action sequences that would become the genre's standard. Dirty Harry also juxtaposes scenes of Harry and Scorpio (and in some cases, shots) in a one-to-one correlation. This brings parity to the men and grounds their relationship as the center of the film.

The violence of Dirty Harry erupts on a cycle. Each action sequence begins almost exactly ten minutes after the previous one began. With few exceptions, the audience never has to wait more than eleven minutes, or less than eight, for a new sequence. This pattern includes an extended sequence in which Scorpio sends Harry running from phone booth to phone booth to rescue a kidnapped teenager, and which climaxes in a blaze of violence almost ten minutes to the second from when the sequence began. This climax represents the first face-to-face confrontation between Harry and Scorpio. Significantly, it occurs at about the film's one-hour mark, the point at which film narratives often take a critical turn. During this sequence's climax, set under the giant cross in Mt. Davidson Park, Scorpio brutalizes Harry, Chico fires at Scorpio, Scorpio guns down Chico, and Harry stabs Scorpio in the leg with a concealed knife. All three men fall. And now that Harry and Scorpio have met, Siegel, his writers, and editor Carl Pingitore intensify the film's pattern of cutting from its hero to its villain and back to suggest parity between them. In fact, in the aftermath of the Mt. Davidson Park violence, the filmmakers alternate shots of a wounded Scorpio and of a wounded Harry, then of Scorpio rising, and of Harry rising. Chico, still alive, is omitted.

For the rest of the film, this crosscutting of shots is inflated to a juxtaposition of scenes. After Harry later tortures Scorpio for information about the abducted girl (balancing Scorpio's earlier beating of Harry), the audience follows Harry into the district attorney's office, where Harry confronts him and the appellate court judge. From here, Siegel cuts to Scorpio in a playground—watching children—and then shows Harry watching Scorpio. From the playground, we cut to a strip club where Harry is once again watching his prey. Scorpio pushes past Harry, and in the next scene, we follow Scorpio as he is beaten by a man he has paid to disfigure him. After the beating, we cut to Scorpio being admitted to the hospital, where he tells the press that this was done to him by "Callahan, a big tall cop . . ." It is noting that Siegel has just presented two Scorpio scenes in a row, but follows them with two Harry scenes:

Harry with police officials, and then Harry with Chico and Chico's wife. Next comes a slow dissolve to the school bus Scorpio hijacks, which marks the second of the film's captivity scenarios.

This structure creates a balance between Harry and Scorpio, and suggests that they are linked. The connection is established with the film's first images: from an inspector's shield situated against a plaque memorializing slain San Francisco police officers, Siegel dissolves to a matching close-up of the muzzle of Scorpio's rifle. The curves of the shield and of the muzzle overlap. It fits that so stark a film would open by both contrasting and connecting the icons of its hero and villain.

Few would argue that *Dirty Harry* is an ambiguous film. Still, it never fully resolves whom its violent cop more closely resembles: the system he represents or the maniac loner he pursues. This dynamic drew criticism, but is also one the studio was willing to exploit. In its unfavorable review, *Daily Variety* reduces Harry and Scorpio to "the sadist-with-badge" and "the sadist-without-badge."[10] Even cheekier, the studio's trailer embraces the fact that the film's cop and criminal are not as easily discernable as are good and evil. The opening makes Harry and Scorpio *both* look like rooftop snipers. "This is about a movie about a couple of killers: Harry Callahan and a homicidal maniac," the narrator says, then clarifying, "The one with the badge is Harry."

None of this should surprise us. Harry is, after all, the "Man Who Knows Indians," only in the film's 1970s San Francisco, "Indians" are now crazed Caucasians. "You're crazy if you think you've heard the last of this guy. He's gonna kill again," Harry assures the district attorney. "How do you know that?" the district attorney asks. Harry answers, perhaps recognizing himself in the *other*: "'Cause he likes it." An earlier draft of the script written by John Milius, Terrence Malick and Harry Julian Fink makes an even finer point of Harry's Western-derived duality by describing him sniffing the air at the outset of his inspection and likening him to "a cavalry scout in modern dress." Later, wielding a packing knife, Harry tells the killer (who in this version of the story is a vigilante killing criminals), "I'm not going to kill you . . . I'm going to scalp you" (ellipsis in original).[11]

Either way, Harry is alone in his awareness that forces such as Scorpio must be fought. To Kael, Harry's understanding is his dirtiness, "the moral stain of recognition that evil must be dealt with;" she writes, "He is our martyr—stained on our behalf."[12] Here, Kael does more than just skewer *Dirty Harry's* concoction of fantasy and politics; whether intending to be flip or not, she taps into one of the genre's key underlying archetypes by invoking the sacrificial hero.

To film scholar Rikke Schubart, two themes are central to action films: passion and acceleration. The latter pertains to speed, pyrotechnics, and the kinetic, sensory stuff to which action films are commonly reduced. The former, however, pertains to emotion, psychology, and mythology. She writes that the passion theme "links the hero to society, to hierarchy and the law, to martyrdom and masochism (the prototype is Christ)."[13] Schubart draws on French anthropologist Rene Girard's "sacrifice plot," in which societies sacrifice scapegoats to avoid social crises. For Schubart, the action film's "passion plot" shares the three parts of Girard's sacrifice plot and adds a fourth: a hero is marginalized, chosen to handle a crisis, sacrificed, and finally, resurrected to claim his vengeance. *Dirty Harry* follows this structure. He is set apart from fellow officers and looked down upon by many of his superiors; these superiors enlist him to deliver ransom money to Scorpio; he is beaten by Scorpio, admonished by the same superiors, and then removes himself from the case by telling them that they can find "another delivery boy." Finally, with no official mandate, he returns to kill Scorpio.

Moreover, underscoring the role martyrdom plays in *Dirty Harry*, the film visualizes (and verbalizes) the point by making much use of Christological imagery and references. After Scorpio claims his first victim, Harry finds Scorpio's ransom note and utters his—and the film's—first line: "*Jesus.*" This is mirrored toward the end of the film when Scorpio, having hijacked the school bus, looks up to see Harry waiting, standing monolithically atop a railroad trestle. Astonished, Scorpio whispers "*Jesus,*" and except for a dashed off "drop the gun, creep" much later, this is the last word Scorpio says (ever). Moreover, during an earlier shootout, Scorpio destroys the neon letters of a "Jesus Saves" sign with glee (and automatic fire) while keeping Harry and Chico at bay.

Siegel invokes not only the name of Jesus, but also the icon of the cross. In the middle of the film, the two violent encounters between Harry and Scorpio are staged against crosses. In the first, Scorpio beats Harry at the base of Mt. Davidson Park's giant cross. From Harry's point of view, the audience peers up at the cross; it is distended, even bizarre. In the second, Siegel's use of the cross is subtler, though also linked to violence: as Harry tortures Scorpio—stepping on the leg that he has already shot and, before that, stabbed—Scorpio is splayed on a football field. The yard lines appear like crosses, but Scorpio is positioned such that the crosses appear on a diagonal, skewed.

The brutality Harry suffers in the park also evokes martyrdom. As Schubart argues, "to be an action hero was not only a question of . . . beating and gunfire; it was also a question of being violently beaten, sensing violence on your own flesh."[14] While the beating of the protagonist had long been a convention of hardboiled fiction and film, here, its ritualistic aspect is elevated to quasi-religiosity. But this must be clear: the religiosity of Dirty Harry does not serve any theological point. Its purpose, one suspects, is to enhance the mythos of the movie. It figures that religion, so resonant with the mythic and with notions of martyrdom and resurrection, would be so pronounced in Dirty Harry, the genre's first true archetype. "Passion" would become a convention of the genre, although it would not be rendered with the same intensity until the action films of the 1980s. These films would depict the super-bodies of Sylvester Stallone, Arnold Schwarzenegger, and others subjected to masochism, resurrection, and torture bordering on the fetishized. In the meantime, action filmmakers would continue expressing passion for other things: vigilantism, hardware (especially weaponry), and the action movie's generic forebears.

If, in the 1960s, Clint Eastwood succeeded John Wayne as a Western icon, then in the 1970s, Wayne attempted to emulate Eastwood as a hero of the budding action genre. John Sturges's McQ (1974) marks the first of two action/late police procedurals Wayne would make during the twilight of his career. As in Dirty Harry, the heroics of McQ's titular rogue cop straddle an antiquated genre (the Western) and an emerging one (the action film). "The easy willingness with which it would suspend civil rights in the name of law-and-order, something it shares with most of the other cop films," writes New York Times critic Vincent Canby, "may well be a true reflection of our times but it is also a philosophy inherited from one kind of narrative, the classic Western."[15]

But as viewed through the lens of John Wayne-as-urban avenger, the film's affinity for Western tradition is less striking than its enthusiasm for action film modernity. Several times, Wayne's Lon McQ trades one weapon for a more advanced model: first, his revolver for an automatic pistol; later his automatic pistol for an Ingram 9mm machine gun. The scene that introduces the Ingram displays the genre's zeal for weaponry. When Wayne tests the Ingram in a backroom firing range (his license to carry a weapon has been revoked by his superior) the gun is dubbed the "Equalizer." With clear admiration, the characters introducing McQ to his new toy prattle off its specifications in an exchange that recalls Dirty Harry and its first sequel, Magnum Force (1973), and that future action films would imitate. We are told that the gun weighs six and a quarter pounds, and that "those thirty-two slugs came out in a second and a half."

Though the body of the film places less of an emphasis on the Ingram than, say, Dirty Harry places on Harry's .44 Magnum, McQ's publicity materials suggest Warner Bros.'s eagerness to make the Ingram an icon—or at least, for the purposes of branding, to represent the whole of the film with this weapon, the film's most propulsive element. In the studio's pressbook and theatrical programs, as well as in the film's print advertisements contained therein, the film's title treatments are all the same: the title "McQ" appears in bold, military stencil, and alongside it is the Ingram, complete with extension. Often accompanying the strong graphic, is the tagline, "His gun is unlicensed," accenting Wayne's vigilantism and the enhanced destructiveness he can deploy in its service.[16]

Wayne's follow-up, *Brannigan* (1975), expresses a similar fascination with the gun-as-icon. A fish-out-of-water story, the film finds Chicago cop Lt. Jim Brannigan (Wayne) dispatched to London to retrieve a fugitive. Through the clashes between Brannigan and Scotland Yard Commander Charles Swann (Richard Attenborough) over the former's insistence on carrying a sidearm, the film agitates over the gun. *Brannigan* foregrounds the gun in a striking main title sequence that echoes the opening of *Magnum Force* and predicts those of *Cobra* (1986) and *Ricochet* (1991). To composer Dominic Frontiere's swinging score, close-ups of a gun and ammunition appear. The camera isolates the gun's parts by zooming in on the trigger, and then on the muzzle, which the filmmakers further privilege with a superimposition of the film's title. Similarly emphasized are the gun's barrel, its hammer, the grip (emblazoned with the Colt logo), and a bullet.

Of *McQ* and *Brannigan*, the former makes a stronger display of modernity. In addition to McQ's Ingram, the film emphasizes his Green Hornet car, and subjects it to a crushing demise reminiscent of the punishment visited upon the bodies of Harry Callahan, his *noir* ancestors, and his action movie descendants. As Pauline Kael summarizes, "In the most ludicrous single sequence, two huge trucks, specially equipped with murderous battering rams, come at Wayne's Green Hornet, one from the front and one from the back, and they crush the little car like cheese in a grilled sandwich."[17] This and the film's climactic beach chase are clearly meant to be among the film's show-stopping moments. Indeed, McQ's Green Hornet and the film's car chases factored into its publicity, if not as pervasively as the machine gun. *Motor Trend's* March 1974 issue dedicated a feature story to a "behind-the-scenes look at the filming of the spectacular chase film that makes 'Bullitt' and 'The French Connection' look like Sunday drives."[18]

While ending with a violent car chase at a decrepit factory (not the last time an action movie's climax would be staged in such an environment), *Brannigan* remains gentler in tone than *McQ*, as one of its standout sequences is a bar-room brawl the lieutenant instigates. Complete with a player piano and swinging doors through which Brannigan enters the room, the film converts this British pub into a Western saloon. The nod to Wayne's legend is so overt, *The Hollywood Reporter* refers to the scene as "a John Ford brawl in a local pub," while *Variety* regards it as "an inside joke."[19] This sequence illustrates the good cheer with which the filmmakers inflect their violence and also nostalgia for Wayne's earlier roles. But as evidenced by *Dirty Harry*, the action film can use Western references ironically—that is, for more than nostalgia, or differentiating the traditional from the modern, then from now. Michael Winner's *Death Wish* (1974) distends the Western even further, and in its own ironic way, foregrounds the Western more than *Brannigan* would the following year.

Death Wish, based on Brian Garfield's 1972 novel, is the story of Manhattan architect Paul Kersey (Charles Bronson, a former Western and war film star), who turns to vigilantism after his wife and daughter are savagely attacked and the police can do nothing. Following his wife's death and daughter's catatonia, but before setting out to prey on New York's predators, Paul accepts an assignment in Arizona. Here, Paul's client takes him to Old Tuscon's "famous movie location and studio," a fake Western town where occasionally, Westerns are filmed and stunt shows are performed. During one such performance, the filmmakers suggest that Paul is more engaged than the other spectators. Winner presents Paul in a number of low angles that exaggerate his likeness as Paul listens to corny "movie" dialogue, and in close-ups that emphasize his wincing at the stuntmen's punches. Stressing not the show, but Paul's reactions to it, Winner makes it something surreal. The soundtrack enhances this effect: the stuntmen wear microphones that produce a strange reverb, enhancing the phoniness of the show.

Back in New York, after internalizing this Western performance, Paul becomes a vigilante, celebrated by the public and the media alike. Here, Winner continues to make ironic use of the Western, which he now connects to urban vigilantism. Paul's final campaign against New York's criminal element takes place in a park, where he is critically wounded. Pursuing the final mugger, Paul waits atop an industrial structure the camera never fully reveals. From this elevated position, he looks down on his target. Invoking a thousand Westerns and the stunt show he saw earlier, he invites the street punk to a fast-draw. "Fill your hand," Paul says. "Huh?" asks the mugger. Here, the film implies that the mugger is excluded from the older combatant's references by his youth, and possibly by his minority status. "Draw," Paul instructs, but before the guns can blaze, he faints, thereby subverting one of the Western's fundamental conventions: the showdown. Underscoring this, as Paul falls back, he reveals a wooden structure below, a structure that resembles a Western façade. Interestingly, this is the most brightly lit part of this otherwise noir-ish frame.

Later, in the hospital, Paul is confronted by Inspector Ochoa (Vincent Gardenia), who has been pursuing "The Vigilante." This confrontation is, in fact, one of the few instances in which the two adversaries meet, but the connection between them is grounded in the film's story structure and editing. Roughly imitating Dirty Harry, from the time Ochoa is introduced, his scenes follow Paul's in a near one-to-one correlation. Thus, he, and not the criminal element, is Paul's true adversary. But Ochoa, like many movie cops, has been restrained by his superiors. With New York's crime rate falling, they do not want Ochoa to arrest this killer, but instead, to quietly discourage him and allow the city's would-be muggers and rapists to think that they are stalked by a .32-toting vigilante. At Paul's bedside, Ochoa declares, "We want you out of New York. Permanently." Ochoa has nearly left the room when Paul speaks. "Inspector. By sundown?" Ochoa smiles. On him, as opposed to the young mugger, the reference to the Western is not lost.

The frustration with which Paul seethes, the violence he lets loose, and the Western code of vigilante action he invokes and embodies all constitute a new Paul Kersey, one built on the ruins of his previous liberalism. Early in the film, Paul accedes to his colleagues' charges that he is a "bleeding-heart" by telling them that sure, his heart "bleeds a little for the underprivileged." Of course, this changes in the wake of the attacks on his family and the police department's ineffectiveness. Thus, unlike the vigilantism of Harry Callahan and many of his imitators, Paul's is given a point of origin. This makes Death Wish even more reactionary than Dirty Harry, in which there is no real exploration of the hero's politics or motives. (In fact, when Chico's wife asks Harry why he stays on the police force Harry answers, "I don't know, I really don't," emulating the Western's many laconic gunmen, including High Noon's.) Death Wish is therefore about progression—downward though it may be—while Dirty Harry is about stasis. Indeed, until the bus sequence, Dirty Harry's most movement-driven episode is the phone booth relay, in which the motion is less propulsive than retarded. There is no mistaking that Death Wish is the beginning of Paul's story—a beginning that would propel him through this film and four follow-ups (1982, 1985, 1987, 1994); Dirty Harry, on other hand, could have just as easily been one of its own sequels.

Paul's liberal nature is elaborated upon in Arizona, at the firing range where we first see Paul handle a gun. Here, Paul reveals to his client that he had

"Print the Legend": The antiheroism of Paul Kersey (Charles Bronson) enters public discourse in Death Wish (1974). (From the author's collection.)

served in the Korean War as part of a medical unit, as a conscientious objector. His father had been a hunter, he explains, and had raised Paul with "all kinds of guns." His mother hated this, so when his father was killed in a hunting accident, his mother "won the toss." Ever since, Paul has resisted guns—despite his being an excellent shot, a part of his early rearing that no progressive ideology ever expunged. In this respect, Paul fits into an archetype already examined: the hero who embodies both that which he upholds and that which he abhors. The Searchers's "The Man Who Knows Indians," who, in Dirty Harry became "The Man Who Knows Criminals," becomes in Death Wish, "The Man Who Knows Liberals."

Ultimately then, Death Wish does not merely criticize liberals—a charge many critics have leveled against Dirty Harry. Instead, it converts its liberal, in a manner articulated two years later, in The Enforcer (1976), the third Harry Callahan film. As Harry's partner, Frank DiGeorgio, dies from wounds sustained in battle, DiGeorgio's wife reflects, "It's a war, isn't it? I guess I never really understood that." This is echoed in Winner's later Death Wish 3 (1985), when Kersey's love interest, a criminal defense attorney, confesses, "Sometimes I feel like I'm on the wrong side, defending creeps. . . . Damn it, people have got to start to fight back and hard! The whole thing is just out of balance" (emphasis in original). Kersey replies, "Some people would say that was an extreme position."[20]

Though the original Death Wish is the movie with which today's audiences most readily associate Bronson, he was already proven as a star at the box-office and as a gunfighter on film—in Western, war, and urban varieties—prior to making the movie. Hence critic Stanley Kauffmann's remark, "You'll miss the 'in' joke if it's your first Bronson [film]—this outlaw with an office job and a Riverside Drive apartment learning how to kill" (emphasis in original).[21] For a star working in the closely related Western, police procedural, and action film genres, innocence lost by previous characters is not easily regained. It may be an irony inherent to genre filmmaking: regardless of how Westerns and action films may champion the individual in the face of an arbitrary system, the characters' journeys are always, to one degree or another, predetermined.

But a genre film's mythos is also a product of the visual landscape that frames the action and the characters' development. In Death Wish, that landscape is New York–noir, dark and punishing from the opening credits. In contrast, the film's pre-credit sequence finds the Kerseys on a Hawaiian beach in a scene more akin to From Here to Eternity than anything to be found later in

Death Wish. Paul wants to make love with his reluctant wife. "We're too civilized," she says. Moments later, a harsh cut relocates the couple to a taxicab caught in the strangle of Manhattan traffic, underscored by Herbie Hancock's discordant music. The cut also establishes the jarring style of Bernard Gribble and Winner's editing. Winner's Manhattan is a fragmented space—fragmented editorially, musically, *psychically*—and nothing, not the fact that it is a self-contained island nor that it is laid out on a grid, is enough to repair the schisms, the disorder.

In fact, the space seems bound together only by its shadows. They help make the city a wilderness, and as such, characterize the parks and alleys that become Paul's hunting ground as much as (if not more than) they are the criminals'. This photographic scheme is *Death Wish*'s primary *noir* referent, although a secondary one is its depiction of race. As in many films of the genre, the majority of the villains—and crucially, the most depraved—are white, which is presumably intended to blunt the edge of this reactionary entertainment for more politically sensitive viewers.

Critic Frank Rich sees this strategy as transparent, and decries *Death Wish* as "a work of honest-to-God idiocy," in which, "lest the film be accused of preaching minority genocide, its creators have made sure that the targets displayed reflect what seems to be an exact racial breakdown of the population of New York City."[22] More significant than the races of the extras Paul dispatches is the fact that those who attack the women of his family are white (one is Jeff Goldblum in his first screen role). Before raping the women, one assailant even spraypaints a red swastika on the Kerseys' white wall in what is staged as just a bit of background action. The attackers' race, racism, violence, and sexual depravity make these "freaks," as they are designated in the end credits, close cousins to Scorpio (again, who *Dirty Harry* bills only as "Killer"), to the other maniacs who pick up Scorpio's bloody mantle, and to their sadistic progenitors from *film noir*.

His prey both white and black, Paul hunts at night, when his city is at its most *noir*. But unlike a true *film noir*, in which this style would saturate the film's entire world, here, different sorts of atmosphere characterize the interiors. These interiors, perhaps even more than the exteriors, support *The Hollywood Reporter*'s observation that "Arthur J. Ornitz's photography relies heavily on wide angle lens, giving the right sense of nightmare and distortion."[23] The most distorted spaces are institutional ones, appendages of *the system*: the hospital to which his wife and daughter are taken and the police precinct from which Paul receives no help. The hospital waiting area is enormous and antiseptic. Spying an injured man, Paul articulates what the visual implies, that the system is distanced from the citizenry: "Somebody oughta come," Paul says. "There's a man over there; he's bleeding and nobody comes." Similarly, the 21st Precinct is wanly lit, modern, and spacious (unlike the New York City police precincts of *Coogan's Bluff* and *The French Connection*). The set seems to recede from the people occupying its foreground. Indeed, the institutional spaces of the precinct and the hospital are almost all background; the foregrounds lack much detail or set dressing, and consequently, the sense of completeness—or at least of normalcy—that characterizes Paul's home and office.

These are the stages against which Paul makes the transition from social advocate to society's avenger—environments of the *noir* world to which invoking the Western (through such spaces as the Old Tuscon Amusement Park, and the unspoiled Arizona landscape itself) is then a reaction. As a civilian—indeed, a liberal!—with no inspector's shield or cop's badge to complicate his allegiances or duties, Paul crystallizes both the urban vigilante and the ambivalence with which he can be received. But in this early stage, the genre has still other depictions of vigilantism, including the vigilante as *enemy*, as seen one year earlier in *Magnum Force*.

Originally titled *Vigilance*, this first sequel to *Dirty Harry* marks the return of Harry Callahan as he investigates the murders of San Francisco's most nefarious: organized crime bosses, narcotics traffickers, pimps. To the audience, the killings seem initially to be the work of a lone motorcycle cop. Ultimately, we discover that the vigilante is actually a team of rogue officers acting under the command of Harry's superior, Lieutenant Briggs (Hal Holbrook). It falls to Harry to dispatch Briggs and the vigilante cops, and to restore the system. This is a strange reversal of the original film, though mitigated by the fact that *Magnum Force* is co-written by John Milius, whose original, unproduced *Dirty Harry* script featured a similar vigilante villain.

The world of *Magnum Force* is not the *noir*-ish backdrop of *Dirty Harry*, *Death Wish*, or *McQ*. Virtually all of the action takes place during the day (and therefore probably cost less to produce). Instead of expressionistic shadows, director Ted Post stages his actors against industrial backdrops. Frequently, machines and instruments (including weapons) are the most commanding part of the frame, even when relegated to the set-dressing. *Magnum Force's* world is nearly as imposing as those of the film's more *noir*-inspired counterparts and outright *noir* antecedents but has no sense of emanating from the characters. Thus this aesthetic is iconographic, but as impersonal as the machines that define it.

Following the murder of Harry's friend and fellow cop Charlie McCoy (Mitchell Ryan), by one of the vigilante officers, Harry and McCoy's widow watch as McCoy's body is loaded onto an airplane for transport. When the scene begins, the camera pans with the casket as it moves up a conveyor belt into the plane. The casket clears the frame, revealing Harry and Carol McCoy (Christine White) framed against the plane's hull. They walk toward the car waiting for Carol. The camera pans with them, and when they stop, they are now framed against the plane's engine. On the soundtrack, we hear the noise of the engine idling—a backdrop for the dialogue, just as the engine is a backdrop for the actors. Standing with them is Officer John Davis (David Soul), who unbeknownst to Harry, killed McCoy. After Carol leaves, the camera moves around Harry and Davis, again framing them against the engine, but now looking past the characters directly into the engine's mouth. Davis regrets that he had not been there to aid McCoy and feels responsible. Harry considers Davis. Both men wear sunglasses. Their eyes—and with them, their thoughts—are hidden from view.

As Harry's investigation continues, he compares slugs taken from the victim's bodies to those discharged from Davis's gun. Standing near the center of a small ballistics lab, Harry is surrounded by weapons and cartridges. A high, overhead angle reveals scores of handguns laid out on the tables around Harry; the camera's wide-angle lens creates a slightly fish-eyed, or distorted, effect. As Harry peers through a microscope, the filmmakers cut to a low angle that furthers the cramped effect, but this time shows rifles racked up behind Harry. Although rifles, pistols, and ammunition are icons of the Western and of American individualism, the numbers in which they appear here and the manner in which they are laid out suggest mass production. They do not evoke the individualism inherent to the Western myth (and the previous Dirty Harry film), but rather, an industrial, if still violent, world.

This modern aesthetic is also embodied in the backdrops of several major action sequences. In the first, Harry foils an airplane hijacking from inside while the plane taxis (the airline is "Sovereign Airways," an amusing name given the period's high number of skyjackings). The second and third are set on the docks: a shootout between mobsters and the police, and later, a final confrontation between Harry and the vigilantes. With Phil Sweet (Tim Matheson) having been "sacrificed" by his brethren earlier, three officers remain. Harry kills the first, Mike Grimes (Robert Urich) by ramming his commandeered car head-on into Grimes's motorcycle: destruction of the mechanical that borders on glee. Harry and the surviving officers then enter a decrepit battleship, where, amid shadows and rusting steel, Harry kills the next in hand-to-hand combat. Emerging from the ship, Davis engages Harry in a motorcycle chase, in which the officers (or more to the point, their bikes) jump and race around the docks. Davis does not complete his final jump; he plunges into the water, to his death. Harry comes upon the scene and finds Davis's white motorcycle helmet, overturned in the foreground. He kicks the helmet off the dock, recalling his final act in *Dirty Harry*.

This gesture is significant apart from its connection to the previous movie. Throughout *Magnum Force*, Post has presented the white motorcycle helmet and other elements of the motorcycle cop's uniforms as icons. They are not icons of justice, however (that is what Harry's .44 Magnum and Eastwood himself are for), but icons of terror. The black uniform, boots, gloves, the white helmet, the sunglasses—they all suggest a violent force that is not animated by any personal or individual will. This costuming radiates the fearsomeness of the shock trooper, of the automaton. In fact, when the vigilante cops stalk their prey, composer Lalo Schifrin underpins his music with a martial percussion line. So charged is this iconography, it predicts—or may well have inspired—its use in both the low-budget exploitation film *Assault on Precinct 13* (1976) and the mega-budgeted spectacle *Terminator 2: Judgment Day* (1991).

Magnum Force makes the eeriest use of this iconography when the vigilante cops, hoping to recruit Harry, approach him in his parking garage. Harry does not hide his disdain. "You . . . *heroes* have killed a dozen people this week," he says. "What are you going to do next week?" Post and editor Ferris Webster (who edited every one of the fourteen films in which Eastwood starred between 1972's *Joe Kidd* and 1982's *Honkytonk Man*) cut to a new angle that shows the three cops in a diagonal line stretching across the frame and receding into its depth. There is no part of the frame the vigilantes have not captured when they answer Harry: "Kill a dozen more."

The audience has already seen that Harry understands these officers more than he lets on here. Earlier, Harry tells his partner, Early Smith (Felton Perry, also of the same year's *Walking Tall*),

> It's not hard to understand how this could happen nowadays, the way things are. As incredible as it seems, there may be a whole sub-organization within the police force. Sort of a death squad like they had in Brazil some years back.

Harry's reference is to the death squads formed by Brazilian police, which, according to historian Anthony Burton, were a form of counterterrorism that eliminated perpetrators of urban warfare and "signed" their acts (over 1,000 murders between 1964 and 1970) with some iconography of their own: a skull and crossbones.[24]

By citing the Brazilian death squads, Harry puts his nemesis in a larger historical context, a favor he did not extend to Scorpio, even though Scorpio had been inspired by the very real Zodiac Killer. But in Harry's analysis, there is something clinical, something detached. This is curious, given how his own vigilante actions in both films suggest that he and these cops should reflect each other. Harry's speech is more dispassionate than his declaration in *Dirty Harry* that Scorpio will kill again because he likes it and the implication that Harry identifies with the maniac. Oddly then, Harry seems more detached from the vigilante cops of *Magnum Force* than he does from the deranged sniper of *Dirty Harry*.

In Harry's garage, the costuming and composition of San Francisco's death squad are disquieting because they suggest, even if subliminally, that these vigilantes, lacking the individuality—but not the violence—of the frontier hero, can reproduce themselves infinitely. As a foil for Harry, these cops are an inversion of Scorpio. That psychotic had been a single (and singularly) evil entity indulging in multiple modes of destruction. The cops of *Magnum Force*, on the other hand, are a mob. They have no specificity (no faces, no eyes), but they are possessed of a single purpose and almost single modus operandi. What the villains of these two films share is the suggestion of their homosexuality, which in many action films, and their *film noir* progenitors, is equated with sexual deviance. Believing them to be nothing more than talented rookies, Harry asks Smith what he knows about the group. Smith tells him, "They stick together like flypaper, you know? Everybody [at the Academy] thought they were queer for each other." Harry answers, "If the rest of you could shoot like them, I wouldn't care if the whole damn department was queer." And it is no coincidence that of the four, the most effeminate, the blonde Officer Davis, is the ringleader and also the most violent. Nor is it a coincidence that in the next sequel, *The Enforcer*, Harry growls, "You fuckin' fruit" when dispatching the film's flaxen-haired, light-eyed maniac. (With a rocket launcher.)

There are, however, more fundamental connections between the first two *Dirty Harry* films than what they suggest about their villains' sexuality. *Magnum Force* makes no apologies for how it fetishizes guns—indeed, while many action films derive their titles from their characters' names or occupations (*Dirty Harry, McQ, Brannigan, Rambo, Cobra, Robocop, Braddock, The Enforcer, The Terminator, The Specialist, The Punisher, Van Helsing,* etc.), *Magnum Force* is named for its hero's sidearm. In fact, the film's opening credits appear over a single shot of a hand holding the Magnum against a red background. Studying the gun's profile (thereby taking advantage of the widescreen frame), the camera slowly zooms in on the gun. Director Ted Post's credit is set apart from his collaborators' as, just before his credit appears, the thumb cocks the hammer. The gun then turns to the camera. With the credits over, we hear a truncated version of Harry's famous speech from the last film. "This is a .44 Magnum and could blow your head clean off. Do you feel lucky?" The gun fires.

Warner Bros. seized upon Harry's Magnum, one of the most striking emblems of the last film (and now the franchise) to market *Magnum Force*, the first of four sequels. Throughout the studio's press book, different advertising images all emphasize the Magnum. Some show it to be breaking out of a frame-within-the-frame, and exaggerate perspective so that Harry is in the distance but the muzzle looms in the foreground. Many of the other ads show the gun in Harry's hand, in two or three positions simultaneously, suggesting the motion of Harry swinging the gun up into combat-readiness. The last position is rendered with the boldest ink, and affords a view of the gun's underside and considerable length.[25]

As the scene in the ballistics lab suggests, however, Harry's Magnum is not the only weapon with which *Magnum Force* concerns itself. Rather, the film romances weapons in general. Reminiscent of *McQ* and *Dirty Harry*, and in advance of such scenes from *Taxi Driver*, *The Terminator*, *Blue Thunder*, *Lethal Weapon*, and others, Harry and the rookies exchange banter about guns and their specifications: "What kind of load do you use in that .44?" "A light special. This sized gun gives me better control and less recoil than a .357 Magnum with Woodcutters."

Guns drive not just the dialogue, but also the formal properties of the filmmaking itself, such as camera movement, composition, and editing. At a supermarket, a would-be armed robber aims a shotgun at Smith and orders him to his knees. As Smith complies, the camera peers at Smith down the barrel of the gun, and even tilts with it as it tracks Smith. The filmmakers cut to a new angle (this one from behind a two-way mirror), composed such that its elements are connected by guns: Harry's gun is aimed at the robber; the robber's gun is trained on Smith.

In contrast to the suspense created by these images, the violence of the vigilante cops is rapidly cut, letting loose a fierce catharsis. When one of the policemen shoots naked partygoers in a swimming pool, for example, the sequence consists of twelve cuts in ten seconds. These cuts include three inserts of the machine gun muzzle discharging. The final insert is a close-up as the weapon unloads into the camera. Cut for maximum impact, this sequence is the most intense of the film's assassinations because of the destruction visited upon the setting. The machine gun blasts bodies, windows—a low angle nicely exaggerates this particular bit of devastation—and the water itself.

The next entry in the Dirty Harry franchise, James Fargo's The Enforcer, continues its predecessors' fascination with weaponry. In a pre-credit sequence, Fargo introduces Bobby Maxwell (DeVeren Bookwalter), ringleader of The People's Revolutionary Strike Force—a band of urban guerillas reminiscent of the 1970s' Symbionese Liberation Army. Fargo and editor Ferris Webster cut among shots of Maxwell stalking a truck driver and armed with a mini-shotgun, an extreme close-up of Maxwell's hazel green eyes, and a close-up of his knife, outfitted with what seems to be a brass-knuckled handle. Maxwell stabs the driver and shudders with almost orgasmic release. When Maxwell shoots a second driver, Fargo and his special effects technicians take pains to show the driver's beer bottle explode when struck by the shotgun shell.

Harry's first major action sequence displays a similar affinity for exploding glass. Foiling a hostage situation, Harry crashes a car through a liquor store window, and then kills one criminal with three gunshots that smash bottles before finding their target. Later, a chase over San Francisco rooftops finds Harry firing at his quarry. The shots cut down a television antenna, while Harry's target escapes by crashing through a skylight.

Such instances of mayhem show off not just the weapons, but also the effects they have on other objects, animate and inanimate alike. This is a form of spectacle, as is the evolution of the weaponry itself. We have already seen this in the case of Harry's Magnum, as well as McQ's machine gun—a more sophisticated piece of hardware than that borne by the Duke's Western characters. In The Enforcer, an antitank rocket launcher serves this purpose. Two scenes showcase this weapon: the first is a military demonstration Harry and his new partner, Inspector Kate Moore (Tyne Daly) attend, where the rocket launcher is introduced. Intentionally or not, the film articulates the state of war between the police and the criminals depicted elsewhere, when Harry asserts that he is "already checked out" on the rockets.

The second sequence is the film's climax, set on Alcatraz Island, in which Harry kills Maxwell by shooting him with a rocket, blowing him apart against the island's rocks and metal scrap—the detritus of industrialization, echoes of Dirty Harry, Brannigan, and others. The evolution of Harry's weaponry will continue into the next entry in the series, Sudden Impact (1983). In several scenes, Harry's .44 Magnum is replaced with a semiautomatic version. When the gun is introduced during target practice—sunlight gleaming off the barrel in two places—Harry's friend brags about his own shotgun by remarking: "you'll have to strain the remains to get fingerprints." Harry replies, "Well this is the .44 Magnum Automag. It holds a 300 grain cartridge and if used properly, it can *remove* the fingerprints." As Harry speaks, he looks into the camera and holds his new weapon upright, as if he were its official spokesman.

Demolition of the mechanical and the manufactured is so heavily emphasized in Eastwood's follow-up to *The Enforcer*, the film all but abandons most other forms of violence. Eastwood directed *The Gauntlet* (1977), in which he also stars as Ben Shockley, a broken-down, alcoholic Arizona cop dispatched to Las Vegas to retrieve a witness, Gus Mally (Sondra Locke). Throughout the journey back to Phoenix, the pair is forced to utilize (in some cases, steal) various modes of transportation, including a car, a motorcycle, an ambulance, a train, and finally, a bus that Shockley reinforces with one-quarter inch steel. They resort to this because corrupt local police forces—including Shockley's own—are trying to kill Shockley and Gus at every point on the journey.

Their flight, and its attendant mayhem of course, is mostly set against a desert landscape—a contrast to the urban, industrial environs of *Magnum Force* and others. But by using this setting's vastness as a stage for the filmmakers' enthusiastic destruction of the mechanical, *The Gauntlet* demonstrates the action genre's ambivalent relationship with hardware. After all, for a film about two people trying to survive the murderous intentions of two states, the violence visited upon people's bodies is minimal compared to that sustained by property. For two uninterrupted minutes, gunfire pulverizes Gus's house; after the police cease fire, the structure actually collapses. Similarly, at the state line, the police shoot at a constable's car that has been commandeered by Gus and Shockley. The bullets, fired by silhouetted policemen and from darkened police cruisers (in imagery that predicts a SWAT team's assault on the title character of *Robocop*), ravage the car for thirty-two seconds. Later, a helicopter chases our hero and heroine as they try to flee on a stolen motorcycle. From the helicopter, gunfire rains down on Shockley and Gus, who evade the chopper and cause it to get tangled in power lines. The helicopter explodes, but then, as if the sequence still wanted for a coup de grâce, an electrical tower collapses. Finally, and most memorably, is Shockley and Gus's slow roll into Phoenix, as police blast away at the bus he has armored. The bus is demolished; our heroes are not. Such calamitous spectacle, along with the film's "road movie" format, is likely what inspired the *Los Angeles Herald Examiner's* critic to remark, "*The Gauntlet* is Clint Eastwood's Road Runner movie."[26]

Less cartoonish is Black Sunday (1977), a film similarly concerned with spectacle and vigilantism, while also aligned with the disaster films of the decade. Directed by John Frankenheimer (whose French Connection II motivated producer Robert Evans to hire him), Black Sunday follows the struggle of Israeli commando Major David Kabakov (Robert Shaw) to stop Palestinian terrorist Dahlia Iyad (Marthe Keller) and her American lover, former U.S. military captain and prisoner-of-war Michael Lander (Bruce Dern). Their plot is to convert the Goodyear blimp into a weapon that will kill multiple thousands of Americans at the Super Bowl in Miami. "The Paramount release looks like a good [box office] prospect," Daily Variety assessed, "though unmeasurable [sic] and subliminal human revulsion may work against it."[27]

At the time of the film's release, many critics linked Black Sunday to the disaster films best typified by The Poseidon Adventure (1972), The Towering Inferno (1974) and Earthquake (1974), a linkage that is not unfair: one of the film's most powerful images comes from its finale, in which the blimp, out of control, flies into the stadium, topples its press box and towering lights, and scatters panicking fans. Indeed, the film's print advertisements showcase the blimp's "attack" on the stadium and the fleeing attendees. The copy reads, "It could be tomorrow!"—a message which, even taking into account the decade's high level of worldwide terrorism, is even more ominous in a post–September 11 world. But unlike the era's classic disaster films, Black Sunday trades on the promise of spectacle more than it does the spectacle itself. Most of the drama of The Towering Inferno, for instance, stems from the characters' attempts to survive the fire, not to keep it from happening; in Black Sunday, however, the hero's project is to prevent the disaster—an explosion that would perforate the Super Bowl spectators with some 80,000 nails.

If this potential for disaster—rather than a disaster actually unleashed—leaves the film with any void, this void is filled by classic action character types: the vigilante law enforcer, the sidelined partner, the terrorist, the outright maniac. In Black Sunday, these types are given specific cultural, historical, and political contexts, which action moviemakers are usually more reluctant to explore. The terrorists in the film, as well as in the novel on which it is based (the first by Thomas Harris, author The Silence of the Lambs), belong to the Black September movement, which did exist in the early 1970s. Black September's tactics included murder and hijacking; its most infamous act was the killing of the Israeli athletes at the 1972 Munich Olympics.

Critics seized upon Black Sunday's novelty of presenting terrorists who have an actual agenda—in this case, the cessation of the United States's aid to Israel. *The Hollywood Reporter* notes that the difference between the villains of *Black Sunday* and others is that "this terrorism is not the work of a mindless, anonymous, trigger-happy kook."[28] One early scene shows Dahlia even lamenting the impending massacre. Indeed, the film's most disquieting dynamic is that for all of Dahlia's fanaticism, her relish for killing is outstripped by her American lover's. Dahlia and her comrades are not the terrorists of *The Enforcer*—a group modeled after the Symbionese Liberation Army, and divested of any ideology. Most members of *The Enforcer's* People's Revolutionary Strike Force use the rhetoric of freedom fighters to cover up what is nothing more than their greed. This will become a staple of the genre in the 1990s, when much action movie terror is conducted with no underlying political conviction. This could be interpreted as skittishness on the part of the studios, a skittishness that may have briefly dogged the development of *Black Sunday*. When *Daily Variety* reported that veteran screenwriter Ernest Lehman would be adapting Harris's novel, the trade paper specified that the book "deals with Arab terrorists threatening to kill 85,000 spectators to cause cutoff of U.S. aid to Israel, but [Paramount's] announcement describes the film's terrorists as only 'a radical group.'"[29]

Political conviction is not solely the domain of the terrorists, however. Although Kabakov confesses to his young partner, Robert (Steven Keats), that he has become weary of the war he has spent thirty years fighting, he still sees Israeli sovereignty and survival as a global matter in which he is personally vested. Recovering from injuries sustained in a bombing attempt, Kabakov reveals that his parents, wife, and two sons are dead. He has one daughter living in Jerusalem, he says, then adds, "Jerusalem, *Israel.*" At his bedside is FBI agent Sam Corley (Fritz Weaver), who will become Kabakov's de facto partner after Robert's murder. Commenting on Kabakov's predilection for vigilante action, Corely says, "In your own operational circle in Israel, I understand that behind your back they call you 'The Final Solution'—a man who takes things to their ultimate conclusion and beyond." This moniker casts Kabakov as the generic loner willing to go to extremes, willing to do what the society under his protection is not. However, derived from the name given to Hitler's genocidal plan for the Jews, the nickname also casts a shadow over this resolve, and taints Kabakov's willingness with a grim historical irony. Kabakov compounds this irony when he answers, "Some of them say that to my face." Here, Kabakov signals that he accepts this mythic persona out of political necessity. This makes Major Kabakov unique among the movie vigilantes considered thus far—heroes whose wars are ideological, but rarely political.

The apotheosis of this more apolitical vigilantism might not be that of Harry Callahan or Paul Kersey, but instead, that of *Taxi Driver*'s Travis Bickle (Robert De Niro). Directed by Martin Scorsese, *Taxi Driver* (1976) is not strictly an action film—its generic composition and frankly, its artistry, are too complex to justify such a reduction. It is, however, one of the 1970s' seminal vigilante films, a trend that contributed more to the formation of the action genre than did any other trend in American films of that decade.

Perhaps it is ironic that while set against a distinctly late 1970s Manhattan, Travis's vigilantism exists outside history. Christopher Sharrett notes the refusal of the film and its antihero to "examine events in a political/historical context, opting instead for a perception of all reality as angelic/demonic."[30] Sharrett's terminology is significant: while many critics have singled *Taxi Driver*'s references to the Western, the mythology Sharrett examines is that of the apocalypse. He observes:

> Ever since the Puritans, the apocalyptic view of history and human destiny has been a controlling force in American art . . . Martin Scorsese's *Taxi Driver* . . . a preeminent example of apocalyptic art of the 1970s, suggests very well the original Puritan belief in a divinely-ordained historical destiny, which, when violated or ignored, will cause a cataclysmic retribution. *Taxi Driver* proposes that the divine contract has been undone and that Manifest Destiny is at an end. As the film deconstructs and debunks the conventions or various film genres, it provides not ideological criticism but the ahistorical and fatalistic vision of apocalypticism.[31]

Taxi Driver's suggestion that this divine contract has been undone and that Manifest Destiny has reached an end resonates with the anxiety expressed in 1960s' and early 1970s' Westerns over the closing of the frontier. It also resonates with the era's assault on "white male privilege"—in American society and in film—wherein the positions of authority traditionally enjoyed by white males came under fire by feminists and minority groups. This anxiety has been the subject of much of the writing devoted to *film noir* and the action film; similarly, Travis's response to the erosion of order, both the divine and the patriarchal varieties, makes up much of *Taxi Driver*.

Travis is a New York City cabbie and Vietnam veteran. He is a loner, estranged from society, from himself, and increasingly, from reality. Jilted by Betsy (Cybill Shephard), the one thing of beauty Travis had found in a city that disgusts him and practically bursting from the pressure to "go out and really *do* something" with the "bad ideas in [his] head," Travis arms himself. Heavily. His first attempt to "do something" is a failed assassination attempt on Betsy's political idol. Ultimately though, Travis channels his fury into the slaughter of the pimps and criminals surrounding Travis's new friend, Iris (Jodie Foster), a twelve-year-old prostitute.

Indeed, Scorsese's New York is a Sodom or Gomorrah of the modern world. And because Travis can make no meaningful connections with others, he expresses himself most pointedly through voiceover narration. This is rationalized not as a recounting of his story to another (as in so many films noir), but as entries in his diary, as Travis's talking to himself. His disgust is already roiling when the audience first joins him in his cab. In voiceover, Travis echoes an almost identical thought (and scene) from Dirty Harry, in which Harry, looking out the car window at a tableau of urban inequity, remarks, "These loonies. They ought to throw a net over the whole bunch of 'em." Travis's reflection, however, is less distanced: "All the animals come out at night. Whores, skunk pussies, buggers, queens, fairies, dopers, junkies. Sick, venal. Someday, a real rain will come and wash all the scum off the streets." The slang that propels the first part of this monologue (which, like all slang, is specific to a time and place) makes Travis's concluding thought all the more striking for its apocalyptic force. Indeed, many cultures outside, and even predating, the Judeo-Christian sphere have used flood myths to depict divine purging.

The imagery of apocalypse Travis invokes is grander than the modern setting in which he dwells. Similarly, his psychosis is larger than any simple psychological defect. According to producer Michael Phillips, "Paul Schrader, who wrote the screenplay, deliberately avoided defining the roots of Travis' schizophrenia, because all attempts become clichés. *Travis symbolizes the universal psychotic*" (emphasis original).[32] This aligns Travis with the Scorpios of the world as much as it does the Inspector Callahans; and if there is an element of Scorpio in Harry Callahan, then in Travis Bickle, there are elements of both.

As the film progresses, Travis increasingly sees himself as the agent of this apocalypse. To enact this myth—or any myth—there must be at least an element of the ritualistic. Travis's most striking rituals are those that prepare him for his final act of purging the city's scum. The first is buying his arsenal, a scene that both visually and verbally displays the same obsession with guns as seen in other vigilante films. The other rituals are stitched together in a montage: Travis exercising (honing his body), practicing at a firing range (honing is skill), rigging contraptions to conceal and quickly deploy his weapons (honing his method), and holding his hand over the flame of his stove (honing his will, symbolically purging his impurities).

Travis also hones his purpose and, with it, his identity. "Listen you fucks, you screwheads," he declares in his voiceover. "Here is a man who would not take it anymore. A man who stood up against the cunts, the dogs, the filth, the shit. Here is someone who stood up. Here is—." In this montage, Scorsese includes inserts of Travis's diary pages. We see in Travis's handwriting "Here is," but the voiceover does not complete the sentence. Instead, Scorsese cuts to Travis drawing his gun. The gun is the noun, the end of the sentence. The gun is what Travis is.

Despite Travis's declarations of who he is, it is clear that he is losing himself. This unraveling, as much as the film's final bloodletting (the colors of which had to be desaturated in order to avoid an X rating from the Motion Picture Association of America), has led some critics and scholars to recognize the film's affinity for the horror genre as much as its kinship with the Western. As influences on Travis's deterioration, Sharrett weights the two genres equally. Likewise, *Daily Variety*'s review deems Paul Schrader's screenplay "a sociological horror story."[33] Richard Corliss's review for *New Times* notes, "*Taxi Driver* is an urban horror movie, and by its climax Travis has become *Psycho*'s Norman Bates transformed into an urban guerilla." Corliss then claims that this climactic scene is "a blood ballet that's half-Peckinpah and half *Night of the Living Dead*." He concludes by arguing, "If *Taxi Driver* becomes a hit, it won't be because it's brilliantly made but because it feeds the *Death Wish* fantasy of too many Americans."[34] Even harsher is Arthur Knight, whose review for *The Hollywood Reporter* argues that Travis "strongly resembles Charles Bronson in *Death Wish*, except that Travis is a sentimental idiot."[35]

Many of *Taxi Driver*'s shades of horror can also be cast as elements of *film noir*. Noir's influence on *Taxi Driver* has a long history: while still a film student at UCLA, Schrader, an enthusiast of the genre, wrote "Notes on Film Noir," an essay that would help drive the interest in *film noir* through the 1970s. As for how *Taxi Driver* embodies *noir*, Sharrett provides a lucid accounting: "the morbid atmosphere of the film; the focus on misdirected or perverse sexuality, the chiaroscuro urban setting, psychology as a theme, and . . . the contribution of [Bernard] Herrmann's score."[36] Indeed, at the time of the film's release, the *Los Angeles Herald Examiner* called *Taxi Driver* "1940s *film noir* stripped of its glamorous allure."[37]

The film's twelve-year-old Iris, as both the locus for the film's "misdirected sexuality" and the object of Travis's rescue (that is, the justification for his rampage), connects *Taxi Driver*'s noir-esque world to the Western myth underpinning it. Examining the film's complicated generic matrix, Sharrett juxtaposes these *noir* elements with Western themes such as vengeance, rescue, and the return of the war veteran. Occasionally, these traditions emerge in the form of recognizable, if distended, Western iconography. *Taxi Driver* is informed by the Western genre as a whole, but if it has any one point of reference, it is John Ford's 1956 classic *The Searchers*, in which Civil War veteran Ethan Edwards searches for his nieces, abducted by Comanche Indians in 1860s Texas. Comparing *Taxi Driver* to *The Searchers*, Daniel Boyd observes that both Ethan and Travis are "first seen wearing the uniform of a war over . . . and in each case, it is the uniform of the defeated side."[38] Likewise, Iris's pimp, Sport (Harvey Keitel), calling attention to Travis's cowboy boots, likens Travis to Western gunfighters.

Sport is a reference to another character from *The Searchers*: Scar, the Indian chief who abducted Ethan's nieces, Lucy and Debbie, thereby triggering his six-year search. Lucy is found dead after being sexually violated. Debbie, however, grows to womanhood. The audience learns that Ethan intends not to rescue Debbie, but to kill her: better she die than live as a Comanche (that is, sexually corrupted by one). Likewise, Sport has corrupted Iris, both as her pimp and as her lover. But in selling her childhood by the half-hour, he purchases Travis's fury, which Travis visits upon the sleazy building where Sport conducts his business. Travis stalks his way through his rescue attempt, killing all but Iris and himself (though he does attempt suicide) in a rampage that is as stilted as Ethan and the cavalry's is propulsive.

But if Travis is willing to assume aspects of Ethan Edwards—from his costuming to his violent retribution—he also goes a step beyond anything Ethan would have done: Travis shaves his head, adopting a Mohawk haircut. Sharrett sees two dimensions to the Mohawk: "[it] is the caricatured rendering of the psychotic Vietnam veteran. [It] also actualizes the image of the Indian as demon/victim."[39] Occasionally in the action genre, villains will sometimes appropriate and corrupt icons of heroes or of society; consider Scorpio's peace symbol belt buckle in *Dirty Harry*, the vigilantes' helmets and uniforms in *Magnum Force* (and that appear again on the murderous T-1000 in *Terminator 2*), a tin star worn by the maniac Luther in *The Warriors* (1979), and the cowboy boots worn by an American terrorist in *Die Hard* (1988). Appropriated by the *other*, the icon becomes hollow.

In *Taxi Driver*, however, instead of the villain adopting the symbols of the hero, it is the hero (or more precisely, antihero), who adopts the symbol—and presumably, the spirit—of what has traditionally been the enemy. On one level, this is simply making overt what might have otherwise been too latent:

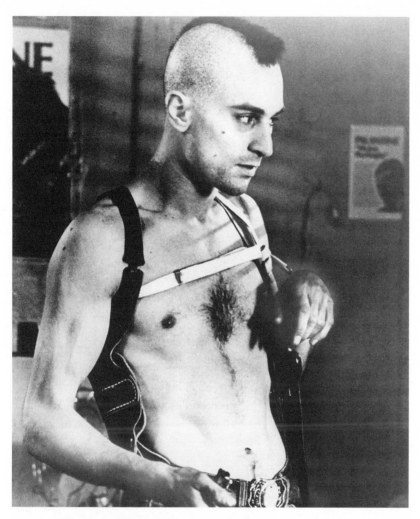

The Lone Gunman: *The title character of Martin Scorsese's
1976 film* Taxi Driver, *disaffected cabbie Travis Bickle (Robert
De Niro), prepares for his violent catharsis and makes overt
the Western's "The Man Who Knows Indians" archetype.
(From the author's collection.)*

that the character of Travis is founded on the Western's "The Man Who Knows Indians" archetype, the psychology of which is mirrored by the classically *noir* theme of duality. Visually, however, this imagery is so extreme, it pushes past the level of archetype and into a darker realm—one where the irony is not that the villain claims the icons of the righteous, but rather, that the supposed righteous bolsters himself with the totems of a traditional enemy. This is especially significant when considering genre films of the late 1960s and 1970s, a period of confused generic conventions, and distrust of the ideologies they had so often embodied.

Colliding and reorienting generic conventions is a form of spectacle unto itself, one which the action genre often uses to inflate the myth of vigilante action. Essentially an exploitation film, John Carpenter's low-budget *Assault on Precinct 13* follows a similar pattern of blending genres and movie references and creates a sense of ritual experienced by the characters and by the audience. The film is set in "Anderson," a Los Angeles ghetto with a new police precinct set to open and the old one preparing to close. On the outdated precinct's last night in operation, only a new lieutenant, two secretaries, and two death-row inmates occupy the building. Soon, it is besieged by punks—scores and scores of punks. They seek to avenge themselves on the police and also claim the civilian who, outraged by the murder of his daughter, killed a gang leader and sought refuge inside the precinct. With the civilian unconscious, the other five (and that number dwindles) must repel the horde. This scenario recalls how David Sumner (Dustin Hoffman) repels the villagers in Sam Peckinpah's *Straw Dogs* (1971). In the film's third act, Hoffman's mathematician uses his ingenuity and previously untapped capacity for violence to defend those inside his country home, and in the process, finds the inner warrior beneath his outer weakling.

As many critics and Carpenter himself have attested, *Assault on Precinct 13* is heavily influenced by Westerns, and is specifically derived from Howard Hawks's *Rio Bravo* (1959), a film in which John Wayne and company must defend a jailhouse from an encroaching enemy. But Carpenter's affinity for Western settings is not limited to the jail. Anderson itself recalls a Western landscape. Like a desert, it feels flat and barren, which is striking for a movie that is set in the urban jungle. Modern cities call to mind the vertical, while Anderson suggests the horizontal, the frontier on which so many Westerns were set. However, economically depressed and overrun by crime, Anderson does not seem to be a frontier as much as it does a margin; it does not suggest Manifest Destiny so much as it does dread made manifest. Thus, with the establishing shots of the community, Carpenter begins to subtly stitch the Western and the horror film into the canvas that will be the action's backdrop.

This is intensified by the ritualism with which Carpenter presents the gang. First, there is the blood ritual in which several gang members participate. After the film's opening, in which six or seven youths are ambushed and fired upon from elevated positions by anonymous police officers (almost identical to the vigilante cops of *Magnum Force*), we soon see a racially integrated group of gang members prepare for battle by cutting open their arms and pouring their blood into a glass bowl. Later, when the gang begins its assault, one of the convicts recognizes the symbol the gang has lain before the precinct—the gauntlet it has thrown down.

Here we are told that this gang fights for the sake of fighting, kills for the sake of killing. It has no ideology, no higher rationale. When the gang members advance, they are photographed from a distance, so as to deemphasize their individuality. When they try to breech the precinct walls, they are repelled by the heroes' gunfire, but just as quickly, replenish their numbers. When the gang members open fire, blowing out windows and riddling walls, they do so with silencers. Without the sound of the gunshots, the damage inflicted on the precinct seems to have no tangible cause, instead taking on an almost metaphysical air. The film suggests the gang and the destructiveness it wields are forces of nature, like the rampaging Indians of so many Westerns.

The Indians of such films and the "Indians" of *Assault on Precinct 13* each embody their wilderness, but whereas the actual Indians are rooted in nature, the gang members in this film are decidedly unnatural, even unholy. They are like zombies: slowly moving but never stopping—not living, not dead, and not killable. They are, in the words of critic J. Hoberman, "as implacable and mindlessly malevolent as a squadron of [George] Romero ghouls."[40] Nature and the undead are thus interchangeable in their assault on civilization.

As the film synthesizes the Western and horror, it also synthesizes horror and *noir*. Carpenter makes heavy use of slashing horizontal shadows, which are justified by the Venetian blinds hung throughout the set. These shadows maximize the atmosphere for a film made on a minimal budget, but as staples of *film noir*, they also elevate the film by situating it within a generic tradition (and in the process, demonstrate why genre citation is often the last refuge of the underfunded).

In the aftermath of one assault, the gang makes one of its less overt but more disquieting gestures by removing the bodies of the fallen and hiding all signs of disturbance. The action is even more unnerving for taking place offscreen; the audience does not see it. The removal of the corpses (by what are essentially corpses themselves) resonates with horror, but the consequence—the appearance of normalcy to anyone glancing in the precinct's direction—is suggestive of the home invasion cycle of *film noir*. Typified by John Berry's *He Ran All the Way* (1951) and William Wyler's *The Desperate Hours* (1955), these are films in which fugitive criminals lay siege to a home, hold some of the family members prisoner and send others out into the world to suggest that all is normal, to prevent suspicion. No one hears the family; no one knows what is happening. Stifled shouts, shifting alliances, the destabilizing of otherwise secure spaces: these are the components of the *noir*–home invasion film's choking suspense.

One mark of the home invasion film is the pretense of normalcy, which the gang affects outside. But *Assault on Precinct 13*'s affinity for the home invasion film does not stop at the precinct walls. Rationality (a counterpoint to both the wild and the undead) begins to break down inside the building as well, allowing the *noir* of the outside to seep in through the fissures. Another convention of the home invasion film is the breakdown of alliances, the fallout of which leaves the family members unable to trust one another. Carpenter develops this tension within the group—especially between Lieutenant Ethan Bishop (Austin Stoker) and convict Napoleon Wilson (Darwin Joston), the film's main good guy-criminal whom Bishop arms; and to lesser extents, between Wilson and the other inmate Wells (Tony Burton); and between the group and the weak-willed secretary Julie (Nancy Loomis).

Even during the gang's primary assault, when it is certain that Bishop, Wilson, Wells, and heroic secretary Leigh (Laurie Zimmer) are firing at a common enemy, Carpenter edits the sequence to exploit the uncertainty of their alliance. Four heroes unleash their firepower; obviously, they are firing out at the precinct's perimeter, with each one probably defending one wall. To make this clear, a filmmaker would compose and edit the shots so that the characters' gunfire seems to be aimed outwards. Carpenter, however, does something else. His characters seem to face toward the center of the frame. As a consequence, they appear to be firing not out toward the perimeter, but *in* toward the *center*: in other words, at one another. And as Carpenter accelerates the sequence, he eliminates shots of bodies falling, such that a shot of one character firing is answered by a shot of another character seeming to fire back. And as the sequence intensifies, so does the soundtrack. Unlike the gang members, whose guns are silenced, the defenders of Precinct 13 each have different guns, and each makes a different report until the sound becomes catharsis and discord all at once.

If *Assault on Precinct 13* is an action film in which the Western, horror, and *film noir* are tangled together, then Walter Hill's *The Warriors* (1979) is one that grabs from the Western, *noir*, martial arts movies, jungle adventures, and the combat film. The plot is simple: the Warriors, a New York gang, is framed for the murder of a messianic gang leader and has one night to fight its way through rival gangs and the police, from the Bronx back home to Coney Island. *The Warriors* is not reserved when it comes to style; indeed, it is the excessiveness of the costumes, of the fight choreography, and of Andrew Laszlo's cinematography that somehow enables the film's grab bag of generic referents to hold together.

The Warriors is a rare action movie in that there is virtually no gunplay. Guns are used only twice, both times by Luther (David Patrick Kelly), the villain. The first time is when he assassinates Cyrus (Roger Hill), a gang leader who wants to unite all of the gangs and overthrow the police. The second is when he fires at Swan (Michael Beck), the Warriors' "war chief," during their standoff at the film's end. Between the movie's inciting moment of violence and its final one, virtually all the fighting is hand-to-hand. In the park, rival gang members surround one of the Warriors, who then fends them off in the style of a martial arts movie. Other than hands, the weapons most stressed by the film are the baseball bats wielded by the Baseball Furies, a frightening tribe whose face-painted members dress like the New York Yankees. The Furies perform feats with their bats that border on the acrobatic, but the Warriors manage to turn the bats against their owners. Both gangs twirl and strike with the bats as if they were staffs in a kung fu film. Another gang, the Gramercy Riffs, also recalls the martial arts movie. The Riffs often appear in red robes, standing in columns before their black-clad leaders. These soldiers answer their leaders in unison, always ready to do their leaders' bidding.

The Warriors also inherits from *film noir* and from the Western. Derived from *film noir* is Luther, whose sadistic indulgences and flaxen hair make him the bastard son of *noir* aesthetes and heir to Scorpio. Meanwhile, the Lizzies are femmes fatale masquerading as juvenile delinquents. They seduce a faction of the Warriors only to try to murder them. The film's Western references are more inverted: ironically, as the most savage of the savages, Luther has a sheriff's tin star affixed to his leather jacket. But the end of the film offers the hero a chance to reorient some iconography of his own. The climactic standoff between Luther and Swan, set against the Coney Island shore, is a Western-esque fast draw. Luther fires a gun; Swan flings a knife. His arm speared, Luther falls to his knees. Swan grabs Luther's hair, pulls it back, and wipes the bloody knife clean against it. The image suggests a scalping, but one commit-ted by—not to—the white hero.

In *The Warriors*, gangs are the savages, and the city is their wilderness, "a hostile neon jungle" and "an exotic, almost alien world of unknown dangers," according to *The Hollywood Reporter*.[41] While our heroes would like nothing more than to take the nearest B-train out of Indian country, the city seems to exist solely as a stage for gang action, and as a space that exists only to be tra-versed. This effect is completed by the film's almost total lack of extras. There are no "civilians" on these streets, only combatants. Thus the city is a ritual-ized space; it exists as a dream state. And as a dream state, spatial orientation begins to fold in on itself, despite the linearity of the Warriors' journey. As the *Village Voice* noted in 2001, "For the beleaguered Warriors . . . urban space sud-denly decays from an orderly and marked set of territories into a carnivalesque and almost incoherent series of scrawls. Allies become enemies, seduction suddenly warps into violence."[42]

The carnivalesque that this critic and others have observed is also a key component of the film's spectacle. According to Pauline Kael, "this picture isn't a melodrama; it's a fantasy spectacle that has found its style in the taste of the dispossessed—in neon signs, graffiti, and the thrill of gaudiness."[43] As spectacle, this clashing that Kael suggests is inherent to the film's atmosphere parallels the filmmakers' patchworking of multiple genres: both make public display of the modes of expression themselves. Kael's remark raises an addi-tional question: if, for all its graffiti and neon, the world of *The Warriors* is the world of the dispossessed, then whose world is that of say, *Magnum Force*, driven as it is by industry? In this context, the industrialization that *Magnum Force* and its ilk display would further entrench these films in the conservatism with which the action genre (the *Dirty Harry* series in particular) has so often been charged.

However, this is not to hold up *The Warriors* as any great bastion of progres-sivism. It is true that the Warriors are racially integrated, "an improbably harmonious mixture," according to critic David Denby, one that "possibly re-flects commercial calculation: the movie is designed to do well in *all* the neigh-borhoods" (emphasis in original).[44] But it is the Warriors' cumulative identity that is most important. In fairness to Denby, this does not escape him. He writes, "In the past, Hill has made films in semi-mythical style about loner outsiders. . . this time he's celebrating a loner gang."[45]

While Denby's skepticism of the Warriors' racial complexion might be jus-tifiable, this "improbable mixture" also reflects the multiracial platoons of

"Warriors, Come Out to Play-yaaaaay": *In Walter Hill's* The
Warriors *(1979), tribal warfare comes to the streets of New
York City as a Warrior battles a member of the Baseball
Furies. (From the author's collection.)*

World War II combat films (which may represent an even greater fiction than does a multiracial street gang). This is articulated by critics as well as by Paramount's publicity machine. According to Paramount,

> Lawrence Gordon's production of 'The Warriors,' presented by Paramount Pictures, is not an attempt to depict any real-life gang or actual incident. The aim of the film is to capture the flavor of what it has always meant to be a member of a gang—the tribal feeling of going into battle together, of loyalty, of support and shared goals.[46]

Denby recognizes the film's tribal aspect, but sees it as an attempt to compensate for weak character development. He writes, "Hill doesn't even bother to develop the relations among the gang members—it's the gang as spiritual entity that counts."[47] Perhaps *Los Angeles Herald Examiner* critic Michael Sragow offers the most succinct evaluation of the film and also of the departure it marks from the generic tradition with which it might be most readily (but myopically) associated: "Unlike most movies about violent [juvenile delinquents], *The Warriors* doesn't deal with youthful revolt, but with straight-out war."[48]

Indeed, war had come to the streets of New York. And to those of San Francisco. And of Los Angeles and Chicago. And to the desert of the southwest and to the skies over Miami. Waging this war was the urban vigilante, cop and otherwise. Like many veterans and historians of that era's real-life war, the vigilante would tell you that powers greater than his own (bureaucratically that is, not mythically), allow him to fight, but not to win. What he might not tell you is that what makes him such a potent weapon in this war—apart from the potent weapons he brings to it—is also what makes him so disdained by the system: those elements of the enemy, of the *other*, that resonate with the hero's own nature.

Needed but not wanted, the vigilante hero draws his strength not from the community, but from generic traditions that predate the action film. Often, the stars and filmmakers who crafted these heroes (and villains) had been part of those traditions themselves, having worked in Westerns before adopting this newer urban format. Both archetypes, the hero and the villain go to war with each other against backdrops of modernity and industry. This underscores the timelessness of their conflict because theirs is the conflict between civilization and savage, between order and anarchy, the conflict of the Western and prior to that, of frontier literature dating back to the seventeenth century. Only, in the 1970s, the frontier was closed and Hollywood filmmaking often distrusted and distended traditions of genre. Perhaps it is strange then, that during this time of generic confusion, the Western, *film noir*, and others coalesced into what in the following decades would become one of Hollywood's most archetypal, and most exported, film genres.

In the 1980s, the vigilante tradition would persist, partly as a strata of exploitation movies that reinforced the genre's increasingly spectacular productions. A roster of such films—most of them schlock—would include the *Death Wish* sequels; *The Exterminator* (1980); Abel Ferrara's *Ms. 45* (1981), a well-crafted gender-bending thriller also known as *Angel of Vengeance*, in which a mute woman descends into vigilantism after being raped twice on the same day; and the aptly titled *Vigilante* (1983). For this last film, the advertising copy says it all: "Attention criminals! The cops turn their backs. The courts set you free. If they can't stop you . . . we will!" The sentiment is reiterated toward the bottom, just above the credit block: "We are armed. We are ready."[49]

But prior to these films new action stars were already on the horizon—ones whose personae would dovetail with the conservative politics and paramilitary culture of the new decade. These would be the first action stars to enjoy fame not previously established in Westerns, war films, or police procedurals. And as the action film further established itself and outgrew its more direct connections to the Western, we find a fitting elegy in the June 1979 death of John Wayne. The passing of the Western's greatest icon at this particular moment is of course a coincidence; nonetheless, it marks a poetic close to this transitional era of film—and film genre—history.

2 Automatons
Rise of the Killing Machines

It can't be bargained with. It can't be reasoned with. It doesn't feel pity or remorse or fear. And it absolutely will not stop. Ever. Until you are dead.
—Reese (Michael Biehn) in The Terminator (1984)

To the urban rot that the 1970s action hero set out to stem, pastoral images of farms, suburbs, and churches would certainly have been a counterpoint. In 1984, such images were not the stuff of a new trend in the genre (although the genre *was* changing); rather, they were part of Ronald Reagan's campaign to retain the presidency of the United States. The theme of his reelection campaign, "Morning in America," suggested economic and political, but moreover, moral rebirth. It was charged with promises for the future, while invoking an idealized past. "Morning in America" was therefore the perfect backdrop for the decade's new species of action hero, personified by new superstars Sylvester Stallone and Arnold Schwarzenegger. This model of hero signified a previously unseen standard of masculinity and tapped directly into the warrior myths and racial politics of America's frontier past. With over-the-top stunt sequences and pyrotechnics, he wrought destruction that was proportional to his overdeveloped physique, weaponry, and combat skills.

All of these were the action hero's weapons, and as society's exceptional—but still underdog—savior, he deployed them against an enemy whose savagery resonated with the decade's anticommunist ethos. In 1983, Reagan set a tone for the next several years when famously casting the Soviet Union as the world's "Evil Empire." This followed Reagan's sharp midterm decline in popularity and America's slide into a recession. Reinvigorated, this Cold War paranoia nourished the era's action films. Reaganite entertainments, to be sure, these movies stress the threat posed to society by an enemy, often a horde, that is *other*; a group whose evil is a byproduct of its psychological, political, or racial composition. In response, the hero's mission becomes one of extermination. Richard Slotkin explains that such notions of the "savage war" have been both "mythic trope" and "military doctrine" in America and lie at the heart of America's "myth of the frontier"—a foundational myth characterized by "separation, temporary regression to a more primitive or 'natural' state, and *regeneration through violence*" (emphasis in original).[1] For the action hero, this purging regenerates not only his own spirit, but also the community's. "Morning in America" indeed. But while the nation's political climate fueled the 1980s action film, the genre's popularity also informed the Reagan administration's rhetoric, as when Reagan would invoke Harry Callahan's "Make my day" (from 1983's *Sudden Impact*) or joke about *Rambo* as a blueprint for hostage recovery.

It might seem curious then, that at the outset of this era—an era in which American and male identities were fused and revitalized—Sylvester Stallone's first entry into the action genre underplays, and even undercuts, this new masculinity. The film is Bruce Malmuth's 1981 directorial debut *Nighthawks*; until then, he had been known mostly for his Excedrin commercials (as might befit an action film director).[2] Although *Nighthawks* precedes the *Rambo* trilogy (1982, 1985, 1988) and *Cobra*, films that better represent both Stallone's persona and the decade's action filmmaking, *Nighthawks's* subversive quality may be seen as a riff on Stallone's hard-body persona established in part by his portrayal of Rocky Balboa in *Rocky* (1976) and *Rocky II* (1979).

One might expect gender-bending from an actor already established in the action genre, such as Clint Eastwood, director and star of *Sudden Impact*, in which Harry pursues his female doppelganger: a rape-victim-turned-vigilante. But from Stallone, still early in his career, this is surprising. Throughout *Nighthawks*, in which Stallone and Billy Dee Williams play New York City cops pursuing international terrorist Wulfgar (Rutger Hauer), Stallone's character, Deke DaSilva, hesitates to use deadly force and is eager to communicate with his fashion designer ex-wife Irene (Lindsay Wagner). In one scene, he softly emotes to Irene just moments after being framed behind a lingerie-clad mannequin. Moreover, the film is bookended by images of Stallone in drag. The first sequence begins with DaSilva, undercover as a woman, waiting for would-be muggers to spring. The last shows DaSilva in a nightgown and wig, a trap for Wulfgar. As Wulfgar stalks forward with a knife, DaSilva turns, an insane sight with his long blonde "hair" and dark, fully-grown beard.

Of course, these jabs at masculinity frame (and occasionally punctuate) what is otherwise a masculine world. This is embodied in the film's dark color palette, which is driven by browns, blacks, blues, grays, and rust and also in its industrial backdrops. One sequence takes the viewer on a tour of this world, as Deke and his partner, Mathew Fox (Williams) chase Wulfgar from a nightclub, through a construction site, down a tunnel, onto the subway platform at the 57th Street station, onto a train, and finally, onto the platform at 42nd Street.

Wulfgar eludes them, but not before slashing and disabling Fox. This, along with the murder of their superior, triggers a transformation in DaSilva. At a firing range, the camera pushes in on him as he shoots, possessed. Red lights fan and flare over the gray ceiling and walls, predicting the imagery of *Cobra* and a score of others. DaSilva is now warming to the violent agenda of Peter Hartman (Nigel Davenport), his British mentor and founder of ATAC, their counterterrorism squad. As Hartman explains earlier, ATAC, or Anti-Terrorism Action Command, "has been formed because of a serious lack of ruthlessness on the part of the police." Behind him, a film shows the recovery of dead hostages. Off to the side is a pull-down display of various handguns.

Before transforming, DaSilva resists what Hartman advocates: killing Wulfgar. "How do you expect me to understand that you're training us to be nothing but assassins?" DaSilva protests. "And the only difference between him and us will be the badge . . . I didn't join the force to kill people." Here, DaSilva opposes the 1970s vigilante cops who preceded him and the generations of Western gunfighters and *film noir* antiheroes who preceded them. He sounds more like an urban pacifist than pacifier. This is despite the fact that, consistent with these genres' tradition, DaSilva is a war veteran: he served in the army in Vietnam and, as Hartman reveals, scored "fifty-two registered kills in combat."

But in the war on Wulfgar, it takes the attack on Fox, Hartman's murder, and lastly, a hostage crisis on a Roosevelt Island tram to fully stir DaSilva's inner combatant. Once it is awakened (recalling the converted liberals seen in the last chapter), DaSilva, in a brief montage charged with ritual, prepares himself by donning his uniform: black clothes over which he zips an ATAC jumpsuit, black gloves, and a black ATAC cap. This is his armor, his insulation. It is also a shade of the wardrobe Stallone will wear in *Cobra* and of the ones worn by Schwarzenegger in the *Terminator* films (1984, 1991, 2003), *Eraser* (1996), and so on. Such costuming evokes a certain hunter-ethos, but more importantly, an emotional and even physical impregnability. A fear of the *other*, defined by race or by a substitute for it, infuses these films with its fear of bodily corruption. The hero's clothing constitutes protection. Nothing gets in. But neither does anything get out, as such wardrobe also signifies the hero's self-containment and, by extension, emotional reticence. As much as action filmmakers of the 1980s seek to dazzle audiences with the exposed bodies of their heroes, how they *cover* these bodies also comes to be a potent, if more subtle, convention of the genre.

This threat of corruption is most often manifested in the suggestion of sexual and/or biological impurity, as we saw with the *film noir*-derived aesthetes of the 1970s. Wulfgar continues this trend, telling his plastic surgeon, "I want to be beautiful" and hooking the inside of the surgeon's mouth with one of his surgical instruments. Wulfgar is also seductive and destructive toward innocent women whom he perceives can help him. Most egregious, however, is his crime of stroking a baby's head while holding hostages on the Roosevelt Island tram. The villain's taking or touching children is a trope of the genre. In the case of a *Commando* (1985), a *Lethal Weapon* (1987), or *The Last Boy Scout* (1991), in which the heroes' daughters are kidnapped and menaced by the villains, this device personalizes the conflict between the hero and his enemy. In the case of a *Dirty Harry*, a *Nighthawks*, or a *Wanted Dead or Alive*, however, the threatened children are anonymous. Thus, they are not the hero's children, but society's, so to threaten them is to threaten society at its most innocent.

On the tram, Wulfgar tries to explain himself to DaSilva: "We're not that different, Deke. I do not enjoy killing, but it's my job . . . I represent oppressed victims who have nothing. I speak only for them. I'm their voice. I'm a liberator." Only the film never specifies who these "victims" are. *Wulfgar's* victims include citizens of London and New York. In these cities, Wulfgar follows his acts of terror by declaring to the media, "There is no security"—a mantra that is all menace and no real politics.

Moreover, Wulfgar, a blonde German who answers to an unseen Arab, then prattles off the names of terrorists he wants released in exchange for his tram hostages. The list includes an Arab, a Russian, a Chinese man, and a Latino. This multiethnic roster anticipates the one used as a ploy by Alan Rickman's apolitical terrorist leader Hans Gruber in *Die Hard* (as well as the terrorists of *58 Minutes*, the 1986 novel on which *Die Hard 2* would be based). In both films, the multiculturalism of these "comrades" suggests a lack of ideology: one cannot imagine a cause that would be common to terrorists of such disparate regions. At the same time, this pluralism recalls the platoons in the combat films of World War II, in which the American military was integrated onscreen at a time when it was not yet integrated in the field. Thus, while in the World War II combat film pluralism may have represented America's ideal view of itself, as invoked by these 1980s action film villains, it represents an ideological vacuum. It also suggests the array of enemies aligned against America and its righteous action heroes. The rosters dictated by Wulfgar and Gruber resonate with the warning issued to Arnold Schwarzenegger in *Commando*: "You've made enemies all over the world, John. It could have been the Syrians, the South Americans, the Russians, or a terrorist group. They're gonna find you."

The tram is the Nighthawks's most memorable set piece, driving film critic Peter Rainer to write, "These days, with the drama of the American hostages still fresh, the sight of frightened hostages being threatened and abused at gunpoint in a movie has unnecessarily unpleasant overtones."[3] (On a related front, Variety's Todd McCarthy wrote a profile on Hauer that notes how Wulfgar was loosely based on international terrorist Carlos the Jackal.)[4] Other critics, however, cast the film in more mythic terms: "the story remains one good guy's triumph over evil," claims Daily Variety.[5] At least one shot in the sequence would support this latter view: a long shot in which the tram seized by Wulfgar and a helicopter manned by DaSilva face each other. The chopper, with "ATAC" emblazoned on its side, looks less like something deployed by the NYPD or FBI than it does like something issued by toy companies Kenner or Hasbro. Magnifying the characters into their vehicles, the standoff anticipates similar ones in Stallone's Rambo: First Blood Part II and Rambo III.

Nighthawks is rare among the action films made with these new stars in that its hero engages in few showstopping feats. It would fall to Ted Kotcheff's First Blood (1982), based on the David Morrell novel that introduced the character John Rambo, to unite two key aspects of Stallone's persona: the underdog and the superhero. In the film, Rambo, a disaffected Vietnam veteran, is hassled and then arrested by a small-town sheriff, Teasle (Brian Dennehy). Rambo escapes from Teasle's custody into the Oregon woods. A manhunt begins that quickly envelops the region's state troopers, army reservists, and Colonel Sam Trautman (Richard Crenna), the man who recruited, trained, and then commanded Rambo in Vietnam.

First Blood establishes Rambo's underdog standing with the opening image. Rambo walks a long road, deep in the distance, while a minimalist version of Jerry Goldsmith's main theme is rendered with mournful guitars and horns. This image is echoed later, when Rambo rejects Teasle's directive to stay out of town, and instead, walks back over the bridge at which Teasle has left him. Crossing this gauntlet, Rambo starts toward the viewer in an extreme long shot. In both images, the landscape dwarfs the hero.

As the film progresses, Rambo asserts his mastery over the landscape and, ultimately, over the forces arrayed against him, even though they keep increasing in number and in armaments. If Rambo exaggerates masculinity, this is partly because the town against which Rambo struggles is a parody of it. The town of Hope, Oregon, is situated at the base of a majestic wilderness. (The very name suggests regeneration while also sharing the name of Hope, British Columbia, the town where *First Blood* was filmed.) The filmmakers use this setting to take jabs at the rugged outdoorsman image and sensibility, as appropriated by domesticated, small-town dwellers. A cigarette billboard declares, "Take the Road to Flavor," while the bank is named "Mountain State Savings." Most overt, however, is the sporting goods store Rambo raids and destroys in his final rampage: "The Outpost," trumpeted by a gaudy neon sign with electric arrows. Standing in The Outpost's doorway, Rambo makes a consumer culture seem as freakish as he is now. Although more dirt and blood and shadow on Stallone would have heightened the monstrousness and the irony of this image, the implication is still clear: in a town of would-be warriors, the *real* man is Rambo.

After Rambo returns to town and razes it, he surrenders to Trautman. The credits roll over a freeze-frame of Rambo being taken into custody. So ends the first film in what would become Stallone's second major franchise: in the finale of *First Blood*, as at the close of the first *Rocky*, Stallone's character loses. In fact, *First Blood*'s print advertising tied the film's hero to the star's *Rocky* alter ego. The ad shows Rambo holding an M60 machine gun, and under the name "Stallone"—writ large—appears the tag line "This time he's fighting for his life."[6] In all the *Rocky* and *Rambo* films (eight movies in total between 1976 and 1990, with *Rocky Balboa* and *Rambo IV* in production and pre-production as of this writing), Stallone's superheroism is therefore founded on an underdog quality that gives such daring—or destructiveness—its divinely sanctioned purpose. And if this is central to his persona, then it is also central to why the Reagan era was so conducive to Stallone's popularity—both before and after Reagan's "Evil Empire" speech. Reagan was president of one of the world's (and the Cold War's) superpowers, but by making the menace posed by the Soviet Union such a driving factor in his politics, he projected a United States threatened by a formidable enemy. Thus, in the popular imagination, America could be both David and Goliath, while onscreen one of its most popular heroes, John Rambo, made war as their bastard son.

The character's mythos became conflated with that of Reagan's America in the sequel, *Rambo: First Blood Part II*. But at least one critic saw both sides of the dichotomy as early as *First Blood*. The *Los Angeles Times*'s Sheila Benson describes Stallone as "the most put-upon stoic since Billy Jack," but *First Blood* as "the best use of Stallone's outsize[d], outrageous presence."[7] Embodying this dichotomy is the first superheroic feat Rambo performs after his escape from police custody. To evade one of Teasle's sadistic officers, Rambo leaps from a cliff into the treetops below. He succeeds, avoiding the gunfire, but fails, spearing himself with a branch. He later masters the leap, jumping from a hillside onto the top of a moving Army jeep, commandeering it. With *Rambo*, producers Mario Kassar and Andrew Vajna expand on this stunt work. Among other feats, Rambo leaps from a Vietnam waterfall as Russian explosives turn it into an inferno.[8]

Of course, Rambo's stunts are not limited to high falls. Also in the sequel, he drags an American prisoner of war through a rice paddy as enemy mortars explode around them. In another scene, he kills all the riverboat pirates who have betrayed him, blows up an enemy boat with a rocket launcher, and then jumps into the river just before the riverboat is rammed by the other boat's flaming wreckage. And as if this were not enough, Rambo's female co-combatant, Co Bao (Julia Nickson), exclaims, as if in a Saturday morning cartoon, "You made it, Rambo!"

Rambo is superheroic even when captured. He refuses to give information to the Russians, even while being subjected to electroshock treatment (as Mel Gibson's Martin Riggs will be in *Lethal Weapon*). Rambo is strapped to coils and springs in a set that resembles something from a 1930s Frankenstein film. Unbroken, Rambo goes on to withstand scarring with a heated knife. He agrees to talk only when *another* American is threatened with torture and death—punishments that apparently, only Rambo can endure.

The image of the electroshock treatment and equipment, in addition to conjuring the genre's enthusiasm for torturing, even violating its heroes, underscores Rambo's likeness to machinery, always one of the most important facets of the character. In October 1981, one month before the filming of *First Blood* began, *Daily Variety* ran a two-page ad, which featured Stallone in one panel, and in another, Kirk Douglas wearing what would be Richard Crenna's costume (Douglas was originally cast as Trautman but left the film during production due to "creative differences"). The ad's copy reads, "He's a machine . . . programmed to kill . . . Impossible to stop!" (ellipses in original).[9] The film itself takes a more ambivalent view. Trautman, heralding Rambo's survival skills and abilities to live off the land and ignore weather, links his charge to nature while Teasle casts Rambo as something automated: "Colonel, you came out here to see why one of your machines blew a gasket."

But like many of the mythic elements of *First Blood*, Rambo's machine-like nature would truly come into its own in *Rambo: First Blood Part II*—especially in the film's climactic scene. Having been left for dead in Vietnam while on the cusp of rescuing POWs, Rambo has been betrayed by his government a second time. He returns to base in a commandeered Russian helicopter; storms into the hangar, which is lined with computer equipment; and, bare-chested, devastates it all with a machine gun he famously holds in one arm. In light of author Yvonne Tasker's claim that the muscles of Stallone and Schwarzenegger are less functional than they are just excessively visual, the image becomes surreal: we are watching hardware use hardware to destroy hardware.[10]

Stallone would follow Rambo with Rocky IV (1985), the next film in the series to show the boxer machining his body, and the following summer's Cobra, which returns Stallone to Nighthawks's brand of urban action and imperviousness. Later, with Rambo III, Stallone again illustrates the notion of Rambo-as-man-as-machine. It is fitting that this is the last major Stallone film to offer this view of his physique, as Rambo III is also one of the era's last "Evil Empire" fantasies. The movie, in which the veteran frees a captured Trautman and the oppressed people of Afghanistan, opened on May 25, 1988. Like the previous installment, Rambo III was primed to launch the year's summer movie season with a Memorial Day opening weekend (in this case, along with "Crocodile" Dundee II). This time, however, the timing was not so ideal: less than two weeks before the release, the Soviet Union began to withdraw troops from Afghanistan, where they had been stationed throughout the 1980s. Moreover, Rambo III was released against a backdrop of warming relations between the United States and the Soviet Union. Neither would help the film's performance.

Director Peter MacDonald opens Rambo III by intercutting between the establishment of Colonel Trautman and shots of Rambo's forearm, his wrist being wrapped, his torso from behind as he removes his necklace, and then again from behind as he tightens his headband. This montage, like ones from the preceding film, do not merely show the character, but assemble him; this string of shots builds to a reveal of Rambo that is the sum of the images that preceded it. But Trautman, in trying to describe his recruit in the most elemental terms he can, later uses a metaphor that would seem to undercut this notion. Trautman denies having created Rambo, a denial that does not quite ring true in light of the previous two films. As demonstrated in First Blood and its first sequel, it is clear from Rambo's actions as well as Trautman's pride in them that not only is Rambo a machine, but that Trautman is its engineer. But this time, in this scene from Rambo III, Trautman instead likens his charge to a sculpture, for which "the rough edges"—that is, everything that was not his inner warrior—needed merely to be chipped away. The implication is troubling: that killing is not a function for which some are tooled and prepared, but an elemental state to which they can be reduced. The metaphor is still mythically charged, however: action movies can depict the hero's tapping into his primal nature as a process of stripping-down as often as they cast it as one of building-up—and sometimes do both in the same film (*Rambo* and *Commando* for example).

Still, the film's imagery belies Trautman's metaphor. If the editing treats Rambo like a machine, so do the compositions. One finds Rambo firing a mounted machine gun at Soviet helicopters as they attack his Afghan allies; the camera pans from the massive weapon to Stallone's massive arm, buckling from recoil. For the film's climax, Rambo, having commandeered a tank, and his Russian nemesis, piloting a helicopter gunship, charge each other. The vehicles spit gunfire and artillery. They collide. In the aftermath of the explosion, the tank is still intact. Rambo emerges. This showdown echoes the helicopter showdown of *Rambo: First Blood Part II* and the helicopter/tram standoff of *Nighthawks*; in all cases, the machines signify the characters.

The language the writer/actor himself uses to describe his character betrays Rambo's link to the mechanical. In an article by the *Los Angeles Times*'s Pat Broeske, Stallone claims that "Rambo is geared, built, tooled—whatever term you want to use—for geopolitical situations," while *Time* quotes Stallone as saying, "Rambo is a war machine that can't be turned off."[11] In addition, Stallone's physique was incorporated into the film's publicity, as was the process by which it was "built." As the *Los Angeles Times* reported from the *Rambo III* set, "A trainer is on hand for daily hour-long sessions at the hotel, where Stallone does about 60 sets of exercises, 10 repetitions per set, with 90-pound weights. Which means he's starting his day by pumping 54,000 pounds."[12] When the film was released, critics were not as enraptured. "Together with his fellow film makers, [Stallone]'s made what may be a $60-million monument to himself," claims Michael Wilmington, also writing for the *Los Angeles Times*. "It's an awe-struck memorial to his musculature, a would-be pop 'Iliad' loony with self-love—a carnival of carnage that reduces history, politics, and warfare to foils of the greater glory of Sly."[13]

Stressing the genre's link between suffering and narcissism, Rambo repairs one of his more gruesome wounds, in a scene that elaborates on a similar act in *First Blood*. Whereas the original film shows Rambo sew shut a wound he sustains to his arm, here, injured during a rescue attempt, Rambo strips off his tank top, pulls a sliver of wood through a wound, fills the wound with gunpowder, and ignites it. Flame sizzles through, and cauterizes, his entry and exit wounds. Not only is Rambo a machine, he is one that can perform its own maintenance. This scene, like others in wilderness-set action films, displays

Rambo's masculinity not only through his masochism, but also through shedding his clothes. This should be intuitive, given Stallone's hard-body status. But it is worth pausing to note that in his urban action films, namely *Nighthawks* and *Cobra*, and in those of his contemporaries, the opposite is also true: rather than the exposed body, it is costuming, and the insulation it offers, that signifies masculinity. It would fall to Bruce Willis's John McClane, running barefoot and later bare-chested through *Die Hard*'s corporate skyscraper to project an image of the wild onto the modern.

Prior to *Die Hard*—and to *Rambo III* for that matter—*Cobra* achieved similar mythic ends by using different visual means. *Cobra* reunited Stallone with *Rambo* director George Cosmatos, and marked Cosmatos's first time filming on American soil. The film follows LAPD Detective Marion "Cobra" Cobretti (Stallone) as he protects a witness from the "Night Slasher" (Brian Thompson) and his murderous cult, against whom Cobra's "investigation" becomes a campaign of extermination. Described by Cosmatos as "a *film noir* of the '80s," the film's style is marked by visual excess and excessive consumerism.[14] As critic Vincent Canby points out, "Mr. Stallone never bears his chest in 'Cobra,' but he models a lot of designer jeans and distressed leather jackets. Like the late Grace Kelly, he also has a fondness for mini-length gloves."[15] In Canby's final assessment, "Like so many other aspects of our public life today, 'Cobra' is an exercise in style for its own sake."[16]

Many of the clothes, weapons, and vehicles that compose *Cobra*'s world are cast as extensions of Cobra himself. One such object is his car: a customized 1950 Mercury. The film's publicity suggests that the filmmakers' aim was to compliment the "unprecedented" weapons Cobra carries and the "original designs" he wears, with an "innovative car."[17] "Unprecedented," "original," and "innovative" make for an interesting choice of words, as Cobra's partner, Gonzales (Reni Santoni, also the partner in *Dirty Harry*) remarks that "[Cobra] looks like a fugitive from the fifties." Indeed, *Cobra*'s connection to that decade— a decade of consumerism, militarism, and Dwight Eisenhower—runs deeper than the film's gray coupe and tossed-off asides. In both its style and content, *Cobra* embodies the zeitgeist of the 1980s; and as film scholar William J. Palmer has pointed out, the 1980s were in many respects a "sequel to" (though he really means "remake of") of the 1950s:

In both the fifties and the eighties, eight years of the American presidency were occupied by a smiling, grandfatherly figure. . . . Both decades politically embraced the ascendancy of style over substance. . . . Both had the

The Well-Armed, Well-Insulated Hero: *In* Cobra *(1986),*
Sylvester Stallone's "Zombie Squad" detective Marion
Cobretti faces one of the film's many violent psychotics, this
time to secure the release of supermarket hostages. (From
the author's collection.)

previous decade's war to remember and get over. . . . Both were acutely nuclear holocaust conscious. . . . Over the course of both decades, America and Russia continuously confronted one another. Eisenhower's fifties had Joseph McCarthy and the U-2 spy plane incident, while Reagan indulged early in his "evil empire" rhetorical saber rattling. Ironically, in the eighties, as America and Russia confronted each other and jockeyed for position, Japan moved in and claimed the spoils of victory.[18]

It should not be surprising, then, that the imagery of *Cobra* is punctuated by political iconography. Cobra's house is decorated with not one, but two American flags, while a framed picture of Reagan hangs on the wall of the homicide squad room. When Gonzales uses one of the squad's phones to relay information to Cobra, the photograph is closer to the camera than the actor is! Writing for the *Village Voice*, critic J. Hoberman calls the photo "hilariously Orwellian."[19]

Disquieted by *Cobra*'s conservatism, Hoberman assesses the film (or is he indicting its audience?) when he writes, "Cobra is a glorified terrorist. The difference is he's one of ours."[20] If Hoberman's language seems extreme, it should be noted that Cobra is armed more like a terrorist than a conventional police officer. This is an important point as, to a large extent, it is by our action hero's weapons that we know him. Cobra is a stylish avenger, to be sure, and the variety of his weapons—to say nothing of the amount—is a component of his style. This is by design. The film's publicity claims that when writing the screenplay for *Cobra*, Stallone specified what weapons his character would carry, "knowing that they would provide insight into the nature of his character."[21] Stallone selected a .45 ACT (Automatic Colt pistol) with a 9mm conversion unit, as well as a JATI 9mm submachine gun. The publicists go on: "Stallone made sure that Cobra's version of the JATI is even more unique. Cobra's weapon also mounts a laser—rendering accuracy even more precise. The dramatic visual impact of the laser also heightens certain dramatic moments in the film."[22] Such claims that the weaponry "provides insight" and "heightens drama" are specious; they read like a publicist's attempt to soften the filmmakers' fascination with weaponry, and/or their presumption that the public has one, too.

Yet the publicists disguise such a fascination only so much, given how thoroughly they detail the weapons' backgrounds and specifications. They describe the unique knife wielded by the film's Night Slasher: "The dagger is 12⅝ inches long, with a blade of 440c stainless steel. The handle is made of 6061T6 aluminum which has been anodized black."[23] This use of jargon is practically compulsive. With the possible exception of the blade's length, these details are likely meaningless—even incomprehensible—to the layperson (6061T6 *aluminum?*). But comprehensibility might not be the aim. This terminology might have been aimed at the uninitiated, to give those interested in, but ignorant of, the specifics of weapons and hardware a sense of empowerment—not an actual command of the jargon, but the sense of one, to be sure.

Cobra's JATI and Colt .45 are similarly described, including their lengths and weights. Additionally, both weapons are military-issue, as are the hand grenades he uses against the Night Slasher's gang. The JATI had been designed in 1980 for use by "police and security forces, commandoes, tank crews, air forces, navy crews and logistic troops." As the featurette then explains, "The aim was to build a light, easy-to-use and highly controllable short-range fully automatic weapon."[24] The Colt .45 has a longer history, having been adopted by the U.S. Army in 1911. According to scholar James Gibson, this weapon served the Army and the Marine Corps through the two world wars, Korea, Vietnam, and all other conflicts until it was replaced, after three quarters of a century of service, by the 9mm Beretta in 1986.[25] This was also the year of *Cobra*'s release. The following year, the Beretta would become the weapon of choice for premier action producer Joel Silver, who would issue it to the heroes of his hit *Lethal Weapon* and *Die Hard* films.[26]

These films, like all action films, fetishize their guns, but none to the extent that *Cobra* does. In fact, *Cobra* fixates on its hero's firearms as much as the *Rambo* films do on their hero's muscles. All of Cobra's weapons are lovingly displayed when Cobra prepares for an assault on the motel where he and Gonzales are hiding their witness Ingrid (Brigittte Nielsen) from the Night Slasher's gang. Getting ready, Cobra strips off his jacket to reveal an impressive array of arms beneath: the JATI and magazines slung over his shoulders, four grenades affixed to his jeans, and the Colt .45, which he quickly sweeps into his hand. This formidability is what led *The Hollywood Reporter*'s Duane Byrge to remark, "[Cobra]'s a one-man battalion . . . Anyone remembering with relish Harry Callahan's magnum [sic] will get off on Cobra's firepower."[27] Once the attack begins, Cobra and Gonzales will repel the gang members in a sequence that resembles a shooting gallery or a video game and that echoes *Rio Bravo* and *Assault on Precinct 13*.

The weapons adorn Cobra's body, thereby serving a function positioned queerly between props and costuming. Cumulatively, they go a long way in constituting Cobra's iconic stature, but by obsessing over them individually, Cosmatos and Stallone make each weapon iconic in its own right. Among the

JATI's most privileged moments is the montage in which Cobra, anticipating the attack on the motel, assembles the weapon. The montage makes the assembly process a ritual; through this ritual, the weapon is made to embody the warrior aspect of Cobra's character (not that his character has many other aspects) as well as of Stallone's persona. Training montages, stripping away clothing and equipment, and other ritualistic images transform Stallone's other major heroes—namely, Rocky and Rambo—from underdogs to supermen. This transformation is an important part of these heroes' mythos. But unlike Rocky and Rambo, Cobra is iconic (and impenetrable) from the start, established in his black leather jacket and gloves and sunglasses. Instead of his body, it is his *gun* that is in the process of becoming. Together, the process and the montage end with Cobra activating the JATI's laser-sighting; so while ritual and rhythm drive the sequence, technology is its conclusion.

The introduction of the Colt is more abstract and is given the privileged position of opening the film. The main title sequence begins with a black background and an extreme close-up of a painted King Cobra head. The camera pulls back to reveal the Cobra painted on an ivory grip, a black leather gloved hand closing around it, the hammer of the gun as it is raised, and the Colt's profile, with a finger on the trigger. The gun turns toward the camera. The muzzle and the camera seem to move toward each other. Over all of this, the audience hears Stallone recite a voiceover: "In America, there's a burglary every eleven seconds, an armed robbery ever sixty-five seconds, a violent crime every twenty-five seconds, a murder every twenty-four minutes, and two hundred and fifty rapes a day." The gun fires. A bullet whirls toward us, and the image cuts to the main title. Just as Cobra's weapons recall Harry's Magnum, the main title sequence of *Cobra* echoes that of *Magnum Force*, in which the camera gradually pushes in on a profile of the Magnum until the gun turns on the audience, and, from offscreen, Clint Eastwood recites an abbreviated version of *Dirty Harry*'s "Do I feel lucky?" speech.

Both of these heroes belong to the action film's urban vigilante tradition; but if Harry is its archetype, then Cobra is its apotheosis. Many critics have commented on how Cobra is modeled after Harry. More striking, though, is how *Cobra*'s villains synthesize the enemies from Harry's first two adventures. With the Night Slasher and his gang, Stallone and Cosmatos graft onto a lawless horde the psychosis that the genre so often assigns to its Aryan aesthetes. The result is an army (*Magnum Force*) defined not by a sense of duty or ideology but by its violence and insanity (*Dirty Harry*). It is the most frightening aspects of both; it is psychosis in numbers.

The action filmmakers who shape Scorpio and his ilk use mental illness to signify the *otherness* that Westerns and combat films often signify with race. This is taken to an extreme with the Night Slasher—so much so that the film depicts him as being, not racially, but somehow biologically, *other*. In one defining image, the camera starts on his massive knife being sharpened against a block. The camera then pans to a filthy tank top, tilts up along his muscular torso, and finally stops on his sweat-soaked face. At first glance, his bulging jaw makes him look positively simian, as he does later when, disguised as a hospital janitor, he walks with his shoulders hunched. In such images, the Night Slasher seems to occupy a lower state of evolution. This is supported by his guttural voice; his constant, heavy sweat (it sprays when he talks); and the mania with which he and his cult "prey on the weak" in their hope to affect a "New Order"—an agenda that as screenwriter, Stallone does not define beyond its necessitating Cobra's righteous and widespread purging.

The difference between how the filmmakers present the Night Slasher and how they present Cobra (Yvonne Tasker describes Cobra as being "not pathologised" but rather, "hidden" beneath his costuming and his built body)[28] embodies the difference in moral worth between the archetypes of villain and hero, as articulated by James Gibson:

> The villain's murderous rage is a natural part of his pleasure in transgression. . . . In contrast, the hero's rage comes from his constant self-denial and personal sacrifice. . . . Only his prowess in combat, a form of impeccable self-control, enables him to protect the boundaries of society against threatening intrusions by the insatiable enemy. At the same time, only by killing the enemy can he release the rage accumulated from a life of emotional self-denial.[29]

In part, the villain is the villain because he is a slave to his desires, while the hero is the hero because he has mastered them. Thus, the loner-hero of so many Western and action films: the man who must have no legitimate outlet for his passions.

Because *Cobra* is an action vehicle for Stallone, his character must be put upon from all sides. In contrast to his reticence are the appetites of the Night Slasher, and also of the other supporting characters: it is Ingrid who makes romantic/sexual overtures toward Cobra, Gonzales who indulges in junk food over Cobra's protests, and Detective Monte (Andy Robinson), the film's wrongheaded, bureaucrat-official, who frustrates Cobra and refuses to believe that they are plagued by more than one killer—even after Cobra and Gonzales are attacked by two vehicles. In fact, it is Monte, not the Night Slasher, who flashes Cobra's most maniacal twinkle. Of course he does: Robinson, who played Dirty Harry's Scorpio fifteen years earlier, gives Monte virtually the same leer.

Naturally, these appetites are secondary to that of the Night Slasher's cult for killing. This is one component of the film's overall obsession with violence and is embodied in the film's editing. In the movie's first sequence, a gunman lays siege to a supermarket. The audience sees multiple close-ups of his shotgun, from medium to extreme, as he draws and pumps it. In fact, in the moments between the gunman's turning toward his first target and his firing the first shot, there are two shots of the gunman and *five* of his gun.

The gunman takes hostages. Setting one free, he then shoots him in the back (for no apparent reason other than the fact that bad people are bad). This is another opportunity for Cosmatos to use his editors to obsess over a violent act. He uses extreme, tilted angles and repeats bits of action, as when two shots show the gunman bringing his weapon into position. Likewise, the first blast fired into the young man is parceled out into four shots, while his corpse falls over *seven*—not including a shot of the hostages reacting and one of the gunman firing again. With such techniques, Cosmatos destroys any sense of psychological equilibrium and, in so doing, creates the need for Cobra to restore it.

Cobra does just that, entering the supermarket and sneaking around toward the killer. Order is restored not only by Cobra's technique, but also by the filmmakers': Cosmatos has linked the killer to fragmented editing and now begins associating Cobra with mythic compositions. When Cobra goes on the offensive, he starts in the frozen food aisle, where doors have been left open. Cobra walks through mist that has pooled above the floor. Mist, like smoke, makes for feral, even primordial imagery, as seen in *Commando* and in the closing moments of *Predator* (1987) and the last *Dirty Harry* film, *The Dead Pool* (1988), among others. In *Cobra*, this motif is repeated moments later, with mist swirling behind Cobra, as he finally faces the gunman (this time they're in the seafood section). Once again, the killer raises his shotgun. Faster, Cobra throws a knife into him, and then, as quickly, aims his Colt. Cosmatos cuts to the gunman stumbling, over which the audience hears Cobra yell, "Drop it!"[30] Cosmatos then cuts back to Cobra as he fires six shots and, having now dispatched the gunman, twirls the Colt on his finger, a classic Western gesture. Cobra then slides it back into his jeans. As punctuation, the filmmakers now cut to an insert of the King Cobra head painted on the Colt's grip.

As the editing of the first sequence is charged with violence, the art direction of the last sequence is a perfect stage for what remains. The final showdown is staged in a foundry. Such industrial settings are staples of the genre, especially as settings for climactic battles. Foundries, factories, basements, chemical plants, shipyards, and the like are prominent in such films as *Wanted Dead or Alive*, *Cobra*, *Commando*, *Robocop*, *Eraser*, two of the *Die Hards*, the three *Terminators*, four of the *Dirty Harrys*, all four *Lethal Weapons*, and others. According to production designer Jackson DeGovia, whose action films include *Red Dawn*, *Die Hard*, and *Speed*,

> Designers like industrial settings because they're massive, they're masculine, and they light well. Switch engines and steel presses; they're the ultimate toys for boys. [Industrial settings] have lots of places to hide, lots of levels. You can be very free there. Nobody cares if you get the walls dirty. They're readily available and they're usually isolated. They are not architecture; they're not made to be pretty, but only to get the job done—more like a landscape, a jungle, than a building. That gives them tremendous scale. The industrial interior is not about human beings. These are the waste products of society. The [industrial setting] has the mystique of the lair, of abandonment. It is Orpheus-into-the-underworld, where evil comes from.[31]

Until that of James Cameron's *Terminator 2: Judgment Day*, the industrial setting of *Cobra* is definitive for the genre, with the foundry's rusty, bolted steel panels, pipes, chains, catwalks, stairs and ladders, rotating lights, fire, steam, sparks, molten metal, and massive machinery that occasionally doubles as battering weapons—all photographed with red gels and blue highlights. It is what Hell would be if Hell was a union shop.

The masculinity of this environment makes it the perfect stage for the final confrontation between Cobra and the Night Slasher. Circling each other like gladiators, the Night Slasher swipes the air with his signature knife (6061T6 aluminum and all) while Cobra wields a chain like a whip. In hand-to-hand combat, Cobra impales the Night Slasher on a hook dangling from overhead and pushes him into a massive industrial furnace. James Gibson describes the act as Cobra "*returning* a member of a devil-worshipping cult to the devil" (emphasis in original).[32] To Gibson, this image is also an example of the "cleansing fires" to which heroes commit their enemies in the films and literature of what he calls the "New War"—a pop-culture phenomenon that places a newfound emphasis on the paramilitary. Central to the New War is the reinvigoration of the warrior figure in the wake of shame and confusion wrought by America's failure in Vietnam. Gibson traces this phenomenon from the early

1970s onward. He cites *First Blood*, *Missing in Action*, *Aliens*, and *Die Hard 2* as examples of films in which the heroes use flame and fireballs to eradicate the enemy utterly. Gibson ties such imagery to archaic rites and religious ceremonies in which fire is used for communal purification.[33]

Indeed, the Night Slasher's fate marks the apotheosis of *Cobra*'s concern with purity, also evoked by Cobra's one-liner, which was widely discussed in the press, even prior to the film's release: "You're the disease, and I'm the cure." This admonition was adapted for the poster, which features a well-insulated, well-armed Stallone. The copy reads, "Crime is the disease. Meet the cure," and then, beneath the title of the movie, a pun based on Stallone's physique: "The strong arm of the law." Throughout *Cobra*, this concern with purity is also expressed more subtly, couched in either style or comic relief. As already discussed, Cobra's outfits exude imperviousness; he even wears his black gloves to eat cold pizza (which he first cuts with a pair of scissors). In fact, Stallone's screenplay utilizes junk food as a motif, but inverts the role it often plays in action and quasi-action films. In such movies as *The French Connection*, *Dirty Harry*, *Stakeout* (1987), *The Hard Way* (1991), and the *Lethal Weapon* series, in which Mel Gibson's Martin Riggs progresses from French fries to chili to dog biscuits, junk food is a mainstay of the hero's diet. In *Cobra*, however, it is Gonzales and Ingrid who binge on sweets and French fries, prompting Cobra to make wry remarks about the virtues of fruit and fiber. More than just a playful spin on a genre convention, this motif dovetails with Stallone's image as a hard body, which in turn manifests the 1980s' obsession with the male body as a site of purity.

Yvonne Tasker seizes upon this in her discussion of the larger-than-life aspects of Arnold Schwarzenegger's persona. In addition to his marriage into the Kennedy clan, she cites "the star's evident physical health, which remains a signifier of *moral* health in western culture" (emphasis in original). [34] In an endnote, Tasker then refers to social criticism that stresses the perceived relationship between physical and moral health in the context of HIV and AIDS, of which the 1980s were the first decade.[35] To that, one might also add Reagan's "War on Drugs" to more fully appreciate the 1980s' concern with corruptors of the body. It seems likely that Tasker would be preoccupied with such an equation when she makes the wider claim that,

Many critics saw the success of Stallone and Schwarzenegger as a disturbing sign, signaling the evolution of a previously unseen cinematic articulation of masculinity. At the same time these figures echo unsettling images from the past, through their implicit invocation of an idealization of the white male body.[36]

As Rikke Schubart's "Passion and Acceleration" article demonstrated in the last chapter, the action genre's theme of "passion" links the brutalizing of this idealized white male body to masochism, martyrdom, and myth. The body is spectacle, and so is the violence that is done to it. But then, so is the destruction that is visited upon cars, buildings, and other such objects—especially as the genre's pyrotechnics become increasingly excessive in the 1980s and beyond. This is the purview of "acceleration," which is marked by "kinetic energy . . . explosions, pure speed, the hard body, invulnerability, invincibility, impenetrability (the prototype is the clone machine)."[37] In the genre's era of hyperbolic bodies, passion and acceleration are closely related: the relish with which Schwarzenegger is punished in *Commando* is the same with which the building is pulverized in *Die Hard*. As the connection between bodies and weaponry has already been drawn, it should be clear now that, as both destroyers and the destroyed, bodies and objects are often equals.

Nowhere is this more literally the case than in James Cameron's *The Terminator* (1984). In his first urban action vehicle, Schwarzenegger stars as the title character—a cyborg sent back from the future to kill Sarah Connor (Linda Hamilton), before she conceives the son who, in the aftermath of a coming nuclear war, will lead the human resistance against sentient, genocidal machines. Schubart regards *The Terminator* as a landmark for the genre, for it is here that "suddenly, acceleration refused to submit to the theme of passion, it tore itself away and became a theme in its own right."[38] *The Terminator* is a taut chase film; it is a foretaste of *Runaway Train* (1985) and *Speed* (1994), and assumes its place in a tradition of films whose hallmarks include the third act of *The Road Warrior* (1981) and even Buster Keaton's *The General* (1927). Like these films' imposing vehicles, *The Terminator*'s Schwarzenegger is a constant onslaught. Seemingly impervious to the weapons of Sarah's protector, Reese (Michael Biehn in the role for which Cameron and producer Gale Anne Hurd originally wanted Schwarzenegger), all the Terminator has to do to accomplish its goal is keep moving toward it. The sound design contributes to the conjunction of Schwarzenegger's formidability and the film's technophobia: when the Terminator is onscreen, a synthesized drone and percussion accompany him, a sound like processed thunder.

Reflecting on *The Terminator* in 1990, *Esquire*'s Michael Hirschorn describes the film as "flush with Reaganite paranoia (even its title is redolent of economic decline)."[39] He argues that its true focus is unchecked technology, as the film's machines have replaced Soviets as the true enemy of the American way. His suggestion that The Terminator is "an expression of its age" resonates with Charles Champlin's observation in the Los Angeles Times that in the hours after Reagan's reelection, The Terminator, a low-budget independent production, was America's highest-grossing film.[40] Champlin also notes the film's sense of paranoia, and ties it to both politics and the film's generic heritage:

> [The film] owes more to film noir than to sci-fi, although it combines both in a way that reminded me of the original "Invasion of the Body Snatchers." And if in its time "Body Snatchers" was a metaphor for the paranoias of the McCarthy days, "The Terminator" rides atop a sort of troika of pre-apocalyptic jitters deep and even subconscious fears of computers getting too smart and taking over.[41]

Like most science fiction-themed action movies, including Robocop and The Matrix (1999), The Terminator couches its futurism in the modern-day urban. Cameron merges them in the nightclub where Sarah, Reese, and the Terminator first collide, a club called "TechNoir." Here, the hard rock and neon of the 1980s are grafted onto the nightclub setting that the action genre had inherited from film noir.

Another setting common to both genres is the seedy motel room or apartment. The Terminator has one—one that serves as a setting for one of the title character's most memorable actions. First, the Terminator climbs in through the window. Outside, a neon sign winks on and off (it seems to say "Bar") as in noir. The room is spare, barely furnished, and seems to be dressed in shades of brown. Damaged from a car crash and a firefight with Reese, the cyborg performs surgery on itself. First, it slices open its arm and manipulates the silver pistons inside. To emphasize this effect, Cameron cuts from a medium shot of the exposed arm to a close-up insert. But the gore and disquieting visual of machinery within flesh is only warming the audience up for what really expresses the talents of make-up effects artist Stan Winston: the Terminator pulls out an eyeball and, reaching into the socket, manually repairs its damaged vision. Although Rikke Schubart has argued that The Terminator is pure thrust, torn free of the genre's fascination with masochism, Schwarzenegger's body (or in this case, prosthetic make-up) is violated as lovingly as it will be in some of his subsequent films.

To go back into the world, the Terminator hides its wound (or gorge) behind a pair of sunglasses. Along with its black leather jacket, the sunglasses help *The Terminator*'s villain predict the fashion sense of *Cobra*'s hero. In both cases, the costuming signifies the reticence that is vital to Schwarzenegger and Stallone's personae. Shielding Schwarzenegger's eyes from view, the addition of the sunglasses to the Terminator's outfit removes one more level of expressiveness—and therefore, adds one more layer reinforcing his juggernaut presence.

Schwarzenegger delivers a minimum of dialogue, and in two of the instances where the cyborg does talk, it does not use Schwarzenegger's voice. Instead, it speaks with the electronically sampled voices of a police officer and of Sarah's mother to further its aims. In Schwarzenegger's voice, one of the Terminator's most extensive dialogue runs is merely the list of weapons he recites to a gun store proprietor. In a monotone, the cyborg demands to see a twelve-gauge Autoloader, a .45 Longslide with laser sighting, an Uzi 9mm, and a "phased plasma rifle in a forty watt range," clearly a weapon of the future. ("Hey, just what you see, pal," the storeowner replies.) The storeowner comments on each selection, demonstrating the genre's passion for weapons. Once outfitted with the store owner's wares, the Terminator is, like Cobra will be, an arsenal unto himself.

All of this—the Terminator's costuming, reticence, weapons, and sheer physique—constitutes more than just a projection of invincibility. They contribute to Schwarzenegger's projection of *otherness*, one that is bolstered by his foreign birth. This *otherness* is reflected in many critics' reviews of *The Terminator*. *Screen International*'s Marjorie Bilbow describes Schwarzenegger as "a menace of superhuman proportions and inhuman relentlessness."[42] The *New York Times*'s Janet Maslin calls the film "a monster movie," and notes that the robotic skeleton to which the Terminator is reduced once its flesh and clothing have been burned away, walks with a "distinctively lumbering gait that matches Mr. Schwarzenegger's own."[43] As *The Hollywood Reporter*'s Kirk Ellis writes, "No doubt about it: Arnold Schwarzenegger was born to play 'The Terminator.'" Ellis deems Schwarzenegger himself to be the film's "most imposing special effect," and notes how being outfitted in so much black and with such firepower makes "the ex-strong man [come] on like evil incarnate."[44] The *London Sunday Times*'s Iain Johnstone puts it even more pointedly: in the cyborg, Schwarzenegger "has found the role for which nature intended him."[45]

Ellis stresses Schwarzenegger's superhuman body less than he does that which accessorizes it. So does the film—which makes for an interesting contrast between *The Terminator*, which couches masculinity as machinery, and Schwarzenegger's follow-up, 1985's *Commando*, which aligns it with nature. A comparison of the title character's departure from *The Terminator* to his entrance in *Commando* makes this point strikingly. In the former, Sarah crushes the Terminator's robotic skeleton in a factory's hydraulic press (a particularly relevant use of a generic setting); in the latter, Schwarzenegger's John Matrix is introduced by shots that show off his sunlit physique as he performs physical labor in the outdoors, near his wood-framed home. This contrast is an even bolder illustration of the dichotomy that underpins Sylvester Stallone's persona, as articulated by Sheriff Teasle and Colonel Trautman's warring language in *First Blood*.

Commando is the first film Joel Silver produced for Twentieth Century Fox as part of a deal that would also generate the *Predator* and *Die Hard* franchises. In *Commando*, Schwarzenegger stars as retired Special Forces operative Colonel John Matrix. Screenwriter Steven E. de Souza claims that the scenario, in which Matrix must use all his skills—and hardware—to rescue his kidnapped daughter from a former subordinate, was inspired by the iconic Western *The Searchers* and the noir-esque *Tokyo Joe*.[46]

Director Mark Lester introduces Matrix in a montage that isolates his body parts. (An extreme close-up of what seems to be a shoulder turns out to be just one bicep.) A wider angle reveals more of Matrix as he carries a log on his shoulder. Matrix walks down toward his home, which is complete with a smoke-puffing chimney, and which is nestled into the landscape. From this idyllic image, Lester cuts back to a shot of Matrix in which sunlight plays on his shoulders and haloes his hair. The image is positively romantic—a love poem to both nature and masculinity, and from it, Lester then cuts to Matrix splitting logs with one axe-stroke each.

This montage is, like those in *Rambo* and *Cobra*, practically ceremonial. What is ritualized is the body, as in this sequence in *Commando*; the body and weapons, as in *Rambo*; or weapons and actual rituals, as in *Cobra*'s gun assembly and the main title sequence (in which members of the Night Slasher's cult gather and clang their axes). In fact, montages are so prevalent in the action, sports, and teen-themed films of the 1980s, as well as in its comedies and love stories, that during this era, the montage is in itself a ritual—in which case the opening credits of *Cobra* represent a ritual *within* a ritual.

These opening moments of *Commando* resonate with the broader claims scholar Richard Sparks makes about heroes: they are, he writes, "outcasts unsullied by attachments or institutional connections, yet they remain 'of the people' and their painstakingly crafted physiques recall in imagination the hardness of men's physical labour."[47] This first montage's emphasis on the male physique and labor predicts a montage in *Predator*, in which Major Dutch (Schwarzenegger) and his commandos make traps out of the jungle for the creature that stalks them. It also recalls the sequence from *Rambo* in which the hero gears up before being airdropped back into the jungles of Vietnam and the training montages in Stallone's *Rocky* films. As previously discussed, the major heroes played by Stallone—Rocky and Rambo—are initially men in the process of becoming heroes, whereas the characters to which Schwarzenegger lends his monolithic presence seem to be born icons. It stands to reason then, that in most of the *Rocky* and *Rambo* films, such montages occur only after the plot is established, whereas in *Commando*, it is how the hero is introduced.

The montage continues through the main credits, incorporating Matrix's daughter, Jenny (Alyssa Milano), with whom he is shown to live in perfect, idyllic isolation. Here, depictions of fatherhood and nature, including sharing ice cream, fishing, playing in the water, and hand-feeding a deer—this is worth repeating: in the beginning of *Commando*, Arnold Schwarzenegger *feeds a deer*—actually undercut the hypermasculinity established just moments before. This is shrewd: not only does it establish the father-daughter relationship at the heart of the film's captivity-rescue scenario, but it also makes room for masculinity to be reinvigorated later. This will happen through the preparations Matrix makes for his private war—especially the other montages that link Schwarzenegger's physique to his character's weapons.

For the film's final act, Matrix arrives on the island where Jenny is held hostage by Matrix's enemy, Bennett (Vernon Wells). In a montage, Matrix readies his weapons, applies war paint, and dons a combat vest that in reality—the studio's publicists make sure to mention—was "in use by the Air Force Para-Rescue Unit and is state-of-the-art for elite force operations."[48] Matrix starts all but naked and constructs himself from the ground up in a sequence that equates preparing one's body with preparing one's weapons. Through the succession of close-ups (there are nearly twenty), this construction is even more ritualized than that of similar sequences in other films, such as *Taxi Driver*. Matrix ties his bootlaces; zips his vest; clips its straps; slides a final shell into his belt; ties grenades into position; sheathes a knife; loads a clip into a silver-plated Desert Eagle handgun; pulls back its barrel; holsters it; greases one muscle, then his face, then another muscle; loads a magazine into an automatic rifle; pulls back another hammer; grips the gun; and then finally, raises a rocket launcher. As he performs this last task, the camera tilts to follow the launcher, and gives the audience its first full, and primal, image of this readied warrior. Behind him, smoke blows across the frame. From above, beams of sunlight fan down. All of this has been scored with a rhythmic, almost tribal music cue by James Horner, and with satisfying clicks and ker-chunks: the bass of battle preparations.

Matrix then stages an assault on the compound of Bennett's employer, General Arius (Dan Hedaya). Wounded during his attack, Matrix enters a shed, where he strips his clothes and tends to his wound. This act predicts Rambo's self-maintenance in *Rambo III*, and illustrates that stripping-down can be as mythically charged as gearing-up. Matrix then fights his way out of the shed with a pitchfork, a hatchet, and a buzz saw blade. Back in the open, Matrix brings to bear his biggest weapon yet: an M60 light–machine gun, like the one Rambo wields during the finale of *First Blood*. In fact, while mowing down enemy troops, Matrix fires the machine gun one-handed—which should be as impossible for him as it should have been for Rambo, who accomplished the same feat in his blockbuster second outing the summer before *Commando*'s October release.

Matrix's use of the M60 after his interlude in the shed lays bare the modular structure of this sequence: each phase of Matrix's attack is delineated by his use of a different weapon. And there are plenty at his disposal. The film's production notes list the weapons Matrix uses to conduct his "final assault." They include "a Valmet full-auto Battle Rifle, a selective-fire Uzi, a Desert Eagle .357 Magnum auto, a 12-guage Remington H70 Laser shotgun, two 60 lb. M-60 light machine-guns, and a Colt M-16, among others."[49] The selection of these weapons reflects the influence of producer Joel Silver. According to de Souza, Silver insisted on using weapons that had never been seen on film before, especially for Matrix's personal sidearm. Before choosing the Desert Eagle, a fifty-caliber automatic pistol with a triangular barrel, Silver selected rifles, handguns, and knives from a virtual arsenal that had been laid out for him on a soundstage. "It was like the scene in *Taxi Driver!*" de Souza recalls.[50]

The variety of weapons used in *Commando* is a significant part of the film's aesthetic, and the aesthetics of weaponry are a significant aspect of Silver's signature style and public persona. The production information for Silver's subsequent productions *Predator* and *Die Hard* also refer to his involvement in arming his films' heroes. This highlights the roles weapons play both as spectacle within the films and as publicity for them—not just here, but in the following year's *Cobra* and *The Delta Force* and others. In so doing, these publicists must have presumed the public to be fascinated with weaponry and that satisfying this intrigue would be rewarded at the box office. This resonates with

James Gibson's concept of pop culture's "New War," of the 1980s' paramilitary vogue.

Of course, this would find expression not only in the films' positioning, but also in their merchandising. In addition to the high-priced replicas of Rambo's knives targeted at collectors (*Rambo III*'s publicity materials claim that one of the limited edition knives sold for over $1,700), more widely consumable items entered the marketplace.[51] According to a Fox press release, even before *Commando* reached theaters on October 4, 1985, a clothing line inspired by the film would "invade department stores throughout the country."[52] The press release continues, stating that the "popularly priced" line would include "olive drab or camouflage t-shirts, baseball shirts, sweatshirts, fatigue pants and cap bearing the name of the film and/or the likeness of the five time Mr. Universe." In the release, Fox's Vice President of Field Operations and National Promotions, Linda Goldenberg then claims, "with 'Commando' we felt that we had a hot merchandising property that could capitalize on the current military look in today's fashion."[53]

The licensee, Sales Corporation of America, Inc., used different designs to target different markets. The first, thought to attract both men and women, utilized the film's logo. Another, aimed at eighteen to twenty-five-year-old males, featured a full-body likeness of Schwarzenegger. The last, aimed at boys aged eight to sixteen, displayed Schwarzenegger firing a rocket launcher.[54] A John Matrix action figure was also released, aimed at an even younger market. A Toys-R-Us ad describes the toy as a "Life-like, articulated figure with weaponry. Comic book. Ages 4-up."[55] It might seem odd that such violent imagery from such a violent property was aimed at children; the film is rated R, after all. But of course, so is *Rambo: First Blood Part II*, which spawned a tremendous amount of similar products including toy weapons and walkie-talkies, sandals for both boys and girls, candy, a Saturday morning cartoon, and a Coleco toy line branded as "The Force of Freedom." The Rambo action figure included an I.D. card that detailed, among other things, Rambo's "Distinguished Physical Characteristics;" "Military Record;" and expertise in Ninjitsu, Karate, Ban Do, mines, plastique, dynamite, booby traps, and "the use of most American and foreign conventional and unconventional weapons." These include the Russian RPG, the American M60, the American Survival Knife, and the Chinese T-Knife.[56] The *Los Angeles Times* quoted Diane Mandell, overseer of *Rambo's* merchandising as saying, "We think 'Rambo' is going to be the 'E.T.' of 1985."[57]

The selling of warriors to children has a certain, if disquieting, logic, given how *Rambo* and *Commando* cast heroism. Writing for the *Washington Post*, Paul

Attanasio claims that Lester "frames 'Commando' as a comic book"—not in terms of his visual style, but in terms of the feats Schwarzenegger/Matrix performs.[58] Attanasio is right. In addition to the enemies he dispatches, Matrix jumps from an airplane landing gear during takeoff; tears the front passenger seat out of a car so he can fit in it; rips a phone booth from the wall with a villain inside; swings across a mall on decorative plastic tubing to the top of a glass elevator; picks himself up after a villain plows through him with a speeding car; and rights an overturned Porche.

Likening Schwarzenegger to King Kong, Attanasio claims that Schwarzenegger is "the most engaging of the new crop of killing-machine leading men, partly because, outsized and inarticulate as he is, you can't imagine him functioning in civilization."[59] The same is true of his enemy, Bennett, who is almost as cartoonish. In fact, if there is anything inherently freakish about Schwarzenegger, it is overcompensated for by the constructed freakishness of Bennett. As much as his physique, Bennett's costuming—chain mail over black—makes the villain look like an action figure. With this depiction, as well as the sexualized malice Vernon Wells brings to the performance (similar to the one he brought to his portrayal of "The Wez" in The Road Warrior) Bennett becomes a caricature of a villain.

This is most fully realized in the film's climax, when Matrix taunts Bennett to fight him hand-to-hand. Bennett's desire to battle Matrix, which he initially resists, is charged with lust. He quivers, shudders, and readjusts his grip on his gun in anticipation. As he utters, "I can beat you," his exhaling is almost orgasmic. He, like the Night Slasher, embodies Gibson's observation that villains take pleasure in transgression. For all the might they wield, they are ultimately consumed by their desire. Lester stages this showdown in the basement of Arius's compound. The fight begins amid crates, mesh screens, steam, and a gigantic fan. It then continues into another section—one of catwalks, pipes, and a furnace. In one shot, the actors are photographed from inside the furnace, and composed behind flames in the foreground. Matrix heaves Bennett into an electrified fence. The current only *increases* Bennett's resolve as he exclaims, "John, I feel *good!*" and renews his attack. This, coupled with the fact that *Commando*'s story is predicated on Bennett's having gone rogue since leaving Matrix's training and command, makes Bennett an action film version of Frankenstein's monster, as are many of those who populate the genre—villain and hero alike.

It is fitting that this industrial set frames the final battle between these two constructed men, but as only one can emerge, it also fits that Bennett is felled

Don't Go in the Basement: *In the industrial setting beneath General Arius's estate, Colonel Matrix (Arnold Schwarzenegger) and his former charge Bennett (Vernon Wells) fight hand-to-hand in the climax of 1985's Commando. (From the author's collection.)*

by the industrial. Matrix tears a pipe from the wall and hurls it into Bennett. It impales him and pins him to a water heater, puncturing it. "Let off some steam, Bennett," says Matrix. Schwarzenegger delivers the line in a monotone, without the wink de Souza's pun suggests. Similarly, throughout this action sequence and others, it falls to the intensity of the editing to suggest the pain Schwarzenegger's acting does not. He does not express suffering so much as he does mere exertion and frustration at not yet having won the fight. Walking away with his daughter and his sidekick (Rae Dawn Chong) at the film's end, Matrix's tale is told by his make-up and costuming more than by his body language. It is as if everything that has happened to him has happened to his flesh, but not to his nerve endings. The irony is that compared to many of his counterparts from the 1980s—and even more of them from the 1970s—he has so much more body to hurt and make suffer! Another irony is that Schwarzenegger's *otherness*, a product of his body, yes, but also of his being a foreigner, would come to represent a brand of heroism that is decidedly American. As de Souza reflects, "It's not funny. That was his plan from day one."[60]

The actor's heroic stature enabled him to insinuate himself into American political life, which only reinforced his adopted American-ness. Just a few years after becoming a United States citizen, Schwarzenegger married Maria Shriver, a member of the Kennedy clan, the nation's most prominent political family. Though the Kennedy politicians are Democrats, Schwarzenegger became an active Republican, serving as the Chairman of the President's Council on Physical Fitness and Sports under the first President Bush, and ultimately, becoming the thirty-eighth governor of the state of California in October 2003 (almost eighteen years to the day that *Commando* was released), defeating Gray Davis in a bid for the Democrat's recall. Schwarzenegger married Shriver just prior to the May 1986 start of production on *Predator*, another of the star's many action films influenced by science fiction. As it happens, *Predator* features not one, but two future governors: Schwarzenegger and former professional wrestler Jesse Ventura, who, as a member of the Reform Party, would be elected governor of Minnesota in November 1998.

Predator is the second of Schwarzenegger's two collaborations with Joel Silver. It is also the first of Schwarzenegger's two films directed by John McTiernan, for whom *Predator* marked his studio feature debut. The film is not just an action movie, but rather a film that represents an unusual tangle of genres, including action, science fiction, horror, and combat. As Major Dutch, Schwarzenegger leads an elite commando unit assigned to rescue a foreign cabinet minister and his aid being held captive by South American guerillas.

But the soldiers' true nemesis is no rebel: it is an alien (Kevin Peter Hall, replacing Jean-Claude Van Damme during production) that stalks them from the jungle roof and hunts them for sport. The alien eliminates one commando after another until only Dutch remains to face it. Their third-act battle is charged with much ceremony, little dialogue, and a thermonuclear explosion triggered by the mortally wounded Predator—and which Dutch *outruns*.

As in *Commando*, Schwarzenegger's character seems a part of nature, especially compared to the heavily technological alien. But as a star vehicle for Schwarzenegger, *Predator* is unique for surrounding his character with a platoon of equally competent, well-trained men, played by actors who give each soldier a distinct personality. In combat film tradition, the group represents a host of races and ethnicities: there are two black men (Bill Duke's Mac and Carl Weathers's Dillon), two white men (Jesse Ventura's Blain and Shane Black's more bookish, bespectacled Hawkins), a Native American tracker (Sonny Landham's Billy), a Latino (Richard Chaves's Poncho), a captured female guerilla (Elpidia Carillo's Anna), and, of course, whatever Dutch is.

The producers and their technical advisors also individualize the characters with their weaponry—about which Twentieth Century Fox's publicists go into great detail. As with *Commando*, Silver was personally involved in the casting of the weapons. For Blain, Silver selected a modern Gatling gun with six rotating barrels. The weapon, capable of discharging 6,000 rounds per minute, had been designed to be mounted on a helicopter; Silver had it rigged to be carried by a man and powered by two twelve-volt car batteries offscreen. The film's publicity makes sure to specify that *Predator* marks the first time the "mini-gun" appears as a field weapon on film.[61]

Weapons consultant Mike Papac, who had run the arsenal at Universal Studios and hunted all over the world, outfitted the rest of the men. Thus, Mac carries the Maremont M60E3, "a light machine gun and the newest squad weapon adopted by the U.S. Marines." Hawkins, Dillon, and Poncho all carry Heckler and Koch MP5 submachine guns, with Chaves also wielding a six-shot grenade launcher. Billy holds an M16A2, then one of U.S. military's newest guns. According to Fox, "His weapon functions as two funs [sic] in one with a pump shotgun underneath." Of course, Dutch's weapon is among the most formidable: an M16A2 with an M203 grenade launcher, which, as the publicists want us to know, is "one of the most effective field weapons in use . . . equipped to fire anything from buck shot to high explosives."[62] One of the M16A2's most powerful appearances does not even involve its being fired: as the commandos hike through a valley in the jungle, the camera tilts up from Dutch's boots to the gun, stretching across the screen. Dutch follows the gun into the frame; he holds it in one hand. In the frame, recalling images from *Commando* and the *Rambo* films, a parity exists between the gun and the actor's arm.

The filmmakers craft two scenes in which the commandos make full use of this arsenal. The first is their raid on the guerilla encampment where the hostages are being held. After Dutch's men eliminate the camp's perimeter guards, Dutch begins the assault. He drops an explosive into the back of a pickup truck and, recalling an early feat in *Commando*, lifts the truck and shoves it downhill. Once it crashes into the camp, Dutch detonates the explosive. His men attack. For a considerable portion of the attack's three and a half minutes, there is none of Alan Silvestri's score; this makes more room for the sound effects designed by Richard Anderson and David Stone. But rather than simply create a wash of gunfire, Anderson and Stone make the report of each weapon distinct, which keeps the viewer (or listener) engaged but not overwhelmed. Their efforts, as much as those of editors Mark Helfrich and John F. Link, dictate the scene's brisk rhythm. The filmmakers use similar techniques later, when, after the Predator kills Mac, the commandos train their weapons on their invisible attacker. This scene contains forty-five seconds of uninterrupted gunfire that devastates their environment. When they finish, it is as if they have shot a hole in the jungle itself.

This jungle clearing is a fitting follow-up to the assault on the guerilla camp. As an indulgence of sheer firepower, the scene is an exercise of sheer testosterone. As such, it is a distillation of the film, as is Dutch and Dillon's earlier reunion, in which they clasp hands in greeting and begin to arm-wrestle. Here, the filmmakers include two inserts of the bulging arms straining against each other. The moment is pure, unencumbered by the geopolitical backdrop that rationalizes the camp attack. In fact, the story will not return to such a state of purity until Dutch learns that the executed foreign cabinet minister and his aide are CIA operatives and that the slaughtered guerillas are Russian military advisors. When he realizes that his team was dispatched not to rescue, but to kill, the captivity/rescue scenario that underlies so much of the genre is exposed here as a fraudulent cover story and thus nullified. After this, the film's violence is instigated only by the most basic motivation: survival—although for Mac, revenge runs a close second.

Predator's reduction from a Cold War covert operation to a stripped-down survival story is what drives the film's third act, an extended sequence in which Dutch prepares for, and wages, a hand-to-hand battle with the Predator. This sequence was filmed after the production's hiatus during which Stan Winston redesigned the creature and Schwarzenegger made his next film, *The Running Man*, released in late 1987. With this last battle, McTiernan and his collaborators, including screenwriters Jim and John Thomas, invest the film with much of its mythological quality. Building to the fight is a montage in which Dutch prepares traps, weapons (including a hand-crafted bow, spear, and stakes) and, finally, his body. Having stripped himself of his shirt, he slathers himself in mud, which foils the Predator's thermal vision and, moreover, makes Dutch seem to be of the land itself. This is intercut with the Predator tending to the trophies of its kills, a ritual of its own. The sequence, which runs for nearly four minutes, ends with Dutch lighting a torch and emitting a sustained battle cry. Later, once the battle is underway, the Predator strips itself down as well: slowly removing its shoulder-mounted laser cannon, and then helmet, the Predator reveals its face to Dutch. These ceremonies suggest a reduction to a primitive state, which in turn suggests the characters' purification.

While advanced weaponry and pyrotechnics drive much of *Predator*'s action, the finale is a contest between two forces of nature. Prior to the film's release, *The Hollywood Reporter* columnist Martin Grove addressed this pairing in terms that apply equally to Schwarzenegger's star persona and the excesses to which evolving genres are prone. Grove quotes an unnamed source who asks, "What else can Schwarzenegger or Stallone fight?"[63] McTiernan offers a broader context when he claims that the film

> combined elements you rarely find together—a classic hero story and a horror story, like the Norse myths where heroes battle against supernatural beings. It also reminded me of old war movies and comic books with men who were larger than life. Arnold Schwarzenegger is one of the very few people in the world who has that quality.[64]

Ironically though, one of the film's greatest strengths is McTiernan's ability to make the audience believe Dutch might lose. This is not merely a function of Dutch's fighting a seven-foot-two-inch alien. *Predator* is the film in which Schwarzenegger begins to loosen in front of the camera, which makes possible his self-parodies and outright comedies that began the following year. McTiernan draws from Schwarzenegger the exertion, suffering, and even weariness that *Commando*'s Mark Lester could not, and that *The Terminator*'s James Cameron sidestepped. Significantly, what may be the best example of this is also the film's final image of Dutch. Flying away in the back of a rescue helicopter, Dutch bleeds, covered in ash, and looks out with glassy eyes that drift to the jungle canopy below. He is not his usual rock, but a shell.

The humanizing of the machine is elevated from affectation to theme in 1991's *Terminator 2: Judgment Day*. Following Schwarzenegger's action films *The Running Man* (1987), *Red Heat* (1988), and *Total Recall* (1990), and his comedies *Twins* (1988) and *Kindergarten Cop* (1990), Schwarzenegger returned to one of his most iconic characters. This time, the cyborg has been sent back in time by the human resistance. The Terminator's mission is to find John Connor (Edward Furlong) and protect him from a new model of Terminator, the T-1000 (Robert Patrick), a machine made of liquid metal that can adopt any form that will help it kill its target. The Terminator collects John and his mother Sarah (Linda Hamilton); together, they spend much of the film trying to escape the T-1000, which is disguised as a police officer. Though *Terminator 2* represents a tremendous advance in computer-generated special effects and, at the time, was widely speculated to be the most expensive film ever made, it is essentially a chase film in the tradition of the first *Terminator*, *The Gauntlet*, Sam Peckinpah's 1972 hit *The Getaway*, and others.[65]

To accommodate the kinder, gentler Schwarzenegger of the late 1980s and early 1990s (the actor had amassed a considerable following among children), director and co-writer James Cameron overhauled the character to make it the hero. To accommodate this new role, Cameron develops the notion that through human interaction, the Terminator can learn to be more human. Thus *Terminator 2* deemphasizes the mechanical dimension of Schwarzenegger's persona in favor of the human aspect of the Terminator machine. It—though perhaps "he" would now be more appropriate—makes jokes, speaks with inflections, and is overall more verbal (especially compared to the first film, in which Schwarzenegger speaks only sixty-five words). Of course, Cameron does not completely divest the character of his mechanical nature. In the kitchen of Miles Dyson (Joe Morton), the man who will go on to create SkyNet, the Terminator slices open his forearm and pulls it off, revealing a robotic arm and hand. Likewise, as the Terminator battles SWAT teams and the T-1000, his flesh is ravaged, revealing the robotic faceplate underneath. The art direction reinforces this side of the Terminator as well, especially in the steel mill where *Terminator 2*'s climax is staged. Here, the T-1000 uses industrial machinery to ram the Terminator, which later finds his arm jammed in a gear. To get free, the Terminator must wrench off his own arm.

The T-1000, on the other hand, is much more fluid. Literally. When damaged, it gels back together; when the Terminator punches it, it simply reforms itself to the side of the Terminator's fist. This contrast illustrates a critical dimension of how *Terminator 2* depicts Schwarzenegger as a machine: obsolescence. The Terminator, a T-800 model, is not the advanced technology that it had been in 1984. That distinction now belongs to the T-1000. Compared to Schwarzenegger's Terminator, Patrick has an ordinary physique; he is an everyman that is far more fearsome than Schwarzenegger's walking juggernaut. Not only does this make the hero the underdog—a dramatic necessity—but it also repositions Schwarzenegger for a post-1980s action audience and for an era wherein heroes would be more common men than supermen. By 1991, the model of hero that Schwarzenegger had represented say, just six years earlier in *Commando* is out of date.

Moreover, dressed in a policeman's uniform, the T-1000 represents another convention of 1990s action movies: the enemy who emerges from the ranks of American military, intelligence, and police forces, as we will see. As such, the T-1000's costuming is part of an "amazing irony" Cameron cites: on March 3, 1991, amateur cameraman George Holliday was videotaping the beating of Rodney King by Los Angeles police officers while *Terminator 2* was in production just blocks away. Cameron claims that the tape and his film both show "a dehumanized police force."[66] Critic Caryn James does not need to look to the King beating to see the film's irony. According to James, *Terminator 2* is "a tricky little morality play in which the good Terminator is disguised as a biker, a bad Terminator looks like a cop, and conventional authority is undermined everywhere."[67] Likewise, the Terminator becomes a protective parent to John, whereas John's mother, attempting to change the future by assassinating Dyson, becomes, figuratively speaking, a Terminator.

The Terminator's protectiveness is one method by which Cameron softens both the character and the actor's images. Another is the self-conscious sense of humor Cameron deploys. Outside a biker bar, where the naked Terminator has acquired clothes and the keys to a motorcycle, Cameron reveals the now dressed cyborg by tilting the camera up from his boots and along his black leather wardrobe, while the soundtrack screams the famous guitar riffs of George Thorogood's "Bad to the Bone." Later, while the Terminator and John gather weapons from one of Sarah's rebel friends, the Terminator takes hold of a Gatling gun, like that used in *Predator*. Establishing the gun, the camera pans across it lovingly as the Terminator picks it up. When he does, John regards the black clad machine and its machine gun. "It's definitely you," John quips. The Terminator grins.

But the joke that most plays on Schwarzenegger's persona comes earlier, just as the film poses its central moral question. Trying to teach the Terminator the value of human life, John has commanded the machine to carry out its mission without killing. John makes the Terminator raise his right and hand and repeat, "I swear I will not kill anyone." While playing this moment, Schwarzenegger looks not at John, but into the camera, as if at the audience. The joke is so sharp, it was used to end the film's theatrical trailer (or, in movie advertising parlance, as the trailer's "button").

Terminator 2 was the biggest blockbuster of its year, grossing over $200 million domestically. There is no denying the importance of the Terminator character to Schwarzenegger's persona, nor that as his persona softened, the character adapted with it. Likewise, as the character changed to accommodate the changing needs of the genre (that is, of the audience), the future imagined by the series also adapted to a shifting geopolitical backdrop. In 1984, the year Ronald Reagan was reelected, the first Terminator specifies that "a few years from now," a nuclear war is fought, though no one remembers who started it. The film clearly implies that either the United States or Soviet Union starts the war. It is only in the aftermath of the war that the machines rise up to exterminate the last survivors. In 1991, Terminator 2 is released, in which the Terminator reveals that after the U.S. military automates the country's defenses, the network, SkyNet, becomes self-aware. When attempts are made to deactivate the system, SkyNet defends itself by launching nuclear missiles at Russia, knowing that the Soviets will respond with a nuclear salvo of their own. Ultimately, Sarah and her comrades destroy the lab where the earliest iterations of SkyNet are being created, as well as the inspiration behind them: remnants of the original Terminator. In this post–Cold War adventure, Judgment Day, the coming nuclear war, is not started by either of the superpowers, but by machines and, in the end, is averted.

Twelve years later, with Terminator 3: Rise of the Machines (2003), the franchise passes from the stewardship of its auteur-creator James Cameron and into the hands of skilled, but hardly visionary, director Jonathan Mostow. Just as Terminator 2 rewrote the mythology of the first film, the third rewrites that of the second. Here, Judgment Day has not been prevented, but only postponed. With the world's computer systems—including those of the American military— falling prey to a computer virus, SkyNet seizes the opportunity to launch the nuclear weapons that will eradicate humanity. In fact, Terminator 3 actually ends with the nuclear war. It very well may be that this ending was selected because it held potential for a Terminator 4 that would chronicle the humans' resistance to the machines, or depict some other spectacular future, and, therefore, not rely solely on Arnold Schwarzenegger. But during the summer of 2003, with the phrase "weapons of mass destruction" very much on the pub-

Gearhead: *Arnold Schwarzenegger as the Terminator in James Cameron's 1991 blockbuster* Terminator 2: Judgment Day. *In this film and in its 1984 predecessor, Schwarzenegger is outfitted—that is, manufactured—with the same imperviousness as Stallone's Cobra. (From the author's collection.)*

lic tongue, it may have resonated for different reasons. In these films, then, World War III evolves as surely as the title character does. It is first envisioned as an inevitable conflict between two superpowers, then as a preventable tragedy triggered by an anonymous machine and, finally, as a tragic ending brought about by an enemy not seriously considered during the Cold War.

The *Terminator* films are among the most central to Schwarzenegger's career, but they are only several of his many films that crossbreed the action film and science fiction. This crossbreeding has allowed him to appear in more spectacular, more high-concept films than his 1980s rival, Sylvester Stallone. Moreover, Schwarzenegger proved more adept than Stallone at satirizing his own image (whether subtly, as in *Terminator 2*, 1994's *True Lies*, and 1996's *Eraser*, or outrageously, as in 1993's *Last Action Hero*), which also explains why Schwarzenegger's stardom has outpaced Stallone's. Still, though Stallone may be a relic of the 1980s action film, both he and Schwarzenegger remain among its icons. Their bodies, prepared for combat and purified by ceremony and by torture, are emblems of the warrior culture that fortified the vigilantism of the previous decade's action films. But if their bodies represent and reinforce the characters' destructive power, then the bodies of another stable of stars, working concurrently, are the instruments themselves. They enact many of the same rituals as the heroes played by Schwarzenegger and Stallone. They are subjected to many of the same punishments. And while their stories resonate with Reagan's "Morning in America," for these martial artists, as for their hard-body brethren, each adventure means enduring a very long day.

Enter the Fists
The Body as the Weapon

"I don't want to see you get hurt!"
"Then don't watch."
—Janice Kent (Leah Ayres) and Frank Dux (Jean-Claude
Van Damme) in Bloodsport *(1988)*

In the 1980s, musculature was not the only form of extreme physicality action stars embodied. Yvonne Tasker distinguishes between stars such as Sylvester Stallone and Arnold Schwarzenegger, who display their masculinity through their physiques, and Chuck Norris and Steven Seagal, who perform it through their martial-arts skills. Visually, these fighting styles—whether karate, aikido, or any other—are marked not just by their sheer speed and force but also by their exoticism. It is a different sort of exoticism than that represented by Bruce Lee in the 1960s or Jackie Chan in the 1990s and beyond: as men of the West using combat skills of the East, Norris, Seagal, Jean-Claude Van Damme, and others straddle two hemispheres, much like the Western's "Men Who Know Indians" straddle two natures.

Like Schwarzenegger, Norris was a superstar in his field prior to entering the film business. Norris studied karate while serving in the Air Force in Korea. After returning to California, he won the karate world middleweight championship and held onto the title from 1968 to 1974, when he retired from the sport, undefeated. On film, his early work was not only as a performer, but also as a choreographer: for 1974's *Return of the Dragon*, Norris staged the fight he shares with no less a martial arts luminary than Bruce Lee. In the late 1970s, he began starring in his own vehicles, with such films as *Good Guys Wear Black* (1978) and *A Force of One* (1979). Promoting *An Eye for an Eye* (1981), Norris told *Screen International*, "The films I want to do are action/adventure films. . . . What Clint Eastwood does with his gun, I want to do with my body as a means of self-defense."[1]

The film's advertising copy is a more sensationalized version of this sentiment: "Chuck Norris doesn't need a weapon," it reads. "He is a weapon." In *An Eye for an Eye*, Norris plays Sean Kane, a superhero loner who resigns from the police force to avenge the murder of his partner (who, in the film's opening sequence, is shot, rammed by a car, and set on fire). In the film's final act, Kane and his old sensei, James Chan (Mako), infiltrate the villain's compound. Meanwhile, the villain, Morgan Canfield (then–B movie fixture Christopher Lee) deploys his army to fight the advancing cops, led by Richard Roundtree. The forces clash while Kane and James further penetrate the compound, which makes the sequence resemble a second- or third-generation copy of a James Bond climax. Inside Canfield's house, director Steve Carver stages the film's final showdown, in which Kane and Canfield's hulking Asian hench-man, "The Professor" (Professor Toru Tanaka), fight hand-to-hand. The fight is so simply structured, it becomes just odd. The Professor throws Kane around the set until Kane delivers three kicks (roundhouse, jumping, and front) to the Professor's head. Each impact sounds like a whizzing bullet. The Professor falls, crashing through a table, defeated. Though victorious, Kane has done nothing resourceful to gain the advantage. This is unlike corresponding fights in the Lethal Weapon or Die Hard films; the outcomes of these battles are shaped, in part, by how the characters utilize what their arenas offer them. In An Eye for an Eye, all that triggers the change in the combatants' fortunes is the film-makers' imposition of slow motion. The Professor is beaten by film technique, not combat technique.

Norris, now as Josh Randall, faces a similar enemy with a similar outcome in Forced Vengeance (1982). Directed by The Enforcer's James Fargo, Forced Vengeance finds Randall fleeing, and then pursuing, the crime syndicate that has de-stroyed his adoptive family over casino ownership. Originally titled Jade Jungle, the film displays a particular affinity for film noir conventions, and represents Hong Kong the way noir had represented Los Angeles, San Francisco, New York, and others. Early on, Randall establishes the city with a voiceover, one of noir's most classic devices: "Fast, hard, and dangerous. Hong Kong is like a slap in the face that makes you feel good. A jaded neon jungle that lives by one law: Make money quick. Any way you can. But it's beautiful." The spirit of this "jaded neon jungle" is to be found in its nightclubs, sleazy motels, and private eye–esque offices. Hong Kong's denizens are similarly drawn from noir con-ventions. Its crime syndicate kingpin is not just a homosexual but one with a predilection for much—much—younger men. And in keeping with noir's tradi-tion of torturing its protagonists, Randall, being taken into custody, is sadis-tically beaten about the stomach and kidneys.

The film's violence is not confined to Randall's beating—and certainly not to the figurative slap of his opening voiceover. The film's frequent brutality is likely what led the *Los Angeles Herald Examiner*'s Fred Rappaport to remark that *Forced Vengeance* "is certainly the crummiest of Chuck Norris's consistently crummy action vehicles, but now and again, it tops itself by becoming literally sickening."[2] Along similar lines, *Variety*'s Todd McCarthy writes of the "Martial arts actioner,"

> In the unlikely event that a film historian stumbles across "Forced Vengeance" 20 years from now, he would probably guess that it was made somewhere around 1974–75. In setting, plotting, themes, and action motifs, latest Chuck Norris pic is incredibly reminiscent of those unlamented Yank-vs.-Hong-Kong-syndicate martial arties of that era, and is just as mediocre as most of them were.[3]

As in *An Eye for an Eye*, vengeance motivates many of the film's beatings, shootings, and chases. Most pronounced are those acts surrounding Kam (Seji Sakaguchi), the film's surrogate for Professor Toru Tanka. Kam rapes and kills Randall's girlfriend in front of an incapacitated LeRoy Nicely (Bob Minor), a close friend of Randall's from their days in the military. "I hope you live long enough to tell Randall what I did to his girl," Kam hisses. When Randall arrives later, LeRoy dies in front of him. The filmmakers next show Randall donning his military uniform, in a ritual that is underscored by a martial rendering of composer William Goldstein's main theme. Also as in *An Eye for an Eye*, the two enemies face each other in a showdown in which, once again, Norris unleashes the power of slow motion (or in which slow motion unleashes him) on his Asian nemesis.

Set against *Forced Vengeance*'s exotic, noir-esque backdrop is a lone visual cue from the Western genre, an iconographical holdout: Randall's cowboy hat. Fargo and company use it as the basis of a running joke, wherein Randall's adversaries repeatedly take the hat away and, in at least one case, stomp on it. "Why do they always pick on my hat?" Randall laments in voiceover. The hat is more than just comic relief, however. It distinguishes Randall as a man of the West—even when in the company of other Westerners. Invoking the Western genre for which Norris had always publicly shown affection, Randall is *Forced Vengeance*'s true American, and with this as the film's center, all of Hong Kong becomes warped around him—or at least it would, if Fargo had created more atmosphere.

For all of Norris's professed love of the Western, he has participated in only a few Western projects. Prior to his CBS television series *Walker, Texas Ranger*, Norris starred in *Lone Wolf McQuade* (1983), which reunited him with *An Eye for*

**The Great White Hope?:
Josh Randall (Chuck
Norris) avenges himself
on Hong Kong mobsters
in Forced Vengeance
(1982). (From the
author's collection.)**

an Eye director Steve Carver. In the film, Norris plays a Texas Ranger who is also a martial artist. The opening credits establish the film's connection to the Western, appearing in a Western font and accompanied by Francesco De Masi's score, which, with its strings and whistling, recalls the spaghetti Western music of composer Ennio Morricone. The first action sequence also calls to mind the Western, as Texas Rangers try to round up horse thieves in the desert. They fail, and it falls to McQuade to recoup the situation. McQuade appears, turns the sequence into a brief martial arts display, and then shoots one of the criminals with an Uzi. This marks the beginning of a shift in Norris's career, in which his films' emphasis on martial arts gradually gives way to an emphasis on guns. This is also borne out by the scheme of *Lone Wolf McQuade's* villain (David Caradine), who plots to sell weapons to Cubans. The shift will continue through *Missing in Action* (1984), *Invasion U.S.A.* (1985), and *The Delta Force* (1986). At the outset of this shift, *Lone Wolf McQuade* holds various modes of hurting people in balance. This is expressed by the set decoration of McQuade's house, in which everything pertains to violence: a heavy bag, rifles, an animal head mounted on the wall.

McQuade's environment is pregnant with aggression, and so is his past. He is a former Marine, a Silver Star winner. This echoes *Forced Vengeance*, in which Randall had served with LeRoy, and with Sam Paschal (David Opatoshu), Randall's adoptive father and martial arts mentor. Randall takes revenge for Paschal's murder (among others), just as in *Lone Wolf McQuade*, McQuade avenges the murder of his paternal Ranger figure, Dakota (L. Q. Jones). In these examples and others, Norris's films privilege not only revenge, but moreover, relationships forged in combat.

It stands to reason then, that the role with which Norris is most identified is that of a soldier rescuing other soldiers: James Braddock of the *Missing in Action* series (1984, 1985, 1988). Norris brings to Braddock the same reserve he brings to his other characters. Reviewing the first *Missing in Action* for the *New York Times*, Janet Maslin observes, "It's possible to watch a Chuck Norris film like 'Missing in Action' . . . and come away with the misimpression that Mr. Norris has not said a word. He does talk, of course, but his real eloquence is exclusively physical."[4] Norris's appearance adds to this impression: his dark sunglasses and now fully grown-in beard and mustache cover much of his face—particularly his eyes and mouth—and therefore limit the actor's expressiveness. For the action hero, as for the Western gunfighter before him, this lack of expressiveness translates into imperviousness. Thus, Norris can take his place alongside Schwarzenegger's Terminator and Stallone's Cobra.

Likewise, Braddock's psychological trauma, the result of having been held by the Vietnamese in a prisoner-of-war camp, is internalized. Director Joseph Zito depicts this psychological scarring in the opening scenes. The first is a firefight between Braddock's men and Viet Cong soldiers (naturally, of all the American soldiers, Braddock carries the biggest weapon—a machine gun outfitted with a grenade launcher). From the end of this firefight, Zito cuts to Braddock waking up in a nondescript room, to television coverage of a Senate hearing on soldiers designated missing in action. This reorients the firefight as a flashback, suggesting the war trauma that also strains other heroes of the era—notably John Rambo, The Terminator's Reese, The Exterminator's John Eastland (Robert Ginty), Blue Thunder's Murphy (Roy Scheider; 1983), Aliens's Ripley (Sigourney Weaver; 1986)—and significantly, scores of film noir protagonists.

With varying degrees of subtly, many of noir's war veterans also suffer from sexual dysfunction, likely connected to a form of battle fatigue. There is a hint of this in Braddock, as well. Preparing to sneak out of a Saigon hotel on a private reconnaissance mission, he begins undressing in front of a woman, Ann (Lenore Kasdorf), who thinks he is trying to seduce her. Braddock gestures for her to turn around. "Would you mind? I'm a little on the shy side," he asks. The joke here is that Norris is an action star who performs with his body and, as such, is a performer of masculinity. Against Ann's incredulous reaction, Braddock changes into black garb and gloves, climbs out her hotel room window, drops from her balcony, and climbs across to the next one. He then performs a series of acrobatic stunts to evade a guard detail and begin his search for American POWs. As in Forced Vengeance, a series of noir conventions follow, which is striking given how it is the Western that is recalled by the film's captivity/rescue scenario and also by Norris's persona. In addition to Braddock's flashback and posttraumatic stress, his adventure leads him into a bar, a brothel, black-market commerce, and a seedy motel where he is savagely beaten. Indeed, Missing in Action's detour into film noir constitutes much of the film's second act.

The filmmakers drop Braddock's sexless reserve into the sequel, this time more stoically. Filmed under the title Battle Rage, Lance Hool's Missing in Action 2: The Beginning is a prequel that chronicles Braddock's imprisonment and escape prior to the events of the first film. Brought before the prison camp's commander, Yin (Soon-Tek Oh), Braddock is told that his wife thinks he is dead and plans to remarry, but if Braddock confesses to having committed war crimes, he will be allowed to contact her. (This predicts Death Before Dishonor, in which terrorists from the fictional country of Jamal use a power drill to torture

Marines into confessing that the United States had brought weapons to Jamal to suppress the people.) Braddock tells Yin that he is happy for his wife and that "If she's waiting for me to sign that confession, she'll have to wait a long time." Norris delivers the dialogue with no passion, no emotion, but in a monotone that signals his imperviousness to Yin's extortion (not to mention Norris's abilities as an actor). This raises a compelling question: in the action film, which represents a higher standard of masculinity, displays of sexual prowess or of reticence?

If the source of Braddock's superheroics is his trauma, their outlet is his rescue of the POWs and annihilation of their Vietnamese captors. He dispatches many with his armaments and, compared to Norris's previous films, noticeably fewer with his martial arts skills. An exception is Braddock's climactic hand-to-hand contest with Yin after Braddock liberates the camp. Yin challenges Braddock "to find out who is the better man" in combat: "No politics. No weapons." The fight is ceremonial, as Braddock dedicates a near-strangulation to one comrade ("This is for Nestor"), a punishing abdominal blow to another ("This is for Franklin"), but reserves an explosion—the fireball that actually kills Yin—for himself ("This is for me").

Still, Braddock—even with his use of an M60 in the first Missing in Action— is no Rambo. He is not *of* the land. Neither is he war personified. He trudges through the landscape and blows it up with grenades. When he runs, it is without urgency. When he mows down Vietnamese soldiers, his arms quiver from recoil as he sweeps the gun back and forth, but his eyes are vacant and the rest of his face seems to register nothing. In this respect, the first two Missing in Actions continue the transition begun by Lone Wolf McQuade and mark the next phase of Norris's career. Through the second half of the 1980s, and in collaboration with producers Menahem Golan and Yoram Globus, Norris seems to grow estranged from his body, relying less and less on exotic fight choreography and more on increasingly sophisticated hardware. This is evident not only in the films, but also in their advertising. Print ads for Forced Vengeance, for instance, display Norris in mid-air, uncoiling, performing a flying-kick. Those for Invasion U.S.A., on the other hand, show Norris standing, firing small automatic guns, one in each hand, a blank stare in his eyes.

Invasion U.S.A., another by Zito, concerns a band of terrorists led by the half-crazed foreigner Rostov (Richard Lynch). They invade America to destroy our way of life by attacking suburban neighborhoods, minority community centers, and shopping malls. As the film's poster trumpets, "No one ever thought it could happen here," a sentiment that evokes nearly the same paranoia—and wording—as one of *Wanted Dead or Alive*'s taglines: "They said it couldn't happen here." Recruited to stop the terrorists is Norris's Matt Hunter (a name that manages to be both hyperbolic and bland), who, having faced Rostov before, has since retired to the Florida Everglades. From the outset, the action genre would make only token use of the police procedural's concern with investigative processes, but *Invasion U.S.A.* excises it altogether. Unlike *Black Sunday*'s Kabakov, who spends much of the film attempting to locate the terrorists and unravel their plot, *Invasion U.S.A.*'s Hunter magically appears when attacks take place, or when they are about to, as if he were Batman or Superman. Hunter and his massive truck are simply *there*, as when terrorists fix a bomb to the side of a moving school bus (inside, the children sing "Life is But a Dream," as did the captive children in *Dirty Harry*). Hunter pulls the explosive free, overtakes the terrorists, and kills them with their own device.

In another instance, Hunter foils an attack on a shopping mall. As terrorists raze the mall with automatic fire and explosives, Hunter's truck, announced by a rack of blazing lights, crashes into the scene. Smashing display after display, Hunter does more damage than the terrorists do. (We have to destroy the mall in order to save it.) Emerging from the truck, Hunter opens fire with small machine pistols without even removing them from his shoulder harnesses. These weapons are now literally an extension of Norris's body, as are the black gloves Hunter wears, his insulation against a contaminated (and therefore contaminating) world that only he can purify. Another extension of Norris is the truck, which belonged to his old Indian friend John Eagle (Dehl Berti). The terrorists kill John Eagle, which recalls *Lone Wolf McQuade* and *Forced Vengeance*, and use machine guns and a rocket launcher to destroy Hunter's two-story Everglades shack. After the onslaught, Hunter pulls himself out from under debris, sets fire to the house's frame, and walks off in a sequence that is so ritualistic, but also so generic, it overshoots myth and becomes caricature.

As a vengeance-seeking loner and a warrior who inherits his heroic purpose from a wiser, older friend, Hunter is sketched much like a Western gunfighter. Indeed, throughout the film, a reporter (Melissa Prophet) calls Hunter "cowboy." A police lieutenant similarly remarks on Hunter's vigilantism as a SWAT team storms his motel room. "I don't know who you are, who you think you are, or who you're fighting for," the lieutenant says, "but it's people like you who've turned this nation upside down. Nobody, but nobody, is above the law." Hunter offers an amused grin, the most emotion he has shown yet. This rant serves to pop up Hunter's exceptionality—a vital aspect of every action hero. Otherwise, it is generic in the extreme. A blowhard official appears here only because the blowhard official is an action movie fixture. As the rest of *Invasion U.S.A.* makes clear, it is not Hunter's methods, but his foreign enemy who is turning the nation upside down.

Indeed, one of the ways *Invasion U.S.A.* defines its hero's uber-American-ness, is to contrast him with the demonized terrorist leader Rostov. In certain low angles, actor Richard Lynch's bone structure appears skull-like. This is fitting, as Rostov has already seen death. Rostov's previous encounter with Hunter, in which Hunter only barely allowed Rostov to live, has left the terrorist traumatized. Now, Rostov breaks down any time he hears Hunter say, "It's time to die," (a one-liner as bland as Hunter's name). Hunter uses this line to taunt Rostov into their final showdown: a Western-style fast draw in which the combatants duel not with six-shooters, but with rocket launchers.

If there is any originality in *Invasion U.S.A.*, it is in Rostov's torment, as it is usually the hero's psyche that is battle-scarred, not the villain's. At the same time, as is typical for the genre, Rostov's *otherness* is the sum of his ethnicity and his psychosis. This also defines the villains in Norris's next movie, *The Delta Force*, in which a U.S. Army antiterrorist team must rescue hostages held by Arab hijackers. The depiction of the hijackers is so racist that *Los Angeles Herald Examiner* critic David Chute remarks, "Of all the movies that have pledged allegiance to the Let's-Get-Tough-American party line, 'Delta Force' is closest in tone to the recent 'Saturday Night Live' *parody* of a Chuck Norris picture, 'Die, Foreigner, Die'" (emphasis in original).[5] Indeed, the first terrorist the audience sees is shown stowing weapons on the plane, sweating, in an extreme low angle that subtly distends his appearance. Similarly, when the terrorist Moustapha (David Menaham) barks orders, his tie is loose, his hair damp and unkempt.

Chute also observes that while the terrorists shriek dialogue such as "'Shut up you American imperialist pig!' . . . the Yank avengers have a crisper line of rhetoric: 'It's a go. *Take 'em down*'" (emphasis in original).[6] The contrast between the terrorists' mania and the commandos' sublimation of emotion to detached jargon recalls the contrast author James Gibson draws between villains who are unable to control their desires and heroes who are defined by their self-denial. In *The Delta Force*, the savagery with which Mustafa beats a Navy passenger who rises to a flight attendant's defense is but one example.

Directed by Menahem Golan, *The Delta Force* was inspired by the 1985 hijacking of a TWA flight that departed from Athens and was diverted to Beirut. In reality, the hijackers killed an American serviceman and scattered the hostages throughout the Beirut area to frustrate any rescue attempt. Ultimately, a negotiated settlement secured the hostages' release. In the film, the airline is "AWT," the flight has the same point of origin, and the hostages are similarly dispersed, but they are rescued by the Delta Force in an extensive third act, which Golan takes credit for inventing.[7]

Opening with a failed attempt to rescue hostages held in Iran, The Delta Force also draws on the Iranian hostage crisis of 1980, which was "a turning point in America's policy on terrorism," according to Golan. "The American people were furious when they realized that the U.S. had become completely powerless against fanatics."[8] The sequence, set in 1980, introduces the Delta Force in what is a prelude to the film's main scenario. The failed rescue attempt results in eight dead and thirteen injured soldiers; the audience never sees a single hostage. But in this failure there is redemption, as Norris's Scott McCoy disobeys orders issued by his superior, Colonel Alexander (Lee Marvin in his final film role), and braves danger to rescue a wounded comrade from an impending explosion.

Even with this small victory, the operation is a debacle, and in its wake, McCoy resigns from the team. Five years later, with the AWT hostages in peril, McCoy comes out of retirement to rejoin Alexander and the men. This calls to mind Invasion U.S.A.'s Matt Hunter, Commando's John Matrix, Rambo's Rambo, and the genre's other avenging veterans who leave their exile (whether self-imposed or not) to rejoin the good war. These heroes are thus reborn and, as such, embody the action film's concern with regeneration.

Of course, no hero is fully reborn until he brings his weapons to bear. In McCoy's case, his primary weapon is a black, high-tech motorcycle, equipped with mini-rockets, machine guns, and a rear rocket launcher. In one of the film's starkest images, McCoy seems to be fused with the bike, as he sits atop it; both are silhouetted by the sun. In the film's climactic hand-to-hand contest between McCoy and terrorist leader Abdul (Robert Forster, in a disconcerting bit of casting), McCoy trounces Abdul but releases him, only to then obliterate him with one of the bike's rockets. Not for the first time in a Chuck Norris movie, artillery is privileged over martial arts. But the film reaches the height of its reverence for military hardware when McCoy, speeding to the AWT plane that the Delta Force has retaken, comes upon a convoy of terrorist vehicles. The convoy stops before the lone McCoy and scatters as he fires on them. The image makes Norris a hero who is one part avenger and one part messiah, as he is often presented in the Missing in Action films. In fact, Norris would reach his most messianic in his final turn as Jim Braddock in 1988's Braddock: Missing in Action III, in which the veteran returns to Vietnam to liberate orphaned children, as the next chapter shows.

A Modern Warrior on His Brand-New Bike: *Major Scott McCoy (Chuck Norris) uses technology more than his body against the terrorists of* The Delta Force *(1986). Note how Norris's image has evolved since the days of* Forced Vengeance, An Eye for an Eye, *and others. (From the author's collection.)*

In the waning years of the 1980s, while Chuck Norris unleashed firepower more than he did his own body, two new martial artists rose to fill the vacuum: Steven Seagal and Jean-Claude Van Damme. Of the two, Seagal represents a more interesting conjunction of star persona and action film mythos. Seagal secured his entrée into the film industry through then-powerful agent Mike Ovitz; the mogul had been a student of Seagal's, a Hollywood martial arts instructor prior to becoming an actor. For his first film, Above the Law (1988), Seagal is credited as one of the film's producers, an author of its story, and its star. His name precedes the title, as if he were already famous. There can be no mistaking that Above the Law was a vehicle intended to not only make Seagal a star, but to position him as one from the start. One approach Seagal and Warner Bros. took was to mythologize the actor. The film's story, in which a former CIA operative-turned-Chicago-cop uses his martial arts know-how to battle government corruption and covert shenanigans, was publicized as originating in Seagal's actual experiences. Having lived and taught martial arts in Japan (as the first non-Asian to open a dojo there, according to Warner Bros.), Seagal claimed to have also worked in "international security" for heads-of-state, including the deposed Shah of Iran in 1979, and as an adviser to CIA field operatives.[9]

Seagal's stories could not be disproved, as the CIA neither confirms nor denies such claims, a fact that Seagal also deployed in the creation of his mystique. With such statements as "I'd be very happy if nobody believes me," Seagal exhibits a cool detachment from this past.[10] This detachment translates into a sense of authenticity—even if it is all manufactured. In recent years, with Seagal's star falling amid disappointing box office returns, allegations of sexual misconduct, and reports of ties to organized crime, skepticism has been leveled against Seagal's purported background. Vanity Fair's Ned Zeman makes a point of mentioning that among the many who doubt Seagal is the woman he was married to when many of these escapades were to have happened.[11]

Perhaps because Seagal entered action films with the pomp of an established star but with no actual history in the genre, Above the Law is obsessed with the past: put another way, the film gives Seagal's character, Nico Toscani, an overabundance of what the fledgling star lacked. Directed by Andrew Davis, Above the Law opens with a series of photographs from Nico's childhood and young adult years. As this montage unfolds—including footage of Nico training Japanese students—the audience hears Nico deliver an autobiographical voiceover that chronicles his family's immigration to America; his fascination with, and study of, martial arts; and finally, his recruitment into the CIA. After this, the film finds Nico and his recruiter, Nelson Fox (Chelcie Ross) in a Vietnamese jungle, circa 1973, where they try to stop CIA honcho Zagon (Henry Silva) from torturing a Southeast Asian civilian. In the aftermath of their skirmish, Nico stalks off into the jungle, declaring, "Nelson, I'm through. I'm finished." To viewers who were acquainted with either Warner Bros.' publicity materials or Seagal's press coverage, this sequence could be imparting Nico's history, Seagal's, or, the likely desired effect, both.

The story then picks up in 1988. Nico and his partner Delores "Jax" Johnson (Pam Grier) investigate what they think will be a large drug shipment, but is actually a CIA plot to assassinate a priest and a United States Senator and cover up the agency's complicity in drug trafficking. When Nico's church is destroyed in an attempt on the priest's life, Nico senses that his past is catching up with him. (Of the C4 used in the explosion, he remarks, "I've used that shit. I know what it smells like, and I know what it blows like.") The investigation goes on to reunite Nico with Fox, and then with Zagon, who, in the film's climactic gunfight, shoots Jax with a shotgun blast. Thinking Jax dead, Nico enters her apartment and reminisces. The camera lingers on framed pictures of Jax, including childhood photographs, in a brief scene that recalls the opening montage.

Later, captured by Zagon's cronies, Nico finally faces—and soon dispatches—his enemy, as Nico pulls free of his bonds after being beaten and injected with drugs. "Get the fuck away from me with that," Nico protests as Zagon approaches him with the hypodermic. After everything to which Nico has been subjected (including beatings, an explosion, and being fired upon as he rides atop a speeding car), what he resists most is the prospect of being violated. Of course he does; *Above the Law* is a product of the 1980s, and Seagal is a product of that decade's action hero vogues.

There is, however, one surprising difference between Seagal and the roster of 1980s action stars he seemed positioned to succeed: the lone wolves played by Stallone, Schwarzenegger, and Norris (and one must not forget Eastwood and Bronson) may distrust bureaucrats, but their politics are still those of the coldest conservatism. Nico's, however, are more radical. His distrust is not of bureaucracy, but of actual government. In the *New York Times*, Vincent Canby remarks that *Above the Law* is "the year's first left-wing right-wing-movie. It's an action melodrama that expresses the sentiments of the lunatic fringe at the political center."[12] Indeed, before killing Zagon, Nico delivers a monologue in which he accuses the CIA of authorizing the assassination of the Senator, encouraging the invasion of Nicaragua, starting wars, and using cocaine money to finance covert operations.

If Canby detects a certain paranoia in the film, it is because in it the enemy is not the former government employee gone rogue, a villain that would have been familiar to viewers of *Commando* and that, beginning with 1990's *Die Hard 2*, would become a staple of the genre in the next decade. In *Above the Law*, the enemy is unaccountable government itself. The film ends by combining its obsession with the past and its obsessive fear of politicians. Nico makes an official statement in which he recounts his military background and involvement in covert operations in Vietnam and Cambodia. He also offers the film's coda: "Gentlemen, whenever you have a group of individuals who are beyond any investigation, who can manipulate the press, judges, members of our Congress, you're always gonna have within our government those who are above the law." The last clause is heard over a shot of the capitol building, even though the story has taken place in Chicago. Over this image, the credits roll.

Seagal foregrounds his apparent concerns with the past and with the government cannibalizing itself and the citizenry in his follow-up, *Hard to Kill* (1990), directed by *Nighthawks*'s Bruce Malmuth. In the film, Seagal plays Mason Storm, a cop who, on the verge of uncovering an assemblyman's plot to assassinate a senator, is attacked by the assemblyman's goons. Storm's family is killed, and he falls into a coma, from which he awakens seven years later. The assemblyman (William Sadler) has since carried out his plot and assumed the Senator's place. Storm retrains himself and prepares to take his revenge. Naturally then, *Hard to Kill*, like *Above the Law* before it, makes spectacle of Seagal's martial arts skills. (Of Seagal's debut film, the *Los Angeles Times*'s Michael Wilmington remarks that "the violence . . . is so nonstop that, after awhile, it becomes almost reassuring."[13]) Seagal's use of aikido, as opposed to the more customary karate, results in fight choreography that is more compact and more exotic than that of Chuck Norris films. Also unlike Norris, Seagal does not rely on slow motion. In one fight from *Above the Law*, for instance, Nico battles four bad guys and slow motion is used only once, to show a thug crashing through a store window.

Exoticism is an important dimension of Seagal's persona. Foreign influence informs not only the violence of his characters, but also their philosophies, costuming, and in some cases, even the films' art direction. For roughly the first half of Seagal's career, the influence was that of the Orient. Inexplicably, however, Seagal made a shift: he discarded his basic black garb in favor of Native American styles, as seen in such films as *On Deadly Ground* (1994) and *Fire Down Below* (1997).

This exoticism is most overt in *Hard to Kill*, in which Storm reconstitutes

"One More Take-Out Order": The one-liner uttered by Mason Storm (Steven Seagal) soon after dispatching this thug in Hard to Kill (1990). (From the author's collection.)

himself against a decidedly Asian backdrop (weakly justified as a house belonging to Storm's new love interest's parents' friend, for whom she is housesitting). Here, Storm regains his strength and skills in a montage that is intercut with flashbacks to his family and newspaper clippings announcing their slaughter. The sequence shows Storm performing strength training, self-applied acupuncture, and martial arts; burning what seems to be incense from the tips of the acupuncture needles—while they are in him—and then running up a small mountain. The sequence's final image is of Storm, silhouetted by the sun, looking down from the mountain's peak.

In the last years of the 1980s, Seagal made his name alongside another rising action and martial arts star: Jean-Claude Van Damme, whose films were of an even lower-rent variety than Seagal's. Born and raised in Brussels as Jean-Claude Van Varenberg, the future movie star had focused on careers in bodybuilding and the martial arts instead of accepting an invitation to dance for the Paris Opera. By nineteen, he would win the European Professional Karate Association's middleweight championship and own a profitable fitness center in Brussels: the California Gym. Pursuing his desire to work in film, Van Damme left his business and his family for a brief, unsuccessful attempt at penetrating the Hong Kong martial arts film industry, and then, in 1982, arrived in America speaking only French and Flemish.[14] As with most movie stars' mythology, minor contradictions dot accounts of his history—although none are as glaring as the vagaries of Seagal's. According to interviews and publicity materials, Van Damme either started studying karate at age eleven or age nine; the gym earned him either $15,000 a month or $7,000 a week; he arrived in America with either $3,000 in cash or $800 (he remembers telling Menahem Golan that it was $40); and he attained his first starring role either at a meeting in Golan's office or by making an impromptu martial arts display in front of a restaurant.

Throughout the early years of Van Damme's career, critics and journalists compared him to Arnold Schwarzenegger. Of his performance in Kickboxer (1989), Variety's Mark Adams notes "Van Damme is a shorter, chunky version of Arnold Schwarzenegger, but without Arnie's developing sense of humor and willingness to poke fun at himself."[15] Indeed, Van Damme never became as natural in front of a camera as Schwarzenegger would, and this could well be one reason why Van Damme never became a superstar on the level of other action stars. Another reason is the high number of low-budget productions Van Damme made even after achieving a certain stardom. The actor claims that this was due to the multiple contracts he had signed prior to the release of Bloodsport (1988). According to Van Damme, each contract called for one film and a number of options that the companies could exercise over Van Damme's successive projects. Thus, he was not available to the major studios he claims were soliciting him. "That's why I made all those movies like *Kickboxer* and *Double Impact*. It was a factory, three movies a year, no cast, first-time directors."[16]

Van Damme began cementing his stardom with *Bloodsport*, the first in a series of low-budget independent films he would make with Golan and Globus's Cannon Films. Filmed in 1986 but released in 1988, *Bloodsport* chronicles the supposedly true story of Frank Dux (pronounced "Dukes"), a martial arts instructor from California's San Fernando Valley who claims to have won the mysterious "Kumite" tournament. According to *Bloodsport*'s publicity, the Kumite is an international martial arts contest staged by the International Fighting Arts Association (IFAA) every five years, a contest "few people know about and even fewer speak about publicly." Cannon's publicists specify that the Kumite Dux won was held in the Bahamas, while the filmmakers staged theirs in the more exotic Hong Kong.[17]

In the film, Van Damme's Dux and his cocky American cohort Jackson (Donald Gibb) fight their way through an international host of competitors. As the film and the Kumite progress, the evil Chong Li (Bolo Yeung) emerges as a titan who stands between our American heroes and the championship. For Dux, the contest becomes personal when Chong Li nearly kills Jackson. The filmmakers use the various fights to lovingly show the martial arts choreography and, more to the point, the impacts they have on the human body. In the final fight, Van Damme performs what will be his signature maneuver: an aerial, 360-degree spinning kick. To finish off Chong Li, Dux performs four of these in a row, spread out over nine shots.

In these sequences, the violence pulls free of any narrative context: it is fighting for the sake of fighting, thinly justified as the characters' need to "be the best." The line drawn by the filmmakers between the good characters and the bad is arbitrary. It is clear that Chong Li is evil—while dispatching opponents, his leer is a skull's leer—but Jackson is just as base, thrilling at the Kumite's bloodletting. Chong Li's villainy is almost entirely a function of iconography rather than ideology: there is Chong Li's maniacal grin, his stance (lumbering toward his opponents like a monster), and his very race, which is a counterpoint to Jackson and Dux's. Chong Li is thus the prototypical villain for the Van Damme action film. The actor's subsequent projects, 1989's *Cyborg* and *Kickboxer*, both distributed by Cannon, also define their villains along racial lines. It is a shrewd if repellant strategy. The *otherness* of the villains augments the us-ness of Van Damme, who, for all of his physical prowess, cannot hide his foreign birth and speak at the same time.

Indeed, Bloodsport establishes the formula of Van Damme's early films, pre-occupied as it is with martial arts displays, racially other villains, the forging of brotherhoods, rituals, and training sequences. In Bloodsport we see Dux's training in a flashback. In one instance, he is tied between two poles. His master, Tanaka (Roy Chiao) pulls a rope, which pulls his disciple's legs and arms apart. Dux suffers, but comes to master his suffering and suppress it. From his compromised position, he even pulls the contraption down. Such acts in Van Damme's Cannon films display a flair for the genre's convention of torturing its heroes, and like the scenes of actual combat, are overstated to compensate for their low budgets and meager production values.

Naturally, the site upon which the filmmakers visit this punishment is Van Damme's body. Bloodsport shows off not only his agility, but also his over-developed muscles ("The Muscles from Brussels" would become one of the star's monikers). In fact, Bloodsport's love scene shows far more of Van Damme's body than it does of his leading lady's. The film's true passion is confined to Dux and Jackson. Toward the end of the film, Dux and Jackson embrace. "I love you, my friend," Dux says, kissing Jackson's cheek. In this scene, the filmmakers insert not one, but two reaction shots of Dux's love interest, reporter Janice Kent (Leah Ayres, introduced when Dux saves her from lecherous Arabs), visibly moved. As in Chuck Norris movies, the true loving relationship is the one forged in battle. It is not surprising that Van Damme's films so revere his body. Its exaggerated, chiseled physique, along with how fluidly it moves, synthesizes the era's action-hero body types: the hard body of Schwarzenegger and Stallone and the martial artistry of Norris and Seagal.

Ironically, while accounts of Van Damme's history are more straightforward than Seagal's, those of the real Frank Dux's, the man on whom Van Damme's breakout role is based, are more suspect than either. While Bloodsport was performing strongly at the box office, the Los Angeles Times investigated the lore surrounding Dux. According to the Times, Dux's story "flourished amid the hazy braggadocio of the American martial arts industry," and that as American interest in martial arts grew in the 1970s, so did the competition among instructors to enroll students. Some instructors resorted to embellishing, and in some cases, outright inventing their own mythologies.[18] The paper claims that Dux's trophy from the Bahamas Kumite was at least partly manufactured in the San Fernando Valley; that the invoice for another IFAA trophy lists Dux as the organization's only contact; and that no trace could be found of Senzo "Tiger" Tanaka, the Japanese expatriate whom Dux claims trained him.[19]

Similar inconsistencies dog Dux's claims about his military career and paramilitary adventures. According to the *Times*, "Dux never ventured closer to Southeast Asia than San Diego," and "his only known war injury occurred when he fell off a truck he was painting in the motor pool."[20] Like Steven Seagal, Dux counters charges of fakery by actually exploiting his lack of substantiating evidence, and spinning it into a still greater mythology: Tanaka could not be located because he had been living under an assumed name; the ceremonial sword Dux claims to have been awarded was sold in a failed attempt to buy freedom for a boatload of orphans—whom he later rescued from Philippine pirates.

As Van Damme would later say of his own background, "I came with my karate because nobody listened to my tongue. . . . So maybe they're gonna listen to my legs, like they listened to the arms of Arnold."[21] It is fitting that *Cyborg*, Van Damme's follow-up to *Bloodsport*, introduces the actor with his leg, exploding into frame to kick a gang member in the face. It is also fitting that having played the self-mythologized Frank Dux, Van Damme now plays a more overtly mythological hero. In the film's postapocalyptic future, Van Damme's character, Gibson Rickenbacker, is a reluctant liberator leading an attempt to rescue a beautiful cyborg from the "Flesh Pirates" that have abducted her.

Although *Cyborg*'s publicity materials, like those of many 1980s action films, stress the movie's weaponry, the movie itself stresses Van Damme's particular talents. Like *Bloodsport*'s director Newt Arnold and the directors of early Chuck Norris films, *Cyborg* director Albert Pyun uses slow motion to capture his star's martial artistry, but in a more stylized manner. In one typical scene, Rickenbacker uses a flying spin kick—and a knife that protrudes from his boot—to slash an enemy's throat. This takes approximately ten shots, the first few of which are in slow motion, while those toward the end last only a few frames.

As in *Bloodsport* and the later *Kickboxer*, and like the action heroes who precede Rickenbacker, the character's explosive violence is balanced by his sexual reticence. His partner in *Cyborg* is a woman, Nady (Deborah Richter), with romantic designs on Rickenbacker. When she sheds her blanket, revealing her naked body, he covers her back up, and instead remembers the more chaste relationship he had with the woman, and the family that had once convinced him to put away his weapons and his warring ways. He would reclaim them only after the Flesh Pirates, led by the sinister Fender (Vincent Klyn), murder the family and torture Rickenbacker in an act that resembles Van Damme's training in *Bloodsport* and *Kickboxer*. We see this in a flashback, as Rickenbacker is forced to pull on barbwire to keep his loved ones from falling to their deaths. Grisly as this is however, it does not compare to a later scene, in which Fender's gang literally crucifies Rickenbacker, as seen in the next chapter. Fender is another Van Damme villain the filmmakers demonize through his appearance. He is black with pale eyes—a counterpoint to Van Damme, a Caucasian with dark eyes. (But in what may be the genre's strangest example of a hero and a villain mirroring each other, screenwriter Kitty Chalmers names each for a guitar.) In his final fight with Rickenbacker, Fender growls and shouts, bares teeth, sports dreadlocks and hyperbolic muscles and, in the style of so many movie monsters, even rises from the presumed dead.

In *Kickboxer*, the star's last film of the 1980s—and the last of his films that Cannon would distribute—Van Damme returns to *Bloodsport's* particular brand of ritualistic violence: the tournament. Co-directed by David Worth and Mark DiSalle, Van Damme plays Kurt Sloane, an American in Thailand who enters a martial arts tournament to defeat the champion "Tiger" Tong Po (Michel Qissy), the villain who crippled Sloane's older brother, champion Eric Sloane (Dennis Alexio). Like the final contest between Kurt and Po (who like his *Bloodsport* counterpart holds himself like a monster), Kurt's training is ritualized, as is the suffering Kurt is made to endure. The most punishing moment occurs as Kurt tortures himself by kicking down a tree. In twenty seconds, he lands twenty impacts, most of which are onscreen and accelerating toward the end of the sequence. The filmmakers stress Kurt's cuts and bruises, as Mylee (Rochelle Ashana), Kurt's supposed love interest and niece of his trainer, Xian Chow (Dennis Chan), tends to them.

The last contest is staged underground, ceremoniously. The ring is an actual circle, not of ropes, but of chains, lined with torches. To ensure more brutality, as well as Kurt's defeat, Po and his underworld bosses mandate that the fight is to be conducted "in the ancient ways." The combatants' hands are wrapped, dipped in resin, and then coated with broken glass. To further handicap the outcome of the match, Po's employers have Eric beaten and kidnapped and Mylee kidnapped and raped. Only after they are recovered in a classical (though hardly classic) rescue scene does Kurt unleash his full fury against Po. Kurt fells the villain with Van Damme's 360-degree aerial kick, which is spread out over seven shots. After the match, Kurt makes a final betrayal of his sexual and romantic reticence. He hugs his brother, then the other men, and then pecks Mylee on the cheek. The film's final image is of the group, but Mylee is on one side of Kurt, while the men are together on the other. Predictably, Kurt focuses his attention on them, not her. This should come as no surprise. Earlier, when Mylee confesses her love for Kurt, he simply rises and leaves.

Many of the rituals in Van Damme's films are the same as those of other 1980s action films, but in the 1990s, they will quickly become anachronistic. This is because apart from compressing time, the training and/or gearing-up montage shows the hero's transformation nonverbally. These montages are therefore well-suited for action stars who are not strong at delivering dialogue. But in the late 1980s, yet another trend of action hero arises, threatening to overtake the superhuman model: more "common men" heroes, played by "legitimate" actors—that is, actors who do not possess overly powerful physiques and who had proven themselves in comedy, drama, or both. Interestingly, the montages in the films of Schwarzenegger, Stallone, and Van Damme do not usually appear in those of say, Mel Gibson and Bruce Willis. Throughout the late 1980s and 1990s, these actors, and others like them, are showcased in many of the era's best and most successful action films. In fact, in 1996, Nicolas Cage would win the Academy Award for *Leaving Las Vegas* just months before the release of his action vehicle *The Rock*.

Mel Gibson's Martin Riggs, one of the heroes of *Lethal Weapon*, produced by Joel Silver and Richard Donner and directed by Donner, is unique for the 1980s action film up to that point. Combining their talents, Donner, Gibson, screenwriter Shane Black, and others all give Riggs a true and turbulent emotional life. Together they humanize the superhuman. Distraught at the recent death of his wife, Riggs constantly flirts with turning his talent for killing inward: one of the film's most compelling scenes depicts Riggs's near-suicide.

Still, the character is an ultimate warrior. Like the men played by Norris and Seagal, Riggs is a martial arts expert as well as a crack marksman. In this respect, he is a synthesis of both phases of Norris's career. In fact, just as the advertising copy for *An Eye for an Eye* read "Chuck Norris doesn't need a weapon. He is a weapon," *Lethal Weapon*'s reads "Two cops. Glover carries a weapon. Gibson is one. He's the only L.A. cop registered as a *Lethal Weapon*." Like many of Norris's characters, and indeed the era's, Riggs is a Vietnam veteran. He is also proficient in all methods of, and tools for, killing people. "It's the only thing I was ever good at," he says from the shadows to his middle-aged partner, Roger Murtaugh (Danny Glover), a fellow veteran. For Riggs and Murtaugh, investigating the murder of Murtaugh's war buddy's daughter leads the detectives to "Shadow Company," a heroin smuggling outfit that had helped the CIA fund the Vietnam War. The drug ring is led by General Peter McAllis-

Jazz Hands!: *In* Kickboxer *(1989), Jean-Claude Van Damme's Kurt Sloane grapples with an opponent. While many of the era's action heroes evoke a sense of martyrdom, Van Damme's pose and the make-up applied to his legs and torso recall one archetypal martyr in particular. (From the author's collection.)*

ter (Mitchell Ryan), and protected by mercenary Mr. Joshua (Gary Busey), the film's psychotic blonde. Mr. Joshua mirrors Riggs—the two even have the same Special Forces tattoo—as, to a lesser extent, the older General McAllister mirrors Murtaugh. Thus, *Lethal Weapon* braids together two *film noir* themes: mirroring and the past's erupting into the present. Here, that past is Vietnam, as ultimately, *Lethal Weapon* pits the good Vietnam veteran against the bad.

As the "lethal weapon" of the film's title, Riggs uses his body to the same ends to which he uses his guns. The climactic fight between Riggs and Mr. Joshua bears this out, as it reveals just how fully the characters command exotic fighting styles. *Lethal Weapon*'s publicity specifies that as early as the film's pre-production stage, Donner wanted this final fight to be unique, "yet also to make a strong statement about the characters."[22] This may well be true, but it is worth pausing to note that in the press, Donner also likens this sequence to John Wayne Westerns and that it has always been a defining mark of Donner's collaborator, Joel Silver, to treat audiences to styles of violence never seen before.[23] Together, three technical advisors and a stunt coordinator (Bobby Bass, who would train the actors to handle their machine guns in Silver's production of *Die Hard*) crafted a savage sequence that runs nearly four minutes, took four nights to shoot, and incorporates three fighting styles: Capoeria, "a fighting art" first developed by West African Angolans to defend themselves against slave traders; "Jailhouse Rock," a style originated by nineteenth-century slaves and that secretly evolved throughout America's prisons; and a form of Jiu-Jitsu.[24]

Then, of course, there is the violence that is done to Riggs. Indeed, the film's first image of him reveals scars all across his back (much like Rambo has), evoking unseen war traumas. Later, Mr. Joshua, who uses a cigarette lighter to singe his own arm in a masochistic display of loyalty to General McAllister, has Riggs tortured for information. Riggs is suspended by chains and subjected to electroshock treatment by Endo (Al Leong). Endo is an Asian torturer who, Riggs is told, "has forgotten more about dispensing pain than you and I will ever know." This torture is consistent with the fact that Gibson is playing an action hero, but also with many of his previous non-action roles. Gibson's characters withstand varying, but always extreme, levels of physical punishment in not only *Lethal Weapon* and the *Mad Max* films, but also in *Mrs. Soffel*, *The Year of Living Dangerously*, and *The River*. Gibson's characters would also be sadistically punished in Donner's *Lethal Weapon 2* (1989) and *Conspiracy Theory* (1997) and in Gibson's own *Braveheart* (1995), for which he would win Academy Awards as both director and producer. Of course, the apotheosis of

Gibson's fascination with torture and martyrdom is his controversial directorial effort, *The Passion of the Christ* (2004). Gibson does not star in this film, but his hand makes a cameo: following protracted scenes of Jesus (Jim Caviezel) begin beaten and flayed, Gibson's hand hammers nails into Jesus during the crucifixion.

But Riggs's body is not merely a repository for *Lethal Weapon*'s violence. Gibson uses body language to express Riggs's vulnerability as well as his inner warrior, his composure often alternating between unease and a fluid malevolence. In the scene in which Murtaugh brings Riggs home to meet the family, Riggs often hangs back or stands in the doorway, uncertain and straddling two spaces. In moments that precede violence, Riggs moves with grace, but with deadened eyes. Gibson's eyes, pale and at many other times flashing, have captured the interest of many of the journalists who have interviewed Gibson over the years. His eyes are central to his performance style and screen presence, as well to the good looks and sex appeal on which Gibson has traded in lieu of a Stallone or Schwarzenegger-esque physique. In assessing Gibson's screen presence, *Vanity Fair*'s Steven Schiff writes, "And like many first-rate movie actors, [Gibson]'s a terrific *reactor*; he can convey a responsive stillness that draws the audience in like a vacuum, so that when he reacts, we react with him, instantaneously" (emphasis in original).[25] Such accessibility on Gibson's part, and the vulnerability of the character, helps create Riggs's everyman aspect.

Another dimension of Riggs's humanity lies in the film's humor, ignited by the much-lauded "chemistry" the partners share on camera. Like the stereotypical old married couple, Riggs and Murtaugh bicker and banter in the mismatched buddy tradition that dates back to early sound comedies. In action movie partnerships, a hero will be assigned his opposite: if one is older or reserved, the other is young or brash (the *Lethal Weapon* series, the two *Stakeout* films, *Tango & Cash*, *The Rookie*, *Bad Boys*, *The Rock*); if one is a battle-hardened cop, the other is a starry-eyed tagalong (*The Hard Way*, *Last Action Hero*, *Showtime*); if one is black, the other is white (*Magnum Force*, the *Lethal Weapons*, *Off Limits*, *The Last Boy Scout*, *Die Hard with a Vengeance*, the two *48 HRS.* films, the 1986 *Running Scared*); if one is American, the other is Chinese (the *Rush Hour* films) or a Soviet (*Red Heat*); if one is a human, the other is a machine (the *Robocop* series), an extra-terrestrial (*Alien Nation*), or the undead (*Dead Heat*).

Author Christopher Ames considers *Lethal Weapon* and its sequels to be part of a trend of interracial "buddy movies" that also includes 1988's *Shoot to Kill* and *Die Hard*. In these films, a violent white man bonds with a "domesti-

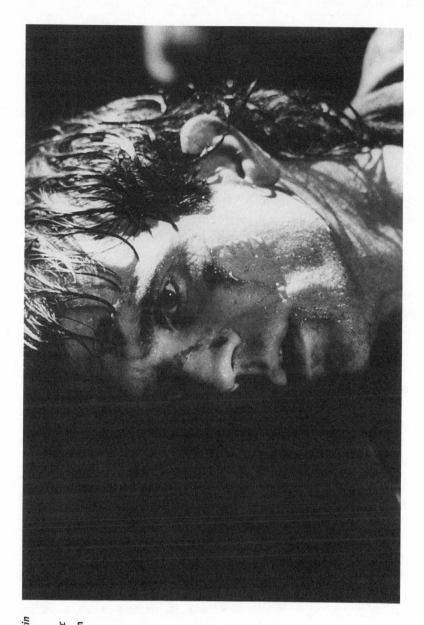

Broken Weapon: *Martin Riggs (Mel Gibson) following the climactic fight of Lethal Weapon (1987). (From the author's collection.)*

cated" black one. From this partnership, the former gets reacquainted with his humanity, while the latter gets back in touch with his inner warrior. Ames maintains that these films invert an American literary myth, one "described by [scholar] Leslie Fielder as the 'idyllic anti-marriage . . . between a white refugee from "civilization" and a dark-skinned "savage," both . . . male'" (ellipses in Fielder's).[26] A shade of the dynamic that Fielder describes, wherein the white man inherits the violence of the *other*, is at play in Norris, Seagal, and Van Damme films, in which the white hero masters martial arts. In *Kickboxer*, for instance, after Kurt defeats a Thai opponent, the Asian crowd chants, "White warrior."

As for the interracial buddy films Ames cites, they retain the mythic transformations of the action genre's literary heritage. Many of them simply invert traditional racial roles and reassign the transformations to the black characters. Thus, the buddies divest the films of much, if not all, of the racial stereotypes that would have been offensive to more modern audiences. It would seem that *Lethal Weapon* achieved this ably: at the twentieth annual NAACP Image Awards, the film won Best Picture, Best Actor for Danny Glover and Best Supporting Actress for Darlene Love.[27] Moreover, *Lethal Weapon* subordinates racial politics to the buddy film's true agenda: male bonding through violence. Near the end of the film, after Riggs and Mr. Joshua's hand-to-hand battle, Riggs and Murtaugh, arms linked, shoot Mr. Joshua—their weapons discharging at almost the same instant. Afterwards, Riggs collapses into Murtaugh's hug, illustrating Ames's further comment that such relationships "are apotheosized in moments of powerful embrace that function like the screen-filling kisses of traditional love stories."[28]

The finale of *Lethal Weapon 2*, one of the blockbusters of 1989, makes this even more literal, as Murtaugh cradles a bloody Riggs after he is wounded in a gunfight that purges Los Angeles of its South African drug dealers. As these villains are also diplomats, and representatives of an oppressive government (South Africa would not end the practice of apartheid until 1994), the sequel makes racial politics more overt, but also more simplified. Here, the interracial partnership is a collective hero, the enemies of which are racist officials beyond the law's reach. Underscoring this point, the office of diplomat Arjen Rudd (Joss Ackland) even recalls the art direction of German expressionist films. Unusual geometric features, high grey walls, and—recalling the Third Reich—an eagle mounted high on the wall surround Rudd, who, administrating his criminal enterprise, is immune to all justice save for Riggs and Murtaugh's vigilante violence.

Of course, the bonding between Riggs and Murtaugh has subtler iterations as well. Just after Riggs and Murtaugh meet in *Lethal Weapon*, they are shown comparing their guns in an exchange that highlights the difference in their ages, but also their shared knowledge of weaponry. "That's some serious shit you carry," says Murtaugh of Riggs's gun. "9mm Beretta, takes fifteen in the mag, one up the pipe, wide ejection port, no feed jams." Murtaugh then reveals that he carries a four-inch Smith and Wesson. Riggs replies, "Six-shooter, huh? A lot of old-timers carry those." For much of this scene, cinematographer Stephen Goldblatt shoots Gibson and Glover in near-silhouette. Both stark and enigmatic, the images are bold graphics, charging the characters' shop-talk with a power bordering on mythos. This is an appropriate image for the first full scene these men share, for the origin of a partnership that will evolve over a four-picture franchise.

As the series progresses, it downplays the first film's darkness and draws out its more cartoonish side. Riggs remains a daredevil, but his antics stem less from psychosis than from a mischievous sense of fun. Likewise, the filmmakers develop the series's humor and over-the-top sensibility through the actors' wordplay and improvisations, but also through zanier set pieces and more formal filmmaking techniques. One of the more significant, if subtle, changes from the first film to the second is that with the sequel, Donner and Goldblatt adopt the more spectacle-making widescreen aspect ratio (2.35:1, compared to *Lethal Weapon*'s 1.85:1 compositions). Musically, composers Michael Kamen, Eric Clapton, and David Sanborn ground *Lethal Weapon 2* as a cartoon—one that just happens to be live-action—by scoring the animated main title in the style of the *Looney Tunes* theme. With the sequel's addition of Leo Getz (Joe Pesci)—and then *Lethal Weapon 3*'s addition of Lorna Cole (Rene Russo) to the series in 1992—the duo of Riggs and Murtaugh often becomes a trio in the tradition of the Three Stooges, whom Riggs imitates and adores (as does Gibson, who produced a 2000 made-for-TV movie about the group). All of this undercuts Riggs's superheroism. But rather than doing so in favor of a return to the grit of 1970s action filmmaking, such uses of humor maintain the sense of an exaggerated reality that marks the *Lethal Weapon* series, Joel Silver's work, and indeed, the 1980s action film.

Donner and his collaborators sustain *Lethal Weapon 2*'s cartoon-like quality for the film's first two acts. The third skews dark and sinister when Riggs learns that one of the South Africans, Pieter Vorstedt (Derrick O'Connor) has killed not just Riggs's girlfriend, but years ago, Riggs's wife as well. Riggs and Murtaugh exact vengeance at a shipping yard, where Riggs and Vorstedt face off in a hand-to-hand contest that recalls that of the first film, save for one significant departure. The choreographers of the final fight in the first *Lethal Weapon* have the characters battle with one overall style, but for the climax of the sequel, stunt coordinator Charlie Picerni has each combatant fight in a style that is unique to him. In this fight, only the foreigner fights exotically. Vorstedt, the film's psychotic aesthete, dances around Riggs and attacks almost exclusively with kicks. Riggs, on the other hand, is not the martial artist of the first film, but a brawler, fighting with more of a "street" aesthetic. Although a departure from how Bobby Bass and the technical advisors had choreographed the fight in *Lethal Weapon*, this is much how Picerni had staged the climactic hand-to-hand combat in the previous summer's *Die Hard*, also for Joel Silver.

Beyond the choreography, the fights are photographed in different styles as well. In the original film's battle, the cinematography is dynamic: the camera moves, light flares the lens, and the actors are composed in close-ups, in which they often seem to strike at the camera. In the corresponding fight in *Lethal Weapon 2*, the cinematography is more staid: the camera movements are less noticeable, and the actors attack each other in medium and long shots. In fact, one of the most brutal images from the fight, and indeed from the entire film, is an extreme long shot in which Riggs climbs atop Vorstedt and pummels him over and over again. Though the camera is farther away here than in the first film, the fight is more intimate. Not only does Riggs fight Vorstedt for revenge, but also the long shots make clear their proximity to each other in this confined space. Also, they are alone—unlike in the previous film, in which the more gladiatorial fight between Riggs and Mr. Joshua is ringed by spectators, including Murtaugh and a host of cops.

As the villains of one of the decade's last action films, Vorstedt and his boss, Rudd (whose diplomatic immunity Murtaugh revokes with a gunshot to the head) provide a transition between the 1980s villain, conjured from Reaganite fears of the *other*, and the 1990s villain, derived from that decade's emphasis on political sensitivity. In short, Vorstedt and Rudd are foreigners we can hate not because we are racist, but because *they* are; indeed, the effects of their drug-running are never made as contemptible as their use of the epithet *kaffir*. For his part, Riggs is the nexus of the 1980s hero, the superman, and the 1990s hero, the common one. He is the warrior we can love because deep down, he is something less than a titan.

As a killer, Riggs may be proficient—and prolific—but he is also one of the few action heroes of the 1980s who is both exceptional and vulnerable. During this decade, the action genre's new stable of stars (in conjunction with the continued output of Clint Eastwood and Charles Bronson) propelled the genre forward through greater levels of exaggeration than the previous decade's films had seen. If the 1980s hero, whether as a martial artist, a hard body, or both, is more superheroic than his 1970s counterparts were, then the morality represented by the 1980s films is equally stark. The hero's vigilante violence, which in the 1970s had been cast as a necessary, if morally ambiguous, solution, had by now become an intuitive one. Although the confluence of masculinity, star persona, myth, technique, and politics that gives form to the 1980s action film would not be seen again, the 1990s would see still greater levels of spectacle. Before that can be examined, however, it will be worthwhile to take a more concentrated look at one of the genre's most mythically charged trends of the 1980s. This trend is composed of films that might seem to be disparate, but that all share a focus on redemption and regeneration, which the heroes find in the wilderness, in the wasteland, and in the aftermath of war.

Into the Jungle,
Out of the Wasteland
Action in the Wild

The ethos of Ronald Reagan and of the action films produced during his presidency were responses to cultural wounds sustained in the past and also to anxiety over a nuclear annihilation in the immediate future. Thus, the genre's emphasis on renewal drives two trends of action films that have traditionally been seen as disparate: the MIA/POW rescue film and the post-apocalyptic adventure. Both trends perpetuate the frontier-hero myth that the genre had inherited from the Western, but compared to their urban counterparts, they do so in a more literal wilderness. Both trends also have heroes who gather the lost and renew the withered. And in both trends one finds slippage between past and future, ambivalence toward the technology that should differentiate them, and awe for the landscapes where they meet.

Critic and poet Michael Ventura recognizes the darkness that underlies these renewal myths—or at the very least, that underlies their popularity. This is a darkness that runs deeper than even the fascist undertones many critics read into them. Writing in 1982, Ventura argues,

> There is a feeling among us that we are already living in the ruins. That the coming catastrophe, spoken of everywhere now, may be just a formality—a bloody ceremony to make official what has already happened. Our civilization reached a state where one of its most commonly held fantasies is to survive the apocalypse and start a *new* civilization! This is extraordinary. [emphasis in original.][1]

This is how Ventura begins his essay on George Miller's *The Road Warrior*, the most emblematic of the decade's postnuclear holocaust fantasies. Produced in Australia, *The Road Warrior* is not an American film in the strictest sense. However, unlike *Mad Max*, the film to which it is the sequel, *The Road Warrior* enjoyed significant support from Warner Bros. and tremendous success at the American box office. It also triggered a host of imitators.

With more gumption than most sequels would show, *The Road Warrior* suggests that in the years since policeman Max Rockatansky (Mel Gibson) avenged himself on the biker gang that ran down his family in the previous film, the world has withstood a nuclear war. Wandering the wasteland, where nomads and gangs war over gasoline—"juice," the lifeblood of this un-civilization— Max comes upon a small community that has established itself around a gas refinery. The settlers agree to trade Max gas for the Mack truck he has recently discovered, a vehicle powerful enough to haul their tanker and lead them 2,000 miles north, out of the wasteland, into their "place in the sun." But a leather-clad warrior-gang led by Lord Humungus (Kjell Nilsson), aims to slaughter the group for its gasoline. The settlers, including the Feral Kid (Emil Minty), a mute boy who tries to bond with Max, look to this stranger to deliver them from this menace. Before the end, Max becomes a postapocalyptic doppel-ganger for Shane, the hero of George Stevens's classic Western. Among the more interesting differences, however, is that in *The Road Warrior*, the commu-nity wants not to defend its turf, but to safely leave it.

This contest is set against great desert vistas and expanses of sky pho-tographed in low angles. The vastness of the landscape exudes mythos; the desert possesses the purity of an elemental state. But the same cannot be said of that which occupies it. The truck, literally the vehicle of the community's deliverance, is first shown sitting idly in the sun, with corpses in the cab, and a tattered banner slung across it reading, "The Vermin Have Inherited the Earth." The letters spill off the edge; the last few have been painted on the passenger-side door. Indeed, many of the objects that compose the film's im-agery suggest scavenging and desperation and represent a collision of styles and sources. The costumes—particularly those of Humungus's gang—are cobbled together with elements that evoke a range of cultures and eras. They illustrate the concept of *bricolage*, both as introduced by anthropologist Claude Levi-Strauss, and as appropriated by film scholars, wherein a culture (or a char-acter) uses objects from the past in ways not originally intended.

In *The Road Warrior*, this concept is illustrated by (among other things) the costume of Humungus's second and love slave, the Wez (Vernon Wells). Wez's outfit clashes leather armor and steel plating with feathers and a Mohawk; it evokes the traditions of Roman gladiators and of Native Americans. The gladiatorial is also a prominent aspect of Humungus's leather-strapped costume, but even more striking is his hockey mask-like faceplate, which is not only more contemporary, but also downright creepy. (The hockey mask would be adopted by the Friday the 13th horror franchise in its third installment the following summer.) Bricolage suggests a lack of stylistic unity, which, in The Road Warrior and its imitators, translates into a lack of moral purity. Humungus keeps Wez on a leash; Wez, in turn, has a love slave of his own, a nubile blonde who is only a little less anonymous than the other rapist, killer gang members. In particular, Miller and costume designer Norma Moriceau use leather and the face mask not just to signify that Humungus and his gang belong to the genre's league of violent, homosexual, sadomasochists, but also to hyperbolize them.

This depiction is not arbitrary. Ventura connects the film's wasteland setting to the sexual proclivities of the gang members who want to dominate it. He writes that their sexuality "is plainly metaphorical: they are sterile, nothing can be created from them."[2] Here, Ventura specifies that it is Wez who, during the film's climactic chase sequence, kills the "Woman Warrior" (Virginia Hey)—the only glimmer of a love interest Miller and co-screenwriter Terry Hayes provide for Max. In killing her, Wez forestalls any hope Max might have had for reestablishing a bloodline. Wez leaves Max no renewal except, ironically, for the spiritual one heroes have always enjoyed by purging the world of men like Wez.

In response to The Road Warrior's archetypes (and no doubt, its success) the filmmakers of the postapocalyptic Spacehunter: Adventures in the Forbidden Zone (1983), Mad Max Beyond Thunderdome (1985), Steel Dawn (1987), and 1989's Cyborg also use costuming to warp the past and to suggest deviance, or at the very least, the bizarre. In Beyond Thunderdome, Miller and Moriceau outdo themselves, integrating dog muzzles, chicken wire, rearview mirrors, and a prosthetic limb into the outfits worn by Max's adversary and her Roman-esque legions.[3] In Cyborg, Jean-Claude Van Damme's nomadic hero dispatches a group of automatons dressed in old military uniforms, helmets, mesh face masks, and in one case, a gas mask. His primary enemy, however, is a gang decked out in leather, with steel plates and tufts of fur. Its leader, Fender, even has a fur-collared jacket, as well as chain-mail and wrist guards that make him look like he has raped the past—medieval times in particular. This connotation is made a bit more literal when Fender and his gang are shown pillaging a small village: they behead its residents and burn its shacks, family photographs, and a wedding cake ornament.

The distant past is also engaged in *Steel Dawn*, but without so pronounced a sense of depravity. The villain (Christopher Neame) and the hero, "Nomad" (Patrick Swayze), are both swordsmen dressed in gladiatorial leather and even wage part of their final duel in a horse corral that the filmmakers use as an arena. That *Steel Dawn* privileges swords, and that *Cyborg* will do the same for knives and bows and arrows, illustrates the premium the postapocalyptic trend places on primitive weapons, a premium that is matched by these films' Vietnam-themed counterparts. If the costumes of these futuristic adventures represent a perversion of the past, then their swords, spears, and bows and arrows signify a more reverent view of it. In this respect, too, *The Road Warrior* is the model. Most of the "settlers" have bows and arrows (the Woman Warrior's is mechanized, predicting Rambo's). The Feral Kid's signature, meanwhile, is his steel boomerang, which he alone masters. Even Humungus's gang fights with contraptions that suggest the primal, such as Wez's wrist-mounted crossbow.

As tools for the subjugation of the lawless, these arms are more reliable than Max's gun, which sputters the first time he tries to fire it, and his police-issued V-8 cruiser—the last of its kind, we are told—which Max himself blows up after it is totaled by Humungus's "dogs of war." These pieces of technology are extensions of Max and the embodiments of a past that never fulfilled its promise. In *The Road Warrior* then, two distinct pasts are at work: one is the past as simply the events that came before, "before" demarcated by the nuclear war; the other is The Past as a state of consciousness, a mythic mental space that, along with that imagined point 2,000 miles to the north, orients us in the wasteland.

On film, this mythic past is often conjured by icons, such as primitive weapons and striking images of the natural world, and by generic traditions. *The Road Warrior's* publicity trades on this by claiming, "[L]ike the classic Westerns and Samurai films, [*The Road Warrior*] is a re-telling of an ancient story—the tale of a lone, dispirited warrior adrift in a dark wasteland who becomes the reluctant champion of a group of idealistic but bewildered survivors."[4] Critics saw more specific referents. The *Los Angeles Times's* Sheila Benson notes "George Miller . . . pits good'uns against bad'uns in a manner John Ford or Kurosawa would recognize."[5] The *Village Voice's* Andrew Sarris remarks, "looking at *The Road Warrior* is more like experiencing a motorized *Stagecoach*."[6]

Sarris's comment applies particularly to *The Road Warrior's* climactic scene, a tremendous chase in which Max drives the tanker, with the settlers flanking him in their vehicles, and Humungus's gang roaring after in pursuit. The scene is noteworthy for more than its extraordinary stunt work and cinematography. It is during this scene that the Woman Warrior is killed, as is Pappagallo (Mike Preston), the settlement's patriarchal leader. Speared, Pappagallo slumps; his car veers off into a dust cloud. Visually, the dust is similar to smoke, mist, light: elements that lend action movies a primordial charge and enshroud the characters who are framed against them—or who vanish into them—in mythos. And should the filmmakers deploy them at the moment of a character's death, as Miller and cinematographer Dean Semler do with Pappagallo's, then the mythos is even more pronounced, as the character seems to be absorbed into the landscape itself.

Another player in this chase is the Feral Kid, who rides in the cab with Max. Throughout the film, the Kid has tried to forge a relationship with Max that would echo the one between the young boy and the gunfighter in Shane. In that film, the young Joey tries to learn heroism from Shane, as the Feral Kid clearly wants to from Max. It is significant then, that during the chase, Miller cuts to a number of reaction shots of the Kid, looking up in awe and delight at Max's feats. Here and elsewhere throughout the film, our sense of Max's heroism is bolstered by the Feral Kid's perception of it. In the voiceover narration that serves as the film's epilogue, the speaker reveals himself as the Feral Kid grown to manhood, now "the leader of the Great Northern Tribe." So Max's lessons, however unintentionally he offered them, did not go unlearned.

As the narrator attests in the film's prologue, Max's adventure in the wasteland helps him "learn to live again" (a figurative rebirth if ever there was one). Max is renewed, even as the tanker itself comes to a cataclysmic end. At the climax of the chase, Max, having outpaced or outright destroyed the cars of Humungus's armada, barrels through Humungus's car, killing him and Wez as one. The tanker then veers down an embankment, overturns, and crashes, its metal rending and its cab plowing earth. When Max discovers that the tanker is not leaking gas, but sand, he realizes that the tanker was a diversion used to draw the marauders' attention. The gas, it turns out, is being smuggled out of the wasteland in the settlers' other vehicles. At the story's end, Max has guaranteed this tribe its future and pointed the Feral Kid toward his destiny, as the sun sets on the destruction both sustained and wrought by the reborn.

The dichotomy of destruction and regeneration that informs Pappagallo's death and the survivors' exodus illustrates that these poles share a fundamental connection—especially when traced back to the biblical source on which postapocalyptic adventures draw. As scholar Mick Broderick notes in an essay on the *Mad Max* trilogy, "Lois Parkinson Zamora has stressed 'the current use of the word apocalypse as a synonym for "disaster" or "cataclysm" is only half correct: the myth comprehends both cataclysm *and* millennium, tribulation *and* triumph, chaos *and* order.'"[7] And compared to the postapocalyptic films that will follow, *The Road Warrior*'s scenes of destruction will remain paramount, but its concern with rejuvenation will seem subtle.

One such film is *Spacehunter: Adventures in the Forbidden Zone*. The story follows Wolff (Peter Strauss), a deep space scavenger, as he braves the hazards of planet Terra 11 to rescue three beautiful women seized by the aging cybernetic dictator Overdog (Michael Ironside). Overdog holds these captives to siphon off their "vitality" and, with it, replenish himself. He seeks to do the same with Niki (Molly Ringwald), a young orphan he captures after she joins Wolff's quest. Near the end of the film, Overdog has Niki placed in the "Fusion Tube." There her essence is drained as Overdog tells her "I am very old, and I need you. I need your vitality . . . [But] the more you give to me, the less there is for you."

To reach this point, Wolff and Niki, separately and together, venture across a world that bears the scars of its apocalypse, and also the influence of *The Road Warrior*'s use of *bricolage*. Terra 11 has been laid waste by an outbreak of "PSI plague," a medical catastrophe that has left its survivors as scavengers and slaves. But that cannot fully account for the film's desolation. After all, *Cyborg* also depicts a world has fallen to a plague, but is set against lush landscapes (provided by Dino DeLaurentis's North Carolina studio and supplemented with rented dirt).[8] *Cyborg* shows us a population that has been decimated, but by an agent that has, logically, left the natural world intact. In *Spacehunter*, however, the planet's postapocalyptic air is largely attributable to a terrain no mere illness could shape. Arid and craggy and pockmarked with precious little water—much of which is noxious—*Spacehunter*'s setting is a desert planet that conforms to the popular conception of a postnuclear holocaust world.[9]

All across this world, the adventurers encounter the weird. One example is the mutant children who surround Wolff, Niki, and Washington (Ernie Hudson), a cohort of Wolff's from their days of military service—much like that privileged relationship among the genre's Vietnam veterans. Niki explains that these children are the creations of Overdog and his second, "The Chemist." The film thus uses its villains to elicit the fear of mutation normally associated with nuclear fallout.

Weirdness is also constituted by the art department's strange combinations of elements. On Terra II, we find a train decked out with a sail and a mast—basically a pirate ship on rails. We find the Chemist's lair, which, like much in the postapocalyptic trend, evokes the past—in this case, a specifically cinematic past: a mad scientist's laboratory, with hints of 1980s pastels. Lastly, we find Overdog's maze, which includes a thicket of iron spikes, jets of flame, a pit of acid, and a metal monstrosity the filmmakers dubbed "the decimator."[10] Niki is made to brave this maze. As she does, Wolff frees the three captured women while Washington liberates Overdog's slaves.

The film spends little time on these slaves. Their liberation seems to be a filmmaker ploy to bolster the heroes' messianic quality—a quality that is often evident in both postapocalyptic and post-Vietnam action films. This is also illustrated in Steel Dawn, which is an even closer retelling of Shane than is The Road Warrior. In the film, "Nomad," the hero who has lost a wife and child (as Max had), comes to an agrarian settlement—a "Purification Farm"—where he is given work helping to farm fresh water. Unlike the settlers of The Road Warrior, those of Steel Dawn are not trying to leave the wasteland. Their vision is to irrigate their valley and build a city. "We must make this land live again," their elder tells them. In adapting (but not greatly modifying) the community of Shane for the world of Steel Dawn, the filmmakers ground this world in the postapocalyptic trend's most overt, if least aesthetic, concern with renewal and purity.

But Steel Dawn is not only Shane in a blasted world. Like Spacehunter, it is The Searchers, too. When Nomad's lover's son is kidnapped, the boy's mother sets off in pursuit. And when her rescue attempt fails, it falls to Nomad to save them both. Having reunited mother, son, and the land they are regenerating, Nomad wanders off into the wild once more, as do the heroes of Shane and The Searchers and of The Road Warrior and Cyborg. These endings point toward two divergent futures: one is the heroes', ripe with the promise of more adventure; the other is the community's, dedicated to building a civilization where there has been none, where there has been only wilderness or ash.

Of course, it is important to note that the postapocalyptic (or at least the dystopian) is also seen in action movies tinged by science fiction and set against urban backdrops. Many of these films collide the anarchy of the postapocalyptic with a sense of totalitarianism. The most overt may be the Terminator films—specifically the sequences set in the future. Additionally, the settings of John Carpenter's Escape from New York (1981) its sequel, Escape from L.A. (1996), The Running Man and Robocop (both 1987), Predator 2 (1990), and

Judge Dredd (1995) all manifest decay. Even *The Warriors* was originally to begin with a card announcing that the film was set in the near future. The flipside of these noir-tinged environments is the tomorrowland of the strangely comedic *Demolition Man* (1993). The film stars Sylvester Stallone as John Spartan, a law enforcer brought out of cryogenic freeze into a future so utopian, it is dystopian: sex is virtual, foul language has been criminalized by the Verbal Morality Statute, and, to acquire his weapons, Spartan must raid a museum armory exhibit. The postapocalyptic is even evoked by the *Death Wish* sequels, set in the present day. As the opening credits of Michael Winner's *Death Wish II* (1982) unfold over aerial views of Los Angeles, we hear the police commissioner announce, "Fear of crime has brought a deterioration of our community. It's almost as if we've been struck by enemy bombs." Three years later, the connection between crime and fallout will become central to the imagery of Winner's *Death Wish 3*, in which the rubble-strewn streets and alleys evoke ruin and rot.

Another trend of action film, concurrent with the postapocalyptic, is also concerned with restoring order to chaos—not the chaos of an imagined future, but the chaos of a past that America had not reconciled: the outcome of, and the government's conduct during, the Vietnam War. The films of this trend are a subset of the action genre, to be sure, but also of a cycle of Vietnam-themed films that include *Coming Home* (1978), *The Deer Hunter* (1978), *Apocalypse Now* (1979), *Platoon* (1986), *Full Metal Jacket* (1987), *Hamburger Hill* (1987), *Casualties of War* (1989), *Born on the Fourth of July* (1989), and others. These and other dramas tend to be either homecoming films or ones that initiate the innocent into the ways of war. The action films, on the other hand, tend to show veterans returning to Vietnam to fight again, often to rescue POWs. Of course, these are also homecomings of a kind, for where else is a warrior at home but at war? Many have remarked that these films process America's still unresolved guilt over Vietnam, but as Michael Ventura notes, it is "not guilt for fighting an unjust war, but guilt for losing one."[11]

Writing in 1986, when these parallel trends were thriving, scholar Elizabeth Traube predicts James Gibson's *Warrior Dreams*, when she claims that these action films trade the Vietnam War for a "fantasy war," but one that "may well have external referents."[12] She cites Nicaragua, as well as the aftermath of the Iranian hostage crisis, as the backdrop against which the POW/MIA films arrive, "amidst Reaganite assurances of the return of American confidence and pride."[13] Another historical referent is the October–December 1983 invasion of Grenada by United States forces to secure imperiled American students (and also overthrow a Marxist government). This invasion is cited in *Let's Get Harry* (1986), not a POW/MIA film in the strictest sense, but one that shares the same ethos. In the film (at one point to have been directed by war and war film veteran Samuel Fuller), four Illinois plumbers venture into Colombia to rescue one of their own, Harry Burck, Jr. (Mark Harmon), when a drug cartel kidnaps him from the power plant he had helped develop.[14] Opening at the power plant, *Let's Get Harry* also shares the postapocalyptic films' interest in regeneration (or in this case, generation).

The POW/MIA action films represent the genre's most distilled rendering of the Western's captivity/rescue myth. Their appearing after an actual hostage crisis testifies to what scholar Catherine Scott considers to be the myth's influence "on popular understandings of America's mission in the world."[15] Scott, whose article "Bound for Glory" analyzes the impact of the captivity/rescue tale on news coverage of the Iranian hostage crisis, is one of several scholars who have traced the archetype back to its use on the American frontier. Between 1673 and 1763, Native Americans took over 1,000 captives, including Mary Rowlandson, the story of whose capture in 1676 saw four editions when published in 1682. Seventeenth- and eighteenth-century ministers then drew from Rowlandson's account the archetype's components of "separation, transformation, and return." From these components, these ministers then drew larger moral lessons and illustrations of spiritual deliverance.[16] It seems inevitable then, that this myth, so deeply rooted in America's psyche, would be applied to the prisoners of war thought to be held in Vietnam. And it is noteworthy that in the movies, these imagined captives, aligned with a tradition rooted in "separation, transformation, and return" would be rescued by imaginary heroes descended from a tradition of "separation, reduction to a primitive state, and regeneration through violence," as Richard Slotkin describes it, and as cited in chapter 2.

The first film of this trend is *Uncommon Valor*, released by Paramount for the holiday season of 1983. It is the story of Colonel Jason Rhodes (Gene Hackman), who, fed up with the government's unwillingness to help him find his MIA son, gathers and trains the members of his son's unit for a covert rescue mission to Laos. The group includes Wilkes (Fred Willard); Sailor (Randall "Tex" Cobb), a violent, hallucinatory ogre; Blaster (Red Brown), a madcap demolitions expert for whom "most human problems can be solved by an appropriate charge of high explosives;" and Scott (Patrick Swayze), a nononsense newbie. Behind the camera, Ted Kotcheff directed *Uncommon Valor* as his follow-up to *First Blood*. Kotcheff also co-produced the film with, among others, another veteran of the Vietnam-themed film—though not of Vietnam—John Milius. This should come as no surprise. As the screenwriter of *Apocalypse Now*, a creator of Harry Callahan, and the director of *Red Dawn*, Milius's stories often involve a hero's journey to find those fallen (or kept) from the light, as well as extremes of jingo-jangle militarism.

Uncommon Valor was a box-office success, performing consistently from week to week after it opened. Paramount's president of marketing at the time, Gordon Weaver, attributed this to the film's "positive ending," "appeal on an emotional level," and also to its revamped advertising campaign. In an interview with *The Hollywood Reporter*, Weaver claims that the initial campaign had emphasized *Uncommon Valor*'s men-on-a-mission aspect, but was reworked to pinpoint the film's "emotional element."[17] For the print ads, the marketing department settled on one iconic image: a soldier with a friend slung over his back and a tagline taken from one of *Uncommon Valor*'s lines of dialogue: "C'mon buddy, we're going home."

Perhaps the task of selling *Uncommon Valor* to Americans was made a little easier by the fact that a real-life version of it had recently occurred. In February 1983, nearly a year before the film opened, news accounts reported that on the night of November 27, 1982, a former Green Beret, Lieutenant Colonel James "Bo" Gritz, led three American soldiers of fortune and fifteen Laotian guerillas into Laos on an operation dubbed "Operation Lazarus." The *New York Times* reports that the nineteen men, funded in part by actors Clint Eastwood and William Shatner—but armed with only four Uzis—entered Laos to rescue up to 120 American POWs that "the raiders" had learned from Laotian refugees were being held in Thailand.[18] The mission ended shortly after it began, when Laotian paramilitary forces ambushed Gritz's group.

Despite this anticlimax, Paramount's publicity for *Uncommon Valor* acknowledges Gritz, by claiming that, "his journey closely paralleled that of Colonel Jason Rhodes and his men in 'Uncommon Valor'—although the screenplay had been written ten months before."[19] Before *Uncommon Valor* was released, however, Paramount was involved with Gritz on other fronts. According to *Variety* columnist Army Archerd, William Shatner purchased the rights to Grtiz's story and began developing it at the studio as a made-for-TV movie to go into production after Shatner completed work on *Star Trek III: The Search for Spock*.[20]

Whereas Gritz's story ends with a capture, *Uncommon Valor* begins with one. The film's first image is of the Vietnamese brush, mist wafting over it. In slow motion, soldiers enter the frame, running into the distance. More shots like this follow, charged with smoke and spray as artillery explodes in the water.

These visual elements, and the mythos they exude, are foregrounded while the sound—shouts and gunfire—is muted and tinny. Next, helicopters touch down. The soldiers charge toward the helicopters, fleeing an enemy Kotcheff does not show. It is as if the landscape itself is after the Americans. Critics often observe that producer Milius's work often bears the influence of John Ford; while this is frequently cast in terms of *The Searchers*, this scene's conflation of the enemy with the natural world recalls Ford's 1934 World War I adventure *The Lost Patrol*.

Colonel Rhodes's son, Frank (Todd Allen), carries a wounded man on his back, toward a helicopter that cannot wait for them. Kotcheff presents a series of one-shots of Frank's buddies, as they watch the melded bodies of their friend with his charge. The helicopters leave, the soldiers reaching out for each other. Frank is captured by the Viet Cong, and the opening credits begin: a sequence that spans ten years as the senior Rhodes travels the globe, making inquiry after inquiry before members of the military and of the government. After the credits, which have brought the audience and Rhodes to the then-present day, we see that Rhodes has exhausted all his favors and his entrée. He now watches the return of POWs on television from the comfort (that is, the confines) of his living room. Situated against his wife's tasteful furnishings, Rhodes is a dead thing waiting to be rejuvenated.

And of course, rejuvenation means action. What makes the action of *Uncommon Valor* unusual, though, is how much of it the filmmakers relegate to the extended training sequence that takes up most of the film's second act. When Rhodes's intelligence provides images of the location where Frank is held, Rhodes's oil magnate friend MacGregor (Robert Stack) provides a life-size mock-up of the camp. This is where the members of Frank's unit reunite—with one another and each with his inner warrior. Before reaching the camp, many of them were grappling with their war traumas (the sensitive and eccentric Wilkes, for instance, has taken to making sculptures, many of which are broken circles). Once they begin their training, however, vigor and good humor flood back into them. During this portion of the story, the soldiers not only thrive, but also have so much fun! This is what makes the second act so surreal: watching actors playing at *playing* at war. Incidentally, the theatrical aspect of this act is echoed in the later *Let's Get Harry*, when the men planning the rescue operation literally hold auditions for the mercenary who will lead them. The sequence is surreal, belonging less in an action movie than in a backstage musical.

The training sequence of *Uncommon Valor* also aligns the picture with World

War II films more than it determines the course of Vietnam-themed action movies. World War II saw a healthy number of war films set in basic training. The same is not true of Vietnam, with Stanley Kubrick's Full Metal Jacket being only a partial exception. After the group completes its training, the men venture to Laos for the final part of the film, where more resemblances to the World War II film emerge. When the soldiers' weapons are confiscated, they pool their money to buy a chest of World War II–era munitions. Used in battle against the Laotian camp guards, these weapons make the attack sequence look like a hybrid of the two wars—an effect that is bolstered by the fact that the hero of Uncommon Valor is not an individual, but a platoon, and a multiethnic, multiracial one at that, including a black soldier and an Asian scout.

The nostalgia these weapons evoke for World War II movies is inseparable from how much more united Americans were and remain in their support for U.S. involvement in World War II, compared to our involvement in Vietnam. Thus, Elizabeth Traube's remark that with these weapons, "drawn from a pre-Vietnam military technology, or, more precisely, from pre-Vietnam films about World War Two, [Rhodes]'s promise about the 'rightness' of the cause is symbolically fulfilled." Traube also writes that as icons, these weapons "evoke traditional military virtues and a time when American wars were cinematically portrayed as just."[21] But one need not consider politics for this dynamic to hold: mythologically speaking, primitive, or technologically outdated weapons, such as the ones used in The Road Warrior and the Rambo sequels, are morally charged by their inherent sense of tradition—especially compared to more modern, impersonal implements of war.[22]

Uncommon Valor makes a final nod to World War II with is its end credits. The sequence is a roll call, in which images of each character from earlier in the film appear along with the actor's name. The final image, over which the rest of the credits scroll, shows Sailor in an earlier scene dancing in silhouette against a brilliant orange sky (which was curious enough the first time around, as the image followed a questionable joke about Agent Orange). This sequence immortalizes the characters—particularly Sailor, who sacrifices himself during the raid—just as the finales of World War II films commemorate their heroes: parading the characters in front of the camera, or reprising them in montages like the end credits of Uncommon Valor, the following summer's Red Dawn, and 1987's Predator.

With the presence (and composition) of a group hero, the weapons it uses, and a credit sequence that immortalizes its members, the filmmakers of Uncommon Valor use a shrewd strategy: mitigating the moral ambiguity of the war at hand with the moral authority of one that, by 1983, already had a forty-plus year history of being mythologized. But nostalgia for the World War II film is only one way *Uncommon Valor*'s makers engage the past; reverence for the natural world is another. The team's trek to the Laotian prison camp takes them through a wilderness that seems to exist outside of politics or modernity. As Rhodes's men hike over a mountain pass, the camera moves in and then pulls away in a sweeping aerial shot that situates the actors deep in the landscape. Other shots, dissolving into one another, show the team mastering the path, hacking through brush, hiking, and crossing a stream.

The soldiers camp for the night. In the morning, their trek resumes. Dissolves now connect shots of the group crossing a barren landscape. Rhodes and his men enter a village, its residents long since the victims of mustard gas, the ground littered with skeletons. One is still dressed, sitting in a chair. The appearance of the soldiers here plays as though they are entering a crypt, intruding upon a past that has been segregated form the rest of the world.

As the journey begins, Laos, a stand-in for Vietnam, is majestic, teeming with life. But in the morning, it is a death-place. Adventure stories have always depicted the jungle with this opposition, which therefore characterizes the Vietnam of our imaginations. But if Vietnam has a privileged place in the imaginations of the audience, then it also has a privileged place in the imaginations of the films' characters. Action films belonging to the POW/MIA strain often pause to show the heroes taking in their first view of the landscape upon their return. The first and last *Missing in Action* films are prime examples. In the first, as Braddock's ally, Tucker (M. Emmet Walsh) steers their boat toward shore, he looks up and says, reverently, "There she is. Vietnam." When director Joseph Zito cuts to Braddock, the hero has already changed into combat fatigues and tied a headband around his head. Zito's use of a low angle exaggerates the sense of mythos. The filmmakers of *Braddock: Missing in Action III* echo this moment when Braddock's pilot, airlifting the hero back to Vietnam, reflects, "Vietnam. I never thought I'd be coming back. I guess we never really can leave, can we?" *Rambo* is more subtle (not a statement one often gets to make), intercutting between shots drawing closer to Rambo steeling himself to parachute into Vietnam and the plane's point of view, gliding through the clouds. Piloting the plane, one of the Special Ops men provides the context: "Back in the badlands, my man." But of course, Rambo is returning to more than the badlands. Passing through the clouds—a surrogate for mist and smoke—Rambo is traveling back to a place, and a state of being, that is more primordial.

The precedent, though, is a moment from *Uncommon Valor.* As the team paddles across a river, Wilkes utters a grim "We're back." This motivates the entrance of James Horner's score; the past often does in this film, as when Rhodes reminisces about his family's legacy of warfare. Wilkes's comment also motivates the cut to a sweeping aerial shot that begins the trek sequence already discussed.

In the nexus of heroes, landscape, and the past, lies the renewal POW/MIA films represent. It is not from actual history so much as from a mythic past that they derive a sense of morality. Of course, showing our soldiers to be the victors this time helps, as does the fact that their mission is to liberate the helpless. "This time no one can dispute the rightness of what we're doing," Rhodes insists, briefing his men. In the film, the heroes of *Uncommon Valor* receive no support from the government; in reality, the opposite was true. According to *The Hollywood Reporter*, the California State Assembly recognized Paramount Pictures and *Uncommon Valor*'s associate producer Burton Elias for paying homage to Vietnam veterans.[23] Similarly, the U.S. Navy recognized Chuck Norris while he was filming *Missing in Action 2: The Beginning.* The men of the S.S. *Dale*, a Navy cruise ship, honored Norris with a plaque while on location in the West Indies island of St. Kitts.[24] Less official but more striking was a 1985 remark by President Ronald Reagan. During a sound check before announcing the release of the TWA hostages (the crisis that inspired *The Delta Force*), Reagan quipped that having seen *Rambo* the night before, he would "know what to do next time."[25]

Critics, on the other hand, were not so enthusiastic about *Rambo, Uncommon Valor* or the first two *Missing in Action* films. Representative of critical sentiment, but especially vivid, is Michael Ventura, who writes, "Go to Washington some night, set up a movie projector in front of the wall on which our Vietnam dead are named, and run *Missing in Action* on *that* screen—nowhere else could the full depravity of the film be sufficiently understood" (emphasis in original).[26]

Like *Uncommon Valor, Missing in Action* tries to make mythic use of the landscape, and through it, connect the hero's quest to his regeneration. To this end, both films feature strong images of their heroes rising out of water. In *Uncommon Valor*, it is Blaster. With his camouflage cap blending into the water, which reflects the foliage above, Blaster surfaces as if of the water itself. In *Missing in Action*, it is Braddock. Dumped into the river when Viet Cong soldiers destroy his raft, Braddock emerges from the river in slow motion, and against this idyllic setting, pumps round after round from his M60 into the three cackling soldiers. The next year, the filmmakers of *Missing in Action 2* expand on the original film's use of water as a pastoral backdrop and its suggestion of rebirth. (Indeed, director Lance Hool would follow this ignoble effort with *Steel Dawn*.) When one of Braddock's fellow prisoners of war escapes from the camp, he rappels down a waterfall. In the water, he hugs a rock in relief. Braddock also ends his extended escape in the river. There he is later reunited with another comrade, who grips Braddock's shoulders and rests his head on Braddock's chest; the moment borders on the amorous.

Seizing upon the mythic qualities with which both the landscape and the very subject of Vietnam have been invested, film critic Stanley Kauffmann remarks that the POW/MIA films "demonstrate that Vietnam today has become a mythological place, somewhat akin to those territories on ancient maps marked 'Here there bee tigers.' . . . Who needs Westerns now?"[27] He makes this comment in his review of 1985's *Rambo: First Blood Part II*, the film that marks the apotheosis of Vietnam as a mythic landscape. Stallone's presence bears some responsibility for this, but so does the cinematography by legendary director of photography Jack Cardiff. A heralded British cinematographer, Cardiff earned his reputation with the Technicolor masterworks he photographed for Michael Powell and Emeric Pressburger. Reminiscent of Cardiff's work on such melodramas as *The Red Shoes* and *Black Narcissus*, his photography in *Rambo* is often marked by a finely calibrated softness and gives a sheen to the film's Mexican locations. It is positively romantic. When applied to Powell/Pressburger's ballets and Himalayan nunneries, such romanticism is one thing, but when applied to *Rambo*'s violence and jingoism, it is quite another: the effect does not undercut these elements of the film, or soften them, but rather, sells them all the more effectively. Thus, the role Cardiff, a foreigner, played in mythologizing Rambo as the uber-1980s American hero should not be underestimated.

Neither should Rambo's use of the land. In one sequence, Rambo stalks Russian soldiers and uses the jungle for cover as well as for weaponry. Here, director George Cosmatos stages an exaggerated version of a similar sequence in *First Blood* and gives the enemy more soldiers than *First Blood*'s Sheriff Teasle has deputies. The scene also carries an added charge by following the death of Co Bao, Rambo's love interest. Rambo has just buried her and, briefly, his own hands, in the mud. Now, going on the offensive, he makes himself one with the earth in order to kill. He does this by reconstituting himself with the mud to which he has just committed Co's corpse, with the amulet he takes from her, and with the headband he fashions from a strip of her dress. In one instance, behind a Russian soldier, an eye opens in the mud itself. It is Rambo. He attacks.

Here and elsewhere, Rambo appears to co-opt the land and warfare themselves, but moreover, to look to them for his very identity. Before Rambo leaves for the mission, Trautman tells him that the old Vietnam is dead, to which Rambo replies, "Sir, if I'm alive, it's still alive." Later, he tells Co, "To survive a war, you gotta become war." He does—through the use of guerilla tactics and his resourcefulness, much touted by Trautman.

What is striking about these skills is that they are more commonly attributed to the Viet Cong than to the American military. Scholars Michael Comber and Michael O'Brien as well as *New York* critic David Denby recognize this. Author Frank Sweeney cites Comber and O'Brien's notion that Rambo resembles the Viet Cong both in his fighting strategies and in his opposition to American authority.[28] In his review of the film, David Denby notes more colorfully,

> The longing to go back to Nam and win that damn war is so strong that the moviemakers have co-opted the enemy's successful strategies—only this is *our* style of guerilla warfare, the American Indian style. The right-wing fantasists who make these movies have taken up Comanche chic [emphasis in original].[29]

To this, we can add Douglas Kellner's observation that Rambo appropriates the motifs of another adversary. He notes that "Rambo has long hair, a head-band, eats only natural foods (whereas the bureaucrat Murdock swills Coke), is close to nature, and is hostile toward bureaucracy, the state, and technology—precisely the position of many 60s counterculturalists."[30] These reversals, through which Rambo becomes a composite of his adversaries, are especially striking in light of critics' charges that *Rambo* would fuel support for more actual military conflicts. This concern was justifiable. As *Time* reports, the U.S. Army hoped to attract potential enlistees by hanging *Rambo* posters outside its recruitment offices.[31]

The franchise's biggest reversal is saved for the mythology on which *Rambo*— and indeed, much of the genre—is founded. *Rambo* is nothing if not an embodiment of the captivity/rescue myth about which Catherine Scott, Susan Jeffords, Richard Slotkin, and others have written. In her article, Scott cites Jeffords's observation that "While the founding of America was carried out through dispossession of Native American lands and wars of extermination, the Puritan captivity narrative reversed the chief protagonists and presented the captives as victims."[32]

It's Not Just a Job, It's a Redemption: By liberating American POWs, Sylvester Stallone's John Rambo helps regenerate a nation's spirit and insinuates himself into its politics with the phenomenally successful *Rambo: First Blood Part II (1985)*. *(From the author's collection.)*

If the captives are victims, then the captors must be victimizers. The victimization Rambo endures after being captured by the Russians and the Vietnamese is emblematic for the genre, and more specifically, for this trend. Rambo's torture echoes that to which the POWs are subjected in *Missing in Action 2* and predicts that which Braddock and his son will face in *Braddock: Missing in Action III*. The latter features a particularly ludicrous bit wherein Braddock is not only shocked with spark plugs, but also tied at the wrists and hoisted so that he must balance on his toes, lest his body drop, and the ropes yank the trigger of a shotgun aimed at his son's face. This trial echoes a flashback in Sergio Leone's *Once Upon a Time in the West* and predicts the one in the postapocalyptic *Cyborg*.

Such torture brings out the messianic in the action hero—particularly in those of the POW/MIA and postapocalypse trends. But Rambo and Braddock may not be the most extreme examples. That distinction could belong to Jean-Claude Van Damme's Gibson Rickenbacker of *Cyborg*, who, having been defeated in a beachfront fight, is literally crucified by Fender and his gang. The cross to which Gibson is lashed and spiked, his arms outstretched, is the mast of a ship, skeletal now, bleaching in the sun. His crucifixion lasts through the night and into the next day. But in the morning, Gibson steels himself with memories of Fender's sadistic abuse of his adopted family. Furious now, he actually kicks the cross down. This is remarkable.

The sadism enjoyed by the punks of the anarchical future can resemble the forms practiced by the Russians and Vietnamese of the POW/MIA films' present day. And though these POW/MIA villains' particular brand of evil is a generic fantasy, the enemy itself does have a very real historical referent: the actual war. With the fantasy and reality easily conflated in the public imagination, the torture of Americans in these films does more than augment the hero's stature. Sweeney cites authors Gaylyn Studlar and David Desser's notion that "Vietnam's alleged actions in presently holding American prisoners serves as an index of our essential rightness in fighting such an enemy *in the past*" (emphasis in original).[33] In other words, if our enemies are depraved *now*, we must have been right to fight them *then*.

In *Rambo*, American righteousness is also embodied by the film's ambivalence toward technology—one that does not echo *Uncommon Valor's* so much as *The Road Warrior's*, and that illustrates the fluidity between past and present which the POW/MIA and postapocalyptic films so often highlight. Prior to leaving on his reconnaissance mission, Rambo is told that he is being given the most advanced weaponry in the world (even Trautman tells Rambo to "let technology do all the work"), but also, that he is not to engage the enemy. Before he has even stepped onto the plane, the bureaucrats have restrained Rambo the way the U.S. government has been often charged with restraining its combatants during the war: not letting our boys fight, win, do their jobs. Thus, much of this equipment—which director George Cosmatos and editors Mark Goldblatt and Mark Helfrich have introduced in a loving, ritualistic montage—is really so much deadweight. Moreover, once Rambo is airborne, the gear becomes actually life-threatening (that is, threatening to the wrong life). While attempting to parachute from the plane, the hero's bag gets caught in the doorway. Rambo is dragged. With his knife, he cuts the bag's strap, and drops into enemy territory; the only devices he has to rely on now are his own.

Once on the ground, two of Rambo's most iconic weapons are his knife (reprising its role from First Blood) and his bow and arrow. These are more primitive tools than the ones he had cut loose. His weapons are now jungle weapons for a jungle war, while in contrast, the Russians and the Vietnamese command the most imposing technology: helicopters and tanks that call to mind the machinery that failed the American military during the real conflict—although such vehicles do not fail Rambo when he commandeers them, of course.

But the primitiveness of Rambo's weapons is mitigated by their being mechanized and overdesigned. These qualities are pushed even further in the next sequel, released in 1988. Rambo III's publicity specifies that the film's copyrighted knife is designed and built by "expert knifesmith" Gil Hibben. According to Hibben (who claims to make knives for collectors, hunters, soldiers, and mercenaries), "There really aren't that many new ideas. Knives have been around for over 10,000 years. I've just been creative with matching new materials to the ancient process."[34] At the same time, the new bow, which took fifteen months to design, is more modernized than ever before. And the publicists seem to relish the details: the "Pro Vantage FPS" features a special "overdraw system," "an extruded glass limb design," and a brand new "Advanced Integrated Material System" comprising "strings and cables fabricated from a revolutionary synthetic fiber" that are "60% more durable."[35]

What's more, in both sequels, Rambo fires arrows that are tipped with screw-on explosives—a stylistic and pyrotechnic flourish that distressed Rambo's (and Stallone's) technical advisor, former Navy commando Tony Maffatone. "I was almost in tears about the exploding arrows," Maffatone told Soldier of Fortune.[36] As reported by American Film's Andrew Cockburn, these arrows reflect Stallone's interest in marrying high technology to primitive weaponry.[37] It fits that Stallone should have such an interest, as this coupling embodies the superhero/underdog dichotomy that has underpinned Stallone's persona since the first *Rocky* films. The technological aspect of Rambo's weapons mirrors the formidability of Stallone's body, while their primitive base evokes the more classic struggle of a man outmatched by the elements.

This dynamic expresses more than just Stallone's persona. The merging of the superhero and the underdog, the technological and the primitive, also distills a particularly American self-image. Though not unrivaled, the United States had enjoyed a position of economic, industrial, technological, and military supremacy in the world throughout the Cold War. But as noted in chapter 2, the era that saw *Rambo*'s blockbuster success also saw our perception of America's formidability mitigated by a sense that was orchestrated or at least augmented by the Reagan administration, of the great and terrible adversaries gathered against us, and of our moral duty to face them. Those subscribing to this worldview reserved for the United States the same meaning, the same great mythos that we grant the loner or the meek who stands up to the mighty. Naturally, other politicians have capitalized on this—before and after Reagan—to say nothing of how foundational this sense of struggle has always been to our mythology and pop culture. To this end, there has always been a deep need in the national psyche to believe that our country's strength is derived not mainly from industrial or economic supremacy, but from more modest origins or even from a divine source. If we can believe that we possess a national purpose that is divine in nature (hearkening as it does back to Manifest Destiny and beyond), then we can believe our power is naturally moral. And if it is naturally moral, then we may shut away what ambivalence attends our disproportionate influence in—and over—the world. This is how we rationalize our might, how we make our great power more palpable to ourselves, and how we reconcile our status as a modern empire with our humbler past. On a smaller scale, this dichotomy is at the heart of Stallone's persona; on a yet still smaller scale, this dichotomy is what Rambo's souped-up knife and tricked-out bow and arrow embody. Thus, if it is by our hero's weapons that we know him, as the action genre would have it, then the lesson of *Rambo* is that by his weapons, we can also know ourselves.

These are the implements of Rambo's guerilla war. But his is not the only guerilla war that the genre depicts, nor is the Far East the only theater in which it is fought. While not a POW/MIA film, John Milius's *Red Dawn* (1984) is a wilderness adventure that imagines a platoon of American teenagers resisting Soviet and Cuban invaders during World War III. As in *Rambo*, *Uncommon Valor*, *The Road Warrior*, and others, the action of *Red Dawn* is staged against a majestic landscape—not a jungle or a desert wasteland, but the Colorado mountains into which the teenagers flee after their town is overrun by foreign troops. In the mountains, the teens regroup, led by the slightly older and far more rugged Jed Eckert (Patrick Swayze). They then name their guerilla band "Wolverines" for their high school sports teams and stage a series of counterattacks.

According to Milius, Red Dawn is "about the country itself—about our sense of invulnerability, about our deep identification with the land, and our attachment to where we live."[38] In the film, this theme is crystallized, albeit darkly, when Jed is asked why a captured Russian soldier must be executed, what makes "us" different from "them." Jed answers: "Because we live here." And the mountains, town, and outskirts of Red Dawn's "here" is indeed land worth getting attached to, suggesting the purity and clean living that are themselves besieged. Of the location, production designer Jackson DeGovia says, "I love that land. That prairie grass. That's original. . . . It's one of the little corners of America that's still splendid in its isolation."[39] To capture this splendor, Milius and cinematographer Ric Waite use angles and lenses that emphasize the ground as an expanse of earth stretching to meet a continent's worth of sky (as during the Wolverines' first ambush). At the same time, the mountains are more than mere backdrop. They provide a constant sense of elevation that in turn suggests a spiritual—that is, regenerative—charge.

Milius also evokes the notion of purity (or of purification) with the various ways the teens fuse themselves with the landscape. Jed and his younger brother Matt (Charlie Sheen) initiate Robert (C. Thomas Howell) into the ways of the wild through the ritual of drinking the blood of the first deer Robert shoots. This begins the film's reduction of Robert to a survivalist and bloodthirsty guerilla who carves a notch into the grip of his AK-47 for every enemy combatant he kills and who then carries out the execution of a traitor when even Jed cannot bring himself to do it. But the relationship between the teens and the natural world is not always confined to the symbolic. As the Wolverines' campaign progresses, the camouflage they steal improves. In time, they come to master the land (and their enemies) such that they acquire the uniforms and other resources to blend into nature with each successive season.

In its majesty, the landscape dwarfs even the Soviet hardware that dwarfs the Americans who are driven before it. Thus the landscape, even with its changing seasons, is monolithic. And in this stature lies a sense of timelessness. Here and there, however, there are exceptions. Jed and Matt encounter the most striking example when they venture back to town. On its outskirts lies a graveyard of overturned vehicles. "It's like it's been here for a thousand years," remarks Matt. Like the dead village in *Uncommon Valor*, an abandoned silo in *Spacehunter*, and the beached, skeletal ship in *Cyborg*, this wreckage suggests an intrusion of the past upon the present. *Red Dawn*'s abandoned wrecks, and the town itself, with its icons appropriated by the invaders, is charged with a sense of a *pre*-postapocalypse—one that is reinforced when we learn that tactical nuclear strikes have destroyed select targets in offscreen America. This calls to mind Michael Ventura's notion that the apocalypse has essentially happened, with or without the part that entails the actual annihilation. As downed Air Force Colonel Andy Tanner (Powers Boothe) reports to the Wolverines, in other parts of the occupied United States, "pyres for the dead light up the sky. It's medieval." Rhetorically, he asks, "Who knows? Maybe next week it'll be swords."

The Colonel's historical referent is grimmer than the ones used by both MGM and at least one of the critics who attack *Red Dawn*. The film's publicity specifies that *Red Dawn* was "inspired in part by the exploits of intrepid Yugoslavian and Greek partisans/resistance fighters during Nazi occupation of World War II."[40] David Denby finds this ironic. He and other critics dismiss the film as a right-wing, even fascist, fantasy. Still, some of its imagery and much of its heroics are, Denby claims,

> drawn from the history and heroic mythology of the international *left*. *Red Dawn* recycles legends about the desperate partisans (often Communists) fighting the Nazis . . . it replays scenes from Hollywood's tear-stained anti-Fascist films such as *The Moon is Down*, *Hangmen Also Die*, and *O.S.S.* (emphasis in original).[41]

Here, Denby anticipates the same appropriation of leftist motifs by right-wing heroes that he will observe the next summer in *Rambo*. The *Los Angeles Herald Examiner*'s David Chute also sees this paradox when he calls *Red Dawn* "a patriotic pig-out," and then notes, "[This is] the kicker: John Milius is pumping up America's patriotic spirit by putting *us* in the position of the insurgents, the Viet Cong" (emphasis in original).[42]

In light of all this, it should not be surprising that *Red Dawn*'s conservatism is the aspect of the film most attacked by critics. This is especially—but by no means exclusively—true of more liberal publications. The defunct *Los Angeles* free weekly, *New Times*, decries, "John Milius' 1984 NRA recruitment feature perfectly captures every right-wing paranoid delusion of the day."[43] Indeed, one of the invaders' first actions is to visit the local sporting goods store and obtain copies of "Form 4473," and from them, determine which townspeople are gun owners. More vivid is the L.A. Weekly's Ginger Varney, who maintains that Red Dawn "is interesting only as an accurate image of the America that must exist in the minds of Ronald Reagan, Jeane Kirkpatrick, and the more zealous among the Pentagon's budget promoters."[44] Indeed, the film was endorsed by no less a figure than General Alexander Haig. Haig had served in Japan, Korea, Europe, and Vietnam. He also served as a military advisor and Chief of Staff to President Richard Nixon, as Secretary of State to Ronald Reagan, and at the time of Red Dawn's release, on MGM's board of directors. Following a private screening of Red Dawn, Haig is quoted as saying:

> This is one of the most realistic and provocative films that I have ever seen. . . . [Its lesson is] the importance of the maintenance of American strength to protect the peace that we have enjoyed throughout history. It is in order to preclude such a scenario that the U.S. maintains its military posture.[45]

Haig also claims to have been "particularly impressed by the technical quality of the equipment that was used."[46] Credit for this belongs to DeGovia, who claims that the most fascinating aspect of designing Red Dawn was researching the Russian hardware—and that this part of the process enabled him to lose himself in the film's politics. "I bought into it completely. The research I did into the Russian military at the time was incredibly sobering. They had really good equipment, and they had a lot of it," DeGovia recalls. "And compared to the American gear, the Russian stuff was very rugged, very reliable, easy to fix, easy to run. It looked wicked and had a lethality that was fun to reproduce."[47] Along with DeGovia's reproductions of the ZSU-24 anti-aircraft gun, or of Soviet tanks (for which he used the chasses of American military cargo carriers), his re-creation of Russian camouflage illustrates his point well. According to DeGovia, "it's very geometric and comes to sharp points. That splinter camouflage was so different, really beautiful."[48]

DeGovia acknowledges that politically, Red Dawn is extremely right-wing, and recalls Milius's involvement with "the Soldier of Fortune crowd and people who called themselves mercenaries," but denies, as so many critics avow, that the film is fascist. "Fascism," DeGovia says, "is corporate authoritarianism and oligarchy. It's basically hooked in with business, mercantile, corporate power. . . . [Red Dawn] is more libertarian, which is about individual freedom and not very interested in big government or big business."[49] Many critics stop short of this distinction, however. In fact, some have reprinted Milius's description of himself as a "Zen-anarchist" as "Zen-fascist."

Still, Milius does provide such critics with some ammunition. Critic J. Hoberman, in his article, "The Fascist Guns in the West," links *Red Dawn*'s "chaste atmosphere" (as well as Chuck Norris's "imperviousness to sex" and the use of Rambo's love interest as a pretense for vengeance) to Susan Sontag's notions of fascism. Hoberman quotes from Sontag's essay on Leni Riefenstahl: "fascist films are concerned with 'the rebirth of the body and of community,'" and that "'the fascist ideal . . . is to transform sexual energy into a "spiritual" force, for the benefit of the community.'"[50] More concretely, Hoberman lists elements of *Red Dawn* that differentiate the film "from traditional Hollywood agitprop and relate it to the mythology of right-wing German nationalism," including "the film's radical subservience of love to patriotism, marked lack of religion, naked hatred of politicians, and subliminal backdrop of Alpine purity."[51]

Hoberman begins his list by charging that the film's opening image, the main title sequence in which the camera flies down through a cloudbank, recalls the opening image of *Triumph of the Will*, the Nazi propaganda film. But by looking only at the opening credits, Hoberman looks at only half the equation. *Red Dawn*'s main title sequence may echo the opening of that fascist hallmark, but the end titles are a roll call, in the fashion of *Uncommon Valor* and in the tradition of anti-fascist World War II films (this time using still photos instead of footage). And while the music that accompanies the main titles is a bass-heavy dirge by Basil Poledouris, the end credits are set to bombastic, martial statements of Poledouris's main theme. There is no mistaking that these credits mark the film's final celebration of its hero, which, less than any one of the characters, and in keeping with the war film tradition, is the platoon itself.

Only in *Red Dawn*, the platoon is a platoon of children. It is worth pausing here to note how prevalent teenagers and groups of teenagers are in Hollywood films of this period, including such coming-of-age comedies as 1982's *Porky's* and *The Last American Virgin*, 1983's *Fast Times at Ridgemont High*, 1984's *Sixteen Candles*, and the apogee of this trend, 1985's *The Breakfast Club* (not to mention a score of horror franchise films, including those of the *Friday the 13th* and *A Nightmare on Elm Street* series). In this light, *Red Dawn* emerges as perhaps the ultimate *zeitgeist* film for the first half of the 1980s. World War III as fought by the Breakfast Club: had screenwriter Kevin Reynolds not hatched the idea, it would have probably generated itself.

But unlike their counterparts in the films that made John Hughes and the "Brat Pack" famous, many of the teens in *Red Dawn* do not come of age by learning about themselves or by finding romance, but rather, by dying mythic

World War III as After School Activity: *The "Wolverines" of John Milius's 1984 occupation fantasy* Red Dawn *gather in a pre–guerilla war pose. (From the author's collection.)*

deaths. When Robert, who transforms from wide-eyed kid to dead-eyed warrior, is killed by a Soviet gunship, he disappears into a dust cloud; when Toni (Jennifer Grey) is mortally wounded, she asks Jed for a hand grenade, lest she be taken by the enemy. Her pretense is that she does not want to be made to talk; but her request, echoing so many Westerns' "save the last bullet for yourself" ethos, resonates with the fear of sexual violation by the *other*. (Earlier, the film had already depicted enemy soldiers as lecherous and would-be rapists). In his review of the film, Hoberman remarks that the right-wing paranoia underpinning the film is "far more xenophobic than anti-Communist."[52] Toni's death, even more than the geopolitics Milius concocts, bears Hoberman out.

More poignant than Robert or Toni's death are Matt and Jed's, or more to the point, the preparation for them. Matt paints the brothers' names on Partisan Rock, a massive rock that the Wolverines mark with the names of their dead, *before* he and Jed leave to attack the train station (*Red Dawn*'s third-act industrial setting). During the attack, Matt is mortally wounded. After killing Matt's shooter in a Western-style fast-draw, Jed carries his brother to the park where they played as children. Jed cradles Matt against the snow and the long shadow of a swing set—the same swings the boys' father (Harry Dean Stanton) recalls while interned in a drive-in-theater-turned-reeducation camp. We do not see the brothers die, but they are never seen again.

Two Wolverines survive. Danny (Brad Savage) and Erica (Lea Thompson). Matt purposely leaves behind this pair when preparing for the final raid. "Someone's gotta live, someone's gotta make it," explains Matt. "Me and Jed, we're all used up." This is no accident. Throughout the film, Danny and Erica appear to be the youngest and most innocent of the guerillas, and in the end they are the only survivors. Thus, when Danny says, "We're free now," and Erica repeats "free," relishing the word, it is the group's figurative children—the truest children among a group of children—who have been liberated. The resolution of *Red Dawn* marks the film's final step in promoting renewal, and toward that end, mythologizing the young. This is in contrast to Reynolds's original concept, which, before Milius rewrote the script at MGM's behest, skewed more toward *Lord of the Flies*, and stressed not the perpetuation, but the corruption, of innocence.

To liberate children is to ensure the future, and so it is a means toward renewal. This theme is developed even more overtly in the post-Vietnam *Braddock: Missing in Action III* (1988) and the post–World War III *Mad Max Beyond Thunderdome* (1985). While in *Red Dawn*, children are the heroes, in these films, children exist to be delivered by—and to be a deliverance for—messianic loners, be they liberator-vets or liberator-nomads. As children symbolize the future more than a prisoner of war or even *The Road Warrior*'s multigenerational commune does, the salvation of children makes each of these last two films the apotheosis of its particular strand. It is no coincidence then, that each is the culmination of its series, the third in its trilogy.[53]

"He's fighting for everyone who can't fight back," declares the tag line for *Braddock*. In this sequel, Braddock returns to Vietnam to free the wife he thought was dead, and the Amerasian son he never knew he had. His wife, Lin (Miki Kim) is killed during the rescue attempt, so instead, Braddock leads a large group of Amerasian orphans to safety in Thailand, through the forces of demonic General Quoc (Aki Aleong). The film's publicity material positions the children as "the final legacy of our Vietnam experience," and Braddock's mission as "something of a political metaphor . . . bringing this arduous chapter in American history to a balanced end."[54] As Cannon's publicity department would have us believe, on these children's fate rests America's healing.

Such deliverance could only be the project of a messianic hero. When Reverend Polansky (Yehuda Efroni), who has been tending to the orphans, sees that Braddock has arrived, he whispers, "Oh my god," not unlike Scorpio's "Jesus" in *Dirty Harry*. Not long after, Lin confides in Braddock, "I prayed you would come. And you are here." Subtler, but more resonant, are the visual cues director Aaron Norris provides—specifically, the many reaction shots of minor characters and extras as they watch Braddock, recalling the Feral Kid's hero worship of Max in *The Road Warrior*. When Braddock enters Vietnam, a little naked child watches the black-clad Braddock speed through the lagoon on his black hovercraft. Later, when soldiers stop Braddock's son Van (Roland Harrah III), and Braddock dispatches them in a display of martial arts, director Norris is sure to include reaction shots of Lin watching.

Most overt are the reactions of Van and the children when Braddock battles a soldier trying to rape one of the orphan girls. The two men fight, but the reaction shots do not come until the scene reaches its most violent, when Braddock stabs his foe with the blade that pops from his machine gun/grenade launcher—another weapon that embodies wilderness action films' fusion of primitivism and technology. Once he does, the filmmakers cut to the girl, then to Van, then to the mass of children, watching. From the children, Norris cuts back to Braddock as he fires a grenade into the soldier. The soldier flies across the room and crashes through a hut wall in slow motion. His landing and coming to a rest are covered in no less than five shots; in the sixth, the grenade, embedded in his stomach, explodes. Not only does the editing of this scene illustrate the obsession with which action filmmaking technique renders violence, but it also gives the violence an awe-filled audience. This in turn enhances the moviegoer's sense of Braddock's heroism: the reverence of his onscreen audience helps cue the reactions of those watching from their theater seats.

Of course, Braddock works for the children's hero-worship by leading them from Vietnam to Thailand. The filmmakers depict this odyssey in a montage that shows Braddock leading the children into the jungle, across a rocky riverbed, along the water's edge. The embattled group then reaches an airstrip. Lush vegetation is relegated to the background; the foreground is now taken up by straw and dirt and dust. After Braddock dispatches enemy soldiers and sneaks onto a plane, his wards storm the landing field's barbwire fence, topple it, and run down toward the plane, past ramshackle hangars. Literally and visually, the children are leaving desolation behind. That is, until the plane, leaking fuel from where it has been struck by bullets, crashes. Sheering trees and jungle brush, it lands, a smoking, steaming wreckage. Braddock, armed with an AK-47, then leads the children in a column into the brush, over water.

Eventually, we see the group reach the bridge connecting Vietnam and Thailand, where another audience lends Braddock moral support: American soldiers on the Thai side of the border cheer as Braddock shoots his and the children's Vietnamese pursuers. After Van helps his wounded father take aim and destroy General Quoc's helicopter, Braddock, tattered and bleeding, rises with Van, from amid the helicopter's wreckage. Cheering Americans run across the bridge, across the border. Supported by Van, Braddock leads the children and meets rejoicing Americans on the bridge. Rather than roll the credits here, however, the filmmakers first show one of the little girls as she lingers. She looks at the conflagration behind them, and then turns back toward Braddock and the others. Smiling, she resumes walking toward salvation, and the end titles begin. Thus, it is not with Braddock's perspective, but with a child's, that the Missing in Action series comes to a close.

The same is true of the Mad Max movies. The trilogy's final scene is set in a skeletal—but still standing—Sydney, Australia, where Savannah Nix (Helen Buday), a young woman looking "into history back," reminds an assembly of children of the time before Max delivered them from the wasteland. This is their nightly ritual, so that as they settle into their future, they remember who they were, where they came from, and Max, who sacrificed his own deliverance so that they might come "home."

This odyssey is the focus of George Miller and George Ogilvie's stunning *Mad Max Beyond Thunderdome*, or at least of its second half. In the first, Max comes to Bartertown, a shantytown founded and run by Auntie Entity (Tina Turner), where the economy is powered by trading, and where energy is derived from the methane gas extracted from pig waste. Auntie Entity recruits Max to kill Blaster (Paul Larsson), the waste-mine enforcer and muscle for Master (Angelo Rossitto), a shrewd midget who has been challenging Auntie's authority. Max is to battle Blaster in Thunderdome, a domed arena in which one law ("two men enter, one man leaves") settles all legal and civil disputes. But upon discovering Blaster's childlike nature, Max cannot bring himself to deliver the deathblow. Their deal broken, Auntie banishes Max into the wasteland. Max is near death when Savannah finds him and brings him back to her tribe of lost children. They believe Max to be "Captain Walker," the man who promised to return for them and bring them home. Reluctantly, Max undertakes this charge, which takes him back to Bartertown and into a last showdown with Auntie.

Though they seem to be disparate, both halves of *Mad Max Beyond Thunderdome* focus on renewal. "Look around," Aunty instructs Max. "All this I built. Up to my armpits in blood and shit. Where there was desert, now there's a town; where there was robbery, there's trade; where there was despair, now there's hope. Civilization. And I'll do anything to protect it." Likewise, the children, look to a time when they will leave the wilderness for the big city of "Tomorrow-morrow-Land," a place of technological wonders. But if both halves tend toward renewal, Miller and Ogilvie underpin them with an unusual measure of irony. The progress Bartertown represents is not the reconstitution of any communal spirit, but rather, of industry, of the free market, and of order itself, through intrigue and assassination. In fact, Bartertown is nicely distilled by "Underworld," the mines that generate the town's power: renewal, yes, but one that is derived from refuse.

The children's journey is also ironic. Though deep in the desert, the children live in an oasis. It is a canyon, lush and rich with water ("The Crack in the Earth," according to the film's publicity).[55] The children are one with nature, as suggested by the animal skins in which they dress. This is also expressed by the actors' make-up: red-yellow-burnt-orange mud from a river that runs through one of the film's remote locations, and from which make-up artist Elizabeth Fardon fashioned a body-paint in which the sixty children were covered.[56]

But the children's search for a better tomorrow leads them to the most nightmarish part of the *Mad Max* world. When they reach Sydney, the children find that "Tomorrow-morrow-Land" has been annihilated as much as any other place. It is choked and red with dust and late day sun. And as created by model coordinator Dennis Nicholson and his crew, its buildings are skeletons, its highways collapsed, girders twisted, and cables snapped (all in a scale model that covered some 3,000 feet).[57] Paradise is not their tomorrow, but their yesterday. Sill, Miller ends the film hopefully. In Sydney the tribe perpetuates itself, and moreover, its *sense* of itself, of its history and purpose. Every night, the tribe "does the tell" that they might not forget and lights the city's lights for Max, whom they remember as "him that finded us, him that came the salvage."

For the characters of postapocalyptic adventures, regeneration is not an act of rewriting the past, as it is for the heroes (and arguably, the audience) of these films' POW/MIA counterparts. In fact, for the characters of *Mad Max Beyond Thunderdome*, their renewal depends upon their retaining the past, or at least a memory of it. Co-screenwriters Miller and Terry Hayes express this through their characters' near-obsession with reciting oral histories and with the vernacular in which they speak—undoubtedly what *Screen International's* Marjorie Bilbow is referring to when she remarks that the film "has a weird beauty and a script with passages that delight the attentive ear."[58]

The Thunderdome fight—the scene many consider to be the film's most memorable—is introduced with a bit of business that illustrates Bilbow's point. Before Max and Blaster face each other, armed and bouncing around on elastic straps (aided by special effects coordinator Mike Wood's hand-controlled air cylinders, a technique he borrowed from, of all sources, *Mary Poppins*),[59] Thunderdome's emcee, Dr. Dealgood (Edwin Hogeman), announces the combatants, but also the history of the venue:

> Listen on! Listen on! This is the truth of it. Fighting leads to killing, and killing gets to warring. And that was damn near the death of us all. Look at us now, everyone's busted up and talking about hard rain. But we've learned by the dust of them all. Bartertown's learned. Now when men get to fighting, it happens here, and it finishes here. Two men enter, one man leaves.

The spectators, hanging onto the outside of the dome, now chant "two men enter, one man leaves" like a mantra. Dr. Dealgood continues: "And right now, I've got two men, two men with a gut full of fear. Ladies and gentlemen, boys and girls—dyin' time's here."

Likewise, the children, cut off from the world, use words and sentence structures that are distended from their original forms, some of which have already peppered this discussion of the film. When they do, one can feel the children trying to hold onto historical referents as they slip out from beneath them. In the canyon, Savannah "takes the Tell," and recounts the apocalypse for those assembled, including Max.

This ain't one body's story. It's the story of us all. We got it mouth to mouth, so you got to listen it and 'member. 'Cause what you hears today, you got to tell the birthed tomorrow. I'm looking behind us now, across the count of time, down the long hall, into history back. I sees the end what were the start. It's pocksy-clipse! Full of pain! And out of it were birthed crackling dust and fearsome time. It were full-on winter, and Mr. Dead chasing them all. But one he couldn't catch: that was Captain Walker.

Savannah then chronicles how Captain Walker flew off with some survivors, crashed, and how those who lived made their way to The Crack in the Earth. In time, a small party—including Captain Walker—left in search of civilization, and promised to return for the rest of the children. And now, having maintained their oral tradition—"everything marked, everything 'membered,"—these children look forward to "Tomorrow-morrow-Land," where they believe they will see such features of the old world as "skyrafts" (airplanes), "highscrapers" (buildings), and "v-v-v-video" (television).

This stylized dialogue compliments the bricolage that so characterizes the Mad Max sequels and their ilk and that has filtered down to The Crack in the Earth. During the scene in which Savannah recounts the end of the world, one of the children, Scrooloose (Rod Zuanic), treats a Bugs Bunny doll like a totem, while the others rely on a child's ViewMaster toy to glimpse what they deem canonical images of the world as it once was. "'Member this?" their leader asks. "The 'River of Lights!'" they declare; the image is a time-lapsed photograph of a highway at night, car headlights streaming. And then there is "the sonic": vinyl albums they have never been able to play, or even comprehend. In a later scene, Max shows them how to operate a record player on which a French language tutorial has been left behind. As two of the children listen and repeat, the film makes one of its most poignant uses of language: "Je vais chez moi . . . I'm going home."

The sheer abundance of words in Mad Max Beyond Thunderdome distinguishes it from The Road Warrior, which is often praised for approximating a silent film, so pure is its visual power. (Indeed, Mel Gibson has fewer than twenty lines of dialogue in the whole picture.) Still, neither film uses dialogue to develop character so much as each uses action and, more to the point, imagery. But in *Beyond Thunderdome*, words are given a unique responsibility: to hold onto what can no longer be seen—the world before this one.

Of course, the power of *Beyond Thunderdome*'s astonishing imagery must not be underestimated, for it grounds the film in a mythic past, even as it takes place in a dystopian future. As Max nears death in the desert, the audience gets its first view of the children—one child, really. In the distance, the smeared silhouette of a warrior figure emerges from bright white light, which trails off into a blue tint. Sand drifts across the frame like the smoke we have so often seen. The image is primordial: it is as if the backlit figure is earliest man, behind whom—*before whom*—there is nothing. Complimenting the imagery is the sound. At first, the audience hears only wind and a minimalist snatch of Maurice Jarre's score, but as both the child and the camera approach Max, the music becomes more thematic, more ordered.

The figure turns out to be the young woman, Savannah. Later, because she is the one who found Max, she "takes the tell." Her narration is staged at the mouth of a torch-lit cave. Cave paintings illustrate the tale. Savannah isolates each one with a wood frame as she recites. The last painting is concealed behind a curtain of reeds. When Savannah finishes, the children chant Walker's name, and the curtain is pulled aside. The last image has been freshly painted. It is Max, in a Christ-like pose, with the children standing in a row across his outstretched arms. The crucified pose, so emblematic of Jesus's suffering, here is literally the children's support. It is a striking image, and the filmmakers know it: the camera pushes in on the painting, and then, in the next shot, rotates around Max as the children rise, surrounding him, revering him. Their reverence makes clear that they see Max as their messiah; and their having painted his likeness as the last in a series of images suggests that they see him not only as their savior, but also as the end of their story.

It is this moment—more than anything represented by Bartertown, by the children's eventual escape from Aunty Entity, or by their reaching Sydney—that L.A. *Weekly* critic F. X. Feeney sees as epitomizing the film's theme of renewal:

> Gibson's wince of horror and wonder when he sees the wall painting is especially beautiful and telling: this is the first time in the entire saga that we've seen Max regard himself. . . . [T]his is the first instance in any of the three films in which he has been forced to comprehend himself as *others* see him (emphasis in original).[60]

They Don't Need Another Hero: *Once the Road Warrior, Mad Max Rockatansky (Mel Gibson) listens to the children he will lead out of the wasteland in* Mad Max Beyond Thunderdome *(1985). (From the author's collection.)*

Seeing how the tribe conceives Max restores his sense of himself, just as story-telling can restore a people's sense of its place in a continuum. "To recover oneself is to recover, period," Feeney writes. "The *Mad Max* series needed *Beyond Thunderdome* to bring it full circle—to restore to its people (and us) the idea of a civilization surviving, surviving by (of all things) the firelight of a well-told story."[61]

Whether in Bartertown, The Crack in the Earth, or in a blasted Sydney, the language and oral histories of *Mad Max Beyond Thunderdome* bring to an anarchical future a calming sense of ritual. It is ritual that brings a sense of order to the wild. And it is the wilderness of desert wastelands and Southeast Asian jungles (and in one case, the mountains of the American Midwest), along with the fluidity among past, present, and future that they embody that so distills the mythology of American action films. These, of course, are the myths of the frontier hero who rescues and renews, and of the savage enemy who can be found at the business end of the hero's weapons (primal and otherwise) or, at the very least, of his steely reserve. The irony is that what distinguishes the action films of the previous decade from the Western genre that sired them is their urban settings. But perhaps there is something arbitrary in this distinction: in action movies, and also in *film noir*, the urban setting is a metaphorical wilderness. Films such as *Rambo* and *The Road Warrior* return what had become implicit to the level of the explicit.

Of course, as evidenced by such films as *The Terminator*, *Cobra*, *Lethal Weapon*, the *Death Wish* sequels, and others, the urban model of action film thrived alongside its wilderness-set counterpart. In 1988, however—the same year that the *Rambo* and *Missing in Action* trilogies end—an action film arrives that, more than any of its predecessors, integrates its urban setting and the jungle metaphor on which the film is founded. This enterprise would work so well, it would be more than a box office hit. It would become a template, and from its influence would stem some of the most spectacular, and most insidious, of the genre's entries.

Blowing Up All Those Familiar Places
Terror and the Confined Arena

Ouch. When you get those feelings, insurance companies start to go bankrupt.
—Sgt. Al Powell (Reginald Veljohnson) in Die Hard 2 (1990)

In the action genre, the postapocalypse managed to come *before* the apocalypse. Following the postapocalyptic and paramilitary adventures of the 1980s, the new action film of the 1990s would focus on the taking and the destruction of a narrowly drawn location, be it a building, bus, plane, or prison. What distinguishes many of these films from their predecessors is both their containment and how they replace the foreign villain lost in the post–Cold War era of political correctness. What remains constant, of course, is the genre's visual excessiveness. In the 1990s, spectacular special effects pick up this mantle, which previously had been carried by the extreme physicality and firepower of the 1980s hero. Even their advertising reflects this: the posters and print material for *Above the Law, Braddock, Cobra, Commando,* and the *Lethal Weapon, Rambo,* and *Terminator* films (among others) showcase their stars in their monolithic glory. On the other hand, the print campaigns for *Speed, Con Air,* and the *Die Hards* feature the talent along with their locations in flames, while those for *Passenger 57, Cliffhanger, Speed 2: Cruise Control, Under Siege 2: Dark Territory,* and *Air Force One* all suggest velocity and motion.

Die Hard, directed by John McTiernan, was the breakout hit of 1988's summer movie season and became the prototype for the confined action film of the 1990s. As it happens, it is also one of the last great pre-CGI (computer-generated imagery) special effects productions from Richard Edlund's Boss Studios. The movie was a tremendous, if surprising, success. It inspired two sequels and also *Toy Soldiers (Die Hard* in a boys' school); *The Taking of Beverly Hills (Die Hard* in Beverly Hills); *Passenger 57 (Die Hard* on a plane); *Under Siege (Die Hard* on a battleship) and its sequel, *Under Siege 2: Dark Territory (Die Hard* on a train); *Speed (Die Hard* on a bus) and its sequel, *Speed 2: Cruise Control (Die Hard* on a cruise ship); *Cliffhanger (Die Hard* on a mountain); *Sudden Death (Die Hard* in a hockey arena); *The Rock* (Die Hard in a prison); *Executive Decision* (Die Hard on another plane); *Con Air* (Die Hard on a prisoner transport plane); and *Air Force One* (Die Hard on the President's plane). This format also became commonplace in the straight-to-video market and on television, where it dictated the plotlines of several made-for-TV movies, and even a 1993 episode of *Star Trek: The Next Generation* (Die Hard on the starship *Enterprise*).

Die Hard stars Bruce Willis as John McClane, a New York City detective who wages a Christmas Eve war against the terrorists who seize the Los Angeles skyscraper where his estranged wife, Holly Genarro (Bonnie Bedelia), is a high-powered executive. The terrorists, led by the dapper Hans Gruber (Alan Rickman), are on a mission not of political or religious fanaticism, but of robbery. In fact, Hans uses the rhetoric of political outrage only as a red herring; like *Nighthawks*'s Wulfgar, Hans sends the police scrambling to release "revolutionary brothers and sisters" belonging to a range of unrelated terrorist organizations, but what he really wants to liberate is the $640 million in bearer bonds the building's vault safeguards.

Die Hard originated as the 1979 novel *Nothing Lasts Forever*, written by Roderick Thorp as the sequel to his 1968 bestseller, *The Detective*. As Thorp recalls, the seed of *Nothing Lasts Forever* was a dream he had the night he saw *The Towering Inferno*. In the dream, Thorp saw a man being chased through a building by men with guns.[1] Also according to Thorp, when associate producer Lloyd Levin later showed the book to producer Lawrence Gordon, Gordon looked at the burning building and helicopter on the cover, and said, "I don't need to read it. Buy it."[2]

For Bruce Willis's turn as McClane, the actor received $5 million, a sum that many felt was scandalous and that sent shockwaves through the industry. At the time, Willis was most known for playing a smart-mouthed gumshoe on *Moonlighting*, a romantic comedy series that had been losing viewership and fan support. This, coupled with Willis's less-than-stellar box office clout (his previous two films, Blake Edwards's comedies *Blind Date* and *Sunset*, failed to make Willis a movie star) and a "bad boy" persona of which the public was tiring led to a brief spat of advertising for *Die Hard* that did not even feature Willis. In these ads, the film's primary location, the high-rise, is the star.

To drum up positive word of mouth, Fox released *Die Hard* in waves, a strategy normally used for smaller dramas rather than summer action fare. On July 15, 1988, the film opened in just twenty cities on 21 screens, but on July 21, for the film's second weekend, that figure jumped to 1,200 screens.[3] The year surrounding *Die Hard*'s release had seen films from all the genre's luminaries, including Schwarzenegger (*Red Heat*); Clint Eastwood (*The Dead Pool*); Stallone (*Rambo III*); Norris (*Hero and the Terror*, and prior to that, *Braddock: Missing in Action III*); and Charles Bronson (November 1987's *Death Wish 4: The Crackdown*). 1988 also saw the first breakthrough films for Steven Seagal and Jean-Claude Van Damme. But *Die Hard* outpaced all of these, grossing a then-impressive $88 million, setting a home video rental record in 1989, and more to the point, becoming a template for the next decade's action films.

Die Hard's aesthetic sophistication distinguishes the film from its contemporaries. The main architects of its style are John McTiernan, directing the film for his *Predator* producers Lawrence Gordon and Joel Silver; cinematographer Jan de Bont, with whom McTiernan would next make *The Hunt for Red October*; and production designer Jackson DeGovia, with whom McTiernan would reunite for *Die Hard with a Vengeance* (1995).

Much of *Die Hard* was shot inside Fox Plaza, then a new, Fox-owned skyscraper on the corner of the studio lot in Century City. According to McTiernan, "We [had] to periodically run downstairs and apologize to the lawyer beneath us, saying 'we're about to fire machine guns; will you excuse us?'"[4] McTiernan's comment seems good-natured enough, but *Daily Variety*'s Todd McCarthy sees a darker side to the action, "a certain perversity in the corporate attitude involved in Fox's setting the picture entirely in its striking new Fox Plaza landmark building, only to completely torch it onscreen."[5] The *Village Voice* critic David Edelstein is even more colorful, calling the skyscraper setting "an apocalyptic toy box," and reflecting, "The people who made this movie must have always wanted to demolish a skyscraper—just ravage the hell out of it—and especially one of those high-tech, glass-and-bronze monstrosities, an *arrogant* skyscraper, like the Trump Tower" (emphasis in original).[6]

Savagery befalls *Die Hard*'s Nakatomi Plaza and also underlies how it was conceived. DeGovia's initial point of reference was the jungle. "When I first read the script, I saw a jungle maze. It reminded me of the book *High Rise* by J. G. Ballard, in which a modern building becomes a tribal battleground. I wanted to make a building where that kind of action could take place," DeGovia says.[7] He would later reflect, "When the building is a jungle, people revert to utter realism, which is savagery. . . . There are entire sequences where McClane moves through the building not touching the floor, like a predator in a jungle."[8]

Several major sequences unfold according to DeGovia's description, and, when coupled with the McClane's guerilla tactics, draw *Die Hard* into a certain kinship with the genre's *Rambos*, *Missing in Actions*, and *Red Dawn*. These sequences include McClane's flight through the building's core; his fight with

Ho-Ho-Ho: *In* Die Hard *(1988), New York City detective John McClane (Bruce Willis) spends Christmas the way an American action hero should: fighting terrorists in his estranged wife's corporate high-rise. (From the author's collection.)*

Hans's towering, Aryan henchman, Karl (Alexander Godunov); and McClane's leap from the rooftop and its aftermath. In the first of these escapades, McClane flees from pursuing terrorists after trying to alert the police. He squeezes through fan blades, dashes along a catwalk, zips down a ladder, works his way into an air shaft, uses the canvas strap from his machine gun to lower himself down, nearly inverts himself reaching for a duct, falls, catches a duct further down, worms his way inside, and finally, drops from an air vent onto the floor of the boardroom. The whole sequence runs approximately six minutes. McClane's bare feet touch the floor three times.

Later, on the "machine floor," the film's requisite industrial setting, McClane fights Karl, whose brother McClane killed in a fight through a jungle-like bramble of metal studs on the thirty-second floor. In the later fight, imagined by McTiernan and co-screenwriter Steven E. de Souza and then choreographed by stunt coordinator Charlie Picerni, McClane and Karl engage this familiar landscape in fierce, unexpected ways. They smash into drums and pipes. They use nooks and staircases and, in one case, a chain. Godunov, a Russian ballet dancer, offsets Karl's brutality with grace, but the character still lacks inventiveness. McClane, on the other hand, is scrappier, a more resourceful street brawler. It is McClane who uses the three-dimensionality of the room, securing his victory. While Karl limits himself to the horizontal plane, McClane, offscreen, climbs onto a pile of crates, and waits like a predator. In fact, when Karl nears the crates, McClane's foot is barely visible to the audience—that is, until it lashes out and catches Karl in the jaw. At the climax of the fight, McClane relies on the vertical again. He lashes a dangling chain around Karl's neck and sends him sailing off, high above the floor.

McClane's next feat is his leap from the exploding rooftop. With a fire hose tied around him, McClane drops approximately ten stories before slamming against the building. He then swings and smashes through a window to get back inside. Here, McClane is Tarzan. And returning to the thirtieth floor (a three-story set built on Fox's Stage 15), the exhausted hero dodges an explosion inside a replica of Frank Lloyd Wright's Fallingwater, an indoor, manmade waterfall. Stalking through Fallingwater's greenery, then diving into its pool, McClane is truly in the jungle, at last. When he rises, the elevator bank explodes. Around McClane, ceramics topple and the sprinklers discharge; it is as if the building has sustained so much damage, it has begun to consume itself.

This is all only a portion of what McClane endures to liberate the hostages— as is the fact that he spends the film barefoot, making his contact with the high-rise that much more tactile. This, and the gradual loss of his clothing, which marks his reduction to savagery (in addition to marking his vulnerability and the film's passage of time), is a further counterpoint to the building's modern look. And just as McClane's ordeal weds corporate modernity to a wilderness past, *Die Hard* inflects the modern action film with nods to its Western heritage. Throughout the film, both Hans and McClane's friend, LAPD Sergeant Al Powell (Reginald Veljohnson), call McClane "cowboy." McClane, recognizing how his predicament recalls the Westerns of his youth, tells Al to call him "Roy," as in Roy Rogers. Hans accuses McClane of being "just another American who saw too many movies as a child," and when he asks if McClane really thinks he stands a chance, McClane quips the now signature one-liner from the *Die Hard* films: "Yippi-kai-yay, mother-fucker," itself a combination of Western bravado and modern profanity.

With the final showdown, the film's derivation from the Western becomes visual as well as verbal. As in *Dirty Harry* and others, the showdown of *Die Hard* cites that of *High Noon*. Here, however, a seemingly unarmed McClane, and Hans, who holds a gun to Holly's head, actually *discuss* it. The fast draw comes after Hans confuses John Wayne with Gary Cooper, and tries to co-opt McClane's one-liner. McClane pulls his gun from where he had taped it to his back. (His 9mm Beretta is a solid, working-class counterpoint to Hans's effete, snub-nosed Walther PPK and Karl's massive Steyr Aug assault rifle.) McClane fires his last two bullets to dispatch the last two terrorists, Hans and Eddie (Dennis Hayden), an American in cowboy boots. McClane then blows the smoke from the muzzle. "Happy trails, Hans," he says.[9]

Die Hard has another, subtler affinity for *High Noon*. McTiernan often uses his compositions to limit McClane's stature and our sense of his command over the space—especially in long shots that highlight McClane's vulnerability. Often, McTiernan pushes McClane to the margins of the frame—usually the left margin, as Fred Zinnemann had framed Gary Cooper in *High Noon*. And like Cooper's Will Kane, McClane often crosses the screen only at critical moments. Alone and outgunned, McClane does not control the frame; it controls him. Additionally, McTiernan and de Bont often use a shallow depth-of-field to trap McClane in the background of the image, while a desk, door, potted plant, or metal studs, take up the foreground.

The filmmakers also use framing devices to restrict McClane. Framing him in doorways or between objects, McTiernan makes *Die Hard*'s hero look smaller, even prior to the terrorists' attack, as in the lobby or Holly's executive washroom. Once the terrorists take their hostages, McClane is framed in doorways *nine times* before beginning his counterattack. As he journeys through the building's core, the framing devices become industrial and menacing, including fan blades and the airshaft. These frames are captured as surely as the building has been. And as McClane conquers the terrorists, he also conquers the terrain. Therefore, his control of a scene dictates his control of the camera—or lack thereof. When Hans reveals McClane's identity, de Bont's cinematography throws the hero into shadow and the space into abstraction. When Powell later asserts his solidarity with McClane, the lighting returns to normal, the room to familiarity, and the camera follows McClane's lead as he rises. Thus, *Die Hard* is not just a story of captivity and rescue; it is also a turf war.

What makes this war so compelling is that the film's imagery and screenplay and Willis's performance (vulnerable, regretful, wisecracking from exasperation, not with other action heroes' ironic detachment) make McClane an everyman, of whom producer Lawrence Gordon says, "He seems to be a man that you believe could lose."[10] How then, to maintain McClane's everyman quality in a big-budget sequel that would automatically mythologize him? Adapting Doug Richardson's adaptation of Walter Wager's novel *58 Minutes*, Steven E. de Souza solves this problem with something of a wink in *Die Hard 2* (1990), originally titled *Die Harder*. Among the first films commissioned by Twentieth Century Fox's new chairman, Joe Roth, the sequel finds McClane battling terrorists who have staged an electronic takeover of Dulles International Airport. The terrorists' goal is to free General Ramon Esperanza (Franco Nero) during his extradition to the United States. Esperanza is a drug-running dictator in the mold of Manuel Noriega, whom the U.S. government arrested in December 1989, while *Die Hard 2* was in production. De Souza claims that he based the film's backstory on America's "Central American meddling"—that is, President George Bush's campaign against Noriega, and the previous administration's involvement in Iran-Contra. "Everything going on south of the Rio Grande we conflated into one scandal," de Souza says.[11]

Just as McClane and Hans had referenced Schwarzenegger, Rambo, Roy Rogers, John Wayne, and the cast of *High Noon*, *Die Hard 2*'s supporting characters reference McClane's celebrity status—the inevitable byproduct of his feats in the last film. This grounds the movie in a "real world" sensibility (though it is often undermined by the sequel's expansive action scenes and gaudier visual style). "The ghost of Christmas past," quips reporter Sam Coleman (Sheila McCarthy). "Nakatomi? L.A.? You're John McClane, right?" Later, the film's bureaucrat police captain, Carmine Lorenzo (Dennis Franz), hotly declares, "Yeah, yeah, I know all about you and that *Nakatomi* thing in L.A., but just because the TV thinks you're hot shit, that don't make it so!"

Even McClane is prone to making such remarks. When he recognizes a man who will turn out to be the terrorist leader, the man tells him, "I get that a lot. I've been on TV," to which McClane answers, almost to himself, "Yeah. Me too." Later, after a devastating gunfight, this stranger, Colonel Stuart (William Sadler), realizes just who his adversary is: "Oh, McClane. *John McClane.* The policeman hero who rescued the Nakatomi hostages. I read about you in *People* Magazine. You seemed a bit out of your league on *Nightline*, I thought."

In the novel, the terrorist leader is German, like Hans. He commands a multiethnic bunch that includes a Japanese revolutionary, an Arab, and two Puerto Rican brothers. In the film, however, the terrorists are uniformly American—ex-American military, to be precise. De Souza remembers conceiving Stuart as "a far right [-wing] cold warrior," angry that with the end of the Cold War, his country abandoned its anticommunist allies. But according to de Souza, English was then still a troublesome language for Finnish director Renny Harlin, who therefore directed Sadler to give a more psychotic and less "sincere" performance, and largely divested *Die Hard 2* of these politics.[12] Stuart's rhetoric contains just a dash of anticommunism; the rest of the film implies that the terrorists are, like Hans was, in this for the money. When Stuart does seem to make a political statement, it is either vague or aborted. In the church where the terrorists establish their command center, Stuart stands at a pulpit: "Gentlemen, tonight the pattern ends. The dominoes will fall no more and the ramparts will remain upright." But when one of his men cuts in, "Sir, General Esperanza's plane just came on the scope," Stuart springs into motion, seeming to forget that he was mid-speech. Later, after Stuart has freed Esperanza, he addresses his men: "Congratulations, gentlemen. You've won a victory for our way of life. You've earned my pride, my admiration, and a kickass vacation." But nowhere in the film does Stuart specify what that way of life is, or that they even have one. In fact, this is less rhetoric than simply bluster.

Having little cause, and no distinct ethnicity, Stuart and his men (including the turncoat Special Forces platoon pretending to fight Stuart) are the prototypes for what the *New York Times*'s Ben Brantley calls "a homegrown" enemy, "a toxic variation on the disgruntled former employee who has defected from the ranks of the police, the military, or Federal covert intelligence."[13] This is an ideal Hollywood villain for a post–Cold War America, in which the climate of political correctness made foreign villains seem anachronistic at best and downright racist at worst. Moreover, so many of these villains fight not as zealots or politicos, but as white capitalists. What they want to liberate is whatever they can take from the vault or extort from governments. The home-grown menace certainly existed in action films prior to the end of the Cold War, as seen in *Magnum Force*, *Commando*, and *Cobra*, and technically, *Die Hard 2* (having been written and largely produced prior to the beginning of the Soviet Union's dissolution), but appears in a true glut of films afterward. Harlin re-visits the domestic enemy in *Cliffhanger* (1993) and *The Long Kiss Goodnight* (1996). The former film, edited, production designed, and executive produced by veterans of each of the three *Die Hard* films, inaugurated the summer movie season of 1993 with its Memorial Day weekend release, which is noteworthy given how that summer is remembered primarily for the Steven Spielberg blockbuster, *Jurassic Park*.

Of course, many other films bear out Brantley's observation. Among them are *The Taking of Beverly Hills* (1991); *Under Siege* (1992); *Speed* (1994); *Under Siege 2: Dark Territory* (1995); *GoldenEye* (1995), which resurrected the James Bond franchise; *The Rock* (1996); *Eraser* (1996); *The Negotiator* (1998); the Steven Seagal vehicle *Exit Wounds* (2001); *S.W.A.T.* (2003); *XXX: State of the Union* (2005); the re-make of *Assault on Precinct 13* (2005); and, to varying degrees, all three *Mission: Impossible* movies (1996, 2000, 2006). The remake of *Assault on Precinct 13* is no-table for how it marries a convention from the 1990s-on to a template from the 1970s, itself a reference to the Westerns of a still earlier period of Hollywood's past. Thus, while *Die Hard* supplies the model for a trend of action films, *Die Hard 2* supplies this trend with its villains. Ironically, de Souza used the Ameri-can military as his terrorists to avoid repeating the first film.[14]

Die Hard 2 also anticipates the editorial pace that will characterize action films later in the decade, while also demonstrating how editing can charge violence with obsessiveness. When the terrorists ambush an airport SWAT team, Harlin and editors Stuart Baird and Robert A. Ferretti fetishize the deaths by devoting multiple shots to each one, much like *Cobra*'s supermarket spree-killing, and by linking several deaths to the destruction of objects. It takes three shots for the first officer to fall and four for the second, who crashes over a ladder (including a cutaway to the terrorist gunning him down). Next, gun-fire drives a terrorist into a bank of phones over three shots—this time in-cluding a cutaway to the SWAT officer firing. After the filmmakers then devote eleven angles to the killing of just two more officers, a final SWAT officer is gunned down over *seven* shots. The first shows the terrorist shooting; the next shows the officer being struck; the next five show him driven through burst-ing planes of glass.

The death toll stands at six until McClane arrives to kill the last three terrorists. From the terrorists' first gunshot until McClane lowers his gun, 224 seconds contain nearly 180 shots: the scene averages 1 shot less than every 1 ½ seconds. Likewise, when the terrorists surround the grounded plane inside which they have trapped McClane, the filmmakers show them firing at the plane in 17 shots over 20 seconds, averaging less than 1¼ seconds per shot. The most comparable scene in the first Die Hard is the computer-floor shootout, in which the shot length is nearly double. Just two years later, Die Hard 2 anticipates the more furious editing of the Jerry Bruckheimer productions directed by Michael Bay and Simon West, which will come to emblemize late-1990s action filmmaking.

Die Hard 2 also stresses characters' reactions to destruction. Presumably, their astonishment is intended to trigger, or at least bolster, the audience's. When the terrorists crash a plane despite McClane's efforts to save it, the crash and explosion are covered in fourteen shots, including ones that show the panic of the passengers and crew, and horrified reactions by McClane, Lorenzo, and airport tower chief Mr. Trudeau (Fred Dalton Thompson). Moments later, an ambulance arrives, and with it, a crane shot that surveys the wreckage and fire and firefighting. This continuous take lasts nearly twenty-five seconds— the flip side of the cutty action sequences.

Similarly, in the film's final act, crowds of people inside the terminal learn that the airport is under siege, and riot. They run, scream, and crash through glass partitions—a fitting climax for the beginning of a new action film model, one that would factor into the coming renaissance of the disaster film. In these trends, reactions to destruction are as pervasive as destruction itself. With the rioters of Die Hard 2, even the response to spectacle is spectacle.

After Die Hard 2 achieved blockbuster status in 1990, Michael Levy, the film's executive producer and president of Silver Pictures, said of the proposed Die Hard 3, "If the first one was The Towering Inferno and the second was Airport, then the third has to be The Poseidon Adventure."[15] Originally, the third installment was to pit McClane against terrorists on a hijacked cruise ship. But Die Hard 3 was in development at the same time as the Steven Seagal vehicle Under Siege, in which terrorists take over a Navy battleship. According to reporter Jeffrey Wells, Die Hard 3 stalled due to acrimony between producers Lawrence Gordon and Joel Silver, and later between Silver and Bruce Willis, who stopped collaborating after Hudson Hawk and The Last Boy Scout (both 1991).[16] Meanwhile, Under Siege continued to gain momentum. Die Hard 3 was cancelled. Wells indicates that by failing to open before Under Siege, the similarly set Die

Hard 3 would have been seen as just an imitation. (If so, the film would have been imitating *Die Hard*'s imitator.) As it happens, there would be a third installment, *Die Hard with a Vengeance*, produced not by Silver and Gordon, but by *Rambo* producers Andrew Vajna and Buzz Feisthans—and released two months before *Under Siege 2: Dark Territory.*

Compared to *Die Hard* by many critics, *Under Siege* reunites Seagal with *Above the Law* director Andrew Davis (who had previously directed Chuck Norris to what is widely considered to be his best performance in 1986's *Code of Silence).* Released in October 1992, *Under Siege* stars Seagal as navy cook Casey Ryback. With the unlikely assistance of *Playboy* centerfold Jordan Tate (Erika Eleniak), Ryback fights the terrorist forces of former covert operative William Strannix (Tommy Lee Jones) and navy battleship executive officer Commander Krill (Gary Busey) when they capture the USS *Missouri,* a 900-foot dreadnaught on its final voyage. Doubling for the *Missouri* during production was the USS *Alabama,* a South Dakota–class ship decommissioned in the 1950s. According to the film's publicity, the film crew renovated the *Alabama* to resemble the *Missouri* by removing the former's 20mm and 40mm guns, and re-equipping the ship with 16-inch ones.[17] Of *Under Siege*'s setting, co-producer Peter Macgregor-Scott invokes Jackson DeGovia's metaphor for *Die Hard:* "A battleship is a maze, a jungle. Actually, it's worse than a maze. . . . It's a maze with the lights turned out."[18]

Ryback becomes as territorial about the ship as he is about his kitchen. Of course, Ryback is no ordinary cook: he is an ex-Navy SEAL. When the Navy brass learns what is happening aboard the *Missouri,* Ryback's dossier is articulated: "Expert in martial arts, explosives, weapons, tactics. Silver Star. Navy Cross. Purple Heart with clusters." Only the *Missouri*'s ordinance is recounted so lovingly (and by the same characters): "Forty thousand rounds of 20mm C-WIZ. There's over one thousand sixteen-inch projectiles. We believe there's fifteen Harpoon cruise missiles still aboard and thirty-two Tomahawks . . . eight of them are specials. Nuclear-tipped. Two hundred and twenty kilotons each."

The *Missouri* is the ultimate warship, and Ryback, its defender, is the ultimate warrior. As the action genre tends toward hyperbole, Ryback is an amalgam of everything that signifies Ultimate Warrior status, even more than Riggs had been in *Lethal Weapon.* It is fitting then, that against *Under Siege*'s backdrop of an industrial setting and nighttime action, Ryback's costuming progresses from a white cook's uniform—including a puffy chef's hat—to an olive tank top, to the all-black garb that merges Ryback with the ship, and with which Seagal came to be identified. The most striking example is when Ryback, in shadows and silhouette, crosses the *Missouri*'s deck to blow up a heli-copter. This is part of his plan to stop the terrorists from "offloading" the Tomahawk missiles; as one might expect, the film in general and Seagal in particular seem to relish tossing off military jargon.

Other people merge with the *Missouri* also, but in less photogenic ways. Ry-back kills one commando by pounding him through a catwalk with a metal rail: death by the industrial. Ending an exotically choreographed knife fight, Ryback smashes Strannix's head through one of the bridge's monitors. "Keep the faith, Strannix," Ryback growls, referencing Strannix's earlier remark that Ryback has "faith," whereas Strannix does not. This had been a response to Ryback's strange reflection,

> All your ridiculous, pitiful antics aren't going to change a thing. You and I? We're puppets in the same sick play. We serve the same master, and he's a lunatic, and he's ungrateful, and there's nothing we can do about it. You and I are the same.

This is a continuation of the antigovernment paranoia Seagal espouses in the earlier *Above the Law* and *Hard to Kill*; here, what it lacks in specificity, it makes up for in bluster. It is also curious that the hero articulates what he and the vil-lain share. Usually, what they share is the will to act savagely, a connection that the filmmakers often leave implied.

Ryback's reflection is also inaccurate. He and Strannix are not the same. Ryback believes in his men and in his branch of service. For Strannix's part, it is not that he lacks faith; it is that he lacks a cause. He has hijacked the *Missouri* as part of a business deal. He will earn millions for the ship's ordinance, in-cluding its nuclear warheads. Strannix calls his "investors," like his counter-part will in *Under Siege 2*, and also instructs a subordinate, "Call Chicago. Sell everything we've got in Macgregor Aircraft. That stock is gonna go to shit when they find out what's going on here."

To throw off the military and the CIA, Strannix blathers about chaos, anar-chy, environmentalism, and revolution. All the while, Krill stifles his laughter in the background, a gesture wildly overplayed by Busey. This bit of action sig-nifies that Strannix's speechifying is all for show. "You think they believed you?" a subordinate asks, underscoring the point. "I don't know," Strannix replies. "I think they believe I'm crazy, probably paranoid, something like that." Here, not only will Strannix commit to no ideology, but the movie will not even commit to his insanity. This role-playing aspect of *Under Siege* is com-plimented by the terrorists' costuming. Taking over the ship during the Captain's birthday party, the terrorists board dressed as caterers and a rock-and-roll band; Krill is in drag.

Like the Die Hard films had been for Fox, Under Siege was a tremendous hit for Warner Bros., and the first of two terrorists-take-over-a-something films the studio would open in the fall of 1992. The release of the second, just a few weeks after the first, prompted The Hollywood Reporter's Duane Byrge to comment, "Warner Bros. bellies up to the 'Die Hard' trough once again with 'Passenger 57,' an airplane version of its current hard-hitter 'Under Siege.'"[19] Byrge is not the only critic to liken Kevin Hooks's Passenger 57 to Die Hard; the pithiest might be the Village Voice's Lisa Kennedy, who deems Passenger 57 "a Die Hard meets Die Harder proposition."[20]

A vehicle for Wesley Snipes, Passenger 57 is also the only one of Die Hard's progeny to feature a black hero. In contrast, the film's villain is Charles Rane (Bruce Payne) a notorious terrorist and hijacker who hijacks the plane transporting him to his trial. Rane is an apolitical, upper-crust European, akin to Hans Gruber, but less a sociopath than an outright psychotic. (In one scene, he fondles a flight attendant's breasts with his gun. When she tells him "You'll have to kill me first," he corrects her: "Wrong, Marti. I'm going to kill you during.") Swiped from Die Hard, and predicting Speed, Rane's plot is to blow up the plane as a cover for his getaway.

Unknown to Rane, one of the passengers on this ill-fated Atlantic International flight is John Cutter (Snipes), the airline's new counterterrorism chief. What follows is the contest between Rane's forces and Cutter over the lives of the passengers. In one of the film's more interesting standoffs, Rane and Cutter face each other, each holding a hostage (Cutter's is one of the terrorists) and a gun associated with the other. Rane wields a utilitarian Beretta taken from a slain federal agent; Cutter holds a terrorist's sleek-looking Gloch.

Early in the film, as the passengers board, the filmmakers present a series of close-ups of different parts of the plane. The plane is broken down and fetishized like Schwarzenegger and Stallone's bodies were in montages of the previous decade. Every part is made an icon. Vehicles in Speed, Executive Decision (1996), Con Air (1997), and Air Force One (1997) will be presented with similar awe, just as the camera reveres the Nakatomi building when established in Die Hard and Alcatraz Island in The Rock. These dramatic presentations help the viewer make an emotional investment in the locations, increasing the emotional stakes when these settings meet their cataclysmic ends.

In Passenger 57, Cutter and Rane have their final fight in the plane's cabin, as damage from errant gunfire causes the plane to depressurize. Oxygen masks

An Upright and Locked Position: *Counterterrorism expert John Cutter (Wesley Snipes) prepares to retake a hijacked airliner in Passenger 57 (1992), a film in which, as one critic suggests, Die Hard meets Die Hard 2. (From the author's collection.)*

fall, giving the cabin a jungle-like appearance. They also make the combat more visceral as Cutter and Rane fight through them. Swift editing and a fluidly moving camera enhance this energy. Matters turn nastier when Rane tries to strangle Cutter with an oxygen mask cord and when one of the cabin doors blows out. Papers and other debris fly through the cabin. The space is mad with the sense of catastrophe.

Even taking *Passenger 57*'s ridiculously short running time into account (eighty-four minutes, with credits), *Speed*, the directorial debut of *Die Hard* cinematographer Jan de Bont, is an even bolder exercise in kinetic energy. Another Fox release, the bulk of this 1994 film follows a Santa Monica bus as it careens through and around Los Angeles. Fastened to the bus's undercarriage is a bomb that will detonate if the bus slows to less than fifty miles per hour. (Strangely enough, the film was advertised, among other places, on the sides of buses.) In an unusual bit of structuring, this crisis, *Speed*'s central concept, takes up only the film's second act and is largely disconnected from the others. The first act introduces the film's bomber, Howard Payne (Dennis Hopper) and its LAPD hero, Jack Traven (Keanu Reeves), when Payne rigs an elevator car to explode if the city does not acquiesce to his demands. In the third act, Jack pursues Payne into the L.A. subway system and onto a train that will become a runaway.

Payne is a disabled member of the Atlanta police department's bomb squad and is now using his knowledge to extort the city of Los Angeles. Payne is Colonel Stuart, Commander Krill, William Strannix, and others: the protector from whom we now need protection. When Jack, via cell phone, asks what Payne wants, Payne replies with what might be the genre's most self-conscious quip about its new villains: "Well I want money, Jack. I wish that I had some loftier purpose, but I'm afraid in the end, it's all about the money."

Jack, with help from Annie (Sandra Bullock), a passenger who takes over the wheel for the incapacitated driver, comes to lead the bus's multiracial, multigenerational group of passengers. They resemble the communities of so many 1970s disaster movies, only here the group is all working-class. The bus is working-class, too: a 1970s GMC on the verge of obsolescence. (One can imagine it heading toward its own decommissioning, just as the *Missouri* is at the start of *Under Siege*.) The bus's age and other "warm" design features, such as its rounded edges and soft blue palette, heighten the drama by undercutting the audience's sense of its formidability. This scheme peaks near the end. After everything the bus endures, a rescue vehicle pulls up alongside it. Side by side, they make for a bold composition. Compared to the bus, the rescue vehicle is large and angular, with slashing diagonal lines that make for a striking graphic.

The filmmakers also cement the viewer's investment in the bus by using stark angles and sounds to introduce it, and intercutting them with inserts of the odometer climbing toward fifty. Our first glimpse of the bus is a close-up of the "2525" emblazoned on its back. In fact, throughout the film, de Bont directs our attention to the number, giving the bus more of an identity, and with it, more character. The film's first mythic view of the bus comes soon after. At a construction site, the bus breaks through bright steam and steers past the camera, which pans to follow it. Mark Mancina's music, absent in the preceding moments, underscores this image with ominous, metallic percussion.

Next, de Bont provides an aerial view of Bus 2525's full likeness (which Mancina scores with a full statement of his main theme) and, moments later, cranes up as the bus speeds through the frame, the camera close to the ground and exaggerating the bus's length. From time to time, the filmmakers exaggerate the bus's dimensions to make it imposing and, at the same time, infuse it with pathos. The most strangely poignant example finds the bus charging ahead toward a gap in the freeway, as the emergency vehicles that have been flanking the bus pull away, leaving it to go it alone. This moment also illustrates the bus's most compelling aspect: the underdog/overdog dichotomy that characterizes it. Sometimes, the bus is formidability itself, dwarfing (and smashing) the smaller vehicles that surround it; at other times, the bus is small, exciting our compassion—especially in the aerial shots and others that establish it against its more massive environs.

Following Bus 2525's introductory scene, the bus is forced off the freeway. This begins a progression. On local streets, the bus is at the mercy of the terrain; obstacles that cannot be avoided must be obliterated. This presents a crisis when schoolchildren cross the street and when a woman with a baby carriage strolls into the bus's path. Later, the police direct the bus onto the unfinished 105 freeway. Here, Annie and Jack—and by extension, the bus itself—start to assert themselves on their situation, as when they accelerate toward the gap, jump it, and land safely (if noisily) on the other side. The bus and the characters become most proactive in Bus 2525's last sequence, which begins as Jack directs Annie off the freeway and into the Los Angeles International Airport. Here they can circle the runways indefinitely—or until they run out of gas, which they begin to leak during a failed attempt to disarm the bomb. Accenting this new proactivity, de Bont "cheats" the distance between the bus and an airplane in a dramatic composition: speeding into the frame, the bus

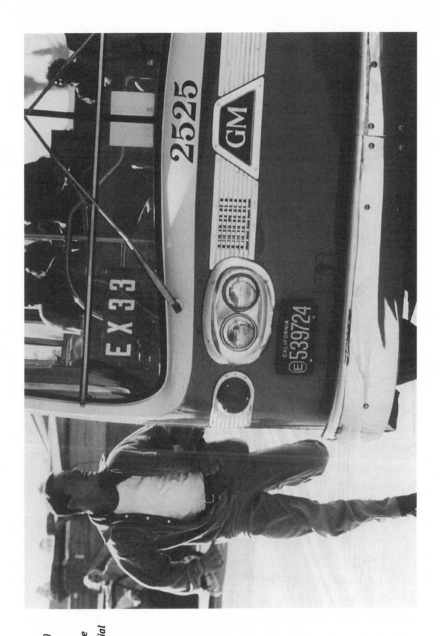

Rapid Transit: Jack Traven (Keanu Reeves) races alongside the imperiled bus of Jan de Bont's kinetic directorial debut, Speed (1994). (From the author's collection.)

seems to cross the plane's path defiantly, a dilapidated David to a jumbo-jet Goliath.

The police seize their chance to save the passengers by transferring them from the bus to the rescue vehicle. Jack and Annie escape moments later, sliding out from under the bus on a hatch that plows through a score of orange cones. The bus careens into a courier plane and explodes. De Bont and editor John Wright parcel out the conflagration over fourteen shots, including several in which the passengers react to the explosion that could have so easily consumed them. The most striking of the reaction shots shows the fireball reflected in the rescue vehicle window, effectively superimposed over the survivors. The explosion and the reactions to it take almost forty-five seconds to unfold: forty-five seconds in which the characters and the filmmakers show reverence for destruction.

Speed was originally developed at Paramount Pictures, which ultimately abandoned the project. The new chairman of Twentieth Century Fox, Peter Chernin, would acquire the script in December 1992, about a month after taking over the studio from Joe Roth. (According to Variety, Paramount's Sherry Lansing tried to greenlight Speed not knowing that her studio had already put it in turnaround.[21]) If this seems shortsighted on Paramount's part, it should be noted that the same summer Speed performed so well for Fox, Paramount released the blockbuster Forrest Gump, which it had acquired from Warner Bros. This was part of a deal that saw Warner Bros. obtain a script by Predator screenwriters Jim and John Thomas. With the Thomas brothers' screenplay, ultimately titled Executive Decision, the studio was back in the hijacking business.[22]

Executive Decision marks the directorial debut of another craftsman, editor Stuart Baird, a longtime collaborator of director Richard Donner and producer Joel Silver. The film is a Silver Pictures Production in which army commandos and a bookish counterterrorism analyst, Dr. David Grant (Kurt Russell), try to retake Oceanic Flight 43, after it is hijacked by Arab terrorists. The terrorists' plan is to land the plane in Washington, where they will blow up a bomb containing enough DZ-5 nerve agent to decimate the eastern seaboard.

Baird and his collaborators do not treat this plane with any special reverence. They save that for the Remora, the high-tech aircraft from which the heroes board Flight 43 in midair. (The Remora, we are told, was originally designed to link-up with the space shuttle while traveling through the lower atmosphere at supersonic speeds.) First announced by the steady, martial beat and bright brass of Jerry Goldsmith's score, the Remora embodies Silver's enthusiasm for exotic, military hardware. According to Silver, doubling for the *Remora* was an actual F-117 Stealth fighter modified with a pressurized sleeve.[23]

But the *Remora* is destroyed during the transfer. Lt. Col. Austin Travis (Steven Seagal) sacrifices himself to get the rest of his men aboard, an act which leaves Dr. Grant with a greater share of a hero's responsibility than he wanted. He, like John McClane, is an everyman, one who becomes a hero by conquering a besieged space. Grant begins his transition as he crosses the area above the plane's cabin by crawling down a zip-line and nearly falling, which would send him crashing down into the cabin. During this feat, Grant's glasses fall and break. While on the surface, this loss seems like a liability, and thus a ratcheting up of the film's dramatic stakes, in actuality, it signifies something more: in the movies, eyeglasses have long been an emblem of the cerebral, especially at the expense of the physical (consider how many romantic leading men have "freed" their leading ladies by removing their eyeglasses before kissing them). The breaking of Grant's glasses marks his transition from a man who knows something about terrorism to one who does something about it. So does his wardrobe: Grant begins his adventure in a tuxedo, but by the time he enters the terrorist-held cabin, he has donned a hooded sweatshirt.

It is in this more utilitarian (more democratic, even!) clothing that Grant faces Nagi Hassan, the lead fanatical hijacker played by British actor David Suchet in a bit of casting that recalls Robert Forster in *The Delta Force*. "Who are you?" Hassan asks. Grant answers, distilling the everyman-as-hero to its core: "No one," he says. In fact, for an action film, Grant is such a "no one," he does not even kill anybody. That task is left to the commandos, but is not the film's only division of heroic labor. Diffusing the bomb, identifying its triggerman, mapping the cabin and isolating Flight 43's audio frequencies, performing reconnaissance, and planning for a surprise assault are among the heroes' tasks in *Executive Decision*. They often overlap, and are executed by distinct characters within the group. Echoing *Toy Soldiers*, passages from *Under Siege*, and others, this reminds us that for a trend of action films largely remembered as being one of lone wolves standing against terror, the films feature a surprising number of buddy and group heroes.

But in the end, with the bomb diffused and the terrorists killed, it is Grant who steps up to effect Oceanic Flight 43's emergency landing. Grant overshoots Dulles and must land at the smaller, private Fredricks Field airport, which he does with mixed results. Passing a "Learn to Fly" sign, the jetliner tears down light stands and crushes small airplanes, which of course, explode. At the end of the runway, Flight 43's wing catches fire. The plane then pitches forward into earth, plows through it, and then—then!—comes to rest. As in *Die Hard, Speed, Daylight, Con Air, Under Siege 2, Speed 2,* and *Air Force One,* if the villains meet a violent end, the location meets a catastrophic one.

As the passengers deboard, a limousine waits to shuttle off Grant and flight attendant Jean (Halle Berry). Just before stepping in, Grant looks at the plane. The filmmakers cut to his point of view: starting on the Oceanic logo emblazoned on the plane's tail wing, the camera then pans to take in the rest of the aircraft. On the soundtrack, distant horns evoke a sense of duty fulfilled and sacrifices made. It is here, in *Executive Decision*'s final moments that the filmmakers venerate the plane. The next music cue provides a different mood as Frank Sinatra's "It's Nice to Go Trav'ling" scores the end credits. Joel Silver had given similar big-band resolutions to the first two *Die Hards* with "Let it Snow! Let it Snow! Let it Snow!"—music that is more jubilant than hard rock songs or the orchestral action scores that tend to be somber, percussive, or both.

Executive Decision, released in the spring of 1996, is restrained for the genre, whereas that summer's *The Rock* is all about excess. Overly stylized and mythological, *The Rock* is the second film directed by Michael Bay and the last Don Simpson and Jerry Bruckheimer would produce together, as Simpson died of a much-publicized drug overdose during post-production. This led many critics to consider *The Rock* a fitting farewell for the duo. As Todd McCarthy writes, "This final outing from the Simpson-Bruckheimer team has the strutting, souped-up hardware-fetishizing personality of their signature productions."[24] Peter Travers, also reviewing Simpson's final production, says of the producer, "He is indefensible as an artist, but indisputable as a showman" (emphasis in original).[25]

The story concerns renegade Marines who seize Alcatraz Island and take its tourists hostage. From the island, the Marines, led by General Francis X. Hummel (Ed Harris), threaten to launch a VX gas-laden missile attack on San Francisco. In response, FBI chemical weapons specialist Stanley Goodspeed (Nicolas Cage), must enlist the help of John Mason (Sean Connery), an incarcerated British agent with intimate knowledge of the prison.

General Hummel's dossier, one Washington insider tells us, includes "three tours in Vietnam, Panama, Grenada, Desert Storm. Three Purple Hearts, two Silver Stars, and the Congressional Medal of—Jesus." Now, Hummel's self-issued orders are to force the federal government to acknowledge the debt it owes the eighty-three disavowed soldiers killed while performing covert operations under Hummel's command. Hummel seeks to ransom eighty-one hostages on the island and millions more in the Bay area for $100 million, much of which will be distributed to the fallen soldiers' families.

Of the 1990s' homegrown terrorists, Hummel is the rare one who actually has a cause. Of course, The Rock compensates for this by denying him the conviction to see it through. Once it becomes clear that Washington will not pay, Hummel reveals that he has been bluffing. But lest the film lack a third act, two of the captains in his squad refuse to stand down. Pushing for the missile strike, Captain Darrow (Tony Todd) declares, "I'm not a soldier. . . . The day we took hostages, we became mercenaries. And mercenaries get paid. I want my fucking money!" Captains Darrow and Frye (Gregory Sporleder) clearly relish violence. Darrow is a knife-wielding sadist and Frye is borderline orgasmic at the prospect of a gunfight between the Captains, Hummel, and Hummel's second, Major Baxter (David Morse).

This is odd, but not unprecedented. Darrow and Frye are extreme capitalists, like Colonel Stuart, Payne, Rane, Strannix, and Commander Krill. One might imagine a mercenary being emotionally detached from his actions, but these men are also possessed by a mania reminiscent of Dirty Harry's Scorpio and Cobra's Night Slasher. It is as if the filmmakers suspect that the audience will not sufficiently hate the villains unless violence gives them pleasure as well as profit; it as if the filmmakers suspect that they have settled for a new, but second-best rung on a hierarchy of evil, so they keep one foot on the old.

Like Under Siege's Ryback, Hummel is not just a veteran, but the veteran. Likewise, Mason is not just a convict, but the convict; not just a spy, but the spy. The film is not subtle in how it mythologizes Mason. He is the only man to have escaped Alcatraz. Also, as a British agent (a clear riff on Connery's James Bond persona), Mason knows "all our dirtiest secrets from the last half-century," as his nemesis, FBI Chief Womack (John Spencer), attests. These include what happened at Roswell and the truth behind John Kennedy's assassination. Even more overt is the montage that introduces him. Light gleams off Mason as the camera isolates him in extreme close-ups, while outside his cell, corrections officers march to collect him. With this scene, Bay and editor Richard Francis-Bruce mix real-time with slow motion; Mason is so mythic, he even bends time.

Hummel and Mason. These are the mythologized forces of The Rock (with Goodspeed caught in the middle, commenting on the action). Naturally, the film also mythologizes Alcatraz itself—every time Bay and Francis-Bruce cut to an establishing shot of the island, in fact. Bay uses two such shots to introduce Alcatraz, which benefits greatly from Bay's main strength: a painter's eye for color. In these shots, for example, the camera shows Alcatraz silhouetted against an orange sky, and then pans across a crumbled wall, the prison in the background. This is all softened by mist that bathes the location in mythos.

Unfortunately for the film, however, Bay does not keep the action contained to the island (and the action that does take place there is considerable, including gunfights, explosions, beatings, severe beatings, an impaling, and a threatened disembowelment). Like *Passenger 57*, *Speed*, *Executive Decision*, *Con Air*, and *Air Force One*, the story begins with an action sequence far removed from the location where the brunt of the film will be set. Here, in a scene that illustrates Bay's approach to editing, as well as Simpson and Bruckheimer's indulgence in visual style and military hardware, the Marines raid a Navy weapons depot. Rapid-fire editing practically atomizes the scene. A pounding rainfall makes for additional motion in every shot. The rain, along with the crashing musical score by Hans Zimmer and Nick Glennie-Smith, makes the noise incessant.

Stylistically, the scene is overwrought—with one bit of business that is outright soulless. One of Hummel's men throws a guard through a guard tower window, after which Bay and Francis-Bruce double-cut the impact; that is, they insert two—*two*—close-ups of the guard's face as he strikes the rain-lashed asphalt, amid shards of glass. Certainly, there have been action films as violent as *The Rock*, but what makes this act so wanton is that it happens not to a character the audience has grown to love or hate, but to one who is inconsequential. We can find an action film's conscience, or lack thereof, in how it treats such non-combatants, because here is how the filmmakers choose to present life and death as an abstract or pure value—that is, as a value uncomplicated by considerations of story. For instance, the last act of *Lethal Weapon* surges with violence—violence at a crowded nightclub and on crowded city streets. But only the police and the villains sustain damage.[26]

With *The Rock*'s first action sequence, such editing—and this is not the only instance—demonstrates a commitment to brutality for the sake of what? Editorial rhythm? Brutality's *own* sake? It serves no narrative purpose, and anyone familiar with gravity can surmise what will happen: the guard will hit the ground. Moreover, given how this beat dovetails with the scene's noise and violence, it is interesting to note how the filmmakers backpedal, trying to soften the Marines' image with such dialogue as "We got thirty minutes until these darts wear off." This is clearly meant to suggest that the Marines are not shooting to kill American Navy men. It would succeed, if only the style did not belie the words.

Compared to the depot raid, the later car chase is as numbing, but not as cold-blooded, which is better than nothing. Before joining an ill-fated Navy SEAL incursion into Alcatraz, Goodspeed commandeers a Ferrari to pursue Mason, who has escaped the FBI's clutches in a stolen Humvee. Among the objects Bay lovingly has them destroy are a water truck, a storefront window, a vegetable stand, parking meters, and a trolley car—"photogenic debris," according to Janet Maslin.[27] The trolley is typical of Bay and Bruckheimer. It explodes—despite being powered by electricity, not gasoline—rises into the air, drops down, and slides into the now vacated Ferrari. Which the trolley crushes.

Here, Bay makes the most of his previous experience directing music videos and, more to the point, commercials, having been the youngest recipient of the Director's Guild of America's Best Commercial of the Year award.[28] The footage of the Humvee and the Ferrari—both totems of excessive consumerism—plays like a car commercial as much as it does a car chase. (An *Entertainment Weekly* feature on Bay states that his only weakness is $200,000 Ferraris.[29]) In fact, Francis-Bruce recalls that while interviewing for the film, Bay told him of his intention to have his own commercial editors take a pass after the film editor assembled his cut.[30] Several of the scene's compositions display Bay's infatuation with his vehicles. However, most of the shots are not onscreen long enough for the audience to register how they are composed. From the moment Mason peels out until Goodspeed surveys the damage, the sequence features about 240 shots. This makes for an average shot length of one and a quarter seconds for five unrelenting minutes. And according to Francis-Bruce, this represents a *tamer* version of the scene than the one originally cut.[31]

Overall, this rhythm is typical for the film. Almost every shot in The Rock lasts no longer than four seconds; many under two. This also represents a broader trend in 1990s action film editing, in which the pacing seems more derived from commercials and music videos than ever before. Many, including Francis-Bruce and Mark Goldblatt—who is credited with editing Bay's *Armageddon* (1998), *Pearl Harbor* (2001), and *Bad Boys II* (2003), and who also cut much of the action in The Rock—have attributed this more accelerated pace to the fact that the movies have been increasingly aimed at viewers raised on music videos and video games, and that these audiences assemble more visual information more quickly. But the aesthetic has also changed because of changes in the technique itself. Digital editing and playback, which boomed in the 1990s, have facilitated the over-cutting Bay's films exemplify. With the

Avid and now Final Cut Pro systems, editors can make more cuts in less time. Also, filmmakers and studio executives see assembled footage on video monitors, which is a different experience than seeing it projected in a screening room. Francis-Bruce claims that on a monitor,

> You have no peripheral vision. [The image] is all right in front of you, so you can absorb it; your brain can actually take it in. But if you're watching it on a big screen, if there's action over *here*, then action over *there*, then eight frames later, action over here again, you're never going to be able to watch it. . . . People don't understand: the big screen is a different medium than the small screen. And now everyone sees the cut on Avids, and are honestly being trapped into thinking it should go faster and faster. Well, that's not necessarily better.[32]

At the time *The Rock* was released, critics were divided over whether its editing cripples the fun or increases the excitement. The *Wall Street Journal's* Joe Morgenstern characterizes the film—indeed, many of Bay's films—well. He writes that *The Rock* lacks "any sense of rhythm or flow that might have minimized the movie's repetitiveness; seeking to sell every shot as an eyepopper, [Bay] delivers a succession of exploding tableaux."[33]

Bay has come to be an emblem for this style of editing, but perhaps unfairly. Certainly, one could find precedents in the violence of such late 1960s classics as Arthur Penn's *Bonnie and Clyde* and Sam Peckinpah's *The Wild Bunch* and also in later films of less consequence, such as *Magnum Force*. More contemporaneous with Bay's work however, at least three action films from the summer of 1990 feature violent scenes with similar shot durations: *Total Recall*, *Robocop 2*, and, as seen earlier, *Die Hard 2*. Likewise, most of the edits in *Predator's* guerilla camp attack are under one and two seconds long. The difference, however, is that unlike Bay's films, these earlier movies do not sacrifice continuity and geography in favor of sensory overload. Bay's association with this style is the result of his pacing as compounded by other techniques. Wild camera movement, driving sound, stark angles, severe angle changes lacking compositional through-lines, and propulsive motion within the frame (such as bursting parking meters and water bottles), make Bay's style not just spastic, but downright aggressive. These devices along with the abbreviated shot lengths, add up to an incessant stimulation that is disorienting, even claustrophobic— no matter how large the stage of the sequence might be.

Bruckheimer's next action production, *Con Air*, released the following summer, is even more hyperbolic than *The Rock*, in terms of its characters, editing, and cataclysmic finale. (It is, as Joe Morgenstern writes, a movie "for audiences that found 'The Rock' too subtle."[34]) The title is taken from the nickname maximum-security prisoners give the "Jail Bird," the U.S. Marshals' transport plane that they hijack. Their leader is Cyrus "The Virus" Grissom (John Malkovich). As John Mason was the ultimate convict and spy, and General Hummel was the ultimate military warrior, Cyrus is the ultimate aberration, enough to make Scorpio shudder. U.S. Marshal Vince Larkin (John Cusack) recites Cyrus's resume: "Kidnapping, robbery, extortion, killed eleven inmates, incited three riots, escaped twice. Likes to brag that he's killed more men than cancer. He's a poster-child for the criminally insane." Forced to stop Cyrus and his cohorts is former Army Ranger Cameron Poe (Nicolas Cage), a parolee flying home to his wife and the daughter he has never met. According to Larkin, Poe is—in contrast to Cyrus, but like so many of the heroes in this trend—"a nobody."

With *Con Air*, British commercial director Simon West makes his directorial debut, just as Bay had for Simpson and Bruckheimer with *Bad Boys* (1995). And as Bay's style exaggerates that of director Tony Scott, who directed *Top Gun* (1986), *Beverly Hills Cop II* (1987), *Crimson Tide* (1995), and other Simpson/Bruckheimer productions, West's style exaggerates Bay's. Of course, all are riffs on the style of Simpson and Bruckheimer (and then of just Bruckheimer): oversaturated frames, overmodulated soundtracks, rapid cutting, and a fetish for hardware.

In *Con Air*, this fetish is reflected in, among other objects, the high-tech military helicopter that fires at the plane and the plane itself—in reality, a C-123K military transport plane rather than the more commercial jetliners the Marshals Service actually uses to shuttle prisoners.[35] West and editors Steve Mirkovich, Glen Scantlebury, and Chris Lebenzon (the last of whom cut nine films for Bruckheimer between *Top Gun* and *Pearl Harbor*) introduce the Jail Bird with five establishing shots designed to make the plane iconic. The sixth shot of the plane is of its interior, and establishes the cage where the *really* dangerous maximum-security prisoners are held. While this shot should ground the audience in the plane's layout (as its counterpart does in *Air Force One*), West's overcutting, like Bay's, only confuses the geography, especially during the action. Achieving this level of disorientation is a particular feat, as the action is confined to an airplane cabin.

Appropriately enough, the takeover scene best represents the whole of *Con Air*'s style. From the moment one convict creates a diversion by setting another on fire until Poe reacts to Cyrus's declaration, "Welcome to Con Air," the scene features approximately 139 shots in 160 seconds: an average of just over 1 second per shot. However, 30 seconds are taken up by dialogue between Cyrus and the pilot. Without this interlude, the action itself unfolds over 133 shots in about 130 seconds. Lest these seem like mere statistics, consider that the average length of the *action* shots is less than 1 second. Moreover, many of these shots are close-ups, rendered by a moving camera; and some are double-cut. Flashing lights and their reflections further compound this visual chaos.

The filmmakers do not confine this frenetic action to the plane. When the Jail Bird temporarily sets down at Lerner Field, Poe ends up outside, where he fights a drug lord's henchmen. The fight lasts only fifteen seconds and contains about twenty-six shots in which Poe dispatches all three men *and* enters into a standoff with Larkin. Poe makes his way back to the plane as a battle rages between the now heavily armed convicts and the police they have trapped in this junkyard. Loaded with explosions, gunfire, industrial wreckage, and even a tractor and plow, the scene is hypermasculine. The movie seems now to be spilling out all over—a crucial irony, given that what is unique to this trend of "*Die Hard*-on-a-Something" films is that it is presumably about containment. Therefore, action scenes such as these, *The Rock*'s car chase, *Passenger 57*'s hospital and carnival chases, and the opening raids of *Executive Decision* and *Air Force One* jeopardize this tension—not just as a matter of style, but also of story structure.

Amid all this, Poe get back on the plane, where he rescues the Jail Bird's captured guard Sally Bishop (Rachel Ticotin), before she is raped by Johnny 23 (Danny Trejo), a convict who has taken his name from having raped twenty-three women. Johnny 23 is also a Native American. *Con Air*, like *The Rock*, is a film about terrorists that minimizes their hostages, but within that context, *Con Air* offers this scene: a distillation of the captivity/rescue tale (complete with Indian savage!), even though the film is founded on a different mythic trope: a man's quest to go home.

Only a film as excessive as *Con Air* would feature not one, but two apocalyptic crash landings. The first is at Lerner Field. Touching down like the Oceanic jetliner in *Executive Decision*, the Jail Bird shears off lights, crashes through barriers, pitches into and plows the earth, and stops just before it would have collided with propane tankers. The second is the Jail Bird's razing of the Las Vegas Strip, which begins as the dropping plane shears off the neon electric guitar atop the Hard Rock Café. Things smash and crowds flee, as if from something biblical. This scene comprises one minute and fifty seconds of destruction, interrupted only by Cyrus's veiled threat of child-rape.

But that's not all. Cyrus escapes the crash, with Poe and Larkin in pursuit. Cyrus's fate is another example of the film's excesses: he is hurled through a glass walkway—which sends him through two panes of glass—into a tangle of electrical wires that electrocute him and onto a conveyor belt that dumps him in an industrial press, the slug of which crushes his head as he watches it fall.

But that's still not all. In the middle of all this comes the film's final explosion. Poe leaps to safety as a runaway fire truck collides with an armored car. West devotes twelve shots to this blaze. The last shot is one of Con Air's most emblematic, if more incidental, images (while also recalling the finale of Die Hard): a blossom of flame fading to reveal a snowfall of cash.

The second hijacking film of that summer, and the last film of the decade belonging to the Die Hard format, Wolfgang Petersen's Air Force One is as regal as Con Air is jarring. Naturally, critics compared Air Force One to Die Hard, and while some reference Top Gun as well, at least one also included a nod to Airport 1975.[36] In the film, Ivan Korshunov (Gary Oldman) and his terrorists—aided by a turncoat Secret Service agent—hijack Air Force One to force the release of Kazakhstan's deposed dictator. President James Marshall (Harrison Ford) fights back to save his wife, daughter, staff, and, as Ivan sneers, baseball glove.[37]

Although the cast's performances are quite earnest, David Denby sees an irony underlying the film's scenario. "We have come full circle," Denby writes,

Ronald Reagan in office struck poses borrowed from the movies he had acted in; now the movies have turned the president back into the law-and-order sheriff Reagan used to play onscreen and given him an Uzi rather than a shotgun to wield. At least the head of the Free World fights like a man.[38]

The Western mythos Denby cites is most overt in the final struggle between Marshall and Ivan. Below decks, Ivan holds a gun to the head of the First Lady, Grace Marshall (Wendy Crewson), while tossing parachutes out of the open compartment and taunting the approaching President. Grace knocks Ivan's gun away, and Marshall attacks. The resulting combat is visceral, even primal—especially given the contrast between the fighting and the President's formal clothing. Until the men begin grappling, the scene is another restaging of High Noon's climax, and thus a return to the standoff of Die Hard. This is fitting, as Air Force One ends the cycle Die Hard began.

The President's plane is "played" by a rented passenger jet painted to resemble the actual Air Force One in four days of consecutive twelve-hour shifts.

The interior is a full-scale replica of the real thing, built on the country's largest soundstage—the same one on which Dorothy strolled down the Yellow Brick Road in The Wizard of Oz.[39] Like many films of this trend, Air Force One is in awe of its setting. Petersen and editor Richard Francis-Bruce establish the plane by making a hard cut to the tarmac, as the camera tilts up to reveal a backlit Air Force One. The cut also motivates the entrance of a martial music cue by Jerry Goldsmith. Francis-Bruce next cuts to a low angle of soldiers standing before Air Force One, as the camera dollies across them. Rounding out this introduction is a sharp low angle, and then a pan along the plane. Emblazoned on the hull, the words "United States of America" are visible for nearly twenty seconds. The filmmakers display more reverence for the plane later, as it prepares to take off. Petersen and Francis-Bruce cut to a low angle of the aircraft getting into position. The camera sweeps around such that the plane's nose cuts an arc across the screen, making for a dynamic frame. Goldsmith's orchestra announces Air Force One's becoming airborne with the stately theme established in the opening credits.

Of course, the plane has earned the reverence that Petersen, Goldsmith, Francis-Bruce, and cinematographer Michael Ballhaus confer upon it. Prior to take off, President Marshall's press secretary, Melanie Mitchell (Donna Bullock) reveals that the plane is bullet-resistant and safe even from the pulse a nuclear blast. "Upstairs is the cockpit along with the most advanced communications center on or above the face of the Earth," she remarks. "We could run the whole country from here. Or even a war, if we had to."

Ms. Mitchell parcels out such information on a tour she unknowingly gives the terrorists, and by extension, the audience. This is more than exposition. It is the device through which Petersen and Ballhaus lay out Air Force One's geography. The steadicam shots composing this tour, and other, similar long takes (that is, long compared to Con Air and The Rock) establish the relationships among compartments, a conference room, the communications center, and other areas. This is crucial for the later action. The film's jeopardy depends on the audience's understanding of spatial relationships. How close is danger? How far is safety? These questions are forsaken in Con Air, The Rock, and others in which the staccato cutting breaks down the audience's ability to grasp the proximity of anything to anything. But in Air Force One, as in Die Hard, the space is clear, and thus the violence more engaging, not an assault in its own right.

An exceptional example of this begins as gunfire forces President Marshall to abandon his first attempt to reach the hostages held in the conference

A Hands-On President: As President James Marshall in Air Force One (1997), Harrison Ford uses the space of his plane against its hijackers. (From the author's collection.)

room. Starting in the left-hand aisle (and facing the camera), Marshall moves several compartments ahead of his pursuers, and crosses to the other aisle. Now in the right-hand aisle, Marshall continues moving forward, and then cuts back to the left-hand aisle to fire a burst from his machine gun. Marshall cuts right once more, evading the terrorists' return-fire. Essentially, Marshall has traced a square through the cabin (or a circle, as the President's movement is traced with the fluidity of the steadicam).

Ensuring that the audience follows Marshall, the filmmakers make clear that the President fights strategically—underscored elsewhere by a military advisor who establishes Marshall as a Vietnam veteran, as a man who "knows how to fight." On the plane, Marshall pauses by the lavatories to think. Francis-Bruce now makes a cut—the only cut in almost one minute and twenty-five seconds of action (compare this to his editing of The Rock for Simpson, Bruckheimer, and Bay). This cut is to a diagonal angle of the cabin. A terrorist enters the frame in the background, and stalks down the left aisle. After a beat, another terrorist appears—this one in the *foreground* and in the *right* aisle. Moving parallel to each other, the two terrorists slink down the cabin toward the lavatories where we assume President Marshall is hiding. In this composition, the terrorists have captured both aisles, thereby countering Marshall's tactic of scurrying between them. This is not only action, nor only suspense. It is gamesmanship. And it is this sense of strategizing that gives the action of Air Force One its sly intelligence.[40]

During a later dogfight that embroils Russian MIGs, American F-15s, and Air Force One (with President Marshall now at the controls), Petersen maintains the film's clarity of space. The American fighters always face screen-right, while the MIGs (their pilots bathed in a sickly green glow), always face screen-left. If anything, once the action involves three parties—not two—and the three-dimensionality of open sky—not the confined interior of the cabin—Petersen becomes even more slavish about preserving geography.

This dogfight marks the first of two action sequences that occur after Marshall has dispatched Ivan—an unusual bit of story structure. The second is a race to transfer the remaining hostages (including the First Family) along a zip-line to a military transport plane, before a crippled Air Force One crashes into the sea. When she does, the plane strikes, kicking up a massive spray of seawater. She bounces; her wings rend and tear free; she tumbles onto her side, then end over end toward the camera as she breaks in half. Petersen and Francis-Bruce spread the crash—a calamitous end to Air Force One—over just two shots that run more than fifteen seconds. With a more leisurely editorial pace, Petersen keeps the energy of the action within the frames, rather than simulated by intense editing. This allows the viewer to appreciate the destruction not only as one grand effect, but also as a progression of smaller well-delineated events. Again, Petersen bests directors such as Bay and West, who overcut their catastrophes. In fact, *Air Force One*'s climactic crash is marred only by the sub-optimal CGI in which it is rendered (sub-optimal even for 1997).

In the "*Die Hard*-on-a-Something" film, the "something" almost always meets with an apocalyptic end, thus becoming the site of spectacle. (Indeed, the scene in which *Speed 2*'s cruise ship plows through a tropical port is longer than *Gone With the Wind*'s burning of Atlanta.) And although it seems that this trend suddenly became passé after 1997, Hollywood's emphasis on spectacular devastation—as well the film industry's search for inoffensive villains—would have more life left in it still. Beginning in 1996, just a year before the *Die Hard* model's terminal summer, Hollywood released a spate of disaster movies that hearken back to those of previous decades. These films and others, like those discussed in this chapter, showcase embattled spaces and their communities. But whereas in the terrorist-themed films, the ultimate destruction of the setting arrives as a third-act catharsis, in the contemporary disaster film, such devastation is the main conceit.

Unmitigated Disasters
Old Formulas and the
New Spectacle

[It's] basically the worst parts of the Bible.
—Dan Truman (Billy Bob Thornton) in Armageddon
(1998)
Doesn't anyone have any missiles left?!
—President Thomas Whitmore (Bill Pullman) in
Independence Day *(1996)*

Die Hard and its imitators take their confined format from the disaster films of the 1970s. In the mid-1990s, the older genre resurfaced as another trend of the broadening category of "action film." Most of these films feature communities coming together while endangered by their surroundings (and the occasional alien armada). Of course, the disaster film had been its own popular form in the 1970s, comprising films with large, star-studded casts, crippled airplanes, capsized cruise ships, and modern cities punished by Mother Nature. Irwin Allen's The Poseidon Adventure (1972) and The Towering Inferno (1974), along with Mark Robson's Earthquake (also 1974) are the most iconic of this form, which is also represented by lesser achievements such as the Airport sequels (1974, 1977, 1979), Beyond the Poseidon Adventure (1979), The Hindenburg (1975), The Cassandra Crossing (1976), The Swarm (1978), Meteor (1979), and, among the last of the cycle, Irwin Allen's aptly named When Time Ran Out (1980). The genre's influence can also be seen in such blockbusters as Jaws (1975) and Superman (1978).

Given this roster (a partial one to be sure), it is not surprising that the disaster film is commonly thought of as a form belonging uniquely to the 1970s. During this period, its course parallels that of the solidifying action genre, until such later offerings as The Swarm, The Concorde—Airport '79, and Beyond the Poseidon Adventure trade the disaster genre's natural threats for enemies and weaponry, thereby dovetailing with the increasingly paramilitary action movie. But the 1970s represent only one wave of the disaster film. Author Stephen Keane suggests that the genre surfaces in different cycles. One can trace these back from the 1970s to the 1950s to the 1930s and then to the 1910s—not long after the advent of motion pictures. Of the earliest entries, Keane writes, "At a time when audiences were shocked and thrilled by mere close-ups and trick photography, a number of Roman epics produced principally in Italy between 1908 and 1914 provided the first notable cycle of disaster films."[1]

The next cycle appears in the thirties, the decade in which Hollywood movies truly acquired their patina of prestige. Most notable are *San Francisco* (1936), about the 1906 earthquake; *The Hurricane* (1937), directed by John Ford; *In Old Chicago* (1938), about the 1871 fire; and *The Rains Came* (1939), which beat *Gone with the Wind* and *The Wizard of Oz* for the first Academy Award for Best Special Effects. Keane defines the next cycle of disaster films, that of the 1950s, as comprising remakes and biblical epics that seize upon new widescreen technologies—most notably Cinemascope. This use of technology was part of an industry-wide attempt to increase big screen spectacle and win back audiences lost to television. This cycle also includes science fiction "B" films, widely seen as embodiments of the era's Cold War paranoia.

Among the most recent disaster epics, two of the biggest are *Independence Day* (1996) and *War of the Worlds* (2005), both drawn from science fiction—arguably the same work of science fiction. In between these blockbusters, Hollywood produced a rash of disaster-driven films, most released in a two-year span that includes *Daylight* (1996), *Dante's Peak* (1997), *Volcano* (1997), *Firestorm* (1998), *Hard Rain* (released one week after *Firestorm*), *Armageddon* (1998), and others. This represents a slate of action films that briefly rivaled the genre's more traditional Western and *film noir*–derived entries. Of the films in this cycle, *The Siege* (1998) is least like a 1950s or 1970s disaster film. Still, *The Siege*, a political action film about the response to terrorism in New York City, grapples with similar issues of community and stages its drama on a canvas as wide as those of *Volcano* and that film's model, *Earthquake*.

At the same time, the increasing spectacle of the action genre makes it harder to differentiate these modern disaster films from their more typical action counterparts—certainly harder than it had been in the 1970s. (Compare *Cliffhanger* and *Dante's Peak* to say, *Death Wish* and *The Towering Inferno*.) This is due in part to the advent of the PG-13 rating in 1984. Prior this development, there was no middle ground between the PG rating, which the disaster pictures tended to receive, and the R rating usually assigned to action movies. Also, unlike previous iterations of the disaster film, the modern one draws from breakthroughs in CGI-technology that is especially well-suited for the disaster and action genres.[2] In the midst of this resurgence, however, critic David Ansen protests:

> The disaster movie is back, though I'm not sure anybody was asking for it. Why the sudden torrent of twisters, volcanoes and alien invasions? We could give you a sociopolitical tap dance about the post-cold-war Zeitgeist, and how we're projecting our fears of communism back onto Mother Nature, but it would be hard to keep a straight face. No, Hollywood is cranking out this stuff because it needs to put its new high-tech toys to work.[3]

Certainly, these films create opportunities for this "flexing of muscle," as *Volcano*'s production designer Jackson DeGovia puts it.[4] Indeed, these films have prompted many critics to decry—not always wrongly—what they perceive to be the subjugation of story and logic to spectacle.

More relevant to this study however, is how this spectacle, relying more on special effects than on bullets and bloodshed, has infiltrated, and even overtaken other action movie modes: for instance, the comparison of *Cliffhanger* to *Dante's Peak* aside, the new disaster films shouldered aside the *Die Hard* model. Moreover, the new spectacle would attract younger viewers and families with more PG-13 rated disaster pictures, comic book adaptations, and other such spectacles. While making for bigger tentpole films than ever before, this would also make the action genre more amorphous than it been since its early years.

Still, Ansen's political reading tracks in the wrong direction. The 1990s disaster film does not represent Hollywood's search for a place to park America's fear of Communism. Since the days of the frontier, Americanism—usually located in the individual—has been defined through conflict. In the 1970s, conflict was plentiful with rising crime rates, a floundering economy, a failing energy supply, and a greatly strained political infrastructure. The adventure-oriented cinema of this period processes this strife mainly through the cycle of vigilante loner films we have seen and the disaster extravaganzas wherein the only way to safety is through community. Then, under Ronald Reagan's stewardship, the 1980s saw the Cold War surge and, with it, a renewed projection of America as a liberty-loving—and defending—superpower.

But in the 1990s post–Cold War zeitgeist, America would no longer have any national enemy against which to define a national "us" (hence the decade's American capitalist terrorists). Also, the rise of political correctness—in addition to rendering many traditional action film villains moot—would do more to insulate groups than unite them, by hardening identity politics and complicating dialogue. So once again, the disaster film emerges as a venue for playing out how communities can form when individuals are imperiled.

Spectacle, nostalgia, fear of the *other*, political correctness, and yes, the abandonment of logic: this is the stuff of which Roland Emmerich's blockbuster, *Independence Day*, is made. Its story spans three days in which aliens arrive and launch devastating strikes from the skies over Earth. In America at least, survivors from different locales and ethnic backgrounds band together. On the Fourth of July, we—that is, a newly reconstituted, regenerated "we"—strike back, pitting fighter jets against space ships. Ultimately, humanity defeats the aliens with a computer virus, a contemporary, if cheeky, riff on H. G. Wells's *The War of the Worlds*, in which terrestrial bacteria fells extraterrestrial invaders. The film is a composite of elements, "a spectacularly scaled mix of '50s-style alien invader science fiction, '70s disaster epics and all-season gung-ho military actioners," claims *Variety*'s Todd McCarthy.[5]

Just as *Independence Day*'s filmmakers combine elements from film cycles that span the generations, they also combine pre- and post-CGI special effects techniques. Emmerich, along with his producer and co-screenwriter, Dean Devlin (with whom he had previously collaborated on 1992's *Universal Soldier* and 1995's *Stargate*), merged digital effects with in-camera ones. According to a feature in *The Hollywood Reporter*, miniature supervisor Mike Joyce oversaw four crews that worked seven days a week for over a year to execute over three hundred miniature effects. These include a specially built, thirty-five-foot section of an alien warship (along with store-bought twenty-inch models of F-18 fighters).[6]

The feature went on to report, "Even the startling Wall of Destruction effect—the fireball seen in the trailer . . . was engineered in-camera," in a combination of "live pyrotechnics and miniature-city models."[7] This is a key effect in one the film's show-stopping sequences: the aliens' first strike. Alien death rays and waves of flame pulverize Los Angeles, New York, and Washington, D.C. Among those claimed by the "Wall of Destruction" is Marty Gilbert (Harvey Fierstein). As the fireball bears down on Marty, stuck in traffic, Emmerich alternates between Marty's astonished reaction, seen through his windshield as it reflects the fireball, and Marty's point of view as the fireball sweeps up cars, and sweeps toward his own.

This intercutting is characteristic of the entire sequence, and of the 1990s' disaster films in general: the filmmakers stress not just cataclysm, but also the characters' reactions to it—even more than the filmmakers of the "*Die Hard*-on-a-Something" films do. The characters' reverence for destruction seems intended to cue the audience's reverence for the special effects. In fact, this attack sequence has more reaction shots than effects shots—a most economic way of furthering our sense of spectacle. Earlier, when the alien craft first appears over New York City, the scene comprises more than a dozen shots, but only three feature the ship. The rest show jaw-dropped citizens and car accidents among distracted motorists. Emmerich makes sure to show a variety of people united in their awe. In one shot, the camera dollies in on several street kids, who are then joined by a businessman (though as the scene progresses, the alien ship does move uptown, and with it, so do the locations).

Of course, there is more to this little apocalypse than the lasers, the avenues scorched by roiling flame, and the characters' reactions to it all. As critic James Wolcott remarks, "it isn't the size of the blasts that 'sells' the movie; it's the iconography of the targets."[8] The film's very first image establishes the destruction of icons as *Independence Day*'s major motif: the camera pulls back from an American flag to reveal a plaque left on the surface of the moon: "We Came in Peace for All Mankind." From here, the filmmakers dissolve to footprints on the lunar surface. Approaching from offscreen, the aliens' mothership rumbles, dissolving the footprints. On Earth, the landmarks destroyed by the aliens include the Empire State Building; the Los Angeles basin, normally alight with electricity, but now aglow with flame; and the Statue of Liberty, shown earlier as the shadow of an alien ship falls over it, and now toppled over. In the background of this frame stands the World Trade Center, with the top quarter of one tower blown off. But the image of the White House, being blasted from above, is by far the film's most iconic. This is no arbitrary designation: the annihilation of the White House is the widely talked-about image that anchors the teaser trailer, released to theaters in December 1995 to promote *Independence Day*'s July 3 opening.

Following the attack, *Independence Day* moves toward the middle, both geographically and politically. With the coastal cities razed, the characters converge in Roswell, New Mexico, where the film espouses bridging racial, religious, and socioeconomic divides, to reinforce traditional values: marriage, family, patriotism, and of course, strength through nuclear bombs. Crossing the desert to this union, Air Force Captain Steven Hiller (Will Smith) joins an armada of RVs resembling a modernized caravan of covered wagons. (In his review, critic Steven Mikulan assigns *Independence Day* to the "Injun Attack" category of science fiction invasion film, and asks why, in just a few days, the blockbuster became "not just the *Star Wars* but also the *High Noon* of our era."[9]) But the bone-whiteness of the sand, especially as seen on the day following the

Apocalypse Wow: From Independence Day (1996) comes this snapshot of alien-wrought devastation. (From the author's collection.)

end of our modern world, evokes not only a landscape of the past, but also the blight of nuclear winter.

The community that forms to resist the aliens includes Hiller, a black man; Jasmine (Vivica A. Fox), Hiller's stripper girlfriend, and her young son; David Levinson (Jeff Goldblum), a wiry Jewish genius; his father, Julius (Judd Hirsch); Thomas Whitmore, the President of the United States (Bill Pullman); the President's young daughter; his spokesperson, Constance (Margaret Colin), who is also David's ex-wife; and others. Different races, different classes, different generations: so far, the stuff of classic disaster movie camaraderie. Unfortunately, Devlin and Emmerich scuttle any meaningful sense of community this group might have embodied with a screenplay that sketches each character simplistically and often for comic relief. Before the story's end, Hiller and Jasmine wed, and David and Constance reconcile. The women's last act of the film is to run into the arms of their men as the men return from their victory. They perform no heroics during the last stand; their role is to wait, and then to revere, not unlike those characters and extras who revere the special effects.

Also sidelined is David's father, a geriatric nebbish, chiefly defined by his Jewishness. A borscht-belt comic would blush at Hirsch's accent and line readings, while the rest of us should at his quip to the duplicitous intelligence official, Nimzicki (James Rebhorn, playing a character named for a New Line Cinema executive with whom Devlin and Emmerich clashed while making *Stargate*). During the preparations for humankind's last stand, Julius gathers noncombatants into a prayer circle. He tries to include Nimzicki, even though the agent has been a constant source of antagonism. "I'm not Jewish," says Nimzicki. Julius regards him; the film's attitude toward inclusion, toward the will to community despite people's differences, hangs on how Julius will answer. "Nobody's perfect," he replies, sidestepping the issue, and offering an old take on an old joke, besides.

Similarly caricatured is the wildly effeminate and hysterical Marty, played by the openly gay actor Harvey Fierstein. During the public's initial panic, Marty anxiously phones his *mother* from where he hides under his desk. Later, trying to escape Manhattan, who does Marty desperately try to reach? His *therapist*. The filmmakers deny him not only heroism, but also dignity.

Russell Casse (Randy Quaid) is the most consistently abused. Until his self-sacrifice during the final dogfight, Quaid performs him as a loony drunkard—much as he does many of his comic roles. A Vietnam veteran, Russell's eccentricity is attributed to posttraumatic stress disorder, though he insists he has been the victim of alien abduction. This invites no small measure of ridicule from other characters—even *after* the alien attack. Though a small detail, this translation of warfare's psychological fallout into the stuff of crackpot tabloidism is a perfect emblem for Devlin and Emmerich's writing: equating the serious with the goofy.

As one of the action genre's heroes, President Whitmore—who, with his family, epitomizes the clean-cut, WASP image—is a veteran. Like President Marshall of *Air Force One*, Whitmore had been a pilot, but in a different war. Whereas Marshall flew rescue missions in Vietnam, Whitmore fought in 1991's Operation: Desert Storm. Naturally. This is the only appropriate war for an *Independence Day* hero to have waged. Fought from great distances, experienced by the public through live, first-person footage of falling smart bombs, it was a video game war now woven into the background of a video game movie. In a quirk of historical irony, Pullman spent his first day of shooting in the town of Wendover, where pilots had trained to fly and drop atomic bombs on Nagasaki and Hiroshima. In fact, the Wendover Airport, where Pullman remembers filming, was the site of the *Enola Gay's* construction.[10] This casts a peculiar light (or is it a shadow?) on the directive Whitmore issues from a desert bunker—a directive that signals this liberal President has grown a spine and that elicited whoops and cheers from theater audiences: "*Nuke the bastards.*"

When America's nuclear counterstrike fails, Whitmore coordinates a massive air strike with the world's remaining military forces. Emmerich shows preparations being made around the globe. On the surface, it would seem that this is another expression of the premium the film places on unity: he even shows Iraqi forces doing their part. But when he cuts to Russia, it is dark with night, lashed with rain, and areas of the frame even glow with red highlights. Accented by the score's sudden darkening and adoption of a Russian-esque male chorus, it is a stereotypically menacing image of our old adversary.

So much for finding new allies in old enemies. As for the new enemy, the aliens are depicted in strokes as broad as their attack is decisive. Consistent with many of the decade's more terrestrial villains, the aliens have no ideology. The President comes to see that Earth is merely one stop on the aliens' campaign of sweeping from planet to planet, consuming the resources of each, then moving on to the next. (This is similar to the virus metaphor the virtual Agent Smith uses to describe humans in 1999's *The Matrix*.) This is in contrast to David, who uses a bicycle instead of a car, decries smoking, champions recycling, and warns of the dangers of nuclear winter. The lack of nuance attending the aliens' plot might have made them seem more monolithic, but given the film's overall sense of hokum, it instead makes them seems more cartoonish. But this does not mitigate their suitability as villains: if any group can be abjectly discriminated against in the politically correct 1990s, it would have to be that of a non-national, non-ethnic environmental poacher.

As the technical genius who decodes the aliens' attack signal, David is the only intellectual the film prizes (consider David's doppelganger, a nearly mad scientist played by science fiction star Brent Spiner, the android of Star Trek: The Next Generation). But in the hands of Devlin and Emmerich, even David's brand of genius skews toward the ludicrous, as he parlays a reference to a head cold into using a laptop computer to upload a virus to the alien mothership. Indeed, the conception of the aliens themselves—designed with massive crania and communicating through ESP—is a throwback to science fiction (notably of the atomic 1950s) in which overdeveloped heads and the mental powers they encase embody cultural anxieties about intellectualism and a distrust of those who harbor specialized knowledge.[11]

Thus, despite its politically correct leanings, Independence Day may well be the most sexist, homophobic, anti-Semitic, and xenophobic movie about world unity ever made. Is it because the filmmakers are sexist, homophobic, anti-Semitic, and xenophobic? Almost certainly not. More likely, it is because their sense of humor is simple-minded, mistaking clichés for some grand comic tradition.

Clearly, Independence Day's faults were not enough to impede it as it rocketed to blockbuster status, broke box office records from the notable ("fastest to $100 million") to the arcane ("biggest contributor to biggest box office weekend at $190 million"), prompted journalists to explain how the film insinuated itself into the American psyche within the first week of release, saw critics discuss even its marketing, and wound its way into the discourse of the nation's presidential candidates.[12] Running for reelection, President Bill Clinton publicly recommended the film—not too bold a stance, as America had already embraced it—while Republican challenger Bob Dole, emerging from a bargain matinee near the Fox studio lot, also endorsed it, assessing, "We won in the end. Leadership. America. Good over evil."[13] Indeed, just as Independence Day is a spectacle film, journalists made a spectacle of the public's reaction to it, thereby giving additional lift to the film's already stratospheric level of success.

Of course, most of the films in this trend take place on a smaller scale. While Independence Day engulfs the whole planet, Twister, another summer blockbuster of 1996, embattles only the American Midwest. Twister, like the following winter's *Dante's Peak*, elevates reverence for destruction from visual motif to part of the plot. (And there is plenty to revere: George Lucas's Industrial Light and Magic assigned a seventy-person team to render the film's 320 special effects shots.[14]) *Twister*'s characters are a motley band that runs toward, not from, tornadoes. Led by Jo Harding (Helen Hunt) and her soon-to-be ex-husband Bill (Bill Paxton), they chase these storms for the science, for the thrill, and for the sheer awe.

"I want to see it! I want to see it!" cries Jo as a tornado rushes toward her and Bill. Even as the funnel hurls debris at them, she cranes her face toward it to look. Later, trying to survive a rare and deadly "F-5" tornado, Bill pauses to watch. "Oh my god," he utters, as it consumes a barn behind them. In such destruction, author Geoff King sees a dichotomy that might explain not just the characters' reverence for catastrophe, but also that of the filmmaker, the genre, and the audience. He writes, "Elemental force . . . is presented as both lethal danger and potential source of redemption, precisely the role played by the wilderness and its occupants in the classic American frontier tradition."[15] This is the same role the wilderness had played in the action genre's POW/MIA and postapocalyptic branches in the 1980s.

This role, along with the vast plains that are *Twister*'s stage and Bill's singular understanding of the tornadoes (by knowing when and how they will turn and gleaning insight from sniffing dirt, he is The Man Who Knows Weather), all evoke the Western. Mark Mancina's score, his second for director Jan de Bont, makes this more explicit, by weaving a variation on his theme from *Speed* around a riff on Elmer Bernstein's music from *The Magnificent Seven*. But a tradition more fundamental than that of the Western also underpins King's danger/redemption dichotomy. It is that of the apocalypse, comprising both disaster *and* triumph, as illustrated in chapter 4—hence *Twister*'s last tornado image: the first people ever to see the funnel from the inside, Bill and Jo watch as the dark cloud screams and swirls around them, and then blows itself out. As the darkness breaks apart, sunlight streams in through the gaps.

Surviving the final tornado, Bill and Jo kiss, signaling the reconstitution of their marriage. Previously, with his marriage to Jo seemingly over, Bill had left the group and soon became engaged to Dr. Melissa Reeves (Jami Gertz), a sex therapist. Throughout the film, Melissa is a misfit among the misfits. With her white business clothes and her coiffed hair, Melissa is not made of the tornado chaser's rough-and-tumble stuff. Moreover, she suppresses it in Bill, who has accepted a job as a television weatherman as part of his new life with her. The break-up of their romance—a chaste one, it seems—allows Bill to return to himself, which means returning to Jo, which means returning to the fold. The storm chasers are very much a family (an extended scene shows them breaking bread around "Aunt Meg's" table). As the group celebrates Bill and Jo's reunion, the finale is more than a boy-gets-girl ending, but also a celebration of a regenerated community.

In typical American and American movie fashion, Twister defines this community against that which does not belong to it. Melissa's appearance casts her as an outsider. So does her role as the film's comic relief: taking phone calls from neurotic patients while chasing disasters. This use of her profession, along with the depiction of Jonas Miller (Cary Elwes), the chasers' rival, makes for Twister's confused stance toward things intellectual. As one of the chasers tells Melissa (who, new to the group, justifies much exposition), "He's a nightcrawler. We all started out in the same lab, but Jonas went out and got himself some corporate sponsors. He's in it for the money, not the science. He's got a lot of high-tech gadgets, but he's got no instincts." Jonas's fleet of black SUVs, compared to the group's more banged-up and utilitarian RVs, accents this, as does the rest of his gear—and the fact that Bill consistently bests him.

As a consequence, Twister pits technology, which the film distrusts, against "pure science," which the film claims to value. This might seem peculiar given that the film's original author is Michael Crichton, whose works often combine sophisticated science with high-concept premises. And even where Crichton shows technology running amok, as in Sphere, Jurassic Park, Timeline, and Prey, it is not to elevate earthy, blue-collar ingenuity. Of course, in a style as characteristic of Jerry Bruckheimer's as it is of Michael Crichton's, the characters still speak in jargon-heavy dialogue. Wearing a tank top and working with her hands does not stop Jo from delivering dialogue such as "Looks like the dry line is stalled. Gimme a sector scan west-northwest, look at mid-levels for rotation, and increase the P.R.F." Surely, using this terminology is a gesture of authenticity, but, going unexplained, one suspects its real function is to sound impressive.

Twister's divestment of science from technology parallels the film's denigration of Melissa's more abstract discipline. What these motifs share is ridicule for anything that mitigates tactile experience—whether it is gadgets that have replaced something as primitive as instinct or the neuroses that confuse something as primal as sex. No, the things to be valued in Twister's world are the natural world (worshipfully photographed in sweeping aerial shots) and the elemental forces that are a product of it, as much as they are a blight upon it.

For all of *Twister*'s vastness, its stage is narrower than that of *Independence Day*. Narrower still is the setting of Rob Cohen's *Daylight*, also released in 1996. *Variety* and *Screen International* are among the publications that have referred to it as *Die Hard-in-a-tunnel*.[16] A more accurate point of reference, however, one many critics also cite, is *The Poseidon Adventure*—the archetype of the 1970s disaster film. In *The Poseidon Adventure*, a band of survivors struggles to escape a hellish, capsized ocean-liner; in *Daylight*, a band of survivors struggles to escape a hellish, blown-up tunnel. But the connection between these two films is more than conceptual, as *The Poseidon Adventure* was the first film set that *Daylight* director Rob Cohen ever visited.[17]

Cohen's personal connection to *The Poseidon Adventure* is a quirk of film history; that *Daylight* swipes many of *The Poseidon Adventure*'s story beats is not. In *Daylight*, shortsighted city officials risk a cave-in by sending extra equipment into the tunnel, rather than waiting and risking traffic jams at other exit points; in *The Poseidon Adventure*, a shortsighted company representative risks the ship by pushing her too fast without ballast, rather than risk arriving only on schedule and not before. In *Daylight*, when policeman George Tyrell (Stan Shaw) becomes paralyzed and knows he will die, he hands the group's leader, disgraced emergency rescue worker Kit Latura (Sylvester Stallone), a bracelet to give to the girlfriend he will not see again; in *The Poseidon Adventure*, when Belle Rosen (Shelly Winters) suffers a heart attack, she hands her group's leader, Reverend Scott (Gene Hackman), a necklace to give to the grandson whom she was on her way to meet. In *Daylight*, after the death of matronly Eleanor Trilling (Claire Bloom), Kit must convince her widower (Colin Fox) to stay with the group, to persevere; in *The Poseidon Adventure*, after Mrs. Rosen dies, Reverend Scott must convince her widower (Jack Albert) to stay with the group, to fight on. In *Daylight*, Kit, at his breaking point, rages against the tunnel: "Keep trying, you piece of shit! Keep trying! You killed everybody else, but you should have killed me!"; in *The Poseidon Adventure*, Reverend Scott, furious at losing another member of his party, cries out: "How many more sacrifices? How much more blood? How many more lives? . . . You want another life? Then take me!" And like *The Poseidon Adventure*—but unlike other contemporary action-disaster movies—*Daylight* also has a theme song: whereas in 1972, Carol Lynley crooned, "The Morning After" (later recorded by Maureen McGovern), in 1996, Donna Summer and Bruce Roberts performed, "Whenever There is Love (From *Daylight*)."

But even these larcenies are superficial, compared to how the ruined industrial setting of one resembles that of the other. For the earlier film, production designer William Creber re-created portions of the *Queen Mary* to scale; for *Daylight*, production designer Benjamin Fernandez constructed a one-third-mile-long section of tunnel that hosted 70 percent of the film's shoot.[18] Both are hell; the only difference is that whereas *The Poseidon Adventure* is, as its print ads scream, "Hell Upside Down!" *Daylight's* Manhattan Tunnel is hell right-side up. What sets this all in motion is an explosion that ravages the tunnel. This conflagration is the film's showcase special-effects sequence. It spans two minutes, in which flames rush and consume scores of trapped cars.

Those not killed watch in awe. This becomes a trope of *Daylight*, as throughout the film, Cohen emphasizes his characters' reactions to devastation. And, as in *Independence Day*, there is much that warrants these reactions. This two-minute inferno leaves a hell of flame and wreckage in its wake. It is into this hell that Kit descends. His only way in is to lower himself into a chasm, between the paused blades of a ventilation fan. When the blades start turning again, Kit twirls on and between them as he drops. Recalling *Rambo*, now more than ten years old, Kit becomes caught in the mechanism, and to save himself, cuts away his utility vest. Kit then falls down a long shaft, and in one shot, toward a black abyss—an especially overt rendering of the descent-into-the-underworld mythos that attends much of *Daylight*. In this scene, the film's signature stunt sequence, Kit lands, fights against suction, and climbs up a ladder from which he hangs upside down, fighting gravity itself.

Kit performs this feat to reach the civilians trapped below. In fact, once the group is formed, many of the subsequent action scenes involve Kit separated and fighting his way back to the group. Such scenes underscore the premium *Daylight* places on community, which is also the most fundamental trope of the 1970s disaster film (other than the disaster, of course). *Daylight's* visuals also accent community. Although Kit is the hero (Stallone was paid $17 million for the role after Mel Gibson and Harrison Ford turned it down), the characters are often framed in group shots, again borrowing from *The Poseidon Adventure* and *The Towering Inferno*. The most notable exceptions to this scheme are the one-shots of individual characters reacting to destruction, as when they watch the tunnel ceiling collapse or when Roy Nord (Viggo Mortensen) looks on as debris from the "Mid-River Shaft" flies down to bury him.

Daylight was originally scheduled to open over the July 4 weekend, when it would have contended—unwisely—with *Independence Day*. This prompted Universal to postpone the release until December 1996, when the film opened as the studio's only end-of-year title. Just a few months later, Universal released *Dante's Peak*, another disaster entry written by *Daylight* screenwriter Leslie

Bohem. This is another film in which both the characters and the filmmakers revere the reckoning, this time in the form of a volcanic eruption that devastates a mountain town.

For the production, the volcano was actually a one-hundred-foot by thirty-five-foot high wood and steel structure built in a Los Angeles airplane hangar and wheeled onto the tarmac to be photographed against the sky. Later, these images would be merged with live-action footage and matte paintings.[19] During its first eruption—at approximately the film's midpoint—volcano expert Dr. Harry Dalton (Pierce Brosnan) and Dante's Peak mayor Rachel Wando (Linda Hamilton) drive through town, giving the audience a tour of the catastrophe, a tour that lasts nearly five and a half minutes. The calamity includes part of a church toppling onto a school bus, buildings falling, and elevated freeways collapsing, which sends fleeing motorists to a bad end. And while much of the film suggests that director Roger Donaldson and cinematographer Andrzej Bartkowiak have a special affinity for using high angles, they use more reverential low angles to show Dalton and Rachel witnessing the initial destruction and for the point-of-view shots themselves.

Of course, Dalton had been warning the residents of Dante's Peak about just such a scenario, and in classic 1970s disaster film style, no one would listen. At a town meeting prior to the eruption, Dalton urges, "All I'm talking about is that you consider alerting the town to the possibility of an evacuation." One of the councilmen replies, "What Mr. Dalton here doesn't realize is that if [industrialist] Elliot Blair gets the idea that there is some kind of problem here, he's gonna take his $18 million, his eight hundred jobs, and he's gonna evacuate."

Even Dalton's own superior at the United States Geological Survey, Dr. Paul Dreyfus (Charles Hallahan) is a skeptic. "You are the best man I've got," he tells Dalton. "But until you can get it in your head that there are politics involved in a situation like this, delicate politics—not to mention economics—you're only gonna do these people more harm than good." By the time Dreyfus shares this with Dalton, Dreyfus has already put his subordinate on vacation, effectively suspending him. Reminiscent of all the bureaucratic police officials who have suspended their maverick street avengers, here is a classic action movie dynamic within a disaster movie scenario.

Later, after the eruption discussed above, the volcano *really* blows, unleashing a pyroclastic cloud of flame and charcoal gray ash that billows upwards and out. The film's publicists note that this is an "incandescent cloud of hot gases, ash and rock fragments that surges down a hill at speeds exceeding

100 mph and at temperatures raging to 475 degrees" (on set, the ash was ground-up newspaper dispersed by enormous air cannons).[20] Rachel and her children—for whom Dalton's steadfastness represents a reconstitution of their broken family—watch awe struck. In the car, Rachel's reflection in the window is superimposed over the disaster; an image Donaldson had already used during the first eruption (and a riff on the bus explosion in *Speed*, which Bartkowiak also photographed). "Don't look back, kids! Don't look back!" Dalton cries. The moment is biblical—especially as the next shot shows their truck speeding down the street just before the cloud obliterates the town. This echoes the exodus from the Manhattan Tunnel that Kit witnesses early in *Daylight*, as well as the one that opens *Dante's Peak*, a scene in which people flee from mud, flames, and falling lava bombs, and which is rendered in a red tint, evoking brimstone.

Heightening the spectacle of this scene, Donaldson seems to enjoy blowing objects (trees and the like) into the camera. He must enjoy it; he does it over twenty times in less than ninety seconds. This is also consistent with the energetic visual style Donaldson employs throughout the movie. His camera is almost always moving, and often composes actors in tilted angles, even for straightforward dialogue exchanges. This style is more aggressive than that of director Mick Jackson, whose *Volcano* marks the second volcanic-themed disaster movie released in the spring of 1997.

With the tagline "The Coast is Toast," *Volcano* was Twentieth Century Fox's failed attempt to drum up summer-event-movie excitement for a spring release. Fox went so far as to position *Volcano* as the first film of the summer, even though it was released more than a month before Memorial Day weekend, which is typically the start of the summer movie season. *Volcano* was also the runner-up in a much-publicized race between Fox and Universal to develop and release their volcano films. The last time Fox had been in a pre-production race with another studio, it had been against Warner Bros., when Warner's virus-themed *Outbreak* outpaced Fox's *Crisis in the Hot Zone*, aborted around 1994. Ironically, when Fox and Warner Bros. were in a similar position twenty years before, the result was their co-venture *The Towering Inferno*. This film was not only a landmark disaster film, but it also established the precedent of competing studio partnerships. The fruits of such partnerships are many, including the disaster films *Deep Impact* (DreamWorks and Paramount) and *Titanic* (Paramount and Fox).

Volcano is not set against any idyllic mountain town, but against the urban sprawl, industrialization, and media-saturation of Los Angeles, when a volcano rises out of the La Brea tar pits and erupts. The city's fate falls to scientist Amy Barnes (Anne Heche) and Office of Emergency Management boss Mike Roarke (Tommy Lee Jones). As the magma runs, Amy and Roarke lead efforts to plug, divert, and dam it. This differentiates *Dante's Peak* from *Volcano*: while the former is more concerned with escape and survival, the latter is more dedicated to containment and fighting. The premium *Volcano* places on industriousness, as much as the modernity of its setting, is what justifies the deployment of machines and cement dividers, and the demolition of a building to stem the lava. Here, the manufactured is used to respond to Mother Nature, not just to antagonize her, as it does in so many other disaster films.

Lava oozes down streets, including the film's biggest set piece, a replica of Los Angeles's 17.2-acre, museum-laden Wilshire corridor. The set was built 80 percent to scale at a McDonnell Douglas aircraft plant by production designer Jackson DeGovia and his art department.[21] Among the sites set ablaze is the Los Angeles County Museum of Art, which, with a wink from the art department, hosts an exhibit of Hieronymus Bosch, painter of hell and brimstone, among other religious tropes.

This is only one example of *Volcano*'s sense of humor, with much of the film underpinned—and at times, undermined—by its attempts to satirize Los Angeles while also razing it. Such irreverence better served Jackson's romantic-comedy/Los Angeles satire *L.A. Story* (1991) than it does *Volcano*, which might have been better off satirizing its genre rather than its setting. In *Volcano*'s opening credits, for instance, the filmmakers poke fun at the city's obsessions with media and with the banal, through news reports that give equal weight to crime and plastic surgery. Later, a media account of looting is underscored by a looter racing through the frame and snatching up Amy's scientific gear as he goes. Still later, during the pre-dawn eruption, a lava bomb sets fire to a billboard trumpeting real-life local celebrity and wannabe star Angelyne.

Lava bombs aside, the menace of *Volcano* is not as propulsive as that of *Dante's Peak*—another difference between the films. Throughout *Volcano*, the magma makes slow, but unrelenting progress, creeping toward the camera. In fact, the filmmakers depict the lava as if it were the monster of a monster movie as much as the disaster of a disaster film. (This is achieved visually, but also by Alan Silvestri's rumbling score, and even in the title of its central cue: "March of the Lava.") According to the director, who imagines the lava to be less a force of nature than a character archetype, "It has all the characteristics of the best movie villain: you can not kill it."[22]

Unfortunately for *Volcano*, the lava's sluggishness is not the only restraint

Urban Meltdown: Lava oozes down Los Angeles's Wilshire corridor in Volcano, the second of two 1997 volcano films. (From the author's collection.)

the film shows. Jackson often frames his actors in matching close-ups and medium close-ups that seem derived from television more than feature films. This is exacerbated by the fact that the film is composed in the more limited 1.85:1 aspect ratio, as opposed to the wider, more rectangular 2.35:1 in which the doom and spectacle of many (if not most) disaster films has been so proudly presented. As DeGovia recalls,

> I was on the 1.85 side of that debate. I thought you needed more headroom. [*Volcano*] wasn't a horizontal movie; it was really a vertical movie. Here we had built all these tall buildings and [in 2.35,] you weren't going to see as much. I think in the end, it was an economic decision; it's a lot faster to light 1.85 for one thing, and they knew they were losing the race [to *Dante's Peak*]. I don't know if I'd come down on the same side of that now, but it seemed like the right idea at the time.[23]

As a consequence, the filmmakers reap the benefits of *Volcano*'s aspect ratio at the expense of its spectacle. The disaster genre has always been an exhibition-ist one, demanding that its filmmakers maximize film technology; since the introduction of anamorphic and other 2.35 formats, it is a genre that has re-sisted narrowness.

In some respects, Ed Zwick's *The Siege* (1998) is the inverse of *Volcano*. The film is not a showcase for special effects, as *Twister* and the volcano films are, but photographed in Super 35mm by Roger Deakins, its 2.35 frame reveals a more low-key form of spectacle: a massive location production that portrays New York City besieged by terrorists and ultimately occupied by the U.S. Army. Following the capture of Sheik Achmed Bin Talal (who, in hindsight, much re-sembles Osama bin Laden), Muslim terrorist cells stage a series of bombings in New York. Combating this threat is a multiethnic FBI counterterrorism squad led by Anthony Hubbard (Denzel Washington), and Frank Haddad (Tony Shalhoub), a Lebanese-American. Joining them is Sharon Bridger (An-nette Bening), a CIA operative who must bridge the gap between her agency and Hubbard's to assuage her guilt at having abandoned these Muslims to Saddam Hussein's persecution after training them to make bombs in their campaign against the Soviets. As the attacks escalate, a U.S. Army platoon led by General William Devereaux (Bruce Willis) occupies Brooklyn, interns its Muslim residents, and declares martial law. Although this is an attempt to root out the remaining cell, it touches off a moral and Constitutional crisis, pitting issues of individual liberty against those of community safety and raising ques-tions as to what constitutes "community" for New Yorkers and for Americans.

While the special effects of The Siege tend more toward action movie fire-fights than they do towering infernos (one shootout involves Hubbard's rescue of captured school children; another cites High Noon), the film's emphasis on the meaning of community resonates with the disaster film canon. Zwick maintains that the film "is not about terrorism; it's about us. It's about who we are and who we choose to be. It asks some important questions: how will we respond to an attack from within—and who will we be when tested?"[24] According to critic Peter Rainer, Zwick "wants to make a cautionary political thriller about the moral consequences of fighting terrorism: Can you slay the monster without becoming the monster?"[25]

This gives The Siege more of a political charge than other "mad bomber" movies of the period, including Stephen Hopkins's Blown Away (1994), a revenge thriller; John McTiernan's Die Hard with a Vengeance, in which the villain's Manhattan bombings (real and threatened) turn out to be a ploy to avenge himself on John McClane, which in turn diverts the police from his robbery of the Federal Reserve; and The Peacemaker (1997), the DreamWorks studio's first release, in which a Special Forces operative (George Clooney) and a nuclear expert (Nicole Kidman) race against a terrorist plotting to detonate a Russian nuclear device in New York.

The Siege asks deeper questions than these other films, though that did not dissuade some Arab-Americans from protesting the film while it was in production and again when it opened, just as Executive Decision had been protested in 1996. According to the New York Times, protesters gathered outside the Criterion Theater at Broadway and 45th Street—just blocks from where a pivotal scene had been filmed—and waved placards decrying what they perceived to be Hollywood's equation of Islam with terrorism. (The shrewdest sign took a different approach to discourage potential patrons: rather than try to stir their moral or political passions, it simply gave away the ending of the movie.[26]) But once the film opened to mixed reviews and uninterested moviegoers, other groups cancelled their demonstrations, electing to let the film die its own death. More heated were international protests, such as those in Cape Town, South Africa. As Daily Variety reports, two theaters withdrew the film after a spate of Muslim condemnation, bomb threats, and a car bomb explosion. Seemingly unaware of the irony, the trade paper comments that the film "has been the target of much anger from militant Muslims, who objected to its portrayal of Muslims as terrorists."[27]

Even with a more high-minded approach to its subject, spectacle still informs The Siege. One of the film's most astonishing images is the suicide bombing of a city bus. The explosion begins in an extreme long shot; the audience not only sees the beginning of the enormous fireball, but also sees it set against a huge canvas, as the police have cordoned off blocks in every direction. As Peter Schindler, the film's executive producer, recalls, "That was the day we shut down the Metro, the highway, everything. For ten minutes, I think from 3:05 to 3:15, we owned that [area]."[28] The explosion was rigged by Con Air's special effects foreman Paul Lombardi, a second-generation special effects man, whose father had laid out the napalm explosion that opens Apocalypse Now.

In The Siege, the bus explosion sequence consists of twenty-two shots, but only three are of the fireball itself. The rest are of people falling, windows shattering, papers blowing—storming—across the frame. Evoking a whirlwind, this last might be the least kinetic, but the most apocalyptic. The final shot is from Hubbard's point of view. Knocked to the concrete by the blast, he sees ashy debris falling in front of the sun—a strangely ethereal close to the conflagration.

Another example of stunning destruction is that of the Federal Building, or more accurately, the aftermath of it. The bombing itself is signified by a dissolve to white as an explosive-laden van crashes through the building's lobby window. When the filmmakers dissolve back, it is to the building's hulking skeleton—in reality, an enormous piece of wreckage built in California's San Fernando Valley, according to Schindler.[29]

This attack, which claims some 600 lives, combines references to what were then two of the worst terrorist attacks on United States soil: the World Trade Center attack of February 26, 1993, a plot masterminded by convicted Sheikh Omar Abdel Rahman, in which Islamic terrorists detonated a car bomb in an underground parking garage between the two towers; and Timothy McVeigh's use of a rented truck and several thousand pounds of fertilizer and fuel oil to bomb the Alfred P. Murrah Federal Building in Oklahoma City, killing 168 people, on April 19, 1995. Schindler recalls production designer Lilly Kilvert matching The Siege's destroyed Federal Building set to photographs of the Oklahoma City wreckage.[30]

In the film, the response to such attacks is also a form of spectacle. After the bombing of a Broadway theater, Hubbard, Frank, and Sharon battle their way to the scene through a gigantic traffic jam, which the filmmakers staged, for a scene that required shutting down Times Square and 42nd Street. This image, while not as dynamic as the bus explosion, or the disasters in The Siege's predecessors, is striking for the size, and also the authenticity, of its action.

Quite consciously, the filmmakers put New York on display in all its formidable, widescreen glory. This effect could not have been achieved so well had The Siege been filmed in say, the less expensive Montreal, where filmmakers are often forced to hide the fact that they are not on location in New York City, Los Angeles, or some other major American metropolis.

Following this attack, Zwick uses reports of skyrocketing hate-crime rates and anonymous voiceovers (call-ins to radio programs, one presumes) to depict the breakdown of New Yorkers' unity. "This is the kind of shit these towelheads do in their own country, and now they're bringing it here," one caller says. Hubbard had tried to counter such sentiment by situating New York within a still broader, international community, one that includes such embattled cities as Rome, Athens, and Tel Aviv, and by emphasizing his city's strength. "This is New York City," asserts Hubbard. "We can take it."

But when the Federal Building is demolished—and with it, Hubbard's infrastructure—the President orders the army to take over, which means laying siege to Brooklyn. The football stadium into which the borough's Arab population is corralled is just one striking image. Another is the march of troops and armored vehicles over the Brooklyn Bridge and onto the streets. According to Schindler, "Originally, we were going to use tanks, but then we found that we couldn't run tanks on city streets because the treads would just tear up the pavement. That's why we had troop movers and Armored Personnel Carriers; they had rubber treads." As the real U.S. Army gave the production no assistance, the filmmakers rented these vehicles from private collectors.[31]

Just prior to the occupation, General Devereaux gives the FBI, the President's advisors, and the audience an indication of the awesome sight we know is coming—and by impressing those assembled with the formidability of the army's resources, he makes overt the genre's fascination with hardware, force, and jargon:

Twelve hours after the President gives the order, we can be on the ground. One light infantry division of 10,700 men. Elements of the Rapid Deployment Force, Special Forces, Delta; APCs, helicopters, tanks, and of course, the ubiquitous M16A1 assault rifle: a humble enough weapon until you see it in the hands of a man outside your local bowling alley or 7-11. It will be noisy, it will be scary, and it will not be mistaken for a VFW parade.

Initially opposing this plan, General Devereaux offers these words as ones of caution. As Devereaux, Bruce Willis is most commanding when expressing

Pre-Occupied: *The United States Army marches into Brooklyn in 1998's politically charged spectacle,* The Siege. *(From the author's collection.)*

this reluctance. Later, as commander of the occupying force, he adopts a fanaticism that is as dead-eyed as his enemy's is wild—and no more engaging.

With this part of the film, several ironies emerge: the first is that the citizens of a city known for its racial and religious divisions unite to protest the treatment of their Arab neighbors, while rifts widen between the FBI and the U.S. Army—those given the singular charge of protecting Americans. At the film's climax, the armed standoff between federal agents and army soldiers brings this tension to its highest pitch. Earlier, however, Zwick expresses it in a single image in which the symbolism is stark. Following the General's torture and execution of an Arab-American citizen, Tariq Husseini (Amro Salama), a disgusted Hubbard exits, walking up the corridor, into the background; General Devereaux walks off toward the camera; and Sharon is left in middle ground, literally and figuratively between these two poles.

The second irony is Willis himself. Ten years after introducing the everyman counterterrorist guerilla John McClane, Willis now plays the invading force. One can even imagine a *Die Hard* sequel in which the filmmakers pit McClane against the General as much as the terrorist cell the General seeks. This is exacerbated by how the filmmakers and the studio try to invest not just General Devereaux, but also Willis, with a sense of gravity. In *The Siege*, as well as Willis's preceding blockbuster, *Armageddon*, Willis is treated as some elder statesman of the action genre. (Notably, this begins after 1995's *Die Hard with a Vengeance*, in which he plays John McClane as decidedly burned out.) In *The Siege* and *Armageddon*, Willis plays authority figures against whom other characters' heroism is often defined. Onscreen and in the advertising campaign, *The Siege* lists him last among the headliners with the venerating "And Bruce Willis," as does *Armageddon*'s print advertising. Naturally, all action stars must contend with their own aging while trying to remain viable, and shifting into a statelier persona may be as valid a strategy as engaging in self-parody, as Schwarzenegger has. But in his action films, Willis and statesmanship do not always make for an easy fit, as his star persona is founded on that of a wisecracking upstart.

As one might imagine, since late 2001, it has been impossible to view *The Siege* without being reminded of the terrorist attacks of September 11. The movie contains a number of images that predict scenes of the later calamity. The film's ruined One Federal Plaza and the work lights surrounding the hole in the ground remind today's viewer of the destruction at Ground Zero and the Pentagon. Also recalling the attacks are the aftermath of the bus explosion, in which an otherwise sunny day is made hazy by ash and debris; our glimpse of a bank of monitors running footage of the bus explosion in an obsessive loop; and the masses of people walking across the Brooklyn Bridge (protesters in the film, commuters in real life).

The Siege also makes a number of even more striking, more unsettling predictions about September 11, its aftermath, and al Qaeda. The exploding bus is the second of the film's two hijacked busses, while the World Trade Center would be struck by two hijacked planes. And as the terrorists explode the bus only after the news media appears, the hijackers of the second plane, intentionally or not, would strike the World Trade Center's South Tower while the media was on site filming the impact on the North. Following the attacks in the film, as was the case in reality, much would be made of racial profiling, rising anti-Arab hate crimes, and slumping retail sales. Also, the film's internment of Arab-Americans in the stadium anticipates the United States' later imprisonment of "enemy combatants" (actual and suspected) in Guantanamo Bay, while the debate over torturing the film's suspects would resonate with the torture scandal of Iraq's Abu Gharib prison.

Still, the most pointed comparisons between The Siege and September 11 may be made between their terrorists. Despite his appearance on a terrorist watch list, the film's Ali Wiziri, one of the bus bombers, had entered the United States from Germany with a student visa. Of the September 11 terrorists, a good number were also in the United States with temporary visas (or applications for them), including Hani Hanjour, who had received a student visa; Zacarais Moussaoui, who obtained a visa while appearing on a French terrorist watch list; and ringleader Mohammad Atta, who, as the head of a Hamburg cell of al Qaeda, had been educated in Germany and whose U.S. student visa application was pending.[32]

Like terrorists such as al Qaeda leader Osama bin Laden, the terrorists of The Siege are former CIA assets. Whereas bin Laden and his Mujahideen brethren were supported and equipped by the United States to drive the Soviets out of Afghanistan (a struggle, it is worth repeating, dramatized in Rambo III), the terrorists of The Siege had served a United States–backed Iraqi sheik in a plot to overthrow Saddam Hussein and are now attacking New York with the bomb-making techniques they learned from Sharon Bridger. Indeed, even the number of terrorists strikes a chord: in the film, General Devereaux declares that "we are opposed by no more than twenty of the enemy." On September 11, New York and Washington, D.C., were struck by nineteen hijackers, with Moussaoui long believed to be the intended twentieth.

Of all the disaster-driven action films to punish New York City in 1998, The

Siege was the third (or the fourth film overall, if one counts the disaster-drama *Deep Impact*). Earlier that year, TriStar Pictures launched the summer movie season with the much-hyped Memorial Day weekend release of *Godzilla*. TriStar acquired the rights to the colossal property almost six years earlier from Toho Co. Ltd. Because TriStar and Columbia Pictures were owned by Sony (and had been since 1989), this acquisition amused some Hollywood insiders. The *Los Angeles Times* quoted one as saying, "When Sony took over TriStar and Columbia, the big joke around town was 'we're gonna see a lot of Godzilla and kung fu movies...' But Sony officials were adamant at the time that they would not enforce their taste on American popular culture."[33]

Indeed, it was not the Japanese corporation, but rather American producers who were first responsible for importing Japan's legendary icon to Hollywood. Producer Robert Fried originally secured the rights from Toho for $50,000. Fried claims it was difficult to interest a Hollywood studio in making the film, but that one studio executive embraced the idea: Sony's Peter Guber. However, the deal Fried had negotiated did not suit the studio's interests in at least one key area: while Fried's deal allowed him to make a single *Godzilla* picture, the studio wanted the right to make sequels.[34] Sony negotiated a new deal with Toho and as reported by *Variety*, TriStar acquired the rights for a sum between $300,000 and $400,000.[35]

TriStar initially planned *Godzilla* as a major release for Christmas 1994. The script then developed by the studio featured the giant, dormant lizard being awakened by alien forces and ultimately ravaging not only New York, but also San Francisco.[36] And because the studio wanted to create a creature that it would own outright, the original script by Terry Rossio and Ted Elliot (writers brought in by Fried's then-producing partner, Cary Woods) imagined Godzilla battling a new monster, a Griffin.[37]

TriStar would not meet this release date. In 1994, the studio signed director Jan de Bont for $4 million, just weeks after he surprised audiences and the industry alike with *Speed*, his directorial debut and upstart little action-thriller.[38] In the few months de Bont was attached to *Godzilla*, he began casting and even shooting some preliminary footage. But his deal with the studio fell apart over the gap between the $130 million budget de Bont wanted (he had just made *Speed* for approximately $30 million) and the roughly $100 million budget TriStar would approve. As the deal was collapsing in early December 1994, de Bont was already considering other projects including *Face/Off* and *Twister*.[39] He would choose Michael and Anne-Marie Crichton's *Twister* and turn their script into the second highest-grossing film of 1996. That year's top-grossing film was, of course, *Independence Day*. Its creators, Dean Devlin and Roland Emmerich, would abandon Fox and the studio's hoped-for sequel to join TriStar and *Godzilla*.

Emmerich and Devlin bring to *Godzilla* the devastation as well as the awe that propelled their ode-to-the-fifties, *Independence Day*. (Similarly, in *Godzilla*, as in the original Toho productions of the 1950s, the monster is the product of Cold War nuclear radiation.) But whereas Emmerich and Devlin reveled in blighting all of America in *Independence Day*, they rewrote *Godzilla* to dispense of San Francisco and the second monster. Instead, they provide one locus for their monster's destructive power: Manhattan. As the gigantic lizard storms ashore, he crushes traffic beneath his feet and gouges skyscrapers with his tail (which, according to the film's outdoor advertising, "is longer than this building"). When the rampage is over, a hole has been punched through the center of the Met Life Building—the first of several icons that join the World Trade Center, the Statue of Liberty, the White House, and others, in the landmark-graveyard of Emmerich and Devlin's work.

Other landmarks fall later—not to the lizard's fury, but rather, to the military's tomfoolery. As part of a campaign to destroy Godzilla, the army takes up a position on 23rd Street. Soldiers and armored vehicles blast away, but miss— yes, they actually *miss* Godzilla—and instead annihilate the Flatiron Building, a New York City landmark since 1902. Enraged, Godzilla turns and roars at his pursuers, hurling vehicles and flame toward the camera, an effect that recalls *Independence Day*'s Wall of Destruction. The army next attacks from the air. Apache gunships bear down on the monster, but when the choppers fire their Sidewinder missiles, Godzilla easily ducks them. They destroy the Chrysler Building instead, to an overwrought snatch of David Arnold's score. The Chrysler Building's iconic top falls to the street, where it shatters over two shots. Madison Square Garden is the next to go—destroyed by the army, this time on purpose. When Matthew Broderick's Dr. Niko Tatopoulos (named after the creature's designer) discovers that the arena is now a lair where Godzilla has laid over two hundred eggs, the plucky scientist calls in an air strike. The final doomed icon is the Brooklyn Bridge, onto which Godzilla chases Niko and the other ragtag protagonists. Here, cornered by the military, Godzilla meets its downfall, but not before taking the bridge's train tracks, cables, and several towers with it. (This is a fitting location for the climax: *Godzilla* and the Brooklyn Bridge both opened just in time for Memorial Day weekend—*Godzilla* in 1998, and the Brooklyn Bridge in 1883.)

As was the case with *Independence Day*, Emmerich and Devlin use a variety of techniques to craft *Godzilla*'s special effects. The filmmakers employed at least eight separate companies to provide model and miniature construction, model and miniature photography, creature fabrication, digital creature animation, digital compositing, and other services. The motion capture system, by which an actor's "performance" of Godzilla was digitally translated into the creature's movements, was created by incorporating technology that had been invented not for movies, but for medicine. According to a senior executive of the effects house's parent company, the system had marked a revolution in brain surgery.[40] If so, this would represent *Godzilla's* most ironic use of technology.

It is *Godzilla's* emphasis on spectacle over story—a charge often levied against disaster and other action movies—that led Peter Travers to remark, in a riff on the film's "Size does matter" tagline, "physical size doesn't always matter, but the size of the vision does."[41] It is also part of what prompted David Denby to deride *Godzilla* as a "boring, meaningless, corporate product."[42] The last part of his litany is especially relevant, as *Godzilla* was conceived as an event film to spawn a franchise as early as 1992, when TriStar first acquired the rights to the character. Once the studio had secured Emmerich and Devlin's participation, however, *Godzilla* became not just a movie, not just a potential blockbuster, but a vortex of marketing materials, promotions, merchandise, and the film itself—the last of which managed to seem both central and, at the same time, marginal.

The campaign began early and intensified as the Memorial Day weekend of 1998 drew nearer. *Godzilla's* first teaser trailer—in which the big lizard's titanic foot smashes through a museum skylight and crushes the skeleton of a Tyrannosaurus Rex—was in theaters to capitalize on the July 3, 1997 release of Sony's *Men in Black*, and also to take a swipe at the film that had been dominating the summer box office until that point, Steven Spielberg's record-setting *The Lost World: Jurassic Park*. As early as May 1997, before the release of *Men in Black* (and *The Lost World*, for that matter), *Daily Variety* reported on its front page that TriStar would open *Godzilla* with $20 million worth of promotional support from Taco Bell. This early alliance was a coup for TriStar, but also for Taco Bell, which was benefiting from an exclusive partnership between McDonald's and Disney, a partnership that prevented the fast-food giant from promoting other studios' properties.[43]

The *Godzilla* campaign relaxed its pace for much of the fall, beginning anew in November. The studio released new advertising materials, and perhaps more significantly, certain details of its marketing and promotional plans. As the *Los Angeles Times* reports,

By the time "Godzilla" hits theaters May 20, Sony will have invested $125 million to produce the movie and at least an additional $50 million to market it worldwide—leading some in Hollywood to believe that number will probably be even higher. The studio's promotional partners, led by such major companies as Taco Bell, Hershey, Duracell, Electronic Arts and toy maker Trendmasters, are kicking in more than $150 million in tie-ins linked to the monster.[44]

These companies would be joined by KFC International, Kirin beer, General Mills cereals, Kodak, Swatch, and Dryer's/Edy's Ice Cream, which created a new flavor dubbed "Godzilla Vanilla."[45] In all, the filmmakers and the studio partnered with over two hundred licensees.

The campaign was dogged by one major complication: the filmmakers' insistence that Godzilla's likeness not be revealed until the movie's opening. In fact, Dean Devlin went so far as to provide each promotional partner with a fake image unique to that company. If any of the images found their way to the public, the filmmakers and the studio would be able to identify and sever ties with the company that had leaked it. One did: Fruit of the Loom, Inc.[46]

While this secrecy fueled the mounting hype, it also meant that images of the title character would not appear on any packaging or with any fast-food premiums. It also meant that many licensed products would not appear in stores until the film's opening day. As *Variety* notes, TriStar's strategy even involved coordinating truck movements so that nationwide, stores received Trendmaster's toy line and more than three thousand items of licensed merchandise precisely at midnight on May 20.[47] More than just a logistical challenge, this also represented a gamble: *Variety* editor Peter Bart notes that approximately 40 percent of all tie-in merchandise is typically sold before a movie's release.[48]

When Godzilla was finally revealed, it was on 7,363 screens in 3,310 theaters (crushing *The Lost World*'s record of opening on 6,190 screens).[49] Putting this in perspective, *Variety* reports that there were then 31,640 screens available in the United States, of which a major release would usually grab between 3,000 and 4,000.[50] It appears then that *Godzilla* opened on approximately twice the number of screens as other major releases and, more impressive still, on nearly ¼ of all screens in the United States.

That weekend, TriStar redeemed the marketing, promotional, and distribution muscle it had deployed over its nearly year-long campaign for a $55.5 million four-day opening. This was the third highest in history, outperformed by just two films: Mission: Impossible and, getting the last laugh, The Lost World: Jurassic Park. Still, these returns were underwhelming. Although at the end of the film's first week, TriStar took out a double-page ad in The Hollywood Reporter, boasting the film's $74,214,18 seven-day gross, the tagline "Size does matter" was conspicuously absent. Moreover, on the ad's reverse side, readers could find an article titled, "'Godzilla': relatively thin lizard [sic]."[51]

Godzilla's opening left a mark on Wall Street as well—though not of the type Emmerich and Devlin would have depicted in their film. The day after TriStar's ad ran in The Hollywood Reporter, the nation's leading movie theater chain, Carmike Cinemas Inc., warned "that its second-quarter earnings would be 'significantly lower' than Wall Street estimates" and cited Godzilla's soft opening. With the announcement, Carmike's stock fell 5.7 percent, representing the biggest drop in exhibition stocks after Godzilla's debut.[52] Later, Equity Marketing Inc., a Los Angeles–based toy maker that had produced Godzilla-themed plush toys, key chains, and mugs, signaled in September that its earnings for the third quarter might drop as much as 87 percent from the prior year. Equity blamed weak sales of Godzilla merchandise, as well as soft Asian and Latin American markets.[53] Producer Robert Fried sees the simultaneous releases of the movie and its tie-ins as a major cause of this failure: "The life of movie merchandising is usually three weeks before the movie opens and three weeks after. If you cut off presales, you've cut out half your sales. There were a lot of excess toys."[54]

The film's domestic gross did not climb much higher than $136 million, well-short of the "benchmark for hit status" that the Wall Street Journal fixed at $200 million. Meanwhile, the film cost $120 million to produce (though Fried claims the figure was closer to $150 million) and another $80 million to market worldwide.[55] This is ironic given how TriStar's refusal to approve a comparable budget triggered Jan de Bont's departure. Fried attributes Godzilla's performance both as a film and as a brand to two major factors: an unwillingness to reschedule the release date, which denied Emmerich the time to finish all the effects and "make a shorter, better film," and the withholding of Godzilla's likeness. Fried maintains that while the film dedicated an unprecedented allotment of screen time to computer-generated imagery, "the ultimate look of the creature while interesting, was not unique relative to what we had seen in Jurassic Park, and I think consumers were let down."[56]

Just six weeks after the loud, but ultimately limp Godzilla unleashed itself on New York City, Armageddon, the second of 1998's two asteroid-themed disaster films, came along to pulverize what was left. Though Manhattan only factors into the film's first scene, the city's three-and-a-half-minute cameo is a memorable one. Director Michael Bay establishes the scale of New York with wide angles that flatter its skyline and extreme low angles that emphasize the city's height. A meteor strike begins soon after: eleven shots of explosions and taxi cab crashes in ten seconds. Bay gives the audience a breather by cutting to one cab, snarled in traffic. Inside, a Japanese passenger (presumably a tourist), asks "Why we not going?" The black cabbie answers as rapid-fire as Bay tends to cut:

> You know why? 'Cause this is New York City. Anything could've happened. Look at that, could've been a terrorist bomb. Could've been a dead body, somebody shot, stabbed. And it's Friday, too. Dude, somebody probably jumped when they didn't get that paycheck.

A second Japanese passenger, a woman, then shrieks in stilted English, "I want to go shopping!" The cabbie yells back, "Me too!" mocking her accent. "But we ain't goin' nowhere, 'cause this is a *traffic jam!*" In the space of this brief exchange, Bay stereotypes New York *and* the Japanese *and* arguably, black people. By then, however, Bay is already on a roll; moments earlier, he had mocked—of all ethnicities—Samoans, with a street vendor whose plastic Godzillas are attacked by a dog belonging to a loudmouth, and black, bicycle messenger.

This meteor strike is but a preview of the next, which soon rains devastation on New York for approximately eighty-five seconds. The sequence contains fifty-four shots, and except for four cutaways to the cabbie, virtually every one features some combination of meteorites, destruction, and panicking citizens. Like Roland Emmerich and Dean Devlin and other filmmakers who trade in disaster, Bay thrashes cultural icons. In this one sequence, meteorites punch through a tower of the World Trade Center, wreck Grand Central Station over six shots, and in three shots, destroy the Chrysler Building. As in *Godzilla*, the building's ornamented top plummets to the ground, but *Armageddon* adds people flying down toward the camera, an especially grizzly effect in a post–September 11 world. The shattering of this steel icon is the climax of the sequence, but Bay returns to New York moments later. Intercut with NASA administrator Dan Truman (Billy Bob Thornton) briefing the military, are two apocalyptic views of Manhattan. The first is a crater in the street surrounded by jets of flame and junked taxi cabs (a smashed police car adds a splash of blue and white to the orange and grey frame). The second is an aerial view of the smoldering city. As the camera pans to the left, the lower right of the frame is captured by a red and black plume. In the upper left is the World Trade Center. One tower has been run through. The other, with its rooftop and upper floors annihilated, gushes smoke.

All of this is but the opening salvo, a storm of meteorites that announce the coming of the big one. *Armageddon's* story, as crafted by Michael Bay, Jerry Bruckheimer, and a stable of nine screenwriters, including J. J. Abrams, *Con Air's* Scott Rosenberg and *Chinatown's* Robert Towne (a Writers Guild of America arbitration ultimately determined the credits), finds an asteroid the size of Texas on a collision course with planet Earth.[57] Harry Stamper (Bruce Willis) and his team of deep core oil drillers, are called upon to become astronauts and rendezvous with the rock before it strikes. After landing, Harry and his men are to drill, plant a nuclear device eight hundred feet below the asteroid's surface, and detonate it via remote control. Harry's mission is to literally "save the planet"—ironic, given that the filmmakers introduce the oil drillers amid a floating Greenpeace protest. In fact, to introduce Harry, Bay makes a too-rare display of wit: after Truman explains the power of the asteroid speeding toward Earth, Bay cuts to a golf ball being whacked from a tee. The golfer is Harry, aiming for the protesters who flank his rig.

Upon its release, *Armageddon* did not enjoy even the mixed reviews of Bay's previous film, *The Rock*. Critics eviscerated *Armageddon*, largely (but not only) because of the furious pace of its editing. *Variety's* Todd McCarthy maintains, "Much of the confusion, as well as the lack of dramatic rhythm or character development, results directly from Bay's cutting style, which resembles a machine gun stuck in the firing position for 2½ hours."[58] The *Village Voice* critic Dennis Lim is also typical of the critical attitude, but uses even more colorful language: "*Armageddon* decisively crosses the line from mindless, relatively painless garbage into a whole new dimension of summer-movie hell. Like being yelled at by idiots for 144 minutes, the *Armageddon* experience is pointlessly traumatizing."[59] Whereas at least some critics held that the editing of *The Rock* intensifies the action, the similarly-paced cutting of *Armageddon* seems to have drawn the ire of a less divided critical community.

Indeed, in *Armageddon*, Bay's approach to editing follows the pattern laid down in *The Rock* and in his first film, *Bad Boys*, but makes this pacing even more rigid. As before, precious few shots last more than four seconds, and many are between one and two seconds long. Editor Mark Goldblatt recalls that in cutting the approximately one million feet of film on a tight schedule and with multiple editors, "Sometimes the editing became impressionistic," and laughingly adds, "They paid us by the cut!"[60]

There is, of course, the rare exception. One is the shot in which Truman tells the President about the asteroid and the destruction it will wreak: "Damage? Total, sir. It's what we call a global killer. The end of mankind. Nothing would survive. Not even bacteria." To this critical bit, Bay and his editors (Goldblatt, Chris Lebenzon, and Glen Scantlebury, as well as "two guest editors") devote a full eight seconds—twice the length of that four-second cutoff.[61] The contrast makes Truman's assessment that much more resonant.

The other major exception is a ten-second shot in which Paris is destroyed by pieces of the asteroid that have sped ahead of the main rock. Two stone gargoyles guarding Notre Dame, each perched at a margin of the foreground, frame the action. This creates a sense of depth as the rest of the city is relegated to the background; the obliteration seems to take place on an even larger scale. This effect, like other instances of destruction in the film, was a last-minute addition to Armageddon. According to the Wall Street Journal, in May 1998, not two months before the film's July 1 release, Disney chairman Joe Roth decided to add more than three million dollars worth of effects shots to the film. The aim was not to simply add more spectacle to the film itself, but specifically, to "provide 'fresh imagery for the last two weeks of the [TV ad] campaign.'" (brackets in original).[62]

According to Oren Aviv, Disney's then–Senior Vice President of Marketing and Creative Advertising, Roth commissioned the new effects as a response to a film that preceded Armageddon by less than two months, Paramount and DreamWorks's similarly themed Deep Impact, in which a tidal wave washes over New York. As Aviv argues,

It is becoming more common for marketing concerns to influence a film's content, but that's not as insidious as it might sound. It's just practical. When you have a movie to market, it's not going to necessarily have a clear sail; it's going to be buffeted on the seas of competition. Joe asked Michael Bay and Jerry [Bruckheimer] to come up with a more spectacular sequence than the [Deep Impact] wave. And I ended up using it.[63]

Armageddon's newly-minted destruction includes that of Grand Central Station, inserted into the early battering to which the filmmakers subject Manhattan; and that of Shanghai, which is represented by wood shacks floating on water, which still manage to explode in massive fireballs.

We are later told that the destruction of Shanghai killed fifty thousand people. As in Independence Day, the film rarely, and never meaningfully, deals with these dead. Death tolls have no resonance but to signify epic destruction; the survivors register neither trauma nor a need to suppress their feelings (following the first attack in *Independence Day*, Hiller and another pilot, played by Harry Connick, Jr., provide some comic relief, but their humor is more jocular than of the gallows variety). In the case of *Armageddon*, the fact that Shanghai's destruction was added so late in the filmmaking process does go a long way in explaining what is essentially the film's non-reaction to the obliteration of fifty thousand people. Nonetheless, it is characteristic of the coldness of Bay's work, as is the fact that the double-cutting of the Navy depot guard hitting the ground in *The Rock* has a complement in *Armageddon*. In the first scene of the film, anticipating the brimstone rain that is about to pummel New York, speeding asteroid fragments kill an astronaut performing a space-walk. After his suit is ruptured, Bay and his editors double-cut the smashing of the astronaut's faceplate.

Not long after this, Truman makes his grave assessments. Although Truman's explanation to the President is one of the few instances where Bay slows down, it uses other means to achieve Bay/Bruckheimer excessiveness. The asteroid in the more scientifically credible and dramatically grounded *Deep Impact* is six miles across and has been detected eighteen months prior to impact; the asteroid in *Armageddon*, however, is the size of *Texas* and will strike in eighteen days. (How did this rock go undetected until less than three weeks before its arrival? "It's a big-ass sky," says an underfunded Truman.) If it is bigger and faster, it must be Bay and Bruckheimer, even when the end of the world is a given and when a little restraint would better sell the realism—and with it the terror—of the scenario.

The design of the asteroid also embodies the filmmakers' tendency toward overstatement. Despite NASA's much-touted involvement, Bay and production designer Michael White abandon science in favor of a more violent aesthetic. According to *Armageddon*'s publicity, White conducted extensive research and determined that "most asteroids look like russet potatoes that, in reality, are not very interesting." In White's words, asteroids are "globular and very flat on the surface with not much personality. . . . We wanted something more menacing so we went through a lot of designs to come up with the shape of the rock, the razor-like barb rock formations and the overhangs."[64]

But Bay undercuts White's efforts by failing to use the asteroid's giant outcroppings and rock spires as markers that help us understand the asteroid's geography; instead, they confuse our orientation. So does some of the mayhem taking place on the surface. Despite the fact that the asteroid is just a rock, vents spew dust and vapor across the frame, nightmarish counterparts to the more mythic smoke and mist. As Harry and his team near their goal of drilling eight hundred feet, fragments storm across the site. They collide and explode for no apparent reason—except of course, for the one articulated by Harry and one of his men, Chick (Will Patton), in an exchange that makes explicit what the film has been implying: "I don't think this thing likes us," says Harry. Chick answers, demonizing their locale: "That's because it knows we're here to kill it." The filmmakers further augment the asteroid's presence by scoring establishing shots of the rock with an ethereal choir. This confers a quasi-spiritual aura upon the object of impending cataclysm and also strikes a sharp contrast to the hard rock songs and score that constitute much of the soundtrack.

Disney's publicity materials for *Armageddon* go into great detail about the filmmakers' consultations with NASA and the authentic hardware they either created or were allowed to use: the filmmakers photographed a space shuttle launch; built an eleven-ton, twelve-foot-high asteroid rover; and, for the first time in film history, photographed a real B2 Stealth Bomber—a precedent that would naturally fall to Jerry Bruckheimer to establish. But neither this, nor the freedom with which the characters sling impressive-sounding jargon (as they do in *The Rock*), disguises the outright hostility with which *Armageddon* regards science and intellect.

Before drafting Harry, Truman holds a meeting during which NASA scientists propose various ways of alleviating the threat of the asteroid. All are ineffectual intellectuals, and Truman dismisses each in turn. The first, stuttering and perspiring, is simply cut off. The second does not fare much better: older, bespectacled, and suggesting that a highly focused laser could break the asteroid apart, he is interrupted by Truman, who shows no patience for the scientist's short stream of big words. The third is similarly depicted as being soft: proposing that sails be attached to the asteroid so that solar winds shift its course, he is a pudgy man whose prop makes a silly noise. Truman vetoes anything that sounds like actual science and denigrates anyone who resembles an actual scientist, at least in comparison to the cowboy-saviors Truman will soon enlist. But what articulates the depths of the film's anti-intellectualism is that the end titles bill two of these scientists as "Dr. Nerd."

In Bay's world, however, it is not only the Dan Trumans who minimize and insult the smart. When it comes to answering critics, Bay himself is one of Hollywood's most outspoken directors. Responding to Peter Travers's scathing review of *Armageddon*, Bay wrote a letter to the editor of *Rolling Stone* asking if Travers knows something "that the other 100 million people around the world who saw my movie don't?" (Incidentally, while Bay claims that Tra-

vers hates blockbusters, the critic had been ardent in his enthusiasm for
Speed and *Air Force One*.) As Bay's letter continues, it seems to suggest that the
film's popularity is tantamount to, or should at least override questions of, its
quality.[65]

Elsewhere, Bay attacks his attackers by claiming that he makes movies for
audiences, not critics. Statements such as "Failure is when no one shows up.
When people—not critics—absolutely hate your movie" typify this stance.[66]
Similarly, Bruckheimer would say of his next collaboration with Bay, *Pearl Harbor*, "'We made it for people, not critics," while another of Bay's colleagues,
producer Tom Gorai, told *Entertainment Weekly*, "Michael's interests line up
perfectly with what the American public wants. I think a lot of directors would
be like that if they could put away their artistic guilt."[67] Such rhetoric is
shameful because with it, the filmmakers falsely polarize critics and "the
masses," and then align themselves with the latter. Bay is therefore positioned
as a vanguard of "the people," standing up for them against some rarified in-
telligentsia. To be effective, this defensiveness can only provoke the public's
latent (and sometimes not-so-latent) distrust of intellectualism.

It should not be surprising then that Bay's style also takes a combative
stance toward intellect, even if this stance is not as calculated as the counterattacks he directs toward his critics. His furious editing does more than dis-
rupt one's sense of geography; his unmotivated blaring of Aerosmith songs
does more than indulge an adolescent aesthetic (Bay's more than his audience's, one suspects). Critic Joe Morgenstern is not overstating his case when
he calls *Armageddon* "a crypto-fascist burlesque." He then clarifies: "Not that
'Armageddon' is pushing a political agenda. . . . But the movie tries, with scary
success, to induce a sort of Orwellian stupor that's the enemy of coherent
thought and feeling."[68]

Of course, not all critics are Bay's enemy. Disney actively courted some to
help deliver what the studio surely hoped would be a record-breaking opening
weekend, when *Armageddon* would open on more than three thousand screens.
The *Wall Street Journal* reports that Aviv solicited mostly television reporters—
even though their stories were not broadcast—to offer endorsements with the
letter O in the middle, such as "Wow!" With this request, Disney's hope was to
combine the reporters' quotes with the poster's main graphic: the fiery ring
through which Earth is viewed.[69] More than the sixty-second Super Bowl spot
for which Disney paid $2.6 million, Aviv's plan, along with Joe Roth's late-
stage commissioning of new special effects to freshen the advertising, illustrate the lengths to which studio executives will go in marketing such tentpole

releases. But marketing did not become a factor only in the later stages of production: the *Wall Street Journal* also claims that Roth wanted to release a movie with the title "Armageddon" before he even had a story concept. To acquire the title, he went so far as to trade two titles that Disney controlled ("Father's Day" and "Conspiracy Theory") to Joel Silver, who had already registered the title "Armageddon."[70]

Like *Independence Day* before it, *Armageddon* razes New York, but also represents disaster on a global scale. Widespread calamity also drives *The Core* (2003), a Paramount release that marks the return of the disaster movie after a roughly four-year lull. In the film, it seems that the molten outer core of our planet has stopped spinning, which is causing our electromagnetic field to collapse. *The Core* presents a solution to this crisis that is similar to the one in *Armageddon*, but instead of drilling into an asteroid and using a nuclear weapon to blow it up, the heroes of *The Core* must drill their way to the core of the Earth and use nuclear weapons to jumpstart it.

Dr. Josh Keyes (Aaron Eckhart) briefs the military that in a few months' time, "as the electromagnetic field becomes more unstable . . . anything, everything electronic will be fried." His colleague, Dr. Conrad Zimsky (Stanley Tucci) further predicts that, "static discharges in the atmosphere will create super storms with hundreds of lightning strikes per square mile." "After that," Josh interjects, "it gets bad." As it happens, the Earth's electromagnetic field is the planet's only protection from solar winds, which, Zimsky tells us, "are a lethal blend of radioactive particles and microwaves. When that shield collapses, microwave radiation will literally cook our planet."

Seeking to restart the core is a group of characters who resemble their 1970s disaster movie brethren. Josh, a geophysics professor, is a roll-up-his-sleeves intellectual, whose rarified education is tempered by a certain working-man ethos. Zimsky is his opposite, a self-interested elitist who puts his own fate above the community's. What's more, it was the weapon Zimsky developed, Project Destiny (Deep Earth Seismic Trigger Initiative) that has caused the core to shut down. This recalls the industrialists and bureaucrats of *The Poseidon Adventure*, *The Towering Inferno*, and others, but with an interesting wrinkle. Whereas the disaster movie canon has the industrialist endanger the community because he cut corners, Zimsky, we are told, developed Project Destiny *beyond* all military-approved specifications.

In addition to Josh, Zimsky, and two other scientists, the team includes astronauts Major Rebecca "Beck" Childs (Hilary Swank) and Commander Major Iverson (Bruce Greenwood). They are certainly exceptional in their own right

(Beck is the youngest astronaut to have reached space and in an early sequence, saves the space shuttle from certain destruction), but because they are more adventurers than academics, they have a blue-collar sensibility. This puts them on the opposite end of the spectrum from Zimsky, with Josh in the middle— just as William Holden's industrialist and Steve McQueen's firefighter define the range of characters in The Towering Inferno, with Paul Newman's architect occupying the middle ground between them. This same dynamic is seen in Earthquake, in which the range of characters is defined by Lorne Greene's industrialist patriarch at one end, George Kennedy's beat cop at the other, and Charlton Heston's engineer in the middle. Portions of this range can be found in Airport, The Poseidon Adventure, and others.

Though the film's basic premise is outlandish, there is some science that supports it. On March 3, 2003, Dr. J. Marvin Herndon announced new findings taken from computer simulations and from helium data derived from oceanic basalts that suggest the Earth's center is a giant, natural nuclear reactor powering the electromagnetic field and that the lifetime of this "georeactor" could be coming to a close. But it would be difficult to set any sort of doomsday clock by Herndon's predictions. "The furnace could expire in as little as 100 years or as long as a billion years," he writes, "the uncertainty is great."[71] The timing of this revelation is noteworthy: Herndon made his March 3 announcement just weeks before The Core's March 28 release. Indeed, Herndon's theory was published in the Proceedings of the National Academy of Science and was also issued as a Paramount Pictures press release—with The Core's title stamped large across the top.

Herndon's theory did not receive much support from the scientific community. In the film, Josh and Zimsky's theory is supported by the only community that counts: the military. The government funds the construction of a vessel capable of penetrating the Earth to its core, and delivering a nuclear payload of one thousand megatons. The characters christen the ship Virgil, after the Greek poet whose Aeneid chronicles, in part, an exploration of the underworld and who appears in Dante's Inferno to give a guided tour of Hell. The ship is made of a metal that converts the immense heat and pressure of the Earth's core into energy that reinforces the ship, a metal named "unobtanium." Virgil, according to co-screenwriter John Rogers (who holds a degree in physics from McGill University), is "the big cheat."[72] According to Rogers, "Unobtanium was an intentional joke. It's a real word used by engineers for a needed material that doesn't exist in our current framework. It was a scientist from [Jet Propulsion Laboratories] who reminded me of it."[73]

This cheat aside, though, *The Core* venerates the scientists—and the science—it depicts. As Rogers explains,

The approach I took was [to emulate] a 1960s movie like *Fantastic Voyage* and *Andromeda Strain*, where square-jawed scientists solve the problem and save the day. I wanted to write the kind of movie that [as a kid] made me want to be a scientist. . . . Somewhere in the '80s, it became all about the butch hero, and science was sent to the sidelines. In our movies today, scientists are just bad; they make clones and doomsday devices.[74]

Indeed, the film's respect for the intellectual is what differentiates *The Core* from *Armageddon*. Otherwise, the two films resemble each other conceptually and also structurally: as in *Armageddon*, *The Core* features three major sequences of calamity set against various international locales while our heroes struggle to save the planet. (In *Armageddon*, the locations are New York, Shanghai, and Paris; in *The Core*, they are London, Rome, and San Francisco.) The first of these sequences is set in London's Trafalgar Square, where a mass of birds flies into statues, buildings, fleeing crowds, a double-decker bus (which overturns), and a bookstore, shattering the window.

The next two sequences are even more special effects-driven. A lightning superstorm strikes Rome, cleaving up a street, exploding the Colosseum, and demolishing the Victor Emmanuel Building, a symbol of Italy's unification. The sequence begins with a nine-second take in which the camera tracks backward to reveal more and more people rising and looking with reverence at some offscreen phenomenon. This cues the calamity that is to come. As the lightning strikes, the Colosseum (actually a half-inch scale model rigged with primer cord) explodes over ten seconds, with twelve shots that were photographed at three hundred frames per second.[75] Naturally, the major camera set-up, in which the icon explodes toward camera, factored prominently in *The Core*'s trailer.

In the final sequence—which shares nearly the same running time as the other two—a hole in the electromagnetic field opens over San Francisco. Solar radiation pours through to bake the city. Underwater, we follow dead fish as they float upward. In reality, these were fish purchased from a seafood wholesaler, filled with compressed air, and photographed in a tank at special effects facility Fantasy II. Into this shot, the filmmakers composited a stylized reveal of the Golden Gate Bridge seen from beneath the water's surface.[76] On the bridge, a radiation beam scalds a motorist and then destroys the bridge, which, in the final shot, collapses section by section in a single eight-second take. According to The Core's visual effects supervisor, Greg McMurry (who also was responsible for parceling out the film's nearly four hundred effects shots to more than fifteen vendors), "I thought of this effect as God's magnifying glass. . . . We went through a few iterations about where this could take place, trying to keep our sensitivity about events. At one point it was a backyard barbeque scene, which was quite horrific."[77]

Such a sensitivity underlies Todd McCarthy's observation that

> watching a disaster movie isn't what it used to be; it's too difficult to invent scenes of calamitous catastrophe that don't somehow produce the uneasy feeling that such things could actually happen. . . . [S]cenes of the Golden Gate Bridge and the Colosseum being obliterated, along with much of the beautiful cities that contain them, just don't provide the escape they once did.[78]

McCarthy also cites an early scene in which the space shuttle Endeavor crash-lands in the Los Angeles River. This sequence might have made moviegoers bristle as the February 1, 2003 disintegration of the space shuttle Columbia was still fresh in the public's memory. Though Paramount did not re-edit the scene or change The Core's opening day (the film had already been bumped from its original November 1 release date to dedicate more time to refining the special effects), the studio did pull the trailer, which highlighted the shuttle sequence.[79] But Rogers, who points out that The Core was released during the second week of the United States–led war in Iraq, recalls the audience's reaction at the film's first public screening: "The crowd went nuts when the space shuttle landed. People forget that the movies are where we work out our id shit. But [as a culture] we have not yet moved through our five stages of death and dying over September 11. I think we're still in anger. Or at least depression" (emphasis in original).[80]

Jon Amiel signed to direct The Core less than two weeks after September 11, which would make him one of the first directors to commit to such a large-scale disaster or action movie in the wake of the attacks.[81] For his part, Roland Emmerich would be one of the first directors to return disaster to the city still healing from that deep blow to its skyline and psyche. While Emmerich's The Day After Tomorrow (2004) imagines a massive—and sudden—climate shift that brings a new ice age upon the Northern hemisphere, much of the film's action and drama are set in New York, where high school whiz kid Sam Hall (Jake Gyllenhaal) and his friends are trapped.

As the New York Times reported just before the film opened, "There was some nervousness about creating the first big-budget movie to devastate New York since the attacks on the World Trade Center. Indeed, in one aerial view, one of the first places struck by a giant tidal surge is that now-vacant part of the city."[82] Emmerich, also the film's co-screenwriter, claims that he deliberated whether or not to set his disaster epic in New York, but decided "New York is such a symbol of Western civilization. . . I finally felt that setting the film in another city would be an even bigger problem, because then the terrorists would have influenced where the catastrophe of weather strikes."[83] In other words, if New York is not destroyed, then the terrorists win.

The film incited some political passions, but their locus was not September 11; rather, it was the environment. In the film, the ice age is triggered by rising global temperatures, which have melted polar ice and disrupted normal ocean currents. This inflamed the passions of many activists and a few whistleblowers, too. When NASA, via e-mail, officially banned any of its employees from granting interviews about, or otherwise commenting on, The Day After Tomorrow, one senior NASA scientist gave a copy of the message to the New York Times. As the Times reported, the scientist claimed to resent "attempts to muzzle researchers dealing with climate change." The Times quoted another scientist, a federal climate researcher, who said, "It's just another attempt to play down anything that might lead to the conclusion that something must be done."[84]

As the Times notes, NASA ultimately relaxed its position, but the film still contains "potential embarrassments" for the White House. One is the direct indictment of an ersatz-Bush administration. Another is that the film's hero (and Sam's father), Dennis Quaid's Dr. Jack Hall, is a paleoclimatologist who investigates prehistoric climate shifts for the National Oceanic and Atmospheric Administration. But according to the Times, "President Bush's proposed 2005 budget for the administration would sharply cut the agency's paleoclimatology program, which began under the first Bush administration."[85]

Fox, anticipating that this fictional ice age could set off a political firestorm, did take steps to contain any possible controversy. As reported in the Wall Street Journal, the film blames the catastrophe on "global climate change" rather than on global warming. "The 'W' word is scarcely used in the movie or its website. Fox fears that if it appears to take sides in the scientific and political debate over global warming, that could spark a media storm and hurt the box office," the Journal reports, citing a source "close to the filmmakers." The Journal goes on to cite a Fox spokesman's denial that the word choice had any connection to the conservative politics of Rupert Murdoch, owner of Fox's parent company, News Corp.[86]

On the left, the progressive organization MoveOn.org dispatched thousands of volunteers to movie theaters over the film's Memorial Day opening weekend with leaflets headlined "Global warming isn't just a movie. It's your future." Likewise, two smaller organizations, Global Exchange and the Rainforest Action Network, organized volunteers to hand out postcards at 110 theaters in 80 cities. The postcards depicted SUVs buried in snow. *Variety* reported on these plans, as well as on their possible financial consequences for the studio: "As a small potential boon for 20th Century Fox, which produced the $125 million spectacle pic, all three groups are encouraging their volunteers to see the movie before they hand out literature."[87]

Meanwhile, as *Variety* also notes, the conservative RightMarch.com created its own flier, reading in part, "Don't let radical left-wing environmentalists fool you. . . . Because the day after tomorrow, radical leftists may have wrecked America's economy."[88] In the film, a Dick Cheney surrogate (and look-alike) says as much. Castigating Jack, Vice President Becker (Kenneth Welsh), growls that the nation's economy is just as fragile as the climate. This vice president is the shortsighted corporate stooge of so many disaster movies. Coupled with the film's depiction of the President as a George W. Bush stand-in (in-over-his-head comportment and all), it becomes clear that Emmerich is blasting the White House—perhaps not as literally as he did in *Independence Day*, but blasting it nonetheless.

The most visible political gesture surrounding the film may have been the rally MoveOn.org sponsored four blocks from the film's May 24 premiere at New York's American Museum of Natural History. Promoting the rally, environmental advocate and former vice president Al Gore claimed that the film "presents us with a great opportunity to talk about the scientific realities of climate change. Millions of people will be coming out of theaters on Memorial Day weekend asking the question, 'Could this really happen?' I think we need to answer that question."[89]

The answer, of course, would be no. The calamity of *The Day After Tomorrow* takes place on a hilariously quickened timetable. Early in the film, Jack warns us that such a climate change could take place over hundreds or thousands of years. As the storms gather force, he revises this estimate to six to eight weeks. He later posits seven to ten days. Ultimately, the deep freeze seems to take forty-eight to seventy-two hours. This, of course, is the film's *Virgil*, its major cheat. Otherwise, *The Day After Tomorrow* has an admirable respect for science and intellect, and prizes problem-solving the same way other action films prize muscle or firepower. Jack, Sam, and even Sam's brainy friend, Brian Parks (Arjay Smith), are treated as heroes for their intellect.

Jack, a member of the rugged elite that also includes characters played by Aaron Eckhart, Pierce Brosnan, Paul Newman, Charlton Heston, and others, is granted extra measures of heroism. "Jack, you've been working for twenty-four hours straight," says one of Jack's Washington, D.C., colleagues, "You're the only one who hasn't taken a break." Here, Jack is set apart from the rest—a classic, if subtle, case of action movie exceptionality. Later, Jack, who has been told by another colleague to "save as many as you can," receives a phone call from Sam, trapped in New York. Jack declares, "I will come for you," and with this assertion, changes his mission at the movie's one-hour mark, which in many movies, is reserved for the moment when the hero stops being reactive and starts taking charge. From here, Jack treks to Manhattan on a personal quest that contradicts his duty to save as many people as possible. If this contradiction is not immediately apparent, it is because *The Day After Tomorrow*, while celebrating the rational mind, is still governed by an emotional logic.

The same logic hides the disconnect in Jack's later line, "Mankind survived the last ice age; we're certainly capable of surviving this one. Depends on whether or not we're able to learn from our mistakes." Though this may seem sensical, the first thought actually does not connect to the second. Judging from the film's final image—the Earth sheathed in ice and snow—mankind will not be burning much fossil fuel anytime soon. Survival in this new world would seem to depend not on learning from our mistakes, but on learning to find shelter and food. However, this cold fact does not lend itself to the movie moralizing that Emmerich seems to prize.

Still, in *The Day After Tomorrow*, as in all disaster films, the political, the intellectual, and the emotional, are all secondary to the spectacle. Here, the spectacle comprises 416 special effects shots crafted by thirteen different vendors.[90] Though catastrophe strikes an Antarctic ice shelf, Tokyo, and Los Angeles, Emmerich visits the brunt of nature's force on New York. In the major sequence, running about two minutes and twenty-two seconds, a wave all but overtakes the Statue of Liberty and floods Manhattan. The sequence begins with an aerial shot of the statue, as the camera revolves roughly 180 degrees around her. A great storm surge rises and washes over her—but never tops her shoulders. In fact, even the spray from the first crash of water never gets above the torch. This one shot lasts a full twenty-five seconds.

The next two shots total twenty seconds and begin a "Wall of Water" effect (so dubbed by an offscreen radio announcer) that is a counterpart to *Independence Day*'s Wall of Destruction. In the first shot, the camera follows the wave in and cuts just as it hits the island. The second shot, from further up, provides even more scale than the first: looking down from a steeper angle, we see Manhattan inundated. On the street, the reactions of a blue-collar bus driver and a well-off passenger cue the wave's cataclysmic effects, as people and vehicles are bowled over. Emmerich then provides another aerial shot—a single ten-second take—as water rushes into the channels of Manhattan's grid. The floodwaters bear down on the main branch of the New York Public Library, with one shot riding alongside the wave as if the camera were surfing. Sam and his friends, including his love interest, Laura (Emmy Rossum, later of Poseidon, Wolfgang Petersen's remake of The Poseidon Adventure), dash for cover inside the library. They race up its main staircase as water—and a taxicab—smash through the windows. The sequence ends with another aerial view, looking down for eight seconds at the New York canals.

The Statue of Liberty reappears later, when Jack and a fellow adventurer discover her buried up to her neck in the whiteout. As the New Yorker points out, this image is unlike its counterpart in Independence Day, in which the Statue of Liberty floats sideways against the background of New York's ruined skyline. Instead, this image from The Day After Tomorrow, with Liberty's torch still thrust skyward, "is more resilient and hopeful."[91] The effect is bolstered by the accompanying swell of composer Harald Kloser's main theme—an anthem crossed with a dirge.

Sam and company spend much of the film's remainder inside the library. Along with the other survivors, they change into whatever dry clothes are available. In mismatching jackets and hats, they look like refugees. The imagery is especially resonant now, in a post–Hurricane Katrina America—not unlike images of the World Trade Center in Independence Day, Godzilla, Armageddon, The Siege, and others. The library itself is an apt setting. Not only is it an impressive set (the library's interior and exterior totaled fifty thousand square feet), but it also represents a repository of mankind's history and accumulated knowledge.[92] Therefore, as the world outside is wiped clear, and as the cold encroaches on the library itself, this place marks a line in the snow: Culture's Last Stand.

Along with the Statue of Liberty and the New York Public Library, other icons are punished throughout the movie: Emmerich destroys the Hollywood sign and the Capitol Records Building with tornadoes that whip through Los Angeles. The Empire State Building freezes. And the American flag itself makes several major appearances. The first is during the film's opening. Emmerich opens The Day After Tomorrow with a single tracking shot over a computer-generated arctic terrain. Virtually all of the main titles appear over this shot.

There's Got to Be a Thawing After: *The frozen torch of the Statue of Liberty as both an icon of disaster and a beacon to the survivors of* The Day After Tomorrow *(2004). (From the author's collection.)*

When Emmerich makes his first cut, it is from this expansive landscape to a frame-filling American flag. Over the flag, a superimposition appears: "Larsen B Ice Shelf, Antarctica." This is a curious juxtaposition that recalls *Independence Day*, which begins with a view of the moon and quickly reveals the American flag staked to the lunar surface. In both cases, Emmerich (a German) opens his films with a non-national environment and brands them as American. Emmerich twists this patriotism later, when Jack's colleague Frank (Jay O. Sanders) comes upon a flag on their odyssey to New York. The camera zooms in on a horrified Frank as the flag itself freezes. Underscored by a dizzying exclamation from Kloser's 130-piece orchestra, this cements the stakes: with his third disaster-"actioner" in less than ten years, Emmerich has taken us from the Cold War to a War on Cold.

The Day After Tomorrow depicts a global (or near-global) catastrophe and focuses it through the lens of the national. So does the following summer's *War of the Worlds*, directed by Steven Spielberg. One of the major event pictures of 2005, *War of the Worlds* pits Tripods from Mars against the defenseless people of Earth, and follows the flight of Ray Ferrier (Tom Cruise) and his children to Boston, where the children's mother awaits them.

Spielberg's *War of the Worlds* is the latest incarnation of this invasion tale, the original being H. G. Wells' classic science fiction novel, first published in 1898. As the director and others have noted, it often seems that the story is adapted anew during periods of acute cultural stress. Wells wrote the novel against the backdrop of unease related to the British Empire's colonialism and industrialization; Orson Welles induced much panic with a Halloween radio broadcast in 1938, when the world's most prominent background noise was the rise of Nazism in Germany; and the 1953 feature film was one of many alien invasion movies through which Hollywood focused Cold War anxieties. Of his 2005 adaptation, Spielberg claims,

> 9/11 reinformed everything I'm putting into [the film]. . . . We now know what it feels like to be terrorized. . . . And suddenly, for the first time since the Revolutionary War, we know what it's like to have our two front teeth knocked out, which is what happened when they took down both towers of the World Trade Center.[93]

Indeed, the 2005 *War of the Worlds* is the rare entertainment in which the traumas of and surrounding September 11 factor not only into the backdrop of the production, but also into the film's atmosphere, visual style, and even its special effects. Both Janusz Kaminski's cinematography and the special effects created by Industrial Light and Magic take a documentary-like approach to the spectacle—an untraditional mode for a summer event movie. ILM animation supervisor Randy Dutram claims that he and his collaborators drew inspiration from footage of the September 11 attacks, the December 2004 Asian tsunami, and combat documentaries.[94]

In fact, Spielberg, the artists under his charge, and screenwriters Josh Friedman and David Koepp craft images and scenarios of the aftermath of the attack that are so authentic that they not only recall these crises, but also predict imagery of Hurricane Katrina, the United States' worst natural disaster to date. War of the Worlds opened just two months before the hurricane struck; after seeing images of the devastated Gulf Coast, viewers watching the film's streams of civilians walk alongside the highway, unable to leave the city, and hearing those survivors referred to as "refugees," would certainly be reminded of the disaster. Critic Scott Foundas takes this further, seeing in the film an even more extensive catalogue of modern horrors, with scenes that cite September 11, the Los Angeles riots of 1992, Rwanda's corpse-littered rivers, World War II battlefields and deportation trains, and even the doom of the Titanic.[95]

Among the images that most evoke September 11 are the film's sky-filling haze, walls of photographs of the missing, and in a particularly telling moment, Spielberg's push-in on a dropped video camera as it records the panic and destruction wrought by the first Martian attack and the first human disintegration by the Martians' heat rays. The video camera may not itself be a totem of September 11, but in the context of this scene, it is an emblem of our obsession with witnessing, recording, and thus ritualizing images of destruction. Moreover, this visual cue—and how it is used to distance the viewer from the action—is merely how Spielberg introduces this notion of bearing witness; he develops it later with chilling effect. In the meantime, Ray is a witness to—and barely a survivor of—this initial onslaught. Only after racing home to his weekend guests (his children) does he realize he is covered in ash. The ash is one of the film's most pointed evocations of September 11, recalling the many televised and still images of World Trade Center survivors covered in the dust of the collapsed towers. Ray then speeds his children away from his New Jersey neighborhood, from the ongoing attack. As people and buildings are pulverized (and preceding one of the film's showcase effects, a roughly fifteen-second tracking shot in which the Bayonne Bridge and several blocks of homes are destroyed), Rachel, played by Dakota Fanning, cries out in close-up, "Is it the terrorists?" The line is especially noteworthy for Rachel's slight qualifier. She does not ask "Is it terrorists?" but rather, "Is it the terrorists?" Though subtle, this distinction is a definitive stamp that marks *War of the Worlds* as belonging to the popular culture of a post–September 11 America.

The attacks of September 11 spawned a host of secondary traumas including deepened political divisiveness, widened religious divides, other terrorist threats, the war in Iraq, the Abu Gharib scandal, and the loss of coalition forces to an Iraqi insurgency. In addition to making specific references to September 11, *War of the Worlds* also manifests this more compounded anxiety—in some cases, more pointedly than in others. Koepp has gone so far as to declare, "The local insurgency always kills you. . . . I view [*War of the Worlds*] as an antiwar film, especially an anti–Iraq War film."[96] In this respect, *War of the Worlds* embodies modern America's most severe domestic trauma (the September 11 attacks), as well as its greatest international crisis (the war in Iraq). Rachel, while putting a fine point on our September 11 trauma, also embodies a more diffused discomfort. In the film's first forty minutes, she reveals that she has claustrophobia, back problems, and a world-weariness that are all especially disquieting when seen in a ten-year-old. Even her wardrobe, a riot of colors and patterns, provokes a general unease—especially in contrast to the more monochromatic clothes worn by her father and brother, Robbie (Justin Chatwin).

Costume designer Joanna Johnston acknowledges that manifesting a sense of cultural unease in Rachel's wardrobe was a subconscious process. More conscious was her interest in designing Rachel's clothes to express the tension between two of the film's main concerns: Rachel's little girlhood on the one hand, and on the other, war. In fact, one of Johnston's favorite (and subtlest) costume elements is Rachel's vest, embodying both facets of the film with pink camouflage. According to Johnston, who researched images of earthquake, flood, and September 11 victims,

> [Rachel] is a bit like an onion, and you can peel her away. That's what's going on in her clothing as well. She was the epitome of a little girl, and had all those characteristics in her clothing: pattern on pattern, color, vibrancy, she knew what she liked. Right alongside that is the fact that in a way, she becomes the thermometer of what is happening.[97]

Johnston designed the costumes to suggest Rachel's sense of style, but also to illustrate a consequence of disaster: "When the chips are down, do the clothes matter? They don't. Rachel's not worried that she's completely ragged. It's about survival."[98] This marks the most intriguing irony in Johnston's work:

standing out from the monochrome of her father and brother, Rachel constantly draws the viewer's eye, yet the purpose of her style is to underscore its own irrelevance, and with it, the loss of the only way of life known to a little girl, her family, her society.

Though not through his clothing, Robbie embodies many of the same anxieties Rachel does. A sullen teenager writing a paper about the French occupation of Algeria, he is not on the run for very long before his frustration turns to bloodlust. Spying a military convoy, Robbie breaks away from Ray and Rachel. He insists that the soldiers have room for him and begs them to let him join their campaign as they roll past. After enduring several more attacks, Robbie once again leaves his family behind, this time not enraged so much as transfixed by the flashes of light and artillery explosions that crown a distant hilltop. He runs faster, ignoring Ray's charge to "stay together," and is soon racing up the hill, trying to keep pace with the military vehicles rushing into the fight. Ray gives chase, and near the top of the hill, tries to pin Robbie to the ground face-down. The camera revolves around Robbie, all but hypnotized by the battle, and settles on his close-up. His eyes are wide and his father's voice is far away. Ray turns Robbie over. The two face each other. "I know you wanna fight," Ray says. "I know it seems like you have to, but you don't!"

Though trying to reach his son, Ray does not hear him. So close to the frontlines, Robbie is not saying "I want to fight." He is saying, "I need to see this." When Ray turns to see Rachel being pulled at by strangers and turns back to Robbie, Robbie is still insisting. "I need to be here. I want to see this. Please let me go," he whispers. "*You need to let me go.*" As Ray's daughter cries out for him, Ray releases his son, but his hands linger over empty space as the boy slips away. Spielberg and editor Michael Kahn cut to a ground-level shot tracking back with Robbie as he crawls forward; Robbie and the camera both leave Ray behind. The filmmakers then cut to Robbie rising and turning; he and his father regard each other one more time against a backdrop of flashing light and haze and screams. Father and son turn away from each other: Ray charges after his daughter while Robbie races into the fray. Cradling Rachel, Ray turns back to the hilltop. Jeeps, on fire, roll down from just over the hillcrest. They are followed by a great conflagration—in reality, a four-hundred-foot-tall practical wall of flames.[99] After a beat, a Martian war machine emerges from the fire, forcing Ray to turn away for the last time.

Here, it is not Robbie's desire to fight that reflects America's post–September 11 mindset; it is the fact that at the top of this war-torn hill, Robbie's attraction to battle is reduced not to bloodlust, but to an irresistible compulsion to *see.*

This need to behold spectacular disaster, taken to the point of self-annihilation, serves as an indictment of our own compulsive intake of such images. This appetite of ours, both fed and deepened by twenty-four-hour cable news channels and the internet, may be best represented by news outlets' constant replaying of footage showing the two airplanes strike the World Trade Center and the towers' later collapse. Robbie's choice to be a witness to disaster rather than a survivor of it, suggests also that in a country oversaturated by media, the need to see has become more base, more primal, than even the need to repel invading hordes.

Until that point, however, Robbie's hunger to fight is a shadow of Robert's in *Red Dawn*. And like Robert's end, which he meets in a mythic dust-cloud, Robbie's presumed death is not seen, but inferred from the hilltop inferno. (In what is widely regarded to be the film's most disappointing moment, Robbie reappears at the film's end, alive and, in the process, blunts what has otherwise been one of Spielberg's edgier tales.) To say that Robbie and Robert parallel each other is not to suggest that *War of the Worlds* directly cites *Red Dawn*; rather, it is but one of the ways in which the two films share a certain, dark kinship. Both films are set against the backdrop of a global conflict but are concerned with the occupation of, and an insurgency within, America. Both films depict a world war through a limited number of eyes: in *War of the Worlds*, the film's point of view almost always shares that of at least one member of the Ferrier family; in *Red Dawn*, the film's perspective is largely that of the insurgent Wolverines—and even where director John Milius cuts to the leaders of the occupying forces, the audience's view of World War III never leaves the areas surrounding the film's mountain town.

Additionally, both films share at least one use of iconography. Early in *Red Dawn*, the camera looks out over the town square, deserted but for occupying troops small in the distance. In the foreground, a statue of one of Theodore Roosevelt's Rough Riders anchors the frame. Likewise, late in *War of the Worlds*, Ray and Rachel enter Boston, where they see a Minuteman statue covered in Martian growth that has withered and died. Both images lend themselves to two opposing readings. On the one hand, they are both pregnant with a sense of occupation, both totems of an indomitable spirit that, it would seem, has at last been dominated. On the other hand, they also suggest the futility of occupation, and a sense of stalwartness in the face of temporary—if terrible—change.

Red Dawn is also an artifact of the Cold War, and while Spielberg's version of *War of the Worlds* is not, the film tradition to which it belongs has formidable roots in the era. Furthermore, while Paramount's 1953 The War of the Worlds and its alien-invasion cousins were made decades before 1984's Red Dawn, the late 1980s saw War of the Worlds come to television, as a syndicated series that ran for two seasons, from 1988 to 1990. Conceived as a sequel to the film (and distributed and co-produced by Paramount Television), the program finds the Martians now able to assume human form. This echoes another of the era's televised occupation-and-resistance science fiction adventures, NBC's V, inspired by the resistance movements of World War II. This "they-are-among-us" conceit, while making for more cost-effective science fiction, also anticipates the remake of Battlestar Galactica, a drama produced with a decidedly post–September 11 sensibility. The 1980s also saw a vision of The War of the Worlds that would never come to be realized: in 1986, between V and the War of the Worlds television series, Paramount began developing a remake of the 1953 film with veteran producer David Picker and director George Romero.[100] As Romero's 1968 zombie classic Night of the Living Dead has been given a number of political and countercultural readings—many pertaining to Vietnam—it is likely that the horror auteur would have made one of the decade's most interesting, and paranoid, invasion stories.

As one might expect, 2005's War of the Worlds has more in common with the 1950s disaster template than with what may be considered the more "classical" disaster movie of the 1970s. For instance, War of the Worlds is not obsessed with community, nor does the film strictly define community as a diverse collection of types. This distinguishes War of the Worlds from Independence Day, a fusion of 1950s and 1970s disaster tropes. In addition, Spielberg's approach to spectacle further distinguishes War of the Worlds from Independence Day and many other modern disaster movies, as well as from many of Spielberg's own films. Not only were the film's forty-seven minutes of effects created in a brief twelve weeks, but as senior visual effects supervisor Dennis Muren also notes, the special effects all unfold within Ray's perspective, and are discovered by the audience only when they enter the frame behind or around Ray.[101] According to Muren, a more traditional "Hollywood" style of filmmaking would have revealed the effects with more reverence. The filmmakers would have shown Tom Cruise, then cut to his point of view of the effect he was revering, cut back to Cruise, then back to the effect coming forward, then back to Cruise as he rolled out of its way.[102]

This "Hollywood" approach typifies many of the era's disaster pictures. The approach taken by Spielberg, however, while sacrificing a measure of awe, gives the action a greater sense of urgency—not to mention a sense of real-

The Insurgency Is in Its
Last Throes: Tim
Robbins, Tom Cruise,
and Dakota Fanning
huddle in the face of
all-but-certain doom in
Steven Spielberg's 2005
version of War of the
Worlds. (From the
author's collection.)

ism. Spielberg makes this the through-line of the film's style, applying this aesthetic not only to the visual effects, but to his direction of the camera as well. Whether they are fighter jets, or Ray's ex-wife standing in his driveway, objects are revealed through camera movement rather than editing. Likewise, during the first attack, the camera makes room in the frame for special effects by tilting up from Ray, then back down, the way a person might crane his or her head.

Realism and the main character's point of view were also important to screenwriter David Koepp. According to the *Los Angeles Times*, on the way to his first meeting with Spielberg to discuss the project, Koepp compiled a list of alien attack tropes that would not appear in the film. As Koepp told the *Times*,

> "I'm sick and tired of watching New York get pummeled in movies and reality. . . . No scenes of beating up on New York. No destruction of famous landmarks. No shots of world capitals. No TV reporters saying what's going on. No shots of generals with big sticks pushing battleships around the map. Let's not see the war of the world. Let's see this guy's survival story."[103]

From the outset then, the filmmakers pursued a strategy that gave rise to their era's most intimate disaster film—a surprising distinction for a movie titled *War of the Worlds*. But with Tom Cruise as the focal point, the film, even while prizing the personal over the spectacle, and viewing a specific historical juncture through a particularly American lens, still became a worldwide hit.

Paramount opened *War of the Worlds* on Wednesday, June 29, less than eight months after the first day of principal photography. Twentieth Century Fox, not wanting to contend with *War of the Worlds*, moved the opening of its *Fantastic Four* to July 8 from July 1, a date the studio had staked out more than a year and a half in advance.[104] Capitalizing on a six-day opening (from Wednesday through the July 4 holiday weekend), *War of the Worlds* grossed approximately $113 million domestically in the first five days, while the foreign box office totaled another $102.5 million in seventy-eight countries. Totaling nearly a quarter of a billion dollars in less than a week, these returns were considered strong but a little below industry expectations—or perhaps the industry's hopes, given that it was looking to *War of the Worlds* to break a much publicized eighteen-week box office slump, the worst since 1985.[105]

As was widely discussed at the time, one factor in the film's failure to break this slump may have been the fact that Tom Cruise's publicity overshadowed that of *War of the Worlds*. In the weeks leading up to the film's release, Cruise garnered much attention (a good deal of it negative) for his well-publicized enthusiasm for Scientology, attacks on psychiatry, and romance with actress Katie Holmes, the female lead of the same summer's *Batman Begins*. The following summer, many within the industry hitched Cruise's public persona to the underwhelming opening weekend of his next tentpole movie, *Mission: Impossible III*. The film's three-day gross of $48 million was more than ten million below industry expectations and the opening of *Mission: Impossible II* six years earlier.[106] The "failure" these films represent also illustrates the insanity of motion picture economics, wherein long-term financial projections derived from opening weekend grosses (network, cable, and home video revenue)—to say nothing of production costs and marketing budgets—can dictate that earning a quarter of a billion dollars in seven days is good, but not good enough.

It was not long before *War of the Worlds*'s foreign grosses outpaced its domestic returns: the film opened in over 90 percent of the globe on the same day; just over a month later, the film had grossed $500 million worldwide, with international grosses beating domestic ones by nearly $100 million.[107] To ensure the film's blockbuster status, distributors, marketers, publicists, and the filmmakers themselves all targeted markets the world over. According to *Screen International*, the film's international distributor, UIP, released teaser trailers in twenty-six different languages. These included Japanese, Russian, Mandarin, Cantonese, Korean, Greek, Portuguese, Spanish, Thai, and, for the Indian market, both Tamil and Hindi. In addition, an alternate English version was created for the Southern hemisphere, replacing references to summer with ones to winter.[108]

Further underscoring the importance of the international market, the first of six *War of the Worlds* premieres was held in Tokyo, as Tokyo attracts the Asian media that serves one of the globe's fastest-growing markets. Representatives from 80 foreign media outlets covered the *War of the Worlds* premiere, taking their places among 80 television cameras and 150 photographers.[109] Holding a world premiere internationally guarantees greater foreign media coverage (indeed, Japan's domestic media treats premieres more as news than as fluff pieces covered only by entertainment press, thereby raising awareness among Japanese citizens).[110] A foreign premiere also compensates for the one pitfall of a "day-and-date" opening, an increasingly popular distribution strategy in which studios release their tentpole films domestically and internationally on the same date: with a worldwide release, foreign marketing and publicity efforts have no material to use from a film's earlier, high-profile debut in America.[111]

The marketing and publicity of *War of the Worlds*, like that of *Independence Day*, *Godzilla*, *Armageddon*, and others, was as titanic as the catastrophes these films depict, and as insistent as the communities forged by the disasters. The contemporary disaster films are action movies that inherited the *Die Hard* model's besieged setting, as well as elements from different disaster cycles. They constitute a sub-strain of the action genre that is at once nostalgic for the movies of other decades and emblematic of its day. The 1990s saw a revolution in special effects technology and the loss of traditional villains, as well as increasing globalization and the continued absorption of studios into multinational corporate conglomerates. Against this backdrop, these new disaster films, in which spectacle trumps story and dialogue and the enemy knows no nationality, were prime Hollywood exports: after all, everyone speaks the universal language of *big fire*.

In these films, the extraordinary and the irrevocable befall the world. But what of action films where the world itself is extraordinary? Such movies, perpetuating but also skewing the genre's most basic models, compose the final trends in this study. Gathering together elements of science fiction, video games, comic books, and here and there, dashes of the apocalypse, many of these films present a vision of tomorrow that is midnight-dark.

Tomorrow's Heroes Today
Action Meets the Fantastic

Fellow executives, it gives me great pleasure to
introduce you to the future of law enforcement.
—Dick Jones (Ronny Cox) in Robocop *(1987)*

Of all the films to use computer-generated special effects, among the most noteworthy is *The Matrix* (1999), one of the last pop culture phenomena of the twentieth century. The film belongs to a major trend in the genre that merges action with science fiction. We have already considered two of this trend's vital (and related) facets: the *Terminator* franchise and the 1980s infatuation with the postapocalyptic. In addition to these, *The Matrix* has science fiction-action progenitors that have not yet been taken into account. These include films that interrogate notions of identity, reality, and more subtly, our troubled relationship with media. In addition to the overtly science fictional, *The Matrix* is also the product of an Asian influence, one that is constituted mainly by the Hong Kong action cinema of John Woo and others. The imagery drawn from this influence is charged with an exoticism that translates into a sense of the otherworldly.

Among *The Matrix*'s sources that critics—and the filmmakers—cite are *Blade Runner, The Terminator, The X-Files, Men in Black, 2001: A Space Odyssey*, Lewis Carroll, *Total Recall*, Greek mythology, Jungian psychology, Eastern philosophy, higher mathematics, comic books, computer games, the Bible, Philip K. Dick, William Gibson's cyberpunk writings, kung fu movies, John Woo films, and even *The Adventures of Buckaroo Banzai*. Written and directed by brothers Larry and Andy Wachowski and produced by Joel Silver, *The Matrix* takes its title from the computer construct that humanity mistakes for late-twentieth-century "reality." In the Matrix, built in the aftermath of an apocalyptic war between artificial intelligence and the human race that created it, we are not actually going to work, to the mall, to the movies. Only our minds are. Our bodies are being fed to machines for energy. But some humans have managed to free themselves. One of these "freed minds" is Morpheus (Lawrence Fishburne), who has spent his waking life searching for "The One"—a messianic warrior whose mind is so powerful, it can bend the Matrix to its will and end the war between man and machine. Morpheus believes he has found The One in Keanu Reeves's Neo (an anagram of "one"), who thinks he is "Tom Anderson," a computer programmer, a nobody. Morpheus teaches Neo that as The One, he can bend, and sometimes break, the "rules" of the Matrix, including the laws of physics.

Outside the computer construct, the real world is as choking a wasteland as that of The Road Warrior, but the Wachowskis trade Miller's arid vistas for their own high-tech dystopia. In this vision, humanity has "darkened the skies" in an attempt to cut off the machines from their solar-derived power; now, the machines "grow" crops of humans for ingestion under inky black, lightning-lashed skies. Morpheus calls this "The desert of the real." Like The Road Warrior and its ilk, the populace of this shattered world looks to a better tomorrow and a savior who they believe will deliver it. The children of Mad Max Beyond Thunderdome had Max; the freed minds of The Matrix have Neo, whose very name suggests renewal.

Unlike George Miller's wasteland, however, this one teems with functioning media. True to The Matrix's computer culture and cyberpunk sources, the Wachowskis use television and computer monitors as a motif. This is no mere quirk of art direction. As Neo and his comrades "interface" with their world, the filmmakers use screens-within-the-screen as transitional devices. In fact, the Wachowskis introduce Neo asleep at his computer, as a message appears on the screen: "Wake up, Neo." Neo wakes, as if psychically connected to the machine. This moment establishes the central theme of The Matrix: the progression from slumber to waking realization to taking charge of one's destiny. At this point, however, Neo is still Tom Anderson, a nobody asleep in his apartment—apartment 101, clearly a nod to the ones and zeroes that compose the language of the digital world.

Later, Agent Smith (Hugo Weaving), one of the Matrix's enforcement "programs," interrogates Neo about Morpheus. The scene is established in multiple master shots displayed all at once on a bank of security monitors. Similarly, the Wachowskis use a television to segue into and out of the virtual tour Morpheus gives Neo of the "desert of the real." The television's homey, old-fashioned design is a counterpoint to the blighted futuristic landscape the screen displays. But the film's most overt example is how the crew of Morpheus's ship, the Nebuchadnezzar, views the Matrix when not plugged into it. They watch it on monitors that stream with columns of code, not actual images. One crewmember, Cypher (Joe Pantoliano) tells Neo, "I don't even see the code. All I see is blonde, brunette, redhead."

During the film's climax, the filmmakers again blur the line between seeing and decoding. During the final fight between Neo and Agent Smith and his henchmen, Neo finally accepts that he is The One. The Wachowskis and editor Zach Staenberg (who won an Academy Award for his work on the film) cut to Neo's point of view: the walls are mere streaming lines of code; his opponents are vaguely human-shaped, composed of light. With an ethereal chorus joining composer Don Davis's orchestra, the moment is one of revelation. For Neo, true sight now means seeing the artificiality of the world, not experiencing any tactility. Compounding this schism is Reeves's performance style. He fights as if disconnected from his body. Of course he does: his "body" is invulnerable, his speed incalculable, he fights dispassionately, not even looking at his targets.

Vision is a component of *The Matrix*'s theme of awakening, a component the Wachowskis and costume designer Kym Barrett make coolly ironic by often hiding the characters' eyes behind stylish sunglasses. These match Barrett's flowing black and vinyl wardrobes, which Neo and Trinity (Carrie-Anne Moss) each accessorize with a small arsenal. These costumes, along with the weapons, hearken back to the black fashions (that is, insulation) worn by Sylvester Stallone's characters in the 1980s. Here, however, they do not flatter the characters' bulk. Instead, the clothes make the characters seem sleek and streamlined.

The Matrix's costuming is one the film's most iconic elements. Perhaps darkly so: in terms of costuming and violence, Neo and Trinity's assault on a building's lobby predicts that of "Trench Coat Mafia" members Eric Harris and Dylan Klebold on Littleton, Colorado's Columbine High School, just three weeks after *The Matrix* opened. And undoubtedly resonant with the adolescent audience that the Motion Picture Association of America deems too young for *The Matrix*, but which sees it anyway, is the fact that the fashions represent the characters' wish-fulfillment: Neo, Trinity, and the rest wear these clothes only while inside the Matrix. That is, to each other and to us, they look the way they *imagine* themselves to look.

These outfits—along with the feats the film's characters perform while in them, and the milieu against which they are set—make the costumes akin to those of superheroes. This is one facet of *The Matrix*'s comic book nature, an aspect of the film that nicely counterpoints its more existential, philosophical concerns and that reflects one of the Wachowskis' earliest influences. In fact, when it came time to sell Hollywood on *The Matrix*, the Wachowskis hired several comic book artists to distill their ideas into a more graphic (and understandable) form.[1] To bring those ideas and graphics to the screen, the directors hired cinematographer Bill Pope, who had shot their previous (and first) film, 1996's *Bound*. Pope recalls that his collaboration with the Wachowskis began because of their shared love of comic books:

> I think they hired me because I read comics and knew what they were talking about whenever they mentioned a particular title. In fact, during our meeting, there was a copy of Frank Miller's *Sin City* on their desk, so I asked, "Is this what you want the film to look like?" We were all impressed by Miller's use of high-contrast, jet-black areas in the frame to focus the eye, and his extreme stylization of reality.[2]

Prior to *Bound*, Pope had shot Sam Raimi's *Darkman* (1990), a comic book–like adventure about a scientist-turned-vigilante superhero. Given its subject matter and over-the-top visual style, the fact that *Darkman* is not based on a pre-existing comic book seems merely to be happenstance.

In addition to the visual style, *The Matrix* borrows at least one classic trope from superhero tales: the origin story. Whether Superman's arrival on Earth, the bite Peter Parker receives from a radioactive spider, or Bruce Banner's exposure to gamma radiation, how the superhero came to be is almost always a cornerstone of his mythology. Similarly, *The Matrix* is the story of Neo's awakening and transformation into the role of violent messiah. This sets many comic book films apart from the traditional action film: Harry Callahan, Cobra, Riggs, Rambo, McClane—few action films explicitly show their heroes transformed from average man to super-avenger, as most of these men are rarified before the film starts. Notable exceptions are *Death Wish*'s Paul Kersey, as we have seen, and *Robocop*'s cybernetic superman, as we will.

In the meantime, the Wachowskis cast Neo's origin tale as a cyber-age Christological allegory; the climactic fight even includes his death and resurrection. But the Wachowskis do not simply lay Neo's path before him. They make his choice to walk that path a theme of the film. The motif is established while Neo, still believing he is computer programmer Tom Anderson, is reprimanded by his boss: "The time has come to make a choice," his superior says. Later, when Neo consults with The Oracle (Gloria Foster), she tells him that he is not The One, but that Morpheus is so committed to believing that he is that he will sacrifice his own life to save Neo's. "One of you is going to die," The Oracle says. "Which one will be up to you."

When Agent Smith captures Morpheus, Neo chooses to reenter the Matrix to save him. And fortunately for Neo, with great responsibility comes great power. As The One, Neo's ability to remake the Matrix translates into an ability to defy fists, bullets, and gravity. Neo's comrades, also aware that the Matrix is just a construct, also possess these abilities, albeit to a lesser degree. This justifies the film's many aerobatics (leaps and high falls), acrobatics (running along walls, performing cartwheels amid gunfire), and other special effects (the film contains around five hundred effects shots).

The Matrix's signature special effect is "bullet time," a form of slow motion in which the camera seems to rotate around an action that often times appears to take place at tremendous speed. These effects were created by a one-hundred-person crew under the supervision of Manex Visual Effects's John Gaeta, and executed by an array of 122 35mm still cameras positioned along a flexible rig. The result would be the equivalent of a single high-speed camera filming at twelve thousand frames per second.[3] Neo's choice to save Morpheus results in a series of action scenes that double as special effects showcases— bullet time and others—including gunfights, an escape from a crashing helicopter, Neo and Smith's hand-to-hand fight on a subway platform (and in midair), and finally, the standoff in which Neo fully accepts his abilities and vanquishes Agent Smith.

Afterward, the film's coda returns to the theme of choice—only now, Neo's role is not to make one, or to learn that he will have to, but to pass the opportunity onto those who will follow him. "I don't know the future. I didn't come here to tell you how this is going to end. I came here to tell you how it's going to begin," he says, offscreen, into a pay phone. "Where we go from there is a choice I leave to you." The filmmakers then cut to Neo, who steps out of a telephone booth, evoking Superman. Neo looks around at the citizenry and slips on his sunglasses. A rapid succession of aerial shots of the city follows. In the last, Neo, small at first, flies up, up, and away. This is the final image of The Matrix, but early in The Matrix Reloaded, the first of two 2003 sequels made back-to-back, the Wachowskis further the depiction of Neo as a superhero, Superman in particular. When asked where Neo is, the Nebuchadnezzar's newest crewman, Link (Harold Perrineau), answers, "He's doing his Superman thing." Similarly, the climax of the film finds Neo flying through an exploding building. Zooming toward the camera, Neo holds one arm back and one forward with his fist clenched, as he apes a pose from 1978's Superman.

In addition to representing the superheroic, the feats of Neo and friends in combat also cite the action cinema of Hong Kong. The film's extensive martial arts sequences, enhanced by Gaeta's bullet time technique, are choreographed by renowned Hong Kong director and stunt choreographer Yeun Wo

Hang-Time: In The Matrix (1999), a film that revolutionized special effects, Neo (Keanu Reeves) and Agent Smith (Hugo Weaving) face off in midair. (From the author's collection.)

Ping, who also trained Reeves, Moss, Fishburne, and Weaving. The Wachowskis drafted Yeun both out of their enthusiasm for Hong Kong action films and also in response to where American action filmmaking technique had led. "American filmmakers have gotten to the point where they create their fights in the editing room. Those types of sequences are just designed for a visceral, flash-cut impact." says Larry Wachowski. "Hong Kong action directors actually bring narrative arcs into the fights, and tell a little story within the fighting."[4] But as the series progresses through The Matrix Reloaded and The Matrix Revolutions, these fights increasingly resemble those performed in video games—especially the extended scenes in which a lone Neo fights dozens, then hundreds of Agent Smith replicas. This makes for some visuals that are initially dazzling, but ultimately repetitive. Compounded by a performance that suggests Neo feels no danger, the fights spiral into pointlessness.

In addition to The Matrix's martial arts, the gunplay also bears Hong Kong's mark. In fact, in the film's opening scene, Trinity holds a gun in each hand— "double-fisting." This is one of Hong-Kong-turned-American action director John Woo's affectations. So is Trinity's choice of weapon: the utilitarian Beretta—a Joel Silver signature, to be sure, but also the only weapon Woo specifically requests and reuses in film after film, according to weapons expert and Woo collaborator Rock Galotti.[5] This 9mm handgun is the smallest weapon Neo and Trinity wield in their assault on the building in which Morpheus is held prisoner by the agents trying to hack into his mind. The lobby gun battle is overpowering as its black clad instigators attack in a collage of slow and standard-speed motion, a scene that Sight and Sound calls "a John Woo set-piece."[6]

A captivity/rescue scenario, Neo and Trinity's recovery of Morpheus even evokes the Western, and the action films influenced by it, as the pair strides into the building like cyberpunk Searchers. The filmmakers even make a small joke out of the Western's role as grandfather to all of this business: when Neo and Agent Smith face each other in the subway station, newspaper blows between them like tumbleweeds, and the score riffs on the music of such Western showdowns. Thus, the Western is one more element the creators of The Matrix add to their mix of styles and archetypes. In fact, though the filmmakers employ some revolutionary techniques, their particular patchwork of influences is not without precedent. In the Reaganite eighties, Dutch director Paul Verhoeven made his American film debut with Robocop (1987), a story that, like The Matrix will later, combines science fiction, the Western, the comic book, and the Christological.

Robocop stars Peter Weller as Alex Murphy, a police officer of the near future's Old Detroit. After crime lord Clarence Boddicker (Kurtwood Smith) and his gang gun down Murphy, Omni Consumer Products, the corporation that runs the police department, resurrects him as the film's titular nearly indestructible cybernetic crime fighter. But as snatches of Murphy's memory flash through Robocop's brain, the cyborg sets out to regain a sense of who he was and avenge himself on the criminals who shot him not-quite dead.

Robocop, like The Matrix, is a creation of comic book enthusiasts. Co-screenwriter Ed Neumeier was reading literary properties for a Hollywood studio—including comic books—when the concept was initially hatched. According to the film's publicity, Neumeier and his writing partner, Michael Miner, then "walked a narrow plotline between a tough, sophisticated adult thriller and the grotesque graphic of the comic book form."[7]

When Robocop opened in 1987 (its July 17 release date caused some industry analysts to wonder if Robocop could weather opening against Jaws: The Revenge), critics seized upon the film's comic book influence and discussed the cyborg as mixtures of superheroes, the Terminator, Frankenstein, Harry Callahan, and Charles Bronson's Paul Kersey. The Los Angeles Times's Jack Matthews describes the main character of Robocop (which he claims is "a terrible title for a movie that anyone would expect an adult to enjoy") as possessing "the determination of Dirty Harry and the invincibility of Superman."[8] The Village Voice's David Edelstein calls the film "a high-tech parody of Stallone or Schwarzenegger" and "a vigilante video game with a satirical, adult comic-book edge," while Daily Variety's J. Galbraith stresses that it is "a comic book film that's definitely not for kids."[9] Writing for the New Yorker, Pauline Kael is among the more disapproving when she holds that Robocop "is deliberately shot in a sicko-sleazo comic-book style."[10]

Robocop is a metallic superhero; his chassis is a creation of special effects and make-up designer Rob Bottin, who had been a disciple of make-up master Rick Baker. The suit—a twenty-five pound casing in which Weller endured temperatures as high as 115 degrees—has since become iconic. It comprises an armored chest plate, a domed helmet with a strip of visor covering Murphy's eyes, black rubber, and a massive gun that fires bursts of automatic fire and slips into and out of a retractable holster built into his leg.

When OCP executive Bob Morton (Miguel Ferrer) unveils the new Murphy in an Old Detroit police station, Verhoeven teases out this revelation by breaking it down into small units. Initially, Robocop's face is kept from us. We see only small images of it on television monitors; in fact, it is his televised image that introduces him to us. We get closer when Verhoeven and cinematographer Jost Vacano show Robocop's profile—but through frosted glass. Next comes an angle of his chassis from behind. All of this is intercut with officers of the Metro West precinct craning for a view, acting as our onscreen surrogates.

Of course, once the filmmakers have fully revealed Robocop, they hitch much of what follows to his monolithic presence. This becomes a key component of the film's comic book aesthetic. In one of the most violent scenes from what is a particularly fierce film, Robocop kills nearly the entire complement of two criminal gangs during a drug raid. He enters the scene by slamming down a massive door. The filmmakers reveal the cyborg in low angles as he walks forward, his iconic form cutting through bright, hazy diffusion. The image is spare but powerful, a bold graphic. An even stronger example of this style is found, not coincidentally, in Robocop's first night on duty. After dispatching a would-be robber in a convenience store (where the magazine rack displays issues of "ROM," the 1979–1986 Marvel comic book about an alien cyborg vigilante, based on a Parker Brothers action figure), Robocop next foils an attempted rape with a castrating burst from his gun. Two punks menace a victim in a wide-open corner of Old Detroit when the shadow of the cyborg falls over the wall behind them and cuts into the light from the police cruiser headlights that frame the action. Other than the wall, which contains the light and Robocop's shadow, the only other major compositional element is a billboard advertising OCP's development, Delta City ("The Future Has a Silver Lining").

This spare composition evokes comic book panels that are driven by mood and iconography. Production designer William Sandell, a comic book fan with a collection of over eight thousand issues, also claims to have designed *Robocop* as "cleanly" as possible: rather than add objects to the film's locations, Sandell sought to remove, or at least minimize, them. "I was constantly finding something with clean lines and adding some neon edging . . . just keeping it real stark."[11] Sandell adopted this strategy largely—but not exclusively—for economic reasons, as *Robocop* is a low-budget, independent production. Still, the greater good of this approach may not have been budgetary, but aesthetic. *The Hollywood Reporter* praises Sandell's "sterile 'Metropolis'-like production design" and Vacano's tilted framing—camerawork that gives the film "a mesmerizing, expressionistic slant."[12] Sandell recalls Vacano capturing many of these angles by crawling on his stomach with a gyroscopic camera constructed by the cinematographer himself—"a poor man's steadicam," says Sandell.[13]

The steel mill where Boddicker's gang kills Murphy, and where Murphy later returns the favor, is one of the film's more elaborate sets, but its creation also embodies Sandell's interest in using stark shapes as compositional elements. While most of *Robocop* was shot in Dallas, this location was a closed-down mill in Pittsburgh. "It was really tragic. We set up a little art department in one of the locker rooms where the guys used to come. Everyone was out of work. You could still see the time cards on the floor and the hard hats," Sandell recalls.

I hired a bunch of these aging, steel mill guys back to work for me. We built a lot of stuff, and then we started moving gigantic shapes around for the climactic scene. . . . They would reactivate these huge cranes to move things as big as my house into place. I was decorating with big cylinders and big tanks and hunks of metal and I-beams, things you can't imagine set-decorating with. They would reactivate these huge cranes, moving parts that were forty feet long and four feet wide and must have weighed tons. Just chunks of shapes to give this deserted steel mill the right shape. But it's hard to go wrong in a steel mill. It's so gorgeous.[14]

This commitment to bold shapes is largely responsible for the graphic compositions with which *Robocop* achieves a comic book aesthetic. Of course, this can also be attributed to the film's over-the-top violence. Unlike the violence of a Michael Bay film or *Dirty Harry* movie, that of *Robocop* is rendered in a range of tones, from horrific to heartbreaking to darkly comic in its excessiveness. One of the most cartoonish instances occurs during the steel mill confrontation, as does one of the grittiest. The first is the always crowd-pleasing plunge of Emil (Paul McCrane) into a drum of toxic waste, from which he emerges melted, only to be splattered across Boddicker's windshield.

The next is Boddicker's own death. Having impaled Robocop, he prepares to deliver the deathblow when Robocop spears Boddicker's throat. Boddicker clutches the wound as it spurts streams of blood. He stumbles in the background and falls. The camera rack focuses to Robocop, calling out to his wounded partner, Ann Lewis (Nancy Allen). Gory though this death is, the moment's real cruelty lies in Vacano's rack focus. In nearly every action film, the villain's death is an ultimate triumph that the filmmakers privilege by affording it its own moment. Here, however, except for a few notes from Basil Poledouris's score, neither the filmmakers nor their title character seem to notice Boddicker's death, and instead move right on to the next bit of business. Hard-bitten, this is a fitting victory for the hero of a story about the subjugation of individual identity to the corporate and the mechanized. This world is so sick, it does not pause to acknowledge the purging of its greatest ill.

But as it turns out, this is not the film's final showdown. That distinction is extended to Robocop and Dick Jones (Ronny Cox), the villainous second-in-command of OCP. When Robocop presents evidence of Jones's criminality at an OCP board meeting, Jones takes the corporate patriarch, the Old Man (Dan O'Herlihy) hostage. What follows is the fast-draw of *High Noon*, *Dirty Harry*, the later *Die Hard*, and so on. The Old Man breaks away, and Robocop blasts Jones. For the last time, Robocop then twirls his gun on his finger—a habit left over from his days as Murphy and borrowed from countless Western gunfighters (though Murphy claims to have borrowed it from his son's television role model, "T. J. Laser," the hero of a science-fiction police show that is clearly Western-derived). This gesture, along with Robocop's vigilantism, a lumbering gait that recalls John Wayne's, and Poledouris's crashing main themes, all create the sense that *Robocop* is, in addition to being a comic book, a Western on the frontier of the future—not just in the broadly mythic manner of say, George Lucas's *Star Wars* (1977), but in a way that pinpoints some of the Western's specific affectations.

A beat after Jones's demise, the film's final exchange brings *Robocop*'s invocation of the Western to a new level of self-consciousness. As Robocop steps toward the door, the Old Man straightens and says, "Nice shootin' son. What's your name?" Robocop pauses. "Murphy," he replies. As he smiles and exits, the next edit is a hard cut to the credits, beginning with the film's title writ large in white, a visual trumpet blare. Only at the end, with this Western-like dialogue, do the characters become aware that their tale has taken place in a Western world. This makes for an interesting comparison to the following summer's *Die Hard*, in which the relationship among the characters, the film's formal elements, and the Western genre is the opposite of *Robocop*'s. In *Die Hard*, only after McClane and Hans have repeatedly acknowledged their scenario's affinity for the Western does the imagery make this relationship overt, in their final showdown. The "real" world of *Die Hard* comes to bend toward the mythic world of the Western—a reward of sorts, for McClane and for the audience. But whereas *Die Hard* does this as a form of wish fulfillment, *Robocop* uses its generic past more ironically (if jubilantly), to underscore the ruin into which its present has slipped. Of course, the irony is manifested in Robocop himself: he is literally a product—a product of a parasitic corporate culture while embodying individualistic, "there's-a-new-sheriff-in-town" justice.

Action Figure as Action Hero: As the crime-fighting cyborg of Robocop (1987), Peter Weller wears a suit that makes literal the machine-like bodies of several other 1980s action hero archetypes and predicts the image of Blade, as seen in the next chapter. (From the author's collection.)

The filmmakers' nod to the Western is a counterpoint to their futuristic imaginings. The future is most overtly embodied in Robocop and in ED-209, OCP's prototypical—and violently defective—"enforcement droid." Subtler, however, is how Robocop embodies futurism in media. As in The Matrix, screens abound, such as the computerized displays that stand for Robocop's vision. Robocop can target, track, record, play back, and display crimes in progress and list his prime directives (protect the innocent, serve the public trust, uphold the law, and classified) as graphics superimposed onto his field of vision. In fact, the audience sees Murphy's transformation into Robocop only as a succession of his increasingly computerized point of view: a progression from vision to video.

Other, subtler uses of screens play a supporting role to Robocop's sight and compose a motif of the art direction. Boddicker assassinates Bob Morton on Jones's behalf, in Morton's living room, which features no less than five television monitors. Before Boddicker's hand grenade detonates, he delivers a video message from Jones encoded on a CD (certainly a futuristic image in the pre-DVD age), which plays on three separate, parallel screens in Morton's home entertainment unit. This unit is a scaled-down version of the bank of monitors that adorns OCP's boardroom.

Elsewhere, Robocop enters his/Murphy's former home, now abandoned and up for sale. Judging from this scene, realtors no longer give tours of homes; instead, their pre-recorded likenesses do so from television kiosks presumably triggered by motion censors. There is no actual human contact, and in this scene, there is not even one full human between the two players. As the realtor prattles, Robocop has flashbacks that heighten the film's already turbulent, noir-esque psychology—a psychology that is obsessed with one's recovery of his identity through the recovery of his past. His circuitry now twisting in torment, Robocop strides from the house. The scene ends with a close-up of the video terminal as Robocop's fist smashes it. As the Village Voice argues, the film's "frustration with video (and its inexpressiveness) becomes an emotional hook."[15] Supporting this claim, the punch is more cathartic than most of the film's killings.

Robocop's near-future is a world obsessed with its media. "Media Breaks," brief news broadcasts complete with commercials (satirical ads within a television program within the movie), punctuate the film, and are anchored by actual television personalities Mario Machado (as Casey Wong) and Leeza Gibbons (as Jesse Perkins). In addition, everyone from the criminal lower class to the corporate elite seems to watch the same vapid sitcom and quote its one-liner ("I'd buy that for a dollar!"). In fact, two of Boddicker's crewmembers are watching it when Murphy appears and shoots, killing one criminal and destroying the TV.

Robocop was a box office hit that gave Verhoeven newfound industry status. He would follow his American debut with Total Recall, a bigger-budgeted science fiction/action extravaganza starring Arnold Schwarzenegger in his first action vehicle of the 1990s. Total Recall reunited Verhoeven with many of his Robocop collaborators, including Vacano, Sandell, Bottin, costume designer Erica Edell Phillips, editor Frank Urioste, and sound editor Stephen Hunter Flick, who earned a special achievement Academy Award for his Robocop sound design.

Based on Philip K. Dick's short story "We Can Remember It For You Wholesale," Total Recall is the story of twenty-first-century everyman Doug Quaid (Schwarzenegger), who, bored by his routine and obsessed with Martian dreams, decides to have memories of being a secret agent on Mars programmed into his mind. Before the memory implants can be completed (so we are told, at least), Quaid finds himself embroiled in interplanetary intrigue that involves Earth, Mars, a tyrannical industrialist, his henchmen, double agents, freedom fighters, mutants, and ancient Martian artifacts—and in which Quaid's ordinary life is just a cover story.

The script is credited to Dan O'Bannon, Ronald Shusett, and Gary Goldman. O'Bannon and Shusett began working on Total Recall in 1976, before writing what would be Ridley Scott's breakthrough film, Alien (1979). For more than ten years, Total Recall would wind a serpentine path through Hollywood's various channels of development and pre-production. One iteration was to begin filming in March 1985 and would have starred Richard Dreyfuss under David Cronenberg's direction; another, scheduled for a December 1987 release, would have paired Patrick Swayze—later replaced by Dennis Quaid—with director Bruce Beresford, who would direct 1989's Academy Award winner for Best Picture, Driving Miss Daisy.[16]

The Total Recalls of Cronenberg and Beresford may have mused on the connections among reality, memory, and fantasy, as much as, if not more than, the actual film does, but they would not have also been the lurid, splashy comic book that is Verhoeven's film. One of the big hits of summer 1990, Total Recall made nearly $120 million at the domestic box office and over $260 million worldwide. The film also won a Special Achievement Academy Award for its visual effects, as the Academy of Motion Picture Arts and Sciences did not even nominate any other films for the category. But as futuristic as Total Recall's effects render the film, the weapons and their muzzle-flashes, like those of Robo-cop, The Matrix, Aliens, and Verhoeven's Starship Troopers (1997), are all contemporary. In such cases, the filmmakers favor the bass, the kinetic force, and the obliterating power of automatic fire over the more overtly science fictional laser beams and blasts, as in the Star Trek and Star Wars films. However outlandish the worlds may be, the violence remains grounded in at least some sense of a more visceral real.

Still, it took five companies to produce Total Recall's effects. One, Metro-Light Studios, created the subway security checkpoint where a gigantic screen displays commuters' skeletons in fluorescent green and their concealed weapons in red. The checkpoint is seen in two sequences that total 42 seconds of the film's 113-minute running time. These 42 seconds represent the only computer-generated imagery in Total Recall—just one year before Terminator 2, three years before Jurassic Park and Cliffhanger, and at the outset of what would be the first decade of CGI-driven Hollywood films.

Like Robocop, The Matrix, and other futuristic action films, Total Recall depicts the future through excessive amounts of media and screens. This full-sized X-ray marks the film's most prominent screen—one that is destroyed when Quaid smashes through it. But lower-concept screens are a constant, if subtler, presence throughout the portion of the film set on Earth. The train Quaid takes to work, and on which he later escapes from Cohaagen's agents, is outfitted with televisions running commercials for Rekall, the company where Quaid tries to buy new memories. Over breakfast, Quaid watches a large television built into the kitchen wall as one of several large panels. As in Robocop, Verhoeven uses the newscast to parcel out exposition and to establish one of the film's villains—here, the Mars dictator Cohaagen (Ronny Cox). Quaid's wife, Lori (Sharon Stone), really one of Cohaagen's agents, enters and changes the channel to a view of the natural world. Instead of a window and nature, there is only a screen and a representation. Similar devices are seen in Superman and the special edition of Aliens, first seen on television in 1991. The reveal always has a slightly comic effect that buffs what is really a cynical edge.

Pursuing Quaid is Richter (Michael Ironside), Cohaagen's second and Lori's real husband. His car is equipped with five monitors (two up front, three back and to the side). Fleeing from Richter, Quaid is given a briefcase left for him by his alter ego, Hauser—the man Quaid had been before Cohaagen blanked his memory, implanted a whole marriage's worth of memories in his brain, and deposited him with Lori. Inside the case is a computer. On its monitor is Hauser. Quaid watches his own likeness guide him through the painful process of removing a tracking device through his nose. In one of the film's more surreal images, Quaid removes the bug while Hauser smiles—leers—as if watching. Viewers of *The Terminator, Commando, Predator,* and others had seen Schwarzenegger tortured so often that by *Total Recall,* the act had become a ritual; as a ritual, the torture offers the audience a strange, even paradoxical brand of comfort. Here, however, Schwarzenegger seems to watch and relish his own torture. It is this aspect of the scene—more than the extraction itself—that makes the act so unnerving.

With the bug removed, and Richter nearby, Quaid breaks the computer. It sparks and sputters. When Richter comes upon it, he vents his frustration by shooting a rat, the carcass of which plops onto the monitor. The splattered rat oozes its way down the smashed computer as it repeats Hauser's instruction to Quaid ("Get your ass to Mars") on a jittering loop. Like the earlier smashing of the security screen, this breakage and the gory decoration betray the same hostility toward media that Verhoeven evokes with Robocop's more visceral hammer-punching of the realtor video terminal. It is with a certain pleasure that Verhoeven seems to punish the motif that so defines these worlds.

In the case of *Total Recall,* this sense of satisfaction is bolstered by Verhoeven's use of the ruined machine's close-up as a transition from Earth to Mars, from the first major section of the film to the second. Appropriately, it also marks a transition between two architectural styles employed by Sandell and his art department. Verhoeven and company filmed *Total Recall* in Mexico, where Sandell found exteriors and designed interiors that reflect a hard-lined, utilitarian aesthetic. As Sandell recalls, "In my design books from the middle-'70s—when life and architecture were bleak—this [style] was called 'the New Brutalism. . . .' It's very stark, and it's unforgiving and mean-spirited, but perfect for *Total Recall.* This isn't a nice place, this world that [Quaid] lives in."[17] The buildings that frame the Earth-bound action are bunker-like, even the high-rises. Lacking an aesthetic (unless one considers "austere" an aesthetic), the architecture lacks any sense of romance or the exotic—precisely what Quaid wants to import into his life, or at least into his memory.

Quaid goes to Mars to recover his identity and to liberate the oppressed. Here, the architecture of such locations as the "Venusville" settlement and "The Last Resort" brothel is more eclectic than that of Earth. David Denby claims that the Mars sets are "extremely tacky—the equivalent of a western frontier town with three whorehouses and no school."[18] Similarly, a correspondent for *Entertainment Weekly* writes, "Mars, consisting of 35 studio sets built at a cost of $100,000 to $300,000 apiece, is a metallic-modular, high-tech/ honky-tonk nightmare."[19] According to Sandell, "We designed [the Mars sets] in a very modular form, taken from a lot of Japanese airport architecture, from Japanese airport lounges, where it's almost like you're in a pod. Everything had to look prefabricated."[20] What the architecture of Earth and Mars share is their dystopian sense of commodification—of aesthetics, of identity, of life itself. This is also a theme of Robocop, even though Verhoeven claims that these two films take place in different futures.[21]

The writers' analogies are apt. The Mars of Total Recall is a frontier, and frontiers give adventurers license to go adventuring. On Earth, Quaid has a few fights and one tight escape, but it is on Mars that he gets to indulge his inclination toward the superheroic—just like in the memories he has purchased. It is on Mars that he becomes a hero to the rebels, and gets the girl, and beats the bad guys (pulling Richter's arms off in the process), and activates an ancient alien reactor that creates an atmosphere for the planet.

But even with all of this archetypal, even cartoonish business, the Mars scenes further the existential questions posed in the Earth sequence: Who are we with memories that are not ours? Who are we without the ones that are? How do we tell the real from the simulated when it all comes down to electrical signals in our brains? More accurately put, these questions carry over until the film's one-hour mark, at which point Rekall's Dr. Edgemar (Roy Brocksmith) arrives to convince Quaid that he is still on Earth, suffering a psychotic break. Quaid is skeptical. "What's bullshit, Mr. Quaid?" Dr. Edgemar asks, "that you're having a paranoid episode triggered by acute, neurochemical trauma, or that you're really an invincible secret agent from Mars, who's the victim of an interplanetary conspiracy to make him think he's a lowly construction worker?" Dr. Edgemar's position seems plausible, but Quaid takes the doctor's nervous sweating as evidence that he is lying and shoots him.

This scene is interesting not just thematically, but also structurally. The filmmakers use the ever-critical one-hour mark to resolve whether Quaid's experiences are real or imagined. After this scene, the filmmakers subsume Total Recall's preoccupation with reality and identity to scene after scene of violent confrontation, save for some business between Cohaagen and Quaid (Cohaagen plans to blank Quaid's memory and return his body to the villainous Hauser personality). This marks a striking parallel between Total Recall and The Matrix: not only do both films deal with memory, reality, and virtual living, but both also consign much of this material to their first halves, while reserving the second halves for long runs of gunplay and hand-to-hand combat.

While The Matrix is more content to leave its issues in the realm of the philosophical, however, Total Recall charges them with paranoia and unstable psychology, much like Robocop does. This aligns Total Recall with the noir tradition, as does its motif of duality and mirroring. Indeed, many of the film's elements exist in dichotomies: Mars/Earth; Quaid/Hauser; the symbiotic mutants George/ Kuato (Marshall Bell); the holographic doubles Quaid and rebel-prostitute Melina (Rachel Ticotin) use as decoys; even the reflections of Quaid, Lori, and Dr. Edgemar in a closet mirror; and Melina and Lori as Quaid's two love interests. This last is a noir convention: two women—one blonde and saintly, the other dark and devilish—pull the protagonist in opposite directions. All Total Recall does to tweak this convention is switch the good girl and the temptress's hair color. Thus, Total Recall is even more noir-like than Robocop, and furthers Verhoeven along a trajectory toward his next American film, Basic Instinct, the notorious 1992 neo-noir.

For his part, Schwarzenegger would follow Total Recall with the action/ science fiction blockbuster Terminator 2 and then several action films that make satirical use of the overblown: Last Action Hero, True Lies, and Eraser, as noted in chapter 2. None of these films would replicate Verhoeven's balance of noir and science fiction. No director would achieve this until John Woo, following his immigration to America.

Woo represents the height of the decade's full-blown fascination with Asian action cinema. In the 1990s, Woo become a celebrity, along with his Hong Kong star Chow Yun-Fat, who would star in Antoine Fuqua's The Replacement Killers (1998), and Jet Li, who would play a villain in Lethal Weapon 4 (1998) and a hero in The One (2001). Most notable of the Hong Kong actors is Jackie Chan, famous both for his Hong Kong productions, including Rumble in the Bronx (released in Hong Kong in 1995, and in America in 1996), Supercop (1992; released in America in 1996), and Jackie Chan's First Strike (1996; released domestically in 1997), and also for his American films, such as Rush Hour (1998), Shanghai Noon (2000), and their sequels (2001; 2003).

Woo's Face/Off (1997) may be his third American film, but it is the first in which the personal style he developed in Hong Kong's action cinema does not seem subjugated to the homogenizing force of American studio control or the MPAA. Indeed, Universal revised Woo's American debut, the Jean-Claude Van Damme vehicle Hard Target (1993) seven times before the MPAA would grant it an R rating.[22] More than Hard Target or Woo's second American film, Broken Arrow (1996), Face/Off exhibits many of the Woo signatures identified by critic Richard Corliss: "the slo-mo, the gleaming candles, the long coats flying in the breeze, the doves flying in a chapel as an omen of death—[woven] around the central fantasy of male bonding gone berserk."[23] The *New York Times*'s Bernard Weinraub dwells less in the visual details of Woo's style and more in its thematics when he claims that Woo's "pre-Hollywood Hong Kong films were almost grandiose in their mix of graphic violence with blatant Chinese and Christian religious symbols and their male-bonding themes of loyalty and honor, whatever the price."[24]

In *Face/Off*, the males are an FBI agent (John Travolta), who, through an innovative surgical swap, appropriates the face, voice, and very life of an international terrorist (Nicolas Cage) in order to infiltrate his organization. After the surgery, the terrorist awakens, steals his enemy's identity, and runs amok both at FBI headquarters and at the agent's home. This premise may be absurd, but Woo is adept at stitching together a world out of hyperboles, here starting with the characters' very names: the FBI agent is the steadfastly named "Sean Archer;" his foe is the decadent sounding "Castor Troy."

Archer is obsessed with Troy not just because Troy is a maniacal freelance terrorist, but also because he killed Archer's young son. In what marks *Face/Off*'s first shootout and display of Woo's stylistic excesses, Archer leads his team in capturing Troy. This, the first action sequence of the film, could well be the last of most others: an all-out war between Archer's forces and Troy's, framed by an industrial setting. Troy taxis his getaway plane down a runway, but veers off, and smashes through a hangar. In several slow-motion shots, he dives from the plane amid a shower of sparks, which, out of focus, dazzle like sequins. In the resulting firefight, Troy shoots one agent, who flies into the recesses of the frame. Soon after, a double-fisting Troy shoots at Archer, who returns fire, all against a backdrop of crates, machinery, and engines. The two end up in Woo's signature composition: the hero and villain facing each other, each with his gun in the other's face, their arms crossing. Archer is saved by a sudden engine blast that hurls Troy down a tunnel. Troy crashes into a grate and is captured.

Even more excessive is the later gunfight between Troy's gang and the FBI, set in a palatial loft. The sequence, which includes a colossal gun battle, a confrontation between Archer and Troy (each now wearing the other's face), and Troy's escape, runs nine minutes; according to the film's publicity, the set was rigged with over five thousand bullet effects.[25] Much of the action in the shootout is rendered in slow motion and in dissolves, which stretches out our sense of time—an effect that is perversely romantic, given the violence.

Ghastlier than this effect, however, is what Woo places at the center of this stylization: a child, caught in the middle of the firefight, trying to drown it out by listening to "Somewhere Over the Rainbow" on his headphones. Moreover, Woo elevates the song so that it dominates the soundtrack during this carnage. Woo claims that Judy Garland's version of the song (the version in *Face/Off* is Olivia Newton John's) was his favorite as a boy, that *The Wizard of Oz* was the first musical he ever saw, and that he would escape into the dream-world of American musicals from the reality of his impoverished, crime-ridden upbringing in Hong Kong. And while it has become a cliché for critics to refer to Woo's action set pieces as "ballets," Woo himself acknowledges "When I shoot action sequences, I think of great dancers, Gene Kelly, Astaire. . . . In action I feel like I'm creating a ballet, a dance."[26]

Here, of course, Woo combines the violent and the sentimental to create something ironic, but more than that, something overwrought. Many critics have singled out Woo's films for being highly emotional, which, in all fairness, was a reasonable claim to have made during the mid-to-late 1990s, when so many of Woo's contemporaries were making more ironic, detached pictures. Still, Woo's penchant for sentimentality often sabotages any sense of logic or emotional consistency. For example, following Troy's capture, Archer and his wife, Eve (Joan Allen) tearfully rejoice; the next morning, however, Archer shames his celebratory colleagues with a roll call of the agents who lost their lives on the operation. Woo's American films use emotion as another form of spectacle—pyrotechnics by other means.

Woo indulges himself in *Face/Off*'s third act, which includes the requisite doves in the church; Christological imagery; an elaborate Mexican standoff; a frenzied, overlong boat chase that leads to a hand-to-hand brawl on the shore (Woo repeats this chase-into-beachfront-fight in *Mission: Impossible II*); and not one but two Western showdowns—one with Archer's wife in the middle, the other with his daughter, whose face Troy licks as the orchestra's string section chitters like insects. Yet somehow, none of this is as excessive as *Face/Off*'s finale, in which Archer returns home, his face restored, with Troy's illegitimate son in tow—the same little boy who had been listening to "Somewhere Over the Rainbow." With almost no discussion, the Archers agree to adopt the boy, and resolve the film by restoring their nuclear family.

As the history of the action genre and many of its influences show, physical violence purges psychological demons. In the genre's violent mathematics, then, Troy's death equals Archer's catharsis. But this coda, in which the Archers fill the vacuum left by the killing of their son by adopting the son of the killer, is positively bizarre in its reach for resolution. It is another instance of

Woo straying so far from the dramatic into the overly sentimental that the scene's emotions are less likely to be felt than observed with confounded fascination—so much so, that there might be something subversive at work: one aspect of Woo's Hong Kong filmmaking that he had to leave behind is the noir-esque fatalism with which he would often end his films. Here, he gives the viewer—and Paramount Pictures—a happy ending that is so happy, it borders on parody.

The adoption of the boy also represents the final bit of crossover between Archer and Troy, a crossover Woo obviously embodies in their identity swap. This makes Face/Off an ideal vehicle for Woo, whose films often pit flawed heroes against noble villains and explore notions of duality. Woo claims this is what attracted him to Face/Off, but he need not have turned to so outlandish a premise to probe these themes.[27] Ever since the far more restrained Dirty Harry, the action genre has always been concerned with duality, a theme inherited both from film noir and from the Western's "The Man Who Knows Indians" archetype.

Initially, Woo declined to direct Face/Off. In 1992, the screenplay was then more overtly a piece of science fiction, set a few hundred years in the future. Woo, who had just recently emigrated with his wife and children from Hong Kong, did not feel he was ready to attempt the ambitious project, then being developed by Joel Silver at Warner Bros.[28] This original iteration of Face/Off did not materialize at least in part because Silver was making another science fiction/action film for the studio, 1993's Demolition Man.[29] Still, even with the contemporary setting of Woo's scaled-down version, the film's driving concept of using medical science to switch people's faces, means that Face/Off would never wholly escape its science fiction origins.

The film also embodies futurism in a place one might not think to look for it: the prison to which Archer, undercover as Troy, is sentenced. Above the doorway of the prison's common area is a giant bank of monitors, on which a nature channel is playing.[30] The simulated nature hearkens back to Total Recall, and before that, Aliens. In Face/Off, the irony is even more pronounced as the monitors are set against the imposing steel of the prison. As so often befalls media in the fantastical action film, the common area monitors are destroyed—here during Archer's prison break—exploding in sparks. This betrays another stylistic device of the director's: what gasoline explosions are to Michael Bay, cascades of sparks are to Woo; whatever bullets strike, they spark.

Erewhon Prison, we are told, is "one big magnetic field." The prisoners wear massive boots that can be magnetized by remote, essentially locking those who wear them in place. The boots also serve as tracking devices by which the guards can always locate the prisoners. Thus, the boots are not just good for stomping; they also represent a paranoid vision of the near future: they see where you go—which, of course, is nowhere. Thus, Erewhon maintains an electronic, panoptic view of its inmates, as though they were enemy blips in a video game.

Other films of this era also make pointed use of such imagery, including Paramount's *Mission: Impossible* franchise. In the first film, a summer 1996 tentpole, Jim Phelps (Jon Voight) supervises his team's deployment via a computer array. Similarly, Luther Stickell (Ving Rhames) monitors agent Ethan Hunt (Tom Cruise) as Hunt later infiltrates CIA headquarters. In *Mission: Impossible II*, Woo's summer 2000 follow-up to *Face/Off*, Luther once again tracks Hunt, this time using a computerized, graphics-driven schematic to monitor his teammate as Hunt breaks into a biotech corporate headquarters to destroy a genetically engineered virus. Throughout the scene, the filmmakers insert full-screen images of the computer monitor. As Hunt's nemesis, Sean Ambrose (Dougray Scott) closes in on Hunt's position, Luther and fellow team member Billy Baird (John Polson) watch anxiously. "Luther, what the hell can we do?" Billy asks. Luther replies, "What can we do? Hope he kills all the bugs before the yellow dot gets to the red one." Hunt receives similar assistance via a cell phone during his run through Shanghai in 2006's *Mission: Impossible III*, just as Neo is directed during the final foot chase of *The Matrix*. But none of these examples, nor the one from *Face/Off* is as outlandish as the parking garage car chase in the James Bond film *Tomorrow Never Dies* (1997). In this sequence, Bond escapes from the henchmen of a media tycoon by diving into his MI-6-issued BMW and driving it by remote control from the back seat. With Bond grinning at the action on a small monitor built into the remote, the scene becomes surreal as Bond "plays" his car chase, as if on a Game Boy console.

This is an apt comparison, as the fantastical action film has increasingly drawn from video game aesthetics as much as those of comic books. Indeed, during this phase of the action film's history, Hollywood produced a slew of action films based on video games. These include *Street Fighter* (1994), the *Mortal Kombat* films (1995, 1997), the *Resident Evil* movies (2002, 2004), the *Tomb Raider*-based *Lara Croft* franchise (2001, 2003), and *Doom* (2005).

Rated PG-13 for "action violence and some sensuality," *Lara Croft: Tomb Raider* begins with violence before its famous archeologist/adventuress heroine is established in any meaningful sense. The opening of the film, which finds Lara (Angelina Jolie) trying to obtain a gem from a seemingly ancient temple, is much like the opening of Raiders of the Lost Ark—except for the giant robot Lara comes to battle. Throughout the fight, director Simon West includes at least six cutaways to the robot's computerized point of view, including one as it "dies." West is also sure to include an insert of each of Lara's gun barrels sliding into place as she reloads, and triple-, quadruple-, and even quintuple-cuts her acrobatics. (Lara, West seems to think, even needs more than one shot to drop her guns back into her holsters.) As if young males 18–34 were not already being sufficiently pandered to, West next establishes Lara in the shower, where he devotes seven shots and twenty-five seconds to her rinsing.

This introductory sequence (the shower notwithstanding) is only a training exercise. Matters are more serious later, when Lara is ambushed at her mansion. Using a bungee cord, Lara tangles with the rappelling invaders in a battle that resembles Mad Max's Thunderdome fight, but with machine guns. Meanwhile, Lara's sidekick, Bryce (Noah Taylor), tries to send to her aid the robot she previously defeated. When "Simon" fails to come back online, Bryce receives an error message: "Game over."

Lara escapes to the garage, where another fight ensues. From his trailer, Bryce serves as her eyes. Echoing scenes from the first two Mission: Impossible films and The Matrix, Bryce watches Lara on his monitors and even directs her. He maneuvers her like he would a video game character, which is apropos given that the film is derived from the phenomenally successful Tomb Raider computer games, developed by Core Design and published by Eidos Interactive. In the short time between the first game's 1996 debut and Paramount's acquisition of the film rights in early 1998, the games Tomb Raider and Tomb Raider 2 sold more than six million copies.[31] The games were so successful—as was the film, with a worldwide gross of $275 million—that Lara Croft herself became the first video game character to secure the representation of a major Hollywood talent agency. According to Variety, Creative Artists Agency signed to represent Lara Croft "with the hopes of introducing the Indiana Jones–like character to non-gamers through sports and apparel, consumer product tie-ins, publishing, and, naturally, her own television series."[32]

The years following the release of Lara Croft: Tomb Raider were studded with video game adaptations. These included Jan de Bont's Lara Croft: The Cradle of Life, a 2003 sequel that underperformed at the box office. The same year saw Uwe Boll's House of the Dead, a big-screen adaptation of the Sega-produced video game. Boll's next two films, Alone in the Dark (2005) and BloodRayne

(2006) were also based on video games (though they were not American studio productions). Perhaps the most highly anticipated video game adaptation to follow the original Lara Croft was Andrzej Bartkowiak's Doom, based on the games developed by Id Software.

First released in 1993, Doom is widely credited with establishing the "first-person shooter" genre of video games, in which action comes directly toward the viewer, who does not see the character he or she plays, but rather, shares the character's point of view, peering down gun barrels in the foreground. After a highly successful launch, Doom was followed by Doom II in 1994, Doom 3 in 2004, and an Xbox version of Doom 3 in 2005. In 1994, Hollywood talent agency ICM sold a four-book series to Pocket Books based on the game; the series was simultaneously optioned by Universal.[33] Eventually, Universal's rights expired. Doom was next optioned as a big screen property by Columbia Pictures, and after those rights expired, by Warner Bros. When that deal also expired, the rights reverted back to Id, which licensed the game once again to Universal—a decade after Universal's first deal.[34]

Doom's 2005 film adaptation finds a detachment of marines led by Sarge (The Rock) trying to contain a crisis at an archaeological research center on Mars. "We got us a game," says Sarge, briefing his men, one of whom plays the year 2046's answer to a modern-day Game Boy. Their mission to rescue six scientists, protect the civilians, and recover the property of "United Aerospace Corporation" becomes complicated as monsters overrun the installation. Among these beasts are the missing scientists who have been infected by a viral genetic mutation. The mutation spreads through the monsters' vampiric attacks on their victims and, it seems, can affect both the living and the dead. Eventually, one Marine remains: John Grimm (Karl Urban), the estranged brother of a UAC researcher. When Grimm sets off to find her, the camera adopts his point of view for his battle with the monsters, mimicking the game's signature style. In fact, Bartkowiak transitions from the third-person to the first by entering into blackness through Grimm's eye. From there, Grimm's "run and gun" runs just shy of five minutes (expanded to just over five on the film's unrated, extended DVD). Throughout the sequence, Grimm's point of view has such a computer-generated sheen, it dovetails with the game not only as a matter of style, but also of production value.

This is Doom's show-stopping sequence—indeed, it was produced by a special "First Person Shooter Unit" directed by Jon Farhat, who also served as the film's visual effects supervisor. It is not, however, the only instance in which Bartkowiak replicates the look of the game. When Sarge first fires the film's signature weapon, the "BFG" (which stands for "Bio-Force Gun," but to Sarge, "Big Fucking Gun"), Bartkowiak shows the energy blast from Sarge's point of view, looking down the gun's barrel. The thunderous pulse of blue energy justifies how lovingly the filmmakers had previously introduced the BFG. In an earlier scene, Sarge enters the armory, looking for something "with a little more kick." He approaches the BFG, but not as reverentially as the camera does: in a shot that lasts twenty-three seconds, the camera makes a fluid advance on the gun and circles it as if they were in a dance, rotating more than 360 degrees around the weapon.

Also emulating the game—if more subtly—is the approach Bartkowiak and cinematographer Tony Pierce-Roberts take to the research installation itself. Their camera will often track forward and back, follow characters through doorways, peer down corridors, or pan to a wall or a corner of a T-junction. While such images are often the perspective of an onscreen character (and therefore not truly first-person), they recall the purposely limited perspective of the game, and also share a certain kinship with Steven Spielberg's approach to the same year's *War of the Worlds*.

The marines' maneuvers in such spaces echo not only the *Doom* video games, but also—and more meekly—James Cameron's *Aliens*. In both films, marines are dispatched to another planet to combat a horde of monsters that has besieged a civilian population and used it to reproduce. In both films, the marines are actually doing the bidding of a corporation, whose desire to possess the monster has triggered this tragedy. In both films, the hero must beat a ticking clock to rescue the sole surviving civilian—one to whom the hero is emotionally connected. Both films are "last stand" stories, like a number of Westerns, and as such, in both films the heroes instruct others to kill them if they are infected (in the case of *Aliens*, impregnated). And both films feature similar design elements, from the monsters to the sets to the marines' machine guns, which are blockish with vaguely triangular muzzles.

Curiously, *Doom* is not the only video game adaptation to so closely mirror *Aliens*. Another is *Resident Evil*, Paul W. S. Anderson's adaptation of the Sony PlayStation/Capcom game. The original game, which sold more than 16 million copies and grossed over $600 million between its 1996 release and the film's 2002 debut, was set in a secluded mountain town.[35] Anderson's film, however, has a much more science fictional setting: a research laboratory hidden deep underground, on the outskirts of "Raccoon City." Anderson sets his action here as a prequel to the game. That Anderson would stress the property's latent science fiction qualities—in addition to its more prominent ac-

. . . Or Are You Just Happy to See Me? Sarge (The Rock) reveres the "BFG," which stands for "Bio-Force Gun" (but not really) in Doom, the 2005 adaptation of the landmark video game series. (From the author's collection.)

tion and horror ones—should come as no surprise, given the filmmaker's career to that point. In addition to having adapted the video game *Mortal Kombat* to box office success, Anderson directed the science fiction horror show *Event Horizon* (1997), produced by Lawrence Gordon and Lloyd Levin. Anderson next directed *Soldier* (1998), in which a veteran must defend his adopted planet from his genetically enhanced replacements—essentially *Shane* in space.

It should be noted here that *Resident Evil*, Anderson's first feature since *Soldier*, is not an American production. Written and directed by a British filmmaker, produced by British, German, and French companies, financed in part by British tax breaks, German subsidies, and German banks, and starring a Russian model, *Resident Evil*'s $30 million–plus budget was financed before any North American distribution deal was in place.[36] Still, while the movie represents a pool of foreign talent and foreign money, it bears no mark of any foreign cinema. Unlike John Woo's Hong Kong action movies or *Night Watch*, a Russian film made to answer Hollywood's action and horror blockbusters (2004, released in America in 2006), *Resident Evil* is all but indistinguishable from American films, in much the same way that, say, the independent *Rambo* films are indistinguishable from actual studio productions. Indeed, what little European sensibility *Resident Evil* could be said to have may just as well be references to the work of Stanley Kubrick. The design and photography of a mansion interior, seen early in *Resident Evil*, resembles the living quarters seen at the end of *2001: A Space Odyssey* (1968). Similarly, the computer that controls the research facility recalls *2001*'s HAL-9000—both in its cool, homicidal intellect and in its spherical point of view, through which the human characters are studied. And when the facility's power fails, laboratory doors open, spilling green water toward the camera; this recalls one of the most notorious images from *The Shining* (1980), in which an elevator opens and floods the camera with blood.

In *Resident Evil*, as in *Aliens* and *Doom*, the military is an extension of corporate authority. Here, a paramilitary unit trapped inside "The Hive," the Umbrella Corporation's underground facility, must battle killer scientist zombies, much as the Marines do in *Doom*. One of *Resident Evil*'s soldiers is Rain (Michelle Rodriguez), a counterpart to *Aliens*'s Vasquez (Jenette Goldstein); each is a Latina with more *machismo* than any of her comrades. But this is not to say that Rain is without fear: "I don't want to be one of those things walking around without a soul," she insists. "When the time comes, you'll take care of it." Here, Anderson invokes a save-the-last-bullet-for-yourself ethos seen so often in Westerns, but in virtually the same language used in *Aliens*: "Hicks, I'm not going to end up like those others. You'll take care of it, won't you?"

Early in the film, the soldiers find Alice (Milla Jovovich), who had woken up in the mansion with no memory of how she got there or even who she is. As a civilian among the military, and as an unstable woman who can only find peace by literally battling her demons, Alice mirrors *Alien*'s Ripley, just as Rain recalls Vasquez. But in Alice's case, regaining her memory and identity through fragmented (and photographically overexposed) flashbacks aligns her with the heroes of so many *noir* and *noir*-derived films. This adds *film noir* to *Resident Evil*'s matrix of science fiction, action, and zombie horror. Additionally, Alice unleashes violence seemingly unaware of her talent for it. In one instance, she kicks a zombie into unconsciousness without quite realizing how she is doing it. This recovery of memory, identity, and violent ability is in league not only with Ripley, but also with *Robocop*'s Murphy, *Total Recall*'s Quaid, and *The Matrix*'s Neo. It also resonates with Hugh Jackman's characters from the *X-Men* movies and *Van Helsing* and Geena Davis's amnesic spy in *The Long Kiss Goodnight*.

Resident Evil is a stylish, if unoriginal, affair. Against the film's cool blue palette, Alice's red dress stands out, always drawing the viewer's eye. Anderson also makes much use of computer graphics to cover exposition and the passage of time. Early on, the soldiers' commanding officer details the relationship among Raccoon City, the mansion, and the Hive. One soldier shows the rest a computer schematic that soon fills the frame. For forty-five seconds, the audience follows the image of the connecting tunnel descending into the Hive. Later, Anderson uses such graphics as a motif: instead of following characters as they move from a lab to a dining hall, we watch a thirteen-second computer graphic simulate their motion; likewise, when Alice and an undercover police officer later flee the zombies, Anderson covers their flight with a computer graphic lasting seven seconds. In addition to lending the film some visual flair, these interstitials keep the film close to the gaming world by depicting the characters as if they were in a game, progressing through its levels.

Much of *Resident Evil*'s imagery may be futuristic, but the style of its violence is contemporary—particularly in how the filmmakers seem to relish it. After waylaying a zombie and taking its gun, Alice is cornered by seven zombie dogs. They snarl and leap. She fires, emptying the clip of all fifteen rounds in ten seconds. The filmmakers cover this in seventeen shots that include several close-ups of the gun's muzzle as the weapon discharges and also of the barrel as a spent round is expelled and a new one slammed forward. In fact, eight shots feature only the gun—which is remarkable when one considers that this leaves just nine shots, or about half the total number, to cover various angles of Alice and seven attacking dogs.

As the sequence progresses, the editing intensifies; it becomes difficult to tell what is a new gunshot and what is being double-cut. As punctuation following this brief sequence, the filmmakers provide two shots of the last spent round falling to the floor. These two shots take four seconds, allowing the eye to rest while still fetishizing gun violence. But when an eighth dog appears, Anderson romanticizes not the gun, but the body. Alice runs up the wall, spins around, and launches herself into the air. She lashes out with a kick that catches the dog in the head, mid-leap, and propels it through a window. This stunt, recalling the martial artistry of The Matrix, lasts nine seconds. That is, Alice spends almost the same amount of time dispatching this last dog as she did killing the first seven.

The zombies are but one class of enemy Alice must face. The Hive itself is a threat, run by murderous supercomputer Red Queen (recalling Aliens's hive, controlled by a Queen Mother). In Resident Evil's opening sequence, a viral agent that turns people into zombies escapes from a laboratory and into the Hive's air supply. The building shuts itself down. Scientists are trapped in a flooding lab. Executives are trapped on runaway elevators. When one elevator finally brakes, its passengers pry the door open; one woman cranes her head out. The elevator then shoots downward and upward, trying to decapitate her. Ultimately, Red Queen gasses the Hive's five hundred scientists and support staff. When the soldiers enter the facility to investigate why, the Hive deploys its defense mechanisms. Its ghastliest is a grid of lasers that slice several soldiers, including the commander, to death. It is ironic that in a big-screen adaptation of such a blockbuster video game franchise, a computer represents so lethal a foe.

To the heroes of Resident Evil, the space itself is a threat quite separate from (if secondary to) the monsters. Anderson repeats this in his next production, Alien vs. Predator (2004). Trumpeted by the tagline, "Whoever wins . . . we lose," Alien vs. Predator is something of a sequel to the two Predator films and a prequel to the Alien series. Written and directed by Anderson, the film is set inside an ancient pyramid where human explorers are caught in a war between the creatures of Twentieth Century Fox's popular Alien and Predator franchises. Like the Hive, the pyramid is subterranean—in this case, buried thousands of feet in Antarctic ice. Even before Anderson made Alien vs. Predator, the New York Times suggested that his penchant for setting his films underground, in tight quarters, or in the black of space may be related to his background. Born and raised in England's coal-mining capital of Newcastle, Anderson comes from a family of miners. "It's the lure of going down there into the dark," Anderson told the *Times*. "It's in my blood."[37]

The pyramid is central to Anderson's story. It is an archaeological discovery that reveals a major ancient Earth civilization from which the others descended. The site has been discovered by Charles Bishop Weyland (Lance Henriksen), head of the Weyland Corporation that will become Weyland-Yutani, the company that figures so ominously in the background of the other *Alien* films. (This also establishes Weyland as the template for the Bishop android, also played by Henriksen in *Aliens* and *Alien 3*.) Weyland forms an expedition party to tunnel into the ice and explore the pyramid. Once the team reaches the site, the pyramid hosts most of the action that follows. More than just a stage, however, the pyramid also becomes a player. During the first major action sequence—a firefight between humans and Predators—the pyramid seals off the humans as massive blocks of stone rearrange themselves and slide into place. From here, the humans must also contend not only with the emergence of the Aliens, but also with the pyramid's reconfiguring itself every ten minutes.

Presenting the characters with unique challenges, the space becomes something to explore and dominate, not unlike the space of a video game. Earlier, one of Weyland's team members even announces that she has found a shaft leading to "another level." This could be read only in terms of architecture or in terms of both architecture and gaming. After all, in a post–*Tomb Raider* age, the pyramid setting and its mystery are more in line with computer games than they are with any of the other six films in the *Predator* and *Alien* franchises. In fact, making spectacle out of even the end credits, Anderson stages the sequence as a first-person tour of the pyramid, much as the *Doom* end titles will treat the viewer to a first-person perspective of the installation.

Anderson's obvious affection for science fiction, horror, and action (not to mention James Cameron's *Aliens*) makes him a suitable choice for *Alien vs. Predator*. So would Anderson's niche as a leading adapter of video games to motion pictures, as there had been several *Aliens vs. Predator* video games before the contest was ever seen in a movie theater. In fact, Anderson would follow *Alien vs. Predator* by directing a trailer for the *Doom 3* game and signing to direct a big-screen adaptation of the *Castlevania* video games—a franchise popular since 1986.[38] Anderson's film comes after a number of video games that have matched up these monsters, including a 1993 Super Nintendo game; Capcom's 1994 arcade game; Fox Interactive's 1999 release *Aliens vs. Predator*; and its sequels, *Aliens vs. Predator 2*, released in late 2001 (with an expansion pack, *Aliens vs. Predator 2: Primal Hunt* the following August), and 2003's *Aliens vs. Predator: Extinction*. The games appeared in a number of formats, ranging from the coin-operated to the desktop PC to gaming consoles such as Sony's Playstation and Microsoft's Xbox.

But the film is drawn from more than the video games. (Indeed, while Anderson brings a video game sensibility to the movie, he does not use their plotlines.) The games were released after Dark Horse Comics published a host of *Aliens vs. Predator* comic books. Not including various trade paperback, hardcover, or "Dark Horse Classics" reprints, this roster includes the original miniseries published between 1989 and 1990; a twelve-issue series from 1993 to 1995 (*Deadliest of the Species*); two miniseries in 1995 (*Duel* and *War*); a graphic novel in 1996 (*Booty*); a four-issue miniseries in 1998 (*Eternal*); and two more in 2000 (*Xenogenesis* and, in an embarrassment of licenses, *Aliens vs. Predator vs. The Terminator*).[39] After the release of the video games and the film, Dark Horse would pit the two species against each other again in 2004 (*Thrill of the Hunt*) and in 2006 (*Civilized Beasts*). It is interesting to note that Dark Horse began publishing *Aliens vs. Predator* titles with only one *Predator* film in the marketplace; Fox's *Predator 2* was just over a year from release. These comic books, taken with the feature films, the video games, several toy lines, a set of trading cards, and a trilogy of novels from Bantam imprint Spectra, make *Alien vs. Predator* an ideal—and sometimes surreal—model of entertainment economics wherein a single property is leveraged across various media and platforms.

Like *Doom*, the film version of *Alien vs. Predator* languished in development for over a decade. According to Jeffrey Wells, who cites Fox and talent agency sources, the studio tried to launch the match-up in 1993, but suspended the project when the producing rights (which involved nearly half a dozen high-powered names) could not be agreed upon.[40] The studio found new motivation, however, in the wake of the video games and the success of New Line Cinema's *Freddy vs. Jason* (2003), in which the notorious main characters of the *A Nightmare on Elm Street* and *Friday the 13th* franchises face off. That film earned $36.4 million when it opened over the second weekend of August. *Alien vs. Predator* opened on the same weekend a year later (on a Friday the 13th, no less), and earned $38.3 million—higher than expectations and better than *Freddy vs. Jason*. (The other movie opening that weekend, also a franchise film, also overperformed: Disney's *The Princess Diaries 2: Royal Engagement*.)

For all of the monsters who do battle in the movie, the film has surprisingly little in the way of teeth. The violence of *Alien vs. Predator* is much softer than that of the six gory *Alien* and *Predator* films that precede it; as *Variety* notes, "This may be the first MPAA rating partially attributed to 'slime.'"[41] When the Predators first attack the humans, five people are killed, but there is hardly any gore—just a bit of blood on one of the Predator's serrated blades. (Compare this to the chest-bursting scene from the original *Alien* or the skinned corpses and butchered bodies of the first *Predator*.) Perhaps to compensate, the filmmakers overdesigned the special effects. When the parasitic "facehugger" aliens leap forward, the motion all but stops and the camera rotates around, in what seems to be an anemic version of *The Matrix*'s bullet time effect. Similarly, when one Predator fires its laser cannon and another detonates its thermonuclear self-destruct system, the blasts are more globular, and have a far more computer-generated look than their counterparts in *Predator* and *Predator 2*. This stands to reason. Between the releases of these films and *Alien vs. Predator* Hollywood became ensconced in CGI; what is notable here is that the filmmakers of *Alien vs. Predator* do not use the new technology to re-create the effects of the preceding films, but to elaborate on them. More to the point, however, by the time the film was made, *Alien vs. Predator* had become a franchise exploited across a range of platforms appealing largely to the young. The filmmakers, making the only non-R-rated feature of the seven starring one or both these properties, would have to find their spectacle somewhere.

The influence of game design on filmmaking is also seen in the same summer's *The Chronicles of Riddick*. Like *Alien vs. Predator*, writer/director David Twohy's film is a PG-13 sequel to an R-rated hybrid of horror and science fiction—in this case, *Pitch Black* (2000), also directed by Twohy, and starring Vin Diesel as convict Richard B. Riddick. A survival tale, the earlier film is set on a desert planet plagued by nocturnal horrors. The sequel is a much larger affair, an epic about a galactic holy war that follows Riddick from world to world as he fights for the freedom of every human soul in the universe.

Pitch Black was produced by Polygram Filmed Entertainment, which was absorbed by Universal in a 1998 merger. Just prior to the film's release, Universal retooled the television campaign to emphasize Riddick and the film's action. The movie opened to nearly triple the $4 million it was expected to gross. Overall, however, *Pitch Black* did not shine at the box office—domestically or internationally—but was a great success on DVD.[42] But with Diesel's next film, *The Fast and the Furious* (2001), Universal had a surprise summer hit. While still releasing *The Fast and the Furious* overseas, the studio began developing a *Pitch Black* sequel with *X-Men* screenwriter David Hayter.[43] Eventually, Universal passed on Hayter's submission, as well as one by Akiva Goldsman, and returned to an earlier, more ambitious pitch by Twohy—a pitch that Twhoy claims was the first of potentially three sequels.[44]

The Chronicles of Riddick would be made for $110 million, approximately five times the budget of Pitch Black. Unlike Pitch Black, but much like Alien vs. Predator, the sequel would be a heavily franchised property. There would be one major difference, however. Whereas the film version of Alien vs. Predator was the culmination of the concept's longstanding history of largely independent products, The Chronicles of Riddick was the springboard for a more streamlined set of titles. An animated short, The Chronicles of Riddick: Dark Fury, was released straight to DVD just four days after The Chronicles of Riddick opened in theaters on June 11, 2004. Directed by Peter Chung, the short features a story by Twohy and the voices of Riddick franchise cast members Diesel, Keith David, Rhiana Griffith, and Nick Chinlund. Chung, the creator of the animated series Aeon Flux, had previously written and directed a segment of The Animatrix, a collection of nine animated shorts expanding on the Wachowski brothers' Matrix universe. With Dark Fury, Chung similarly augments the world of Riddick.

If Dark Fury is a mini-sequel to Pitch Black, and mini-prequel to The Chronicles of Riddick, then the video game The Chronicles of Riddick: Escape from Butcher Bay is an interactive prequel to both. Released on June 1, within the same two weeks as the animated short and the feature film, the game fills in Pitch Black's backstory as the player guides Riddick through his escape from the Butcher Bay penal colony. The game features dialogue spoken and co-written by Diesel. Also, in a gaming industry first, the PC version includes an audio commentary detailing the development of the game, much like the filmmaker commentaries heard on so many DVDs.

Apart from the narrow timeframe in which all of these media were released, what keeps The Chronicles of Riddick bound so closely to the animated short and the video game—especially the video game—is the fact that the film's aesthetics are so driven by CGI, from its more overt special effects to its sets. In fact, the apparent influence of video games on the film was singled out by many critics, from the west coast (Variety, The Hollywood Reporter, the Los Angeles Times) to the West End. Variety's David Rooney argues that the film's look "has the flattened, artificial dimensionality of a videogame," while Jessica Winter asks in London's Time Out, "Is this a movie or a projected video game? The compartmentalized narrative and CGI cityscapes strongly suggest the latter."[45]

Both the quantity and the quality of the CGI imbue the film with a sense that the action is taking place on anything but a physical plane: the expansive views of painterly skies and planetary vistas give the film an animated quality, while the more incidental action (such as a crash-landing on the planet Crematoria) recall video game interstitials that bridge sections of game play with expository, cinematic pieces of business. The Chronicles of Riddick even manifests a video game sensibility with its opening sequence. Here, Twohy establishes the film's villain, the Lord Marshal (Colm Feore) and his legion of "Necromonger" soldiers against elaborate computer-generated sets and with narration by a member of the "Elemental" race, Aereon (Judi Dench). The scene resembles the introductory sequences of many video games. Short and cinematic, these pieces generally parcel out exposition from a more omniscient point of view than the one the user will experience during play.

The visuals in The Chronicles of Riddick are so processed that even its most visceral, physical action feels abstract. On the planet Helion, soldiers attempt to apprehend an uncooperative Riddick. (As they approach, a man cries out from offscreen, "You don't understand—he can help us! He can help us!") Riddick snuffs out the room's candlelight; transplanted eyes enable him to see in the dark, motivating a number of stylized point-of-view shots in this film and in Pitch Black. Riddick then unleashes himself on the soldiers as they fire their weapons. The muzzle flashes create a strobing effect that annihilates any sense of continuity. The strobing also gives the impression that the thirty-second fight contains between 100 and 150 shots, even though the actual number is less. Twohy uses muzzle flashes to similar ends soon after, in a gun battle between Necromonger forces and Helion ground troops.

As for Riddick, he and his cohorts later dispatch two- or perhaps even three-dozen Necromongers on the surface of Crematoria, primarily in hand-to-hand combat. The intensity of the editing makes it impossible to know for sure, as does the scene's confused sense of geography (are those eight bodies on the ground, or four bodies shown twice?). The cinematography compounds the disorientation. The image is distorted, presumably from the heat of the rising sun, which we are told bakes the planet surface with temperatures of seven hundred degrees. Though Riddick is rated PG-13, action sequences such as these highlight the irony that underlies much of the genre's violence as much as, if not more than, the brutality of a Rambo or Predator does. As filmmakers top one another, and as the viewer's tolerance increases, filmmakers try to approximate physical sensation with technique that in the digital age, has become increasingly expressionistic. This technique may seem to make the action more intense, but really, it only widens the gulf between seeing an act depicted and sensing it on one's actual flesh. Unsated then, the audience's appetite for such images grows, and the cycle repeats. It is in this context that the gaming industry's evolution of the first-person shooter, as seen in various *Doom* and *Resident Evil* titles and many others, is so disquieting.

The spectacle of *The Chronicles of Riddick* may sometimes feel abstract, but Twohy does try to ground it all in real mythic and religious archetypes. At first, Riddick's background is a mystery. On Helion (where Keith David's Imam from *Pitch Black* has been telling his daughter bedtime stories mythologizing Riddick), Aereon and others question the escaped convict: "What do you know of your early years?" "Do you remember your home world? Where it was?" "Have you met any others?" "Others like yourself?" Riddick dodges the questions. In keeping with other heroic archetypes, Riddick is a man with a past, but possibly one that escapes even him. Thus, as the action unfolds, Riddick will fulfill his purpose and recover his identity at the same time. *The Chronicles of Riddick* may not put as fine a point on this concept as does say, *Robocop, The Matrix*, or even *Resident Evil*, but it is consistent with them just the same.

As the scene continues, Aereon and Imam teach us about the Furyans, the one race that dared oppose the Necromongers, and a little more about Riddick, who, as it will turn out, is the Furyans' favorite son. Here, while many action filmmakers draw from the archetype of the martyr and from the Christological, Twohy goes back even further: as a Moses of the distant future, Riddick descends from a line of warriors prophesied to overthrow the Lord Marshal, who in turn had newborn Furyan males strangled with their own umbilical cords. Riddick escaped this fate, but only reluctantly accepts his destiny as a liberator. Ultimately, he returns to face the Lord Marshal and frees his people from religious persecution.

Aereon is also a font of exposition during the film's opening. Of the Necromonger leader, she tells us, "He alone has made a pilgrimage to the gates of the Underverse [a dark dimension at the center of the Necromonger religion] and returned a different being—stronger, stranger, half alive and half something else." Recalling the many action movie figures who have been possessed by two opposing natures, would this make the Lord Marshal The Man Who Knows Death? What is interesting here is that in Western and action movies, this dichotomy typically exists inside the hero. Thus, with the Lord Marshal's duality and Riddick's messianic qualities and shrouded past, Twohy gives qualities of the archetypal hero to the film's hero *and* its villain.

A hero's missing past, also draped in religiosity, factors into another one of 2004's summer spectacles, *Van Helsing*. Written and directed by Stephen Sommers, who had also made Universal's *The Mummy* (1999) and *The Mummy Re-*

turns (2001), the film stars Hugh Jackman as a nineteenth-century antiauthoritarian who battles supernatural evils at the behest of an order of monks based in Rome. As one of the monks lectures Van Helsing (and helpfully explains to us), "When we found you crawling up the steps of this church half-dead, it was clear to all of us that you had been sent to do God's work. . . . You already lost your memory as a penance for past sins. If you wish to recover it, I suggest you continue to heed God's call."

Van Helsing cannot remember who he was, or even how old he is (though he does remember fighting the Romans at Masada). As the movie progresses, Van Helsing's missing memory moves from backstory to the forefront, as his enemy, Count Dracula (Richard Roxburgh), reveals his ancient and paternal relationship to the hero. All of this applies equally to Jackman's Wolverine character in the X-Men films, particularly X2. In the sequel, Wolverine's search for his past leads him to an enemy who, long ago, helped make Wolverine the mutant he is today. That Jackman plays both characters, and that X2 was released just one year prior to Van Helsing, makes the derivative nature of the title character that much more apparent.

The saint/sinner dichotomy the monk calls to mind is stressed later, when the woman Van Helsing is sent to protect from Dracula, Anna Valerious (Kate Beckinsale) remarks, "Some say you're a murderer, Mr. Van Helsing. Others say you're a holy man." Summoning the archetype that has defined so many action heroes, Van Helsing answers, "It's a bit of both." Late in the film, the war between Van Helsing's opposing natures reaches the supernatural sphere when Van Helsing is bitten by a werewolf. The theme of duality, so central to the action film and the genres that sired it, becomes literal as Van Helsing waits to transform. "Now you will become that which you have hunted so passionately," says Frankenstein's Monster (Shuler Hensley).

When the transformation comes during Van Helsing's hand-to-hand combat with Dracula, it marks not only this theme's coming to fruition, but also Sommers's overindulgence in computer-generated spectacle. When Van Helsing and Dracula fight, they fight as a werewolf and a winged beast. Ultimately, Jackman and Roxburgh are not even seen. Instead, it is their animated replacements that wage the film's final battle. Sommers, rather than redeem his audience's (presumed) investment in his actors at this crucial juncture, chooses to simply overwhelm the eye with CG creatures to which the viewer has no attachment. It is neither wondrous nor any wonder: this has been Sommers's style throughout the film.

Sommers's choice is a pity really, considering how powerful he makes Jackman's image elsewhere in the movie. The first revelation of Van Helsing is parceled out bit by bit, much as that of Robocop and others have been. We get our first glimpse of Van Helsing on a WANTED poster. The poster is torn from a brick wall and the camera pans to find a shadowy figure seen from behind. He regards the poster and sets off when he hears a woman scream. We next see him from high above; in his black garb and wide-brimmed hat, he all but disappears into the street. Next, the camera tilts from the open-eyed corpse of a little girl to our antihero as he crosses himself. With the brim of his hat still tilted down, hiding his face, he looks up. Only now do we see Van Helsing's eyes—and only his eyes, as the rest of his face is concealed by his costume. Later in the film, Sommers crafts an image of Van Helsing that is similarly dark and even more iconic. After loading his gun with silver bullets, Van Helsing steps forward, in and then out of silhouette. His form, complete with the brim of his hat, cuts against the bright steam. His is a formidable presence—and moreover, it recalls the stylized images from vigilante movies of the 1980s, Sudden Impact chief among them.

Ultimately, Sommers wastes his reverence for his hero, not to mention his lead actor's talents (Jackman would win a Tony and an Emmy in 2004 and 2005, respectively) by sublimating all to spectacle. This begins with the opening teaser sequence, a black and white affair in which rioting villagers lay siege to Dr. Frankenstein's castle. As Van Helsing is a Universal presentation and features a roster of characters from the studio's classic 1930s and early 1940s horror films, this first sequence promises to be a tribute—and insofar as its digital backgrounds evoke the Gothic matte paintings and photography of those classic films, it succeeds. Of course, Sommers modernizes the imagery: as Frankenstein's Monster stands atop a burning windmill, the camera swoops over the abomination and reveals electricity crackling inside its exposed brain case. The mill then collapses with the camera peering straight down; from the wreckage, a gear flies up at the viewer.

This opening teaser recalls those of Riddick, Resident Evil, Doom, and others. In each of these cases, the action establishes the film's tone and locale, is connected to the plot or backstory of what is to follow, but does not establish the main character. (This is unlike, say, the opening teasers of James Bond movies, in which the action is often unrelated to the story, but always showcases Bond.) With this first bit of business, Sommers establishes Van Helsing as having a look and a structure that are two parts action movie to one part video game.

This is borne out in the next sequence, in which the film takes us from Transylvania to Paris. Here, Sommers introduces Van Helsing and pits him against Mr. Hyde—the first classic movie monster (though not originally a Universal one) whom Van Helsing must destroy. Voiced by Robbie Coltrane, the oversized Mr. Hyde is a CG character. As *Cinefex* reports, Mr. Hyde had previously been translated to film only through make-up effects and skilled performances, but Sommers proposed that his Mr. Hyde be an "all-digital 'Super-Hyde.'"[46] Universal resisted the idea, and so, according to visual effects supervisor Ben Snow, "Stephen told us that if we were going to do a CG character, he would have to be really, really cool. One of the keys to that . . . was to make him very agile. Stephen came up with a lot of dynamic stunts for him to do, and his physical ability to do those things had to be incorporated into his design."[47] This explains—though does not justify—why *Van Helsing*'s Mr. Hyde is improbable in every way: his size, his agility, his agility *given* his size. During the fight, the giant jumps and leaps about the bell tower of Notre Dame (which in reality was a warehouse formerly used by NASA).[48] In this cathedral setting, Sommers indicates a deep lack of faith—not in God, but in any plausible physics model. Mr. Hyde's acrobatics and the rubbery quality of his animation both strongly suggest not a classic movie and literary figure, but a video game character. Moreover, they are but early examples of how the filmmakers render the movie's action.

Sommers also uses this battle to establish Van Helsing's arsenal, which includes handguns, hand-wound saw blades, and a pistol-mounted grappling hook. He is later outfitted with an automatic crossbow—the primary weapon he uses to protect Anna's village from an attack by Dracula's flying vampire brides. In this scene, also like a video game, the sky becomes a shooting gallery for Van Helsing, whose targets are largely digital creations. As the attack goes on, Sommers reveals a penchant for animating even his human characters and stunt performers in ways that nature—and logic—never intended. Anna has a particular tendency to somersault her way through action sequences. Likewise, Van Helsing later performs a 360-degree somersault and lands between two horses. Actually, this scene includes two Van Helsings—the CG one who performs the somersault, and the live-action one who takes over from the point at which he lands.[49] The filmmakers have a clear affinity for the flip: *Van Helsing* tallies around twenty-five flips, not counting swings, leaps, high falls, or other acro- and aerobatics—but including a flip performed by a flaming stagecoach.

Naturally, it is during the film's climactic sequence that Sommers sends *Van Helsing* into overdrive—a feat, given how overwrought the action and special effects have already been. A prime example from this last scene is the series of

Something Wicked Came and Went: The overmechanized weaponry and the title character of Van Helsing—a film that, like The Chronicles of Riddick, fell short of becoming a major Universal franchise in summer 2004. (From the author's collection.)

stunts executed by Frankenstein's Monster and Anna outside Castle Dracula. Escaping from the castle, the Monster swings from rope to rope, throwing antiwerewolf serum to Anna, who catches it while performing her own high-wire work. "Frankenstein essentially becomes Spider-Man," Ben Snow quipped to *Cinefex*, explaining that the swinging motions were performed by the Monster's "digital double."[50] This is telling. Frankenstein's Monster is bulky, mechanical, lumbering; Spider-Man is slight, agile, fluid. These characters are opposites, but in their blocking, Sommers and his colleagues make them virtually the same. It is possible that with Universal having invested so much in his tentpole film, Sommers staged *Van Helsing* this way to compete with the *Spider-Man* franchise; indeed, the summer movie season of 2004 saw the releases of both *Van Helsing* and *Spider-Man 2*.

Regardless, equating the abomination that is Frankenstein's Monster with your friendly neighborhood Spider-Man marks a breakdown in how action can be motivated by, and a reflection of, character. Though there is much to malign in the action cinema of, say, the 1980s, films such as *Die Hard* and the first two *Lethal Weapons* demonstrate that character development can include how an action sequence is staged and also how the character moves in ways that are uniquely his, rather than uniquely an animator's. In the digital era, it seems that CGI increasingly tempts filmmakers to ignore this dimension of action filmmaking, to ignore restraint and economy of motion in favor of more spectacular movement. This is unfortunate, as it is this restraint and economy of motion that can give good action films their subtle realism and, as a consequence, their true primal quality. In many modern action films, these qualities are falling into jeopardy, far more than the characters are in any palpable sense. As Syd Dutton, the film's matte painting supervisor, told *Cinefex*, "Working with Stephen Sommers, it was about making it big—bigger, better and more bold. . . . Never once did Stephen say to us, 'I think you've gone too far.' It was always, 'That looks great—make it bigger!'"[51]

Restraint is utterly foreign to *Van Helsing* and was none too relevant to Universal's plans for promoting and franchising it. Eight months before the film was even released, NBC commissioned a pilot from Universal Network Television that, while not technically a spin-off or sequel, "would be set in the same universe" as *Van Helsing*.[52] While this project never materialized, *The Hollywood Reporter* detailed what Universal called "'an unprecedented, companywide synergistic marketing effort to launch 'Van Helsing' worldwide and celebrate the studio's legacy.'" The campaign included Universal's "The Monster Legacy Collection" DVDs, clothing lines, consumer products based on both classic and newly created monsters, attractions at Universal Studios Hollywood and Madame Toussaud's Wax Museum in New York, the *Van Helsing* video game, a straight-to-DVD animated prequel, and promotional partnerships with the Carl's Jr. fast food chain, Toys "R" Us, and appropriately enough, the American Red Cross, in support of local blood drives.[53]

Universal also partnered with cable network TNT, a division of Time Warner. During the first two rounds of the 2004 NBA playoffs, as well as during TNT's *Inside the NBA*, the network aired customized vignettes combining highlights from basketball games with footage from *Van Helsing*. Lest this pairing seem incongruous, Turner Entertainment's senior vice president of sponsorships and marketing, Chris Eames, explained it this way: "We think 'Van Helsing' is going to be a big blockbuster this summer, and it fits the NBA like a glove. . . . We have created a partnership that really exploits the theme of their movie with the themes of our playoff coverage—heroes rise and fall, forces gathering, etc."[54] It is Eames's use of "etc." that underscores just how hollow his sentiment is; it would have been more honest (but almost certainly less advisable) to simply acknowledge that *Van Helsing* and the NBA are both big brands, highly visual and highly corporate.

Then again, the action of *Van Helsing* does recall so much gameplay. *Van Helsing* illustrates how a larger force is currently reshaping action filmmaking: the increasingly intertwined relationship between movies and video games—not just aesthetically, but practically as well. As Graham Leggat, a former film marketer and publicist, and video game columnist, observes, "Huge parts of both industries are rising out of a central industry: digital media. Film and games are drawing from a common pool of technology and software, and technology dictates aesthetics. It's not the only factor, but it's a huge factor."[55]

Indeed, action films have long resembled video games. In *Die Hard* for example, the hero pursues a single goal (freeing hostages), progresses from floor to floor (or level to level), and gains, loses, and regains weapons and other resources. Likewise, the utterly disposable *Death Wish 3* seems to anticipate the first-person shooter, with an extended final sequence in which Paul Kersey, stalking across several city blocks, uses a range of weapons against a vast supply of gang members firing at him from various elevations. Yet it is more intuitive to deem such films as *The Chronicles of Riddick* and *Van Helsing* "video game movies." This is partly due to the use of digital media by both game developers and filmmakers, as Leggat cites. Another factor is the leveraging of properties across various platforms. Of the merchandise and promotional tie-ins attending *Van Helsing*'s release, the most significant may be the video game (some radio commercials advertised them jointly) and the straight-to-DVD animated short, *Van Helsing: Assignment in London*, a prequel in which Van Helsing pursues Mr. Hyde. Visually, narratively, and technologically, the film has more in common with these two products than it does with virtually any other facet of the "synergestic marketing effort."

The *Van Helsing* franchise, like the *Chronicles of Riddick* franchise, follows the model of *The Matrix*, which saw *The Matrix Reloaded* and the Wachowski-created game *Enter the Matrix* both released on May 15, 2003, with *The Animatrix* debuting less than three weeks later on June 3. To *Sight and Sound*'s Jonathan Romney, these products form "a nexus of interlocking fictions which, taken together, lead the consumer down a choice of diverging narrative paths."[56] As a further example of this convergence, the Atari game *The Matrix: Path of Neo* (2005) allows the player to experience Neo's journey toward becoming The One and to fight as Neo in the films' most memorable battles. This game does not expand the universe the way *Enter the Matrix* does, but it does give players the opportunity to spin new outcomes off the trilogy's storyline.

From video to video games, the influences of science fiction and digital technology have blurred the boundaries of the action genre. So has Hollywood's increasing use of comic books as source material—both for content and for style. In such films, as in many of the action films belonging to the fantastical trend discussed in this chapter, the hero himself is a special effect, much as he had been a superman in the 1980s. After an interlude in which movies popularized an everyman hero, the figurative superheroes of the 1980s became the literal ones of the late 1990s and beyond. They have become the newest focal point of our mythic lives. With their great powers comes this great responsibility—and the final trend of this study.

Excelsior!
March of the Superheroes

We're the future, Charles, not them.
They no longer matter.
—Magneto (Ian McKellan) in X-Men (2000)

The futurism and heightened realities of many of the films studied in the last chapter all evoke a certain comic book sensibility. Naturally, this is most manifest in the rash of action films based on comic book properties, one that began in the 1990s. Much of the nineties were glutted with would-be-blockbusters about superheroes, but it was not until the decade's later years that the comic book film became such a pronounced trend in the genre, as the *Die Hard* and new disaster models receded. In addition, it is the decade's later years that saw a breaking of the nearly twenty-year stranglehold that DC Comics had held on the comic book film with just the *Batman* and *Superman* franchises.

Of course, the comics have always provided grist for Hollywood's development machine. Flash Gordon, Buck Rogers, and Dick Tracy all prospered on the big screen in the late 1930s. Batman and Superman joined them starting in the 1940s. Beginning in the 1950s, comic book properties flourished on television. In the 1970s, Richard Donner's *Superman* was Hollywood's one superhero blockbuster, while the major entries of the 1980s would include Richard Lester's *Superman II* (1980), John Milius's *Conan the Barbarian* (1982) and Tim Burton's *Batman* (1989). In the next decade, the *Batman* sequels (1992, 1995, 1997) would succeed the *Superman* series (1978, 1980, 1983, 1987) as Warner Bros.'s—and indeed, Hollywood's—comic book–feature film franchise.

Throughout the 1980s, comic book adaptations were a noticeably different strain of adventure film than the action movies already discussed in this book. In 1989, for instance, *Batman* and *Lethal Weapon 2*, released just weeks apart by Warner Bros., were obviously different kinds of films, even if many people who saw one would also see the other. In the 1990s, however, the comic book film would be increasingly co-opted by the fantastical form of the action genre for at least two reasons: the genre would exhaust the models that differentiated it from superhero adventures (the *Die Hard* model, the buddy film, etc.);

and the genre's aesthetics would increasingly emulate those of the comics, just as it would emulate those of the video game.

The 1980s and 1990s mark a nearly twenty-year span in which just two DC Comics characters largely dominated the comic book film. Other comic book- or superhero-themed adventures rarely became blockbusters or launched franchises. A roster of these disappointments would include *Supergirl* (1984), *Red Sonja* (1985), *The Punisher* (1989), *Darkman* and *Dick Tracy* (both 1990), *The Shadow* (1994), *Judge Dredd* (1995), and *The Phantom* (1996). DC's rival imprint, Marvel Comics, especially suffered, struggling and failing to parlay a single one of its titles into a film series. A 1991 adaptation of *Captain America*, directed by Cyborg's Albert Pyun, did not have a theatrical release. *Fantastic Four* was adapted in the early 1990s by executive producer Roger Corman, but was not released at all—not even on video. And while *The Uncanny X-Men* would eventually become a blockbuster film series starting in 2000, Marvel had sold the rights to Twentieth Century Fox in 1993—a move which *Daily Variety* reported as being Marvel's "aggressive effort to spawn its own franchise to compete with Warner Bros.' 'Batman' and 'Batman Returns'"—with Fox committing to "fast-track" the property to the screen.[1]

In the 1990s, Alex Proyas's *The Crow* (1994), based on James O'Barr's comics, first published in 1989, was the first non-DC property to establish a franchise; like *Robocop* and the later *Blade*, *The Crow* would spawn several sequels and even a television series. The film begins on "Hell Night," the night before Halloween. As denizens of the film's unnamed, uninhabitable city set fires that bathe it in an apocalyptic glow, a crime lord's posse brutalizes and murders musician Eric Draven (Brandon Lee) and his girlfriend. One year later, Eric rises from the dead to conduct a vigilante campaign against the killers.

The Crow is well-known for the grim irony in which an on-set gun accident killed the actor playing the risen avenger, three days before he would have finished his work on the film. Upon Lee's death, production was suspended. Filming resumed at the insistence of Lee's fiancée, Eliza Hutton, and his mother, Linda Lee Caldwell, also Bruce Lee's widow. The film was completed with the assistance of DreamQuest, one of the companies responsible for the special effects of *Total Recall*. The company used computers to remove Lee from certain scenes, and to place him in others that had been filmed after his death; to put his head on another actor's body; and to cast his face as a reflection in a mirror. The effort would prove to be a leap forward in the technique of digital compositing. As DreamQuest executive producer Mark Galvin claimed, "we've opened up a Pandora's box for the digital world."[2]

Apart from Lee's death, *The Crow* is mostly noted for its visuals, trading as the film does on violence, atmosphere, and sensory overload. Proyas, production designer Alex McDowell, and cinematographer Dariusz Wolski recreate the style of O'Barr's comic—a style drawn from Renaissance sculpture, gothic horror, *film noir*, and O'Barr's two years of medical school, according to the film's publicity.[3] Translating the extreme imagery—to say nothing of the violence—of O'Barr's comic to the screen would be, for Proyas, a chance to indulge himself stylistically, as his background in directing music videos had prepared him to do. According to Proyas,

> The comic book is black-and-white, and it takes place in a very black-and-white world of good and evil. . . . We've given it that quality through lighting and being very selective and specific about color. We're not using any blues or greens, giving it a dark, expressionistic look. It's a very aggressive style, driven by rock-and-roll music.[4]

This brooding, high-contrast style is not limited to the tall shadows and narrow alleys of this world. Eric represents his creators' palette at its most distilled. He wears all black, including his long raincoat. His stringy black hair, resembling so much rainwater or blood, hangs over his face, which is made-up in pearl-white with black lips and eyes.

It is debatable whether the risen Eric Draven ever became a true pop-culture icon. What is clear is that the filmmakers treat him as one, as they photograph him in silhouette and inaugurate him with a montage of his dressing and applying his make-up. They also bestow upon him a symbol—the shape of a crow—that Eric leaves drawn on the photograph of a victim, painted on a wall in blood, and outlined in fire on a dock. Left for the benefit of those who will come upon Eric's ghastly work, the crow is a device for mythologizing Eric, and for branding his vengeance. The crow-shape is more than a symbol of justice: it is also its logo.

Terence Rafferty heralds *The Crow*'s stark images, "in which the hero, placed in the evocative ruins, seems to embody the dead-end glamour of all the wounded loners of American movies, the weary gunslingers who have to clean up the town before we'll let them fade away."[5] Even with his otherworldly powers and his over-styled appearance, Eric Draven is still a *noir*-esque vigilante descended from those who anchored the early action film in the 1970s. But unlike the indignation of that era's Harry Callahans and Paul Kerseys, Eric's rage is not society's rage, not *our* rage. It is only *his* rage—if that. David Denby questions the sincerity of the character's emotions by charging that, "Everyone in the movie is angry because rage, as a mood, is highly commercial."[6] Along similar lines, Rafferty claims that The Crow is "so dark, so moody, and so seductively overwrought that it seems to have sprung directly from the fevered consciousness of an alienated sixteen-year-old."[7] Indeed, it is disquieting how snugly Eric's frantic flashbacks to his fiancée's rape and his own murder fit with the film's overall hard rock sensibility. And though the gothic buildings, persistent rainfall, and deep shadows are atmospheric, they do not exude the same low-key dread as does Death Wish's antiseptic hospital.

Denby continues his attack on the void at The Crow's center. Citing how Eric redeems a junkie by literally squeezing the drugs from her veins, Denby reflects that

> As in so many pop artifacts, the dirtier the violence, the more moralistic the framework for it. . . . When Clint Eastwood delivered this moralized sadism 23 years ago in Dirty Harry, smart people knew what to make of it. Dirty Harry was American fascism. When it's done as a cartoon, it's hip, it's style, it's great. But how great an achievement is it to impose style on such degraded material? (emphasis in original).[8]

Peter Rainer has another 1970s referent. He argues that The Crow encourages the audience "to relish the killings 'Death Wish'–style, but [the movie] is so far removed from any social agenda that, unlike the 'Death Wish' films, its squashings and torchings are pure theater. It's a reactionary movie without anything to react against."[9]

As comic books tend toward the young, it would stand to reason that comic book films do, as well. Historically, their violence has been limited to ensure the patronage of young audiences. But The Crow brings to the comic book adaptation a new level of violence, one that narrows the gap between this mode of filmmaking and the more traditional action film. This violence would be matched by Blade (1998), the film with which Marvel spawned its first film franchise and began to supplant DC as the major source of comic book–based content. As Blade, Wesley Snipes plays a human/vampire half-breed, who battles vampires to protect humanity. Like its title character, the film is also something of a hybrid. Blade does not draw strictly from the formula that its comic book film successors do, but instead combines elements of the comic book with those of the more traditional action film, thus marking a transition between the two. (For instance, Blade possesses special powers, but also an arsenal of exotic weapons.) The first in a series of successful Marvel adaptations, Blade's success can be attributed more to its being a high-concept star vehicle than to audience awareness of the character. Blade does not belong to the pantheon of great comic book heroes: he is a minor character from *Tomb of Dracula*, a splattery comic book about Dracula's pursuers, first published in 1973. For the film, much of his character, style, and mythology were newly invented.

More like a traditional action film—and unlike *Spider-Man* (2002), *Hulk* (2003), *Daredevil* (2003), *Batman Begins* (2005), *Fantastic Four* (2005), and to a certain extent, *X-Men* (2000)—*Blade* does not show the hero's origin. It does, however, show his birth, in an opening scene that establishes cinematographer Theo Van De Sande's bleached blue palette, as Blade is born to a bloodied mother. The paleness gives the film a frosty detachment that is the photographic equivalent of Snipes's performance. It also increases the impact of the film's reds—blood in particular.

This palette continues into the first scene set in the present day. A human is nearly feasted-upon in a back alley dance club when director Stephen Norrington introduces Blade. Much as Verhoeven does in *Robocop*, and Sommers will in *Van Helsing*, Norrington withholds the reveal of his title character, reducing him to iconic parts. First, the filmmakers show only Blade's boots and the bottom of his cloak. Next, they reveal more of Blade's body, as the camera tilts up along his back. They then cut to Blade's front; the camera continues tilting upward, taking in Blade's costume, but stopping at his throat. Next come several shots of partygoers reacting to Blade's arrival. They part and recede. Only with this reverence is Blade then fully revealed.

Justifying their regard, Blade then conducts a slaughter. He fires shotguns at vampires who disintegrate upon impact (first their flesh goes, then their skeletons). He also uses an automatic weapon, a sword, a dagger, a double-edged throwing blade, and—finally—a rifle that fires not bullets, but stakes, predicting the automatic crossbow of *Van Helsing*. As much as the computer-generated disintegrations, the weapons themselves are a spectacle, like Schwarzenegger's armaments and Robocop's gun. In fact, Blade carries a handgun that elaborates on Robocop's: massive, blockish, and like the weapons of many fantastical action movies, futuristic in design while discharging bursts of contemporary ammunition. Likewise, the breast plating and sunglasses of Blade's costume resemble Robocop's chassis and visor.

It could be argued that the rest of Blade's outfit—all black, supplemented with black gloves, leather, and again, the sunglasses—predicts the costumes of *The Matrix*, but more interesting is how these features recall the attire worn by the Schwarzenegger and Stallone characters of the previous decade's more

It Takes One to Know One: *As the half-human, half-vampire of* Blade *(1998), Wesley Snipes battles the undead with an untraditional arsenal. (From the author's collection.)*

paramilitary action films. These outfits insulated their wearers from all that is pathological in a world obsessed with purity. *Blade* shares these concerns with purity and pathology, but on a more literal level. As hematologist Karen Jensen (N'Bushe Wright) explains, vampirism is both a sexually transmitted disease and also a genetic defect that requires gene therapy—specifically, reworking the victim's DNA with a retrovirus. It is of the blood itself. Whereas vampirism had been traditionally cast in terms of deviant sexuality and unholy curses, *Blade*'s depiction of the vampiric adds to its inherent debauchery the 1990s' fascination with, and advances in, harnessing genetic power.

One aspect of Blade's backstory that the filmmakers retain from the comic book is that Blade's mother was bitten by a vampire while pregnant, hence the hero's partial vampirism. As Blade's friend and weaponsmith Whistler (Kris Kristofferson) later adds, Blade's vampirism surfaced at puberty. He had been feeding on the homeless until Whistler found Blade and helped him suppress his darker side and turn his abilities against the undead. Thus, Blade is The Man Who Knows Vampires. Not only does this resonate with the action film's Western- and *noir*-derived emphasis on duality, but it also justifies the film's depiction of Blade as superhuman. As Deacon Frost (Stephen Dorff), Blade's enemy, explains, Blade possesses all of the vampires' strengths but none of their weaknesses; like his bloodthirsty brothers, Blade can perform spectacular leaps and is all but invincible, but unlike them, he can also withstand sunlight. This exceptionality sets him apart from other vampires just as Harry Callahan's sets him apart from other cops.

Of course, Blade relies not just on his powers, but also on his weapons. In one instance, as he readies for battle, the filmmakers include a scene of Blade preparing his arms—a scene that draws both from vampire lore and 1980s filmmaking technique. We see Blade prepare silver bullets, stakes to be launched, and vials of Karen's serum: an anticoagulant base that makes vampire blood actually explode. The punctuation mark at the end of this sequence is Blade pulling a drop cloth from his motorcycle. In its sense of ritual, this brief interlude recalls the montages of *Commando*, *Rambo*, and *Cobra*. Also charged with ritualism is Blade's signature weapon, his sword: acid-etched and made of titanium—as an admiring Frost makes a point of telling us—the sword also features a booby-trapped hilt in case anyone other than Blade tries to wield it.

In an assault on the sanctum of a vampire record keeper, Blade uses his automatic weapon and shotgun to decimate vampires and a vampire-controlled SWAT team, in a scene that predicts the lobby assault of *The Matrix*. Even its falling sheets of water predict the blasted columns and plaster of *The Matrix*'s lobby. But even so, this is the narrow view. A more fundamental connection between *Blade* and *The Matrix* is that they both express an apocalyptic sensibility. In *The Matrix*, one form the apocalypse takes is the machines' feeding on humans bred for this purpose; in *Blade*, it is the impending rise of "La Magra," a blood god that will turn all of humanity vampiric. Appropriately, with the films' shared notion of the apocalypse comes a sense of the conspiratorial—a sensibility that can often attend near-apocalyptic fiction. In *The Matrix*, Morpheus tells Neo that Neo has been living in a dream world, that the Matrix is the world that has been pulled over Neo's eyes to blind him to the truth, and spends the film trying to awaken his charge. All of this echoes the previous summer's *Blade*, in which Blade tells Karen, "You'd better wake up. The world you live in is just a sugar-coated topping. There is another world beneath it—the real world. And if you want to survive it, you'd better learn to pull the trigger."

Blade's sense of the end-times is toned down, but still present, in Marvel's next franchise, the *X-Men* series, adapted from the comic book created by Stan Lee and Jack Kirby, and first published in 1963. The title characters of Bryan Singer's *X-Men* are heroic mutants, each of whom possesses a special gift (be it telekinesis, the power to control the weather, or the ability to fire energy beams from one's eyes) that marks them as the next phase in human evolution. Large factions of both the mutant and "human" populations believe that a war between these two sides of humanity is coming. One such mutant is the megalomaniac Magneto (Ian McKellan), who has the power to control metal and magnetic fields. Magneto has concocted a scheme to mutate all of humanity, making all people brothers and sisters in mutation. Opposing Magneto is the mutant Professor Charles X. Xavier (Patrick Stewart), the headmaster of a school for mutant children. Professor X leads Wolverine (Hugh Jackman), Rogue (Anna Paquin), Storm (Halle Berry), Cyclops (James Marsden), and Dr. Jean Grey (Famke Janssen) on a crusade to stop Magneto and protect humanity—even those humans who hate and fear their mutant counterparts.

The initial phase of Magento's cataclysm is to take the form of an energy wave unleashed from the Statue of Liberty upon an assembly of world dignitaries. This radiation will mutate the humans exposed to it. What Magneto does not know (or care about) is that following mutation, the exposed humans die. Emanating from Liberty Island, this protoplasmic glob of light is regeneration and annihilation collapsed into one. It is also a major special effect in a film studded with special effects. In fact, *X-Men* features so many effects shots that the film's hurried production schedule necessitated Twentieth Century Fox's dividing the effects among seven different companies.[10]

As a superhero tale, *X-Men* also features origin stories. The first is Magneto's, which occurs against the backdrop of a more literal holocaust. The film begins in Poland, 1944. Here, the man who will be Magneto is young Erik Lensherr, torn from his family by Nazis. The film implies that what follows is Erik's first use of his powers: as he reaches out for his parents, the iron gate between them rends. This continues until the Nazi soldiers beat him unconscious. The lighting of this scene establishes blue as the film's dominant color. In this instance, the blue makes the yellow of the Jews' Stars-of-David even more pronounced. This blue-yellow dichotomy introduces the film's concern with difference and persecution.

As the film progresses, however, its blue tints serve a different purpose: as part of Singer and cinematographer Newton Thomas Siegel's use of primary colors, they are part of a visual style that invokes a comic book aesthetic. Soon after Erik's introduction, Singer establishes Jean Grey testifying before an antimutant Congress. Similar to the film's Nazi Poland, this Congress is driven by a blue-gray hue. Behind Jean, who is dressed in a stark red, is a gold crest of the Capitol emanating rays of light. This is a particularly comic book–like graphic. Later, during a battle in Alberta, Canada, the chill blue tint contrasts with (and therefore pronounces) the orange of the flames inside Wolverine's burning truck, and the magenta of Cyclops's eyebeams. Alberta is near the remote Loughlin City dive bar where Wolverine had been introduced and where he meets Rogue. Her origin had already been shown in the Meridian, Mississippi, of "the not too distant future," in a scene dominated by late-afternoon yellows, occasionally highlighted by reds.

As Magneto's plot depends on using Rogue's ability to absorb other mutants' powers, the X-Men foil Magneto by rescuing Rogue from his clutches. While the X-Men avert Magneto's apocalypse (recalling the word's dual components, as discussed in chapter 4), the sense of an all-consuming war deepens in *X2*, especially when government forces storm Professor X's school. The sequel is also a darker affair visually—given to more night shoots and dark interiors than the original. Also directed by Singer, *X2* is again characterized by blue, but just as the film adds new characters to the roster, *X2* also adds a new color to the palette: green. Green had been largely absent from the original film, save for the inside of the Statute of Liberty and Wolverine's spastic flashbacks. In *X2*, though, green drives the film's second half, set in the Alkalai Lake industrial complex—a site crucial to the past that Wolverine strives to piece together.

In fact, while *X-Men* begins with the origins of two central characters, Magneto and Rogue, for a third, Wolverine, the film is the *search* for an origin. Wolverine cannot remember who he was before his healing and regenerative powers led to the gruesome experiment in which someone Wolverine cannot recall cut him open and grafted onto his skeleton an indestructible metal frame, including the foot-long blades that spring from his hands. Wolverine's search for himself, begun in X-Men, now leads him to Alkalai Lake in X2, where, as in the last film, a sprawling storyline that culminates in saving the world also contracts into a captivity/rescue scenario. On Liberty Island, the X-Men save Rogue from Magneto; at Alkalai, Wolverine, his comrades, and a few enemies reunite to rescue Professor X from Colonel Stryker (Brian Cox) and his mutant son, Jason (Michael Reid MacKay). Wheelchair-bound and possessed of extraordinary mental powers, Jason is Professor X's freakish mirror image. One of the ways the filmmakers depict Jason as a grotesque (apart from showing his brain fluid) is by making his eyes different colors: blue and green, the colors of the film's first and second halves, respectively.

Another example of X2's chromatic darkness is new team member Nightcrawler (Alan Cumming), a devil-tailed mutant of indigo flesh—darker even than the blue-slathered Mystique (Rebecca Romijin-Stamos). Singer introduces Nightcrawler attacking the White House and breaching the President's office. Battling the President's Secret Service detail, Nightcrawler's use of martial arts and superpowers, coupled with the filmmakers' use of slow motion, recalls the heroes of The Matrix. His attack is not meant to kill but to advance the cause of "mutant freedom." His pro-mutant stance and X2's pre-apocalyptic air are also visible at the abandoned church where Nightcrawler lives (a setting that recalls the churches of John Woo films). A hand-painted banner hangs outside. Reminiscent of The Road Warrior's "The Vermin Have Inherited the Earth," this one reads "Nature Laughs Last."

Of the Marvel comics adapted to the big screen since Blade, only The Uncanny X-Men is concerned with genetics. Nuclear fallout would have been more resonant to an early 1960s readership, hence the radioactive spider and the gamma bomb explosion that transform Peter Parker and Bruce Banner in The Amazing Spider-Man and The Incredible Hulk respectively. In fact, the Hulk, another co-creation of Stan Lee and Jack Kirby, first appeared in May 1962, while Spider-Man debuted in the August 1962 issue of "Amazing Fantasy," a title Marvel was about to cancel. Both of these debuts preceded, by only a few months, the Cuban missile crisis.

For the film versions of these titles, the late-twentieth and early-twenty-first century interest in genetics replaces these radioactive triggers. In 2002's

Spider-Man, it is a genetically engineered species of super spider that gives Peter (Tobey Maguire) the bite that endows him with his strength and spider senses. It also enables him to discharge webs from his wrists, as opposed to firing them from the contraptions he builds in the comic. In the following summer's *Hulk*, Bruce (Eric Bana) is exposed to gamma radiation that brings out his inner Hulk only in combination with his modified DNA—a gift from his maverick scientist father, who had been working for the military to genetically engineer its troops' immunity to biological weapons. Critic Ella Taylor, noting how *Hulk* manifests some of our contemporary anxieties, and echoing the comments of *The Core*'s John Rogers, writes, "It is not, finally, our fighting men who most freak us out, but our scientists, those who divorce thought from feeling, who try to improve on nature, who insist on tinkering with food, sheep and—scariest of all—us."[11]

Peter Parker and Bruce Banner are played by actors, but their superhero alter egos are, for the most part, computer-generated creations. In fact, Universal's publicists make sure that potential viewers know just how computer-generated the Hulk is. Universal specifies that the "meticulous work from the wizards at ILM [Industrial Light and Magic]" included developing and painting one hundred layers of skin (the layers representing skin color, but also wrinkles, wounds, moisture, blemishes, dirt, and more); creating 1,165 muscle shapes for the creature's range of movement; "utilizing 69 technical artists, 41 animators, 35 compositors, 10 muscle animators, nine CG modelers, eight supervisors, six skin painters, five motion capture wranglers and three art directors;" and spending two and a half million hours in front of the computer.[12]

Given that these films chronicle the exploits of characters who have little to no physical being—who are not actually *there*—there is a touch of irony in the fact that *Spider-Man* and *Hulk*, like *X-Men* and *X2*, begin with credit sequences that take the viewer on a dazzling, animated tour of the inside of the mutated body. The main titles of the *X-Men* films are more of the brain than of the blood, as are the main titles of *Fight Club*, released in 1999 and one of the first films to popularize such sequences. In *X-Men*, the camera seems to move through the body and into the neurons. In *X2*, the camera moves from the cosmos, to a constellation of mutants as seen inside Professor X's mind (his invention, Cerebro, connects him to all mutants everywhere), to Professor X's Cerebro headpiece, to the conductor that connects the headpiece to the machine, and finally, into the Cerebro chamber. *Spider-Man*'s main title is more abstract, as the camera seems to move into and out of arteries, as well as webs, costumes, and buildings. The credits speed the viewer through emblems of the movie's themes and settings, as if he or she were on an amusement park ride. The main title sequence of Hulk rockets the audience through computer-generated hemoglobin, while the credits appear in old-fashioned comic book lettering. The same year, another Marvel adaptation, Daredevil, does not treat viewers to a Fantastic Voyage–like credit sequence, but during a pivotal moment in the character's origin, the camera pulls back along young Matt Murdock's optic nerve as it is fried during his blinding.

These flamboyant credit sequences aside, Spider-Man and Hulk, while not strictly adhering to the characters' established histories, remain faithful to comic book–like aesthetics. In Spider-Man, the height of this fidelity may be the poses into which the CG artists manipulate the hero as the film ends with Spider-Man swinging from web to web, building to building, in a succession of iconic poses taken from the comic book. In one pose, he swings with his arms behind him and torso thrust forward; in another, he swings with his body curled and legs extended, one arm forward, one arm back. In yet another, his legs are spread and both arms thrust forward. In the next, he crouches, attached to a pole; and in the last, he swings with his legs spread, his head jutting forward, and his body curling back.

Spider-Man and the Hulk are icons, so much so that the films' print advertisements feature just the characters' likenesses, and do not bother with any tag lines. In Spider-Man's case, his costume—whether drawn, stitched and sewn, or computer-generated—is essential to his iconic stature. Costume designer James Acheson faithfully translates the outfit from the comic book page to the big screen. But by hiding Peter Parker's eyes and covering his mouth, what Acheson gains in fidelity, he sacrifices in the character's expressiveness. Thus, as a presence, the film's Spider-Man becomes more than iconic; he becomes monolithic. The same is true of Spider-Man's nemesis, the Green Goblin (Willem Dafoe). The Goblin's eyes and mouth are visible only in select moments. Otherwise, he, like Spider-Man, is statuesque in a way that is unmitigated even by his aerobatics. Spider-Man and the Green Goblin are freaks and automatons both.

This is all set against a New York City that represents a heightened reality. Director Sam Raimi, who often uses wide-angle lenses that allow for lots of light and deep focus, creates a world of grit and shadow during the film's darker passages, but also one of bright wide angles and gleaming facades. Sometimes, this city, like its friendly neighborhood hero, is a digital creation. This was achieved through "photogammetry" (the same technique used to create the virtual city of *The Matrix)* in which the filmmakers extracted shapes of skyscrapers from photographs of New York.[13]

No part of *Spider-Man*'s New York is more important than the city's heights. When the Green Goblin attacks Manhattan's Unity Festival, Spider-Man engages him among giant balloons and around a building rooftop. Here, the battle is taken to higher elevations, as it will be in *Daredevil, Hulk,* and as much of the action had been in *X-Men* and in 1992's *Batman Returns,* in which the heights of Gotham City are adorned with titanic statues. The heroes and villains of such films stand above and apart from ordinary people, so it is fitting that the filmmakers stage some of the action in the upper reaches of the city, in those parts of the city its dwellers do not go, where its monuments appear like echoes of the combatants.

Spider-Man's first sequel, *Spider-Man 2* (2004), also features action sequences set in the high parts of the city. The rooftops host many of Spider-Man's stunts and also several of his battles with the villain of the film, Alfred Molina's Doctor Otto Octavius (the comic book's "Doctor Octopus"). The first of these fights follows a bank robbery committed by Octavius, after which he flees with Peter's Aunt May (Rosemary Harris) as a hostage. Spider-Man pursues. He and Doctor Octavius—or "Dock Ock" as *Daily Bugle* editor J. Jonah Jameson names him—battle their way up and down the side of a skyscraper. At the same time, Spider-Man must save Aunt May. Before Spider-Man swings her to safety (with the choral section of Danny Elfman's score *aaahhhhing* appropriately), Aunt May dangles from an umbrella she has used to hook a decorative statue. From the moment she catches the statute until she lands safely, her peril, intercut with Spider-Man and Doc Ock's brawl, constitutes a sequence within the sequence.

This blended action takes about fifty seconds and comprises twenty-three shots, of which twelve are dedicated to Aunt May. Within this mini-sequence, then, Raimi gives equal weight to Spider-Man's high-altitude battle and Aunt May's fight simply not to fall. Raimi presents Spider-Man and Doc Ock with a moving camera and expansive frames. In contrast, Raimi composes Aunt May much more tightly, with close-ups and medium close-ups, with inserts of her hands slipping on the umbrella, and of her feet dangling in the air. Such framing heightens our sense of Aunt May's panic and of her peril. Moreover, it allows Raimi to never show Aunt May in the fuller context of her surroundings. This is all the set-up for a punchline, the last close-up of Aunt May's feet: as she finally falls, the camera tilts with her feet—as they drop to a ledge that is just inches below.

With this gag, as with many others in the film, Raimi indulges a subversive sense of humor. Throughout *Spider-Man 2*, Raimi upends the audience's expectations—especially during scenes of great spectacle. Several instances find Spider-Man or Peter performing great feats to soaring music, only for his powers to fail. Similarly, when a car flips into the air, and descends on a crowd, the camera shows the fearful mob, but nothing happens. When Raimi cuts back to the car, it is suspended in webs. This sense of humor is an inherent part of Raimi's style and is also manifested in *Spider-Man 2* by the glee with which people and objects rush the camera, from hurled cars to tossed newspapers to panicked secretaries.

The second near-rooftop fight between Spider-Man and Doc Ock covers a tremendous amount of space, first vertical, and then horizontal. The fight takes Spider-Man from a battle dozens of floors above the ground to the street, where he must skate on his back to evade moving cars. Doc Ock leaps aboard an elevated train, which soon becomes a runaway that only Spider-Man can save. Bracing himself against the front of the train, Spider-Man's mask catches fire. He tears it away. Unmasked, Spider-Man/Peter Parker launches webs at nearby buildings to create a sling to slow the train. He stands in great agony, his arms outstretched, his torso lacerated in two places. As if this wasn't Christological enough, Peter then falls forward, unconscious, and is caught by several passengers. They raise him up, and pass him over their heads, his arms still wide. This invocation of martyrdom and the messianic, whether intentional or not, would have been particularly resonant in 2004, as *Spider-Man 2* opened just months after the release of Mel Gibson's surprise blockbuster and cultural phenomenon *The Passion of the Christ*, which, domestically, *Spider-Man 2* would only barely outgross.

All of Doc Ock's deeds are part of his plan to rebuild the fusion reactor he designed when his only identity was that of scientist and humanitarian Otto Octavius. When Octavius unveils his invention, which he has built to benefit all mankind, the reactor overloads, destroying the lab, killing his wife, and fusing four robotic arms (or "actuators") to his back. As the arms are central to Doc Ock's "look," it is fitting that Raimi introduces them with great reverence. He uses five shots to show the apparatus fixing itself to Octavius's back and an angelic vocal from the soundtrack's chorus. As the arms first activate, the camera tilts upward as they rise above Octavius's head.

After the disaster, the arms begin to operate independently. While doctors try to remove them from a comatose Octavius, the arms attack. In one shot, the frame is split into four panels, each displaying the arms' point of view of a

With Great C.G. Comes Great Responsibility: Peter Parker (if not Tobey Maguire) catches a train in the 2004 blockbuster, Spider-Man 2. (From the author's collection.)

terrified surgeon. Here, Raimi gives the arms their own vision, having already given them their own will. Later, the film suggests that the actuators have possessed Octavius. "Something in my head . . . something talking," Octavius says. As he considers suicide, the arms rise to capture the sides of the frame, surrounding his head menacingly. Their "performance," as much as Alfred Molina's, drives the moment. Octavius then considers another plan: "We can rebuild . . . But we need money." Raimi cuts to a wide shot as Octavius's arms walk him over a fallen beam. Octavius's switch from the first-person-singular to the first-person-plural suggests a newfound inclusiveness; so does the wide shot, as it makes Octavius and the four actuators seem like one against a larger background.

This is but one facet of *Spider-Man 2*'s concern with duality. Naturally, the theme is also manifested in Peter, who, fed up with constant suffering and loss, abandons his heroic alter ego. Much has been made of this storyline, which helped give *Spider-Man 2* a reputation for being one of Hollywood's most psychological comic book movies. Peter comes to this crossroad at the crucial one-hour mark when he realizes that Spider-Man is not something he is, or has to be, but something he chooses to be. Choosing not to be, he declares that he is "Spider-Man no more," invoking the title of *The Amazing Spider-Man*'s July 1967 issue, in which Peter comes to the same conclusion. The movie, in a critical moment, even cites one of that issue's images: the Spider-Man costume stuffed in an alley garbage can.

Ultimately, Peter reclaims the role. Moreover, the film's ending, in which Peter gets to be Spider-Man and gets the girl (Kirsten Dunst's Mary Jane Watson), reconciles both halves of Peter's life. Likewise, Doc Ock reconciles his dueling natures (humanitarian genius and supervillain) by destroying his restored fusion reactor. It is notable that fusion is such a major plot device. Both fusion and fission produce energy, but fusion represents the combining, not dividing, of atoms. And for both the film's hero and its villain, the ultimate project is the fusing of divergent natures. Raimi suggests this early on, with a subtle visual cue. Creating the reaction that will give rise to Octavius's second, malignant nature, Octavius wears protective goggles; one lens is solidly black while the other reflects the fiery glow of the reactor's newly created miniature sun. In the climax, however, Octavius makes himself whole by asserting his will over his arms and using them to destroy his invention—and with it, himself— saving the city in the process.

As for Peter, reconciling the part of his life that is Peter Parker and the one that is Spider-Man—a task that has eluded him for nearly two movies—is accomplished by his final reunion with Mary Jane. While Peter has denied his love for her to protect her from Spider-Man's enemies, Mary Jane chooses to brave the risks. After all, as Mary Jane tells him, "It's wrong that we should only be half alive, half of ourselves." In a way that few other conflicted action heroes have enjoyed, Peter's duality becomes singularity: a full journey indeed. This last scene serves another function. As in the first *Spider-Man*, as well as the first two *X-Men* films, *Spider-Man 2* ends with scenes that establish potential conflicts for the next sequel. In the case of *Spider-Man 2*, this developing action includes Peter and Mary Jane forging a relationship, and Peter's friend, Harry Osborn (James Franco), taking up the mantle of his dead villain-father, Norman Osborn. Comic books can often be structured this way, so that an issue does not conclude with the resolution of its story, but rather spurs readers to read on. This is not quite the same as other franchise films that are more self-contained—even horror films that stereotypically end with Jason Voorhees or Freddy Kreuger returning from the dead. Such endings do not propel a story forward, but instead, simply push a reset button.

In *Spider-Man 2*, hero and villain parallel each other, much as they do in the first film. *Spider-Man's* theme of mirroring is grounded in how it balances Spider-Man and the Green Goblin. Not only do the characters parallel each other with their monolithic appearance, but they also each have an elaborate origin tale. By devoting a surprising amount of screen time to the Green Goblin and his alter ego, scientist-industrialist Norman Osborn, Raimi and screenwriter David Koepp's *Spider-Man* may echo the original *Batman*, but more importantly, the parity between Harry Callahan and Scorpio in *Dirty Harry*. In fact, from Osborn's initial transformation, the camera races back from Peter's eye, as he wakes up the morning after his own. This segue suggests that the narrative link between these characters is, in this critical moment, a psychic one as well.

In *Hulk*, it is not the hero and the villain who share this connection so much as it is the hero's opposing natures. Many critics have commented on the Hulk's obvious debt to Robert Louis Stevenson's Dr. Jekyll and Mr. Hyde (as well as to Willis H. O'Brien's creation, King Kong); nowhere is this more overt— or more visual—than when the Hulk hallucinates, as he clings to a fighter jet that carries him up into the lower atmosphere, to "the top of the world." In the Hulk's vision, Bruce Banner is shaving. He wipes the steam from the bathroom mirror and sees the Hulk's reflection. Director Ang Lee then cuts to the Hulk, standing behind the mirror, looking out at Bruce. The first shot in this couplet would have been enough to illustrate that Bruce Banner has two identities. More striking, however, is the second shot. Staged in an abstract space that gives the vision its hallucinatory quality, this image weights the personalities equally: while the Hulk may be a component of Bruce Banner's psyche, this image suggests that Bruce is also a component of the Hulk's.

According to production designer Rick Heinrichs, a longtime collaborator of Tim Burton's, the bathroom set reflects the influence of comic books from the early period. Today, Heinrichs claims, comic book artists will often situate a lit sky above a darker landscape,

> but if you study the works of artist/illustrator George Herriman, he would frequently switch that to a black sky with a lit landscape. We used that idea in a scene in the bathroom. We had a very dark color up above but a very light green tile below. . . . it's part of that duality thing, that tension between the light and the dark, between the simple and complex, the expected and the unexpected.[14]

Of course, the style of Hulk has more contemporary comic book referents. Some of the film's most outrageous visuals are the ones in which Lee strives for a level of fidelity to comic book aesthetics not yet seen in the genre. Often, Lee depicts action in multiple panels within the same frame—even if the action is only a conversation or a character's exit. The panels mimic the shapes on a comic book page, and also the comic book reader's field of vision, which takes in multiple frames at once. Just as reading a comic book is not a strictly linear experience, neither is watching the succession of images in Hulk. The sequential effect of traditional editing is here replaced by a sense of simultaneity.

As in other films of this trend, the filmmakers use color boldly, to evoke the aesthetic of the comic book medium. Lee and Heinrichs are not shy about using green—certainly the most significant color in the world of the Hulk—especially in the early parts of the film. The filmmakers employ many pale greens, as in clothing, the senior Banner's lab, the teenage Bruce's bedroom, and the hallway of the laboratory where Bruce and his ex-girlfriend, Betty (Jennifer Connelly) work. Immediately following Bruce's first transformation into the Hulk, however, Lee and his collaborators use green more sparingly. From the Hulk's destruction of the lab, Lee cuts to Betty entering Bruce's house, designed in reds and yellows. Bruce wears a blue shirt. Except for some background cereal bowls, the scene is devoid of green. This absence not only makes room for green later, but also demarcates an act break. Subtle though it is, the change in the film's color palette reinforces the change the story has taken with the Hulk's first appearance. Later, the underground military lab to which the Hulk is taken marks an even more cartoonish use of color. Against bunker-gray walls are railings, girders, and ductwork all in vivid reds, yellows, and blues.

But before audiences could take in the splashy color and dazzling, even dizzying, CGI of Spider-Man and Hulk, both films had to fight their way to the multiplexes of the world. According to Variety, in 1985, Menahem Golan and Yoram Globus's Cannon Films was the first to obtain the film rights to Spider-Man. The producers attached Invasion U.S.A. and Missing in Action director Joseph Zito to the project and even placed advertisements in trade publications trumpeting their upcoming "event" film. As that project never materialized, Cannon sold the rights to Carolco, which hired James Cameron to write and direct. But with Carolco's 1995 bankruptcy, the rights, along with the rest of Carolco's library, passed to MGM. In 1998, when Marvel filed for bankruptcy the rights to Spider-Man became even more complicated.[15] As the Los Angeles Times reports,

> Marvel had sold overlapping licenses for a Spider-Man film to three companies on terms that were sometimes contradictory and often poorly documented. Each of the licensees had in turn sold pieces of its rights to others, with the result that MGM, Viacom, Columbia Pictures, Warner Bros. and various Hollywood hangers-on all claimed the right to make or distribute a [Spider-Man] picture.[16]

But Spider-Man's path to Hollywood, now hopelessly split, would take an even stranger turn when one of Marvel's attorneys discovered that the initial sale to Cannon, nearly fifteen years earlier, had never been registered with the U.S. Copyright Office. Thus the sale was invalid—as were all the subsequent sales. The rights reverted to Marvel, which next sold them to Sony for $10 million (more than forty times what Cannon had paid).[17] Sony, which had been embroiled in the contest since Carolco declared bankruptcy, was rewarded for its patience: Spider-Man would gross more than $900 million worldwide.

Hulk did not undergo a development process as tumultuous as Spider-Man's, but the project still stumbled on its way to the screen and again after it opened. The Monday after its sensational opening weekend (a record, of course—this one for the biggest June opening), Marvel's stock fell 11 percent. Daily Variety speculated that even with the film's $62.6 million debut weekend, Marvel shareholders were already anticipating that Hulk's box office would suffer a steep decline.[18] These speculations would prove correct. Hulk's domestic gross just squeaked past its budget.

Of course, this was after Universal canceled its original Hulk adaptation in 1998. The studio made this decision when the budget climbed above $100 million, with just over a month from the start of production on what would have been the directorial debut of Armageddon and Die Hard with a Vengeance screenwriter Jonathan Hensleigh. This was not an uncommon occurrence in comic book–to–feature film adaptations. According to Daily Variety, the large—and costly—demands of computerized special effects slowed the development of Fox's X-Men and Fantastic Four.[19] In time, they would become solid franchises for Fox. But their long roads to the big screen would be much like those taken by Superman, which Warner Bros. would relaunch in 2006 after years of struggle and failure; Catwoman, which Hollywood took over a decade to produce; Wonder Woman, which would spend years languishing in development; and others.

One reason that many comic book properties have had a difficult time finding their way to the screen, and that Marvel has supplanted DC as a source of comic book films, is that DC, as one of AOL-Time Warner's holdings, can shop its titles to only one studio: Warner Bros. Marvel, on the other hand, is not so shackled. Since Blade, New Line Cinema, Twentieth Century Fox, Columbia, Universal, Artisan, and Dimension Films (the unit of Disney-owned Miramax that produces genre films) have all adapted, or at some point been adapting, Marvel titles. According to The Hollywood Reporter, following the opening weekend of the first X-Men (another record-breaker, this at $54.5 million), studio executives were "mining the depths of their development vaults for the next comic book project worthy of fast-tracking to the big screen."[20] Artisan boasted fifteen, including "Captain America," "Black Panther," and, as the article puts it, "even 'The Punisher.'"[21]

Of this lot, The Punisher (2004), chronicling the origin and vengeance of a vigilante hero, is the only adaptation Artisan produced before becoming Lion's Gate. Like other comic book action films, The Punisher is filmed in a stark, graphic style. Making his directorial debut, Jonathan Hensleigh renders the movie in a near monochrome, established with the film's main title sequence, in which animated black-and-white ink drawings depict falling shell casings, which give way to expressionistic white blood cascading down. The blood forms the skull logo that has been the Punisher's emblem since his debut on the comic book page.

Hensleigh's color palette throughout the film also recalls the shadowy visuals of the 2002 graphic novel adaptation *Road to Perdition*, for which cinematographer Conrad Hall's translation of the graphic novel's style earned him a posthumous Academy Award. But a better referent for *The Punisher*'s grayscale is *The Crow*, another vigilante film in which the hero exacts creative vengeance on the criminal underworld. In many respects, Hensleigh's world is simply a less gothic, less supernatural version of Proyas's. Better referents still are the action films of decades past. Much of this nostalgia is by design. "What we wanted to do with this was take action movies back to what they were like in the 1970s and 1980s, without all the special effects, and make a real-life gritty picture," says Hensleigh. To do so, according to *The Hollywood Reporter*, Hensleigh and star Thomas Jane "went wild at Blockbuster," renting the films of Clint Eastwood, Charles Bronson, and others.[22]

Indeed, while the comic book-, science fiction-, and disaster-action films of the 1990s and beyond represent fantastical strains of the action genre, it is these comic book films, including *The Crow* and *Daredevil*, that most strongly recall the vigilante entries with which the genre began in the 1970s. In *The Punisher*, the vigilante is Frank Castle (Thomas Jane), a retired federal agent out to avenge the slaughter of his family at the hands of vengeance-seeking crime boss Howard Saint (John Travolta); in *Daredevil*, it is attorney Matt Murdock (Ben Affleck), who, frustrated with "the system," helps the disadvantaged as a lawyer by day and as a superhero vigilante by night. Daredevil and The Punisher may both be vigilantes, but each draws upon different strengths. Blinded as a youth, Daredevil's remaining senses are all enhanced. "High above the streets, I trained my body and my senses," he tells us in voiceover. "An acute sense of touch gave me both strength and balance until the city itself became my playground. I was the boy without fear." In this portion of the flashback, we see young Matt Murdock training high above the city: the same backdrop against which he will perform his spectacular feats as an adult. (One shot finds Daredevil, high up, crouched between two statues, mimicking their pose.) In battle, Daredevil is partial to elaborate martial arts maneuvers, choreographed at least in part by Cheung-Yan Yuen, who lent his talents as a kung fu trainer and wire specialist to *The Matrix* sequels.

The Punisher, on the other hand, does not have superpowers, but rather, a super arsenal. Like *Lethal Weapon*'s Riggs, *Under Siege*'s Ryback, and *The Rock*'s General Hummel, Castle is an ultimate warrior. He speaks six languages and has served in combat, with special ops, and with a counterterrorism unit. He descends from a line of combatants whose infatuation with weaponry and its particulars recalls action films of the 1980s. In one scene, Castle's father (Roy

Scheider) proudly displays his refurbished 1911 Colt pistols. "I bored the chambers and customized the triggers and added some compensators. They used to be pretty good, but now they're nail-drivers." War has been the Castle family business (Frank and his father even share the same first name). And while 1980s Vietnam represented a homecoming for the POW/MIA films' veterans, the Castles, adjusting to the more fragmented geopolitics of the twenty-first century, seem homesick for the Cold War. "You always told me someone needs to do the fighting," Castle tells Frank, Sr. "That was when the world made sense," the senior Castle replies.

Soon after, the Castles are attacked by Saint's black-clad hitmen. (The costumes may not be the best tactical choice as the assassins are attacking beachfront property. In the middle of the day.) Here, Castle derives his warrior status not only from the violence he can mete out, but also from what he can withstand. During the prolonged attack—the sequence runs nearly ten minutes—the henchmen stab, kick, beat, shoot, nearly torch, and all but drown Castle. Not that Castle doesn't give any back: when killing one assassin by shooting a propane tank (the assassin has taken up a position behind the barbeque), Castle sets off a fireball that Hensleigh covers in an almost laughter-inducing twelve shots.

Of course, the real carnage comes at the end, when Castle makes his final assault on Saint's estate. Castle makes his final preparations in a montage of this avenger readying his weapons and his wardrobe. The montage includes three shots of Castle assembling a newfangled bow, four shots of a shotgun, five of his combination machine gun-grenade launcher, three of his sniper rifle, five of his handgun, and five of his shirt, emblazoned with the Punisher skull logo. (This is soon followed by eight shots of Castle's hand fixing anti-personnel mines to the undercarriages of Saint's cars.) This montage, with its ritualistic editing and satisfying sounds of weapons clicking and black tape ripping, recalls those of *Cobra*, *Commando*, and others. It is also the backdrop for Castle's voiceover narration:

In certain *extreme* situations, the law is inadequate. In order to shame its inadequacy, it is necessary to act outside the law. To pursue natural justice. This is not vengeance. Revenge is not a valid motive; it is an emotional response. No, not vengeance. Punishment.

This rings hollow. Though the two words—vengeance and punishment—are indeed defined differently, *The Punisher* does not examine the distinction so much as use it as a high-minded affectation.

Once the attack reaches its most intense pitch, it is difficult to know for sure how many men Castle kills, as some victims may have only seemed dead at one point and are finished off later. Also, before Castle enters the room where he conducts the majority of his slaughter, he blows it up. Still, the body count is approximately thirteen—or nearly three people killed for every one time Castle is shot. This tally does not include Saint, whom Castle defeats, but does not kill, in a fast-draw. No, Saint meets a more spectacular end, as Castle lashes him to a car on which he plants a mine. Castle allows the car to roll forward and drag Saint behind it. As the vehicle drifts into Saint's car dealership, Castle detonates the explosive, along with the other explosives he had planted. Combining the genre's passion for sadism and iconic imagery, Hensleigh lets the audience hear Saint moaning as he and the cars burn, before the film cuts to an aerial view looking down on the car lot. Amid all the cars, the burning ones form a flaming Punisher skull logo.

Considering Castle's arsenal, his skills, and his use of climactic conflagration, it is no wonder that in a rough cut of the film, Castle's neighbor, Spacker Dave (Ben Foster) observes, "He's like Rambo for real."[23] Likewise, when Castle interrogates one of his enemy's henchmen, the vigilante's developed physique, chiseled features, black tank top, cropped hair with a slight 1950s curl, and guttural mumble all invoke Sylvester Stallone—not Rambo so much as Cobra. Indeed, Hensleigh litters the film with the affectations of 1980s, as well as 1970s, action films. Doing so, he creates a gritty, noisy brand of nostalgia. This includes Hensleigh's vengeance-driven plotline, his visual style, and even his locations—from Puerto Rico and Florida to the shipyard of the film's opening, where a yellow sports car is one of the first objects we see, cutting against the wet, heavily blue-gelled night.

In comic book form, The Punisher first appeared in 1973. Daredevil had debuted earlier, in 1964, but acquired a greater prominence in the late 1970s, when Frank Miller began working on the title. Miller would later achieve greater fame for reinvigorating Batman—both onscreen and on the comic book page—with his articulation of its inherent vigilantism and for his original creation, the stark noir-like Sin City. While the Motion Picture Association of America gave The Punisher an R rating for "pervasive brutal violence, language, and brief nudity" (and while it is much harder-edged than many of its comic book–drawn contemporaries), the film is tame in comparison to the adaptation of Sin City (2005). Rated R for "sustained strong stylized violence, nudity and sexual content including dialogue," Sin City is co-directed by Miller and Robert Rodriguez. The film, like the comic books it is based on, is set in the nightmare-noir town of "Basin City." The city's denizens are stabbed, shot, beaten, blown-up, run over, run through, molested, dismembered, disfigured, decapitated, castrated, eaten alive, and literally pummeled to goo.

Even if none of the characters enjoy a picturesque fate, Miller and Rodriguez convey the ugliness with black-and-white photography that is so stylized, it was admired by even the film's harshest detractors—and spot-colorized for blood, intestines, and other punctuation. The film's basic monochrome gives it an abstract quality that, according to Rodriguez, prompted the MPAA to give Sin City an R rating without asking for a single change.[24] Even if this is so, the style with which the violence is filmed cannot mask the indulgence and redundancy with which it is executed—qualities that eventually make the bloodletting less cathartic than just toxic. Whereas the killings of say, Robocop, are at turns heroic, horrific, tragic, and darkly comic, there is little of that range in Sin City. (Take, for example, its three castrations and several more references to the act.) Still, critics were greatly divided over the film, with some seeing it as high art, others as a low point for Western civilization. Ken Tucker argues that Sin City represents one of the year's "most witty and, yes, most moral movies." [25] Anthony Lane, however, sees a darker side of Sin City's style: "We have, it is clear, reached the lively dead end of a process that was initiated by a fretful Martin Scorsese and inflamed, with less embarrassed glee, by [Quentin] Tarantino: the process of knowing everything about violence and nothing about suffering."[26]

The film is not generally thought of as an action movie. This may be due to its structure. Sin City is an anthology of stories, based on several of Frank Miller's Sin City comics, published by Dark Horse Comics both as miniseries and as graphic novels. The titles adapted for the film include the original Sin City (1993, later retitled The Hard Good-Bye), The Big Fat Kill (1994–1995), and That Yellow Bastard (1996). Each story focuses on a different protagonist: Marv (Mickey Rourke), a hardened ex-convict looking to avenge the murder of a particularly charitable prostitute; Dwight McCarthy (Clive Owen), a fugitive murderer helping a gang of hookers maintain their autonomy and hide the death of a vile cop; and the stoutly named John Hartigan (Bruce Willis), a detective desperate to protect a young girl—and later young woman—from a politically connected sexual predator and killer.

A cop, an ex-con, and a should-be con: each of these men dispenses his own justice partly to prove he is still "worth a damn," a theme the film articulates in all three tales. Though this unusual structure may obscure Sin City's affinity for the action film (as might the film's blatantly noir-derived style), when seen individually, the stories of Sin City distill the action genre's basic, and most base, tropes: sadism, masochism, martyrdom, vigilantism, vengeance, violent salvation, rescuing innocents, and the clash of the subhuman and the superhuman.

Still, it is clear that Sin City is a child of noir—the genre that so influenced Miller's books, which in turn inform the movie. In fact, Rodriguez and Miller translated Miller's comic book panels to the motion picture frame partly by using them as storyboards during production. The result is an expressionistic take on an already expressionistic visual style. This may be Sin City's most admirable achievement: as Stephen Sommers does with the opening sequence of Van Helsing, Rodriguez and Miller use digital technology to recall the artistry of a long-gone period of Hollywood history.

In Sin City, as in classic noir, shadows are significant tropes. In one notable composition, the camera captures an exchange between Shellie (Brittany Murphy) and abusive, corrupt cop Jackie Boy (Benicio Del Toro), by photographing their shadows on the floor, crossed by the horizontal shadows of Venetian blinds. Grimmer is the shot that finds Hartigan hung in a motel room. The frame is practically black; the only light comes from a Venetian blind–draped window, built into a wall that is angled away from the camera. This produces a distortion also seen in the most expressionistic noir films. In Sin City, this distortion is also seen when the camera looks down on Hartigan from the ceiling of his jail cell. A wide-angle lens exaggerates the angle, making the bars seem to stretch out toward the corners of the frame.

Unlike most elements of Sin City's art direction, which are digital creations, the bars of Hartigan's cell are real, as are the dock where he is shot eight times at the beginning of the film, Shellie's kitchen, the hospital where the film's coda is staged, and assorted vehicles and furniture. The only full set to be designed and constructed is the bar that links all three stories (though we do not see the bar in the second story, during this episode we learn that Shellie is a waitress there). The bar, Kadie's Club Pecos, is a purely black space in the graphic novels, but in the movie, is photographed with a pale bronze and rose tint. This makes the bar stand out from the rest of the film's environments, thereby emphasizing it. It is fitting that the filmmakers give the bar this extra emphasis, as it is the only space common to the three stories, and as a bar or nightclub is a central film noir convention.

Another noir convention is the voiceover narration, which Rodriguez and Miller use in Sin City. But unlike the traditional noir voiceover, which is written in the past tense, Sin City's voiceovers are written in the present. Thus, whereas

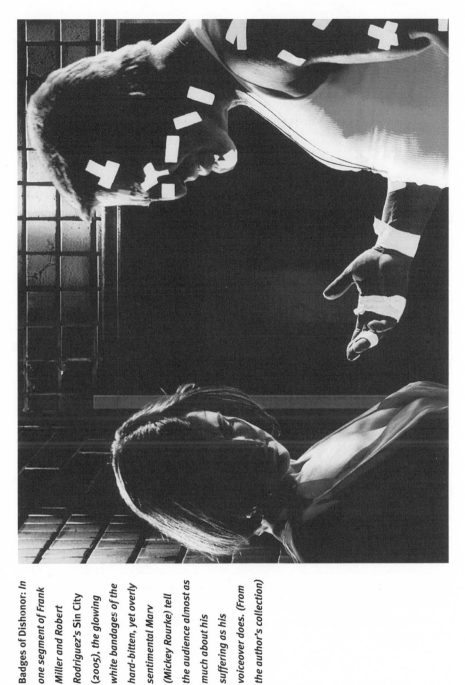

Badges of Dishonor: In one segment of Frank Miller and Robert Rodriguez's Sin City (2005), the glowing white bandages of the hard-bitten, yet overly sentimental Marv (Mickey Rourke) tell the audience almost as much about his suffering as his voiceover does. (From the author's collection)

much of a classic *noir* is often a flashback, *Sin City* is taking place now. As a result, the film trades *noir*'s cold, sure hand of predetermination for the cold, gray heart of nihilism. However, Rodriguez and Miller's use of the voice-over is incessant. And as the voices of Marv, Dwight, and Hartigan constantly buzz in the audience's ear, they detract from the immediacy of the images. This is ironic given their savagery, and unfortunate, given their meticulous, if strange, beauty.

Sin City is not the only comic book–derived film of 2005 to foreground a *noir* sensibility. Another is *Batman Begins*, the first of Warner Bros.'s five *Batman* movies to depict the hero's origin story. But what truly distinguishes *Batman Begins* from its predecessors is that the film is neither a sequel nor a prequel to these other films; rather, it is the launch of a new franchise, independent from what had come before. The film is also distinguished by the dark psychology that not only grips Batman's alter ego, billionaire Bruce Wayne (Christian Bale), but many of Gotham City's denizens as well. Filmmaker Christopher Nolan, who also brought fractured, feverish mindsets to the characters of his neo-*noirs* *Memento* (2000) and *Insomnia* (2002), directed *Batman Begins* from a screenplay credited to Nolan and David S. Goyer, also the writer of the *Blade* films, a *Blade* television series, a sequel to *The Crow*, and adaptations of the comic books *Ghost Rider* and *The Flash*.

Batman Begins also bears the mark of *Sin City* author Frank Miller. Miller had written the comic book miniseries *Batman: The Dark Knight Returns*, published by DC Comics in 1986 and popular for the psychotic leanings it imparts to Bruce Wayne. Miller followed this with *Batman: Year One*, a similarly dark take on Batman's origin story, and one of several sources from which Nolan and Goyer drew for their *Batman* screenplay. In fact, prior to commissioning *Batman Begins*, Warner Bros. had been developing an adaptation of Miller's *Batman: Year One* with Miller and filmmaker Darren Aronofsky, director of the disorienting *Pi* (1998) and the dark *Requiem for a Dream* (2000). Around the same time, the studio was also developing *Batman vs. Superman*. That project, to have been directed by Wolfgang Petersen and released in 2004 (the year that also saw *Alien vs. Predator*), was conceived as a crossover blockbuster to relaunch the two franchises that had served Warner Bros. so well, if with depreciating returns.[27]

Under Nolan's stewardship, part of Batman's origin story is the origin of the iconography that has famously surrounded the character. Through the film's first hour, Bruce's sense of justice evolves, and with it, so do his costume and gear. Nolan uses the Wayne family's corporation to justify the existence of the accoutrements Bruce will use to fight crime. In the "Applied Sciences" division, Lucius Fox (Morgan Freeman) shows Bruce a Kevlar utility harness; a gas-powered magnetic grapple gun; a "Nomex survival suit for advanced infantry" made with "Kevlar biweave" and "reinforced joints" that Nolan will show Bruce spray-paint black over four shots; a material called "memory cloth" that will form his cape; and finally, the Tumbler, an assault vehicle built for the military, but which is fated to become the Batmobile. Many of these items are black or bronze, in keeping with film's color palette.

Like Batman, the Batsuit itself evolves. While in training, Bruce is black-clad with his face exposed. In Gotham, during a preliminary outing, he wears Kevlar armor and a ski mask. It is not until the film's critical one-hour mark that Gotham receives its first visit from Batman per se. At just about fifty-nine minutes into the film, Bruce makes his final preparations, working on his utility belt, the memory cloth, and the "batterangs" which in Nolan's version, are little bat symbol–shaped throwing stars. This takes us into a sequence set at the docks, where, just a minute or so later, one of mob boss Carmine Falcone's thugs finds a batterang that announces Batman's first appearance. Batman attacks, but we catch only glimpses of him until he hoists up a mobster. "What the hell are you?!" the goon asks. The hero, fully revealed for the first time, answers. "I'm Batman."

This "first-night-out" sequence, also a convention of comic book adaptations, includes a train platform encounter between Batman and Bruce's love interest, Rachel Dawes (Katie Holmes). From here, Nolan cuts back to the docks where Jim Gordon (Gary Oldman), Gotham's most honest cop, arrives at the scene. Falcone (Tom Wilkinson) has been fastened to a spotlight projecting the image of his splayed form onto the cloud cover above. Resembling an outstretched bat, this is the origin of the "bat signal" that ends this film, the two Batman films directed by Tim Burton, and that has factored prominently in the Batman comic books and 1960s television series. The sequence ends with a long take looking out over Gotham. For about fifteen seconds, the camera glides in, on, and around Batman, standing statuesque atop a spire.

But all of Batman's armor, weaponry, and mystery do not make him impervious. In one scene, the villainous Scarecrow (Cillian Murphy) sprays him with a fear-inducing hallucinogen and sets him on fire, driving Batman to dive through the window. Batman is aflame for twelve shots; in eight of them, he falls several stories. Included in this mini-sequence is a particularly jarring jump cut between two shots of Batman crashing onto a parked car, from which he tumbles onto the rain-lashed street. Rolling in puddles, he extinguishes the flames. In mere seconds, one of comic and moviedom's most mythic figures is caught between two mythic elements, fire and water. Writhing on the ground, and calling for help from his butler Alfred (Michael Caine), Batman flashes back to Bruce's boyhood trauma in a bat-infested cave. With this brief insert, Nolan combines several *noir* tropes: the flashback, fragmented psychology, duality, and the sadistic punishment visited upon the protagonist.

A later battle at Arkham Asylum, Gotham City's institution for the criminally insane, is similarly staged: tightly framed, quickly cut, and captured with a restless camera that moves about the darkness. Here, Batman unleashes swarms of bats as a diversion. Not only is this a reference to *Batman: Year One*, but it also establishes a motif that would be exploited across much of the film's print campaign (along with the black and bronze palette). Moreover, the style of this action sequence, though visceral, gives one an almost constant sense of contraction, as does the style of other fight scenes in the film. Strangely, Nolan reverses his approach at the climax, when Batman escapes from a runaway train, leaving another villain, Ra's Al Ghul (Liam Neeson), to die. The train falls through a gap in the tracks, crashes, and explodes in fifteen shots (including one brief cutaway to a military weapon) over about twenty-eight seconds. Notably, this is more leisurely paced than most action movie catastrophes. The scene also recalls train sequences from the previous year's *Spider-Man 2* and *The Incredibles*, and also from *Speed* and *The French Connection*.

The violence of *Batman Begins* is part of the film's nexus of justice, vengeance, and vigilantism. This marks a confrontation of vigilantism largely unseen since the action films of the 1970s. Bruce accuses the League of Shadows, which Ra's Al Ghul describes as men who "hate evil" and wish "to serve true justice" as being a band of vigilantes. Ra's Al Ghul denies this charge: "No, no, no. A vigilante is just a man lost in the scramble for his own gratification; he can be destroyed or locked up. But if you make yourself *more* than just a man, if you devote yourself to an ideal, and if they can't stop you, you become something else entirely . . . *legend*, Mr. Wayne." Like the semantic games played by *The Punisher*, this philosophical gobbledygook—and Neeson spouts much more throughout the film—may *sound* good, but does not actually explain the difference between the League of Shadows and vigilantes. After all, if Westerns and action movies have proven anything, it is that vigilantes and "legends" can be, and in fact, are likely to be, one and the same. Less abstract is the conversation surrounding Bruce while dining at a ritzy Gotham City hotel. His dinner companions, unaware of Bruce's alter ego, hotly discuss Batman's vigilantism. Among their remarks: "He's done something the police have never done." "You can't take the law into your own hands." "But he's put Falcone behind bars." "And now the police want to bring him in." "I think the Batman deserves a medal." "And a straitjacket to pin it on."

Curiously, only the members of Gotham's elite harbor this ambivalence. More reverent are the city's working poor—particularly its children. As Batman prepares to face Scarecrow, a little boy spies him in the alley. "It's you, isn't it? Everybody's been talking about you," the child says. "The other kids won't believe me." To the child's delight, Batman throws him a souvenir. Nolan puts an even finer point on such hero worship later. While a bog of Scarecrow's hallucinogen covers the Narrows, the seediest part of Gotham City, Batman races from the Batcave. Nolan enacts the action movie ritual of a quickly cut montage showing equipment being readied (ten shots: two of Batman donning his gloves, two of the batterangs, three of his utility belt, one of his miniature bombs, and two of his grapple gun). On the street, Rachel and the child are besieged by Arkham's escaped inmates, who have emerged zombie-like from the gothic fog. Batman descends, rescuing Rachel and the boy. Rachel holds the child as he whispers, "I told you he'd come." As Rachel watches, Batman flies from the rooftop. After Batman's leap, Nolan cuts to a close-up of Rachel moving forward in the frame, and, after a few shots of Batman flying, cuts to her again. This keeps the initial part of Batman's flight grounded in Rachel's perspective. Even though she has taken a hard line against vigilantism, here, Nolan uses Rachel to venerate Batman, to make him something beheld.

Still, more than the franchise's other directors, Tim Burton (*Batman, Batman Returns*) and Joel Schumacher (*Batman Forever, Batman and Robin*), Nolan darkens the film's hero worship with a gloomy *noir* sensibility. Nolan often evokes this with the *noir* convention of the flashback. In fact, the director seems so taken with this convention that *Batman Begins* features not one, but two varieties of it. The first is brief and fragmented, as when Bruce flashes back to being swarmed by bats, his foundational boyhood trauma. The second is longer and more lyrical, and shows the processes by which Bruce, now a young adult, is forged as a crime fighter. Sometimes, Nolan tangles these flashbacks inside each other, as when Bruce remembers a trip to the opera as a child, and from there, flashes back to the bat attack; or his return from Princeton, and then remembers childhood games with his father. Flashbacks within flashbacks. Indeed, in the film's first act, three timelines unfold: the present, the near past, and the distant past. Nolan's *Memento* has a similar, if more compounded, disorienting quality. In that film, the nonlinear structure is justified by the story's main conceit: a protagonist searches for his wife's killer without the ability to form short-term memories.

It is fitting that Bruce is gripped by such a fragmented psychology; much as he fights Falcone, Scarecrow, and Ra's Al Ghul, Bruce struggles to settle his own mind. *Batman Begins* is the story of a hero, who, traumatized first by bats and then by his parents' murders, must reconcile the fight for justice with the thirst for vengeance. Following this path leads Bruce to imprisonment in China, where the story's present-day timeline begins. In the opening moments of the film, Bruce dreams of playing with childhood friend Rachel on the grounds of stately Wayne Manor before falling into the nightmare of the cave. The adult Bruce wakes, and then, filthy, leaves his cell for the breakfast line where he is attacked. Bruce then rolls, drags, and thrashes seven inmates in the mud. This first sequence marks a departure from the other *Batman* films. Rather than introduce (adult) Bruce as the billionaire playboy, Nolan establishes him as a hardened warrior. This introductory sequence—all of this has taken place in less than the movie's first four minutes—breaks down the clean Batman/Bruce Wayne divide that has been a hallmark of so much *Batman* lore. As this sequence suggests, Batman will not simply be the dark flipside of Bruce Wayne; Bruce Wayne will be a reflection of Batman, much like we saw in *Hulk*'s bathroom hallucination.

The fusion of Bruce's two personae opens the story and reappears close to the end, when Rachel joins him at the ruins of the burned-down Wayne Manor. Here, they enact the superhero movie ritual of realizing that their love can never be. But Bruce does not turn her away because she would never be safe, etc., and so on. Instead, it is Rachel who rejects Bruce, having discovered "his mask." When Bruce insists that Batman is merely a symbol, Rachel pats his cheek. "This is your mask," she says. "Your real face is the one the criminals now fear. The man I loved, the man who vanished, he never came back at all." Rachel's lament anticipates one from Warner Bros.'s similarly themed *V for Vendetta*, in which one character remarks, "When you wear a mask for so long, you begin to forget who you are underneath."

Whether or not Bruce has switched his face and his mask, his embodiment of both personae resonates with critic Caryn James, who places *Batman Begins* in a continuum with other recent tentpole movies. She describes *Batman Begins*, along with *Star Wars: Episode III—Revenge of the Sith*, *Constantine*, and the then-upcoming Russian *Night Watch* as "quasi-spiritual films," arguing, "Their premise is that good and evil are warring in each of us, and that an individual must consciously chose darkness or light."[28] Of course, this has been a theme embodied in the action hero all along and in the Western gunfighter before him, just as duality had similarly been a prominent convention of noir.

But unlike some action heroes, Nolan's Bruce Wayne/Batman finds his dark half by undertaking a journey to which the audience bears witness. His path is first laid before him by Falcone. Bruce, raised by wealthy liberals, confronts Falcone in the nightspot Falcone runs in the Narrows. "Now you think because your mommy and your daddy got shot, you know about the ugly side of life, but you don't," Falcone says. "You've never tasted desperate. . . . This is a world you'll never understand." It is then that Bruce leaves Gotham, Princeton, and all of his privilege for a life of petty crime (and Chinese imprisonment)—all to become The Man Who Knows Desperation, the Underworld.

Bruce is released from prison by Ra's Al Ghul, leader of the League of Shadows and Bruce's one-time mentor, who instructs Bruce to become the thing he fears most in order to become a thing feared by others. The League of Shadows is located high in the Himalayas, and if Bruce wants to learn to fight injustice, he must first prove himself by making the difficult trek. Lending Bruce's travels an icy blue tint, Nolan and Academy Award–nominated cinematographer Wally Pfister imbue the remote locations (shot in Iceland) with a sense of mythos that recalls Clark Kent's northward odyssey in the original Superman. Standing out from the rest of Batman Begins, the cool color palette distinguishes this formative episode for Bruce.

As for the rest of the film, much of its palette is darker, consistent with the film's noir sensibility. But unlike Sin City's black-and-white, Batman Begins is given largely to black and bronze—evoking the darkness, and also the tarnished glory of Gotham City. In one commanding image, the camera pulls back from a young Bruce and his murdered parents. He kneels amid the trash and clutter and shadows of the alley. In the background, we see an open doorway in which steam billows, bronze-lit.

Similarly, when Rachel tries to lecture Bruce on the difference between justice and vengeance, she takes him to the Narrows, where much is shadow and bronze. The tension between the darkness and the nearly light is borne out in the exchange between Rachel and Bruce: "Justice is about harmony. Revenge is about you making yourself feel better. Which is why we have an impartial system," Rachel insists. "Your system is broken," Bruce answers. Your system. Not the system. Not our system. Not even that system. Regardless of whether Bruce becomes a societal protector or mere vigilante, he comes to Rachel's aid later, during his first night out as the fully costumed Batman. The dock where Batman does away with several of Falcone's thugs, and Falcone himself, is photographed in shades of bronze, as is an elevated train platform, criss-crossed by steel beams. Walking alone along the platform, Rachel is approached by assailants whom Batman dispatches without Rachel even seeing him. When she turns, Batman cuts a black figure against a bronze background.

Underscoring the importance of this color scheme to the film is the fact that Warner Bros. remained faithful to it in its print advertising. The studio issued a number of posters in which a bronze sky provides the backdrop for images of the dark knight in various poses: brooding silhouette, carrying an unconscious Rachel, dissolving into a swarm of bats, and in the most engaging, descending toward the camera, cape unfurled, bats flying about, while behind him, buildings stretch skyward. These posters have no taglines. They are driven only by the imagery (including the new bat logo). To the studio's credit, its campaigns for The Matrix Reloaded and The Matrix Revolutions are also faithful to the films, as posters, bus shelter ads, and other print media draw from the films' use of black and green.

As a central part of Batman Begins, the black and bronze palette is established in the film's main title. After the Warner Bros. Pictures and DC Comics logos appear in black and white, Nolan fades to a bronze sky, streaked with sunlight breaking through dark clouds and black bats rushing across the frame. Nolan fades upon a bat symbol that breaks apart before taking solid form. Nolan never shows the words of the film's title. Rather, his only announcement of the film's title is the color scheme and moreover, the symbol. The bat symbol itself is newly designed: more angular and with straighter lines and sharper points than in previous, rounder incarnations.

The main title makes for an interesting pairing with the end titles. Following Bruce's final scene with Rachel, the film's finale finds Batman on a rooftop with Gordon. Gordon laments that the appearance of a costumed superhero in Gotham might be matched by a rise of supervillains. One may already be out there, a murderer and armed robber who, at the scenes of his crimes, leaves a calling card: a Joker. Batman vows to "look into it," and moments later, soars off the roof. Flying, he fills the frame. With a hard cut to black, Nolan begins the credits with simple white print. The first card is the film's title; only now do we see it. Like the makers of many comic book adaptations, Nolan has ended his film with the promise of future conflicts. But with the credits, he adds to this conventional structure a subtle twist. Concluding Batman's origin story with the words Batman Begins, Nolan seems to be suggesting that Batman is beginning now. The finale is no mere coda; rather, the entire film has become a preamble to something bigger.

Bat Out of Hell: *Brooding against a glowing sky, the Dark Knight appears in a stark advertising image from* Batman Begins, *one of several comic book adaptations seen in 2005. (From the author's collection.)*

Like *Batman Begins*, Twentieth Century Fox's *Fantastic Four*, released just weeks later, is PG-13 summer fare. *Fantastic Four* is rated so for its "sequences of intense action, and some suggestive content" as opposed to *Batman Begins*'s "intense action violence, disturbing images and some thematic elements." Still, their tones could not be more different. Whereas one is a brooding *noir*, the other is a light romp, at times bordering on comedy. This is fitting, as *Fantastic Four* was director Tim Story's follow-up to the hit comedy *Barbershop* (2002) and action-comedy *Taxi* (2004) starring Queen Latifah and *Saturday Night Live*'s Jimmy Fallon.

Fantastic Four is based on the Marvel comic created by Stan Lee and Jack Kirby. With the first issue's cover-date of November 1961, the title predates *Spider-Man*, *The Incredible Hulk*, and *X-Men*. In the comic, the Fantastic Four, like their counterparts in other Marvel titles, acquire their powers after exposure to radiation—this time while flying an experimental rocket. Reed Richards becomes super-elastic, acquiring the moniker "Mr. Fantastic." His fiancée, Sue Storm becomes "The Invisible Girl" (later "Woman"), while her younger brother, Johnny Storm acquires the powers of fire and flight as "The Human Torch." Finally, their friend Ben Grimm transforms into "The Thing," a gruff but good-hearted creature whose entire body is made of stone.

In several contemporary film adaptations of Marvel titles, the characters are transformed not by radiation, but by genetic forces. The film version of *Fantastic Four* remains true to the characters' origins in the comic, but uses genetic research to motivate their cosmic ray encounter. The film opens with Reed (Ioan Gruffudd) and Ben (Michael Chiklis) arriving at the company owned by old friend and future enemy Victor Von Doom (Julian McMahon) to solicit funding for their expedition into outer space. The mission will be to study a radiation cloud identical to the one Reed believes triggered the evolution of early life on Earth. In so doing, Reed hopes to, "fundamentally advance our knowledge about the structure of the human genome." Aboard Von Doom's space station, Reed, Ben, and Von Doom, along with Sue (Jessica Alba) and Johnny (Chris Evans) are exposed to the radiation; back on Earth, they begin to mutate, as the radiation has restructured their DNA. Von Doom develops a metallic skin and the ability to manipulate electricity and sets off on a vaguely defined scheme to acquire more power, while the others become the fantastic foursome that alone can fight him.

Unlike Nolan, Miller and Rodriguez, Raimi, Lee, *The Crow*'s Alex Proyas, or even *Blade*'s Stephen Norrington, Story does not employ much of a style. However, as would befit a superhero film, Story has at least *some* appreciation of the iconic: the film's first image is of a thirty-foot statue of Von Doom that play-fully expresses the monumental stature of superheroes and supervillains. Later, when introducing The Thing, Story announces the transformed Ben by first showing his shadow as it cuts into a circle of light cast on a brick wall. This device may not be the most original (*Robocop* uses it, for one), but it is graphic, and moreover, is part of a sequence of shots that is consistent with the action film tradition of teasing out the revelation of the hero. Before show-ing the most visually well known of the Fantastic Four, Story cuts from the shadow to a big-and-tall men's clothing store. We hear an offscreen window smash as Ben breaks in.

The clothing store is where The Thing acquires the trench coat and hat he wears throughout much of the film's remainder. This gives him the look of a movie private eye, on which Story riffs as The Thing sips coffee in a diner window. The green booth where The Thing sits and the green neon lining the window vaguely recall the style of detective films or of *Nighthawks* (the Edward Hopper painting, not the Sylvester Stallone movie). This image may be the film's boldest example of Story and cinematographer Oliver Wood's color scheme. The palette of *Fantastic Four* favors greens and pale blues, supported by doses of red and mahogany, even if this palette is more diffused here than in other comic book adaptations.

The odd juxtaposition of an over-the-top comic book character with the iconography of the down-and-out marks one of Story's subtler efforts at lam-pooning the superhero format—his superheroes in particular. Elsewhere in the film, Story stages a gag in which a pigeon perches on The Thing's shoul-der, only to defecate on it before flying away; later, Story shows the massive Thing juicing a whole bundle of oranges at once. Story also uses Ben for comic relief when the media-crazed Johnny shows him a Thing action figure that even squeaks the catchphrase "It's clobberin' time!" and which Ben crushes. Of course, Story's most overt attempt at comedy is a montage wholly dedi-cated to gags: Johnny dusts The Thing while he sleeps on the couch; Reed walks in on Sue getting out of the shower (she turns invisible, shouting "Can't you knock?"); Reed stretches his face to make for easier shaving; and Johnny spies Reed's rubbery arm stretching from bathroom to hallway closet, retriev-ing a roll of toilet paper and retracting. Such a montage might seem out of place here, as it is more a holdover from 1980s comedies than the ritualistic montages of so many action films. But while Story's attempts to blend com-edy and action may overreach, the likely intention behind them is consistent with much of the genre's recent output. As a good number of the contemporary disaster and superhero films indicate, the action film has long been broadening its appeal by appealing to younger viewers and family audiences.

If the action genre is going through a process of "aging down," and if superhero movies represent one flank of this campaign, it should be no surprise that another flank is represented by the Walt Disney Company. While films like the Pirates of the Caribbean series (2003, 2006, 2007) and National Treasure (2004) might not have been considered "action" films in previous decades, they have gained much ground in earning that designation, largely because the action genre has become an increasingly amorphous class of pictures. "A decade ago, the definition of an action movie was a very specific type of movie appealing to a very specific demo[graphic]," says the Walt Disney Company's Oren Aviv. Since that time, however, the genre has become something else, "an adventure movie that happens to have a lot of action and appeals to audiences beyond the young male."[29] It is worth noting that while Disney was enjoying the success of its summer blockbuster Pirates of the Caribbean: Dead Man's Chest (2006), Aviv, who had been president of marketing for the Walt Disney Company since 2000, and who had additionally assumed the specially minted position of chief creative officer in April 2005, received a much-publicized promotion to president of production. To many analysts, this represented the continuing ascendancy of marketing's influence in the motion picture studios, as Aviv's was Hollywood's second such promotion of the year. (The previous March, Universal announced its appointment of former marketing executive Marc Shmuger, along with Focus Features co-president David Linde, to replace departing studio chairman Stacey Snider.)

This phenomenon Aviv cites is making already anachronistic films such as The Punisher seem even more so. And if this is partly due to the aging down of the action movie, then it is also partly due to another, simultaneous trend: the aging up of another kind of picture. According to Aviv,

> The definition of the family movie has changed. Now you can have spectacular action and adult themes in family films. The perception say, five years ago, was that a family movie was an animated movie my kids wanted to see, that I would have to endure. Now, it's Pixar films, National Treasure, Spider-Man, Pirates of the Caribbean, Lord of the Rings, and Narnia, playing to every age group, every race, every demographic (emphasis in original).[30]

The films listed by Aviv, along with many others—particularly many that belong to the superhero trend—represent the large overlap of the aging-down action movie and the aging-up family film. Interestingly, while superhero movies and Disney films represent two of the most significant influences on the aging-down of the action genre, Disney has not adapted any comic book properties. As Aviv explains, "We prefer to homegrow our own franchises like *National Treasure, Pirates of the Caribbean, The Chronicles of Narnia,* and of course our animated films."[31]

Among the films that best bear out Aviv's observations is *The Incredibles,* an animated superhero tale from Pixar Animation Studios released by Disney as its tentpole animated picture for the 2004 holiday season. Following the G-rated *Toy Story* films (1995, 1999), *A Bug's Life* (1998), *Monster's Inc.* (2001), and *Finding Nemo* (2003), *The Incredibles* is Pixar's first PG-rated feature, rated so for its "action violence." Conversely, *Alien vs. Predator,* released just a few months earlier, is the first PG-13-rated film in two series of R-rated entries. While much still distinguishes *The Incredibles* from *Alien vs. Predator* (and while only the former could be considered a family film), their relationship to their predecessors further illustrates Aviv's points: for the family film and for the action movie, each film represents the move toward newer, wider audiences— spurred at least in part by advances in computer-generated imagery.

Touching on many of the same concepts (and superpowers) as *Fantastic Four,* writer/director Brad Bird's follow-up to *The Iron Giant* (1999) is the story of the Parr family, a family of would-be and used-to-be superheroes who had intended to keep their powers hidden until a new menace rises—threatening first the family and then the world. The Parr family comprises the impossibly strong Bob/Mr. Incredible (voiced by Craig T. Nelson), the seemingly elastic Helen/Elastigirl (voiced by Holly Hunter), and their children. Teenage wallflower Violet (voiced by Sarah Vowell) can turn invisible and manipulate energy much like *Fantastic Four*'s Invisible Woman. Hyperactive Dash (voiced by Spencer Fox), the Parrs' young son, is gifted with super-speed. This foursome is supplemented by baby Jack Jack, who spends most of the film in its margins, only to ignite like the Human Torch during the climax.

While not an action film in the strictest sense (and not based on a comic book), *The Incredibles* makes use of many of the genre's technological and stylistic developments, as well as its thematic concerns. These include computer animation; a sophisticated spin-off video game; elaborate, rapidly cut action sequences; the superhero format; the theme of duality; and the boundaries of, and restraints put upon, heroism. This accounts for the darkness and intensity with which Bird crafts his unusually sophisticated (and Academy Award–winning) animated film. Indeed, *The Incredibles* features action sequences cut much like many of those found in its action film contemporaries—only more finely crafted. A prime example is a sequence in which missiles seek and destroy a jet carrying Helen, Violet, and Dash. With the missiles pursuing, the plane dodging, the "camera" racing between compositions, the quick cutting, Helen's distress calls, the children's panic, the dramatic score, the fraught sound design, and of course, the explosion, the sequence recalls the work of Michael Bay and company, but with far more control, and with it, a greater sense of escalating danger.

The first part of the sequence, from when an alarm first sounds inside the plane's cabin to Helen's execution of her first evasive maneuver, features 12 shots in 20 seconds. The second part, from the first maneuver to a shot of an imprisoned Mr. Incredible, consists of 21 shots in 27 seconds. The final segment, coming out of our last cutaway through the final explosion, contains 23 shots in about 21 seconds. While there is more to the sequence than these three segments, comparing them is useful: with each one, the sequence gets progressively more intense as average shot lengths decrease by one-third of a second—from approximately 1.67 seconds to roughly 1.29 seconds to about .91 seconds.

It is worth emphasizing that these are only averages, and that while some shots may last up to two seconds, others feel practically atomized. Also, unlike traditional filmmaking, in which footage is shot and then cut down, animation requires an even more deliberate approach. Shots are essentially "built" from the ground up, and while the editing of the final images is certainly refined during later stages, by and large, shots are designed to be of a given length.

The action of The Incredibles is unusually visceral for an animated film—and in ways not limited to the pace of the editing. Across a tropical island, henchmen piloting large, flying blades pursue Dash. One of the henchmen punches Dash—a child—in the jaw. During the pursuit, two of these henchmen crash and explode, clearly killed. The second explosion blows Dash into a lagoon. Underwater, the camera looks up at Dash floating, while, above the surface, the fireball blooms. Similar images are seen in True Lies (1994), The Rock (1996), The Transporter (2002), and Poseidon (2006).

Animation has always had a violent streak, but the craftsmanship here is more akin to the action of Bay and West, or Donner and McTiernan, than anything seen in, say, Tom and Jerry. Rather than mallets or meat cleavers, the heroes of The Incredibles must evade machine gun fire and gasoline explosions—and the occasional laser beam and killer robot. Establishing the dire stakes for her children (and for the audience), Helen cautions them about the dangers of leaving their island cave: "Remember the bad guys on those shows you used to watch on Saturday mornings? Well these guys are not like those guys. They won't exercise restraint because you're children. *They will kill you if they get the chance. Do not give them that chance.*" Unusually dark for an animated film, Helen's reference to Saturday morning cartoons helps ground *The Incredibles* in a "real world," much as other action films have done with other film references. Here, however, Brad Bird cites the world of popular culture not with a wink, but with a grimace.

Interestingly, Disney's DVD release of *The Incredibles* includes a short piece, *Mr. Incredible and Pals*, an episode of a faux-television cartoon for which Mr. Incredible and superhero friend Frozone (voiced by Samuel L. Jackson) long ago sold their likenesses. But while *Mr. Incredible and Pals* satirizes animated programs of the 1960s, it also further distinguishes *The Incredibles* from "cartoons." After all, if Mr. Incredible is involved in licensing his image, the film must be taking place in a world of real people, a world of which cartoons are but a part. This is among the more imaginative spin-offs to which *The Incredibles* lends itself. Indeed, as an animated feature that balances a number of intense action sequences, its marketability to families, and the Disney brand, *The Incredibles* is well-positioned for a range of media and promotional opportunities. Among the most prominent may be the video game developed by Heavy Iron Studios, a subsidiary of THQ Inc., which has developed and distributed games based on licensed properties including other Pixar titles, Nickelodeon's *Jimmy Neutron*, World Wrestling Entertainment, Britney Spears, *Star Wars*, *Evil Dead*, *The Punisher*, and *The Sopranos*.

As Heavy Iron's development of the *Incredibles* game coincided with Pixar's development of the film, artists from both companies met regularly. This enabled the game to become a venue for ideas that did not ultimately appear in the final cut of the film. In particular, villains who had been created for the movie, but dropped, later surfaced in the game.[32] THQ's first *Incredibles* game (to date, there have been three) was sufficiently intense to be rated "T" for Teen by the Entertainment Software Review Board, the video game industry's self-regulatory body. According to the ESRB's guidelines, games rated T "have content that may be suitable for ages thirteen and older. Titles in this category may contain violence, suggestive themes, crude humor, minimal blood and/or infrequent use of strong language."[33] With THQ's previous games based on Pixar's *Monsters, Inc.* and *Finding Nemo* having received E ratings (for "Everyone"), the T rating for the *Incredibles* game parallels the PG rating the film received after its five G-rated predecessors.

While the *Incredibles* game draws upon a number of villains, most of the film focuses on one: Syndrome (voiced by Jason Lee), a psychopath whose lifelong desire has been to be regarded as a superhero. We first meet Syndrome as a boy, Buddy, half-crazed with fandom for Mr. Incredible. After the hero crushes Buddy's hope of becoming his sidekick, Buddy goes bad, growing up to amass a collection of lethal, high-tech contraptions and an island base befitting a James Bond villain. Syndrome's plan is to unleash his creations on the public, only to suddenly appear as the first new superhero in a generation and save the day. After he has had his fill of public adoration, he will sell his inventions, become even filthier rich, and watch as people buy their way to super-status. "And when everyone is super," Buddy tells us, "no one will be."

Syndrome's malevolence is twofold. He is quite willing, in fact eager, to kill the Parrs and has already tested his "Omnidroid" robot by using it to lure many of the Parrs' superhero friends to their deaths. And by making everybody super, Syndrome is also plotting to rid the world of all future heroes. But unlike say, the Lex Luthors of the world, Syndrome's aim is not only to rid the world of peace and justice; he also wants to rid it of exceptionality, and with it, all of our romantic associations with heroism. Though Syndrome seems to have many of the accoutrements and all of the megalomania of a Bond villain, it is important to note that he is not bent on world domination. Rather, he wants the playing field leveled. But what Syndrome seeks is the very thing Mr. Incredible rails against. Sequestered in the suburbs by the government, Mr. Incredible harbors a zeal for the good ol' days that finds expression in everything from his nights out with Frozone foiling petty crimes; to his den, decked out in memorabilia and mementos (including a framed magazine titled *Glory Days)*; to his insistence that Dash's fourth grade graduation is not a graduation, but in fact, another of society's "new ways to celebrate mediocrity."

The connection between Mr. Incredible and Syndrome is especially pronounced during a standoff between the archenemies, after Syndrome has captured his former idol. Bird zooms in on Mr. Incredible's eyes, lined by a black mask. Mid-zoom, Bird cuts to Syndrome, similarly masked, with the camera moving in on him. Bird cuts back to Mr. Incredible, with the camera continuing its motion. Bird links the two through the motion of the image, and also by highlighting the resemblance they bear to each other. Indeed, Syndrome represents an interesting spin on a familiar type—not the archetype of the villain, but of the hero. As a villain whose scheme is rooted in his frustrated hero worship, Syndrome skewers the archetype of the protagonist wrestling with opposing natures. Whereas the Western and action film hero has been the

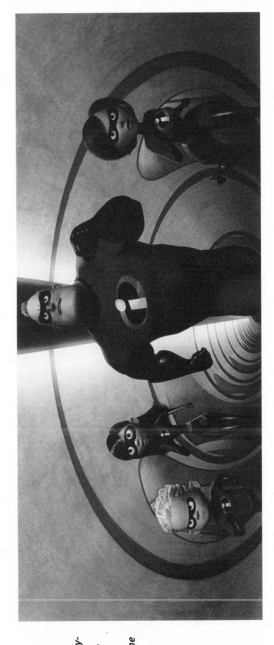

Family Dynamic:
The heroes of The Incredibles (2004), the year's most family-friendly action movie, most intense family film, or both. (From the author's collection.)

Man Who Knows Indians, the Man Who Knows Criminals, the Man Who Knows Psychotics, and the Man Who Knows Monsters, Syndrome is the Man Who Knows Heroes.

In a sense, Syndrome's quest for homogeny simply mirrors the society's ambivalent—and ungrateful—stance toward its champions. After all, *The Incredibles* is set in a world where the government has banned all superhero activity and enacted the Superhero Relocation Program, giving ex-superheroes new, quieter identities. While a clever twist on superhero mythos and the set-up for a number of fish-out-of-water gags (such as Mr. Incredible's oversized bulk squeezed into an insurance company cubicle), this plot device resonates with a number of much bleaker superhero properties such as *X-Men*, *Batman: The Dark Knight Returns*, and most directly, *Watchmen*, Alan Moore's comic in which broken and even psychotic former superheroes have been forced into retirement by the 1977 passage of the Keene Act, which—much like the Superhero Relocation Program—has outlawed all costumed vigilantism.

Watchmen has spent years languishing in Hollywood's development machine, but another of Moore's comic books, *V for Vendetta*, has been adapted by Warner Bros. (although, unlike illustrator David Lloyd, Moore has publicly disowned the film and had his name removed from the credits). In comic form, *V for Vendetta* is mainly thought of as a graphic novel (as is *Watchmen*), despite the fact that it was first published serially beginning in 1982. Producer Joel Silver acquired the rights to the comic in the late 1980s; it would take more than fifteen years for Silver to see the adaptation, written by *The Matrix*'s Larry and Andy Wachowski, come to the screen.[34] Directed by James McTeigue, the Wachowskis' longtime assistant director, *V for Vendetta* is a curious case. With fewer action sequences than most action movies, *V for Vendetta* is not a straightforward action film so much as it is a dramatic political thriller that makes considerable use of action movie tropes. Nevertheless, much of its iconography and thematic concerns compose a long view of the action genre's history.

V for Vendetta takes place against a backdrop that recalls the dystopian tomorrows of so many action films. Here, it is England of the near future—"2020, the year of perfect vision," as J. Hoberman notes—a police state that has outlawed dissent, homosexuality, the Quran, and, it would seem, any popular culture save for the propagandist television network, BTN.[35] Against this backdrop appears a costumed antihero, V (Hugo Weaving), embodying 1970s vigilantism as well as contemporary comic book–derived heroism. Hoping to spark a revolution, V blows up London landmarks to commemorate the anniversary of the 1605 Gunpowder Plot—the thwarted attempt to destroy

Parliament, for which Guy Fawkes was hung. This is the grandest—but hardly the only—example of images and actions that may have motivated Warner Bros. to change *V for Vendetta*'s release date from November 4, 2005 to March 17, 2006. According to *Daily Variety*, the studio, announcing the shift, did not address speculation that the decision was motivated by the then-recent London terrorist bombings of July 7, 2005. (It seems like a plausible assumption, however, especially given J. Hoberman's observation that the film's premiere was scheduled to be held on the 400th anniversary of the Gunpowder Plot.[36]) Instead, the studio cited post-production delays, and as *Daily Variety* further notes, the film would have faced much competition "in the crowded Nov. 4 frame."[37] But while *V for Vendetta* enjoyed an emptier field when released in March, its opening toward the beginning of 2006, rather than the end of 2005, certainly fueled the industry's expectations that *V for Vendetta* would be the year's first blockbuster—expectations the film did not meet.[38]

V has no other name, nor any face other than his Guy Fawkes mask—a seemingly porcelain piece that looks much like the iconic "comedy" mask that, along with its twin "tragedy" mask, so often signifies the theater. The white of his mask is a counterpoint to his black garb, just as the mask's disquieting grin, while complimenting V's theatrical side, is a counterpoint to his morbidity. Putting an even finer point on this schism is the *Village Voice*'s Matt Singer, who reflects that in the comic book,

> Lloyd's ultimate design, dark tunic and cape offset by Fawkes's bleached, perpetually smiling likeness, suggested a composite of Batman and the Joker (an idea Moore would explore further in his graphic novel *Batman: The Killing Joke*, where the eternal foes are depicted as two sides of the same coin).[39]

Warner Bros.'s publicity for *V for Vendetta* draws upon other referents when noting McTeigue's vision of V's costume as "a cross between the actual Guy Fawkes character and a gunslinger."[40] Indeed, less adorned than encased by his white mask and layers of black—his black gloves, his black wig, his black hat—V recalls a related archetype, the impenetrable 1980s action hero. Though drawn from a comic book, V is more like a traditional action hero than a comic book one in that *V for Vendetta* is not V's origin story. Fragmented flashbacks reveal that V was once a prisoner in a government-run concentration camp, where a fire disfigured him and forged his purpose, but this is the film's past; its present does not detail V's process of becoming.

The film does, however, show the maturation of a secondary character: Evey (Natalie Portman), V's young charge. In the film's most disquieting sequence, V dupes Evey into thinking she has been imprisoned and facing execution. The ersatz-prison devised by V, while recalling the computer simulation in which Morpheus trains Neo in the Wachowskis' The Matrix, forges Evey's character. When she is released, McTeigue stresses the movie's preoccupation with two dueling archetypes: the monolithic hero of action films and the burgeoning superhero of comic books. Freed, Evey walks onto the rooftop, into the rain, and into a sequence in which McTeigue intercuts the purifications of his two protagonists. At first, McTeigue composes the characters in a two-shot, but Evey steps forward, into a composition all her own. Reborn, she leaves V behind, and with him, the protective cloak he had tried to put on her. Now that Evey has taken command of the frame, the filmmakers cut three times to flashbacks of V on fire. They cut back and forth between V raising his arms in the inferno and Evey raising hers to the rain.

This sequence also marks the apotheosis of how V for Vendetta braids the past and the present. The bleeding of the past into the present is central to film noir and, not coincidentally, also to Batman Begins. (Indeed, at one point in its development, Moore and Lloyd's comic was conceived as a "thirties mystery strip" set in an authentic 1930s world, and centered around the character "Vendetta."[41]) To a lesser extent, the past is also foregrounded by The Crow, The Punisher, Sin City, and others. Castle's speechifying aside, these films are about vengeance—heroes avenging themselves on villains, and villains on heroes— and what else is revenge if not obsession with one's own history? It is no coincidence that vengeance is a motivation also seen in a number of Westerns. Though many Westerns are set against a backdrop of progress, revenge is among the ways the genre expresses its own concern with events long gone (another being the man-with-a-past archetype that so many gunfighters echo). Is it any wonder, then, that the action film is so widely seen as being conservative? It is descended from not one, but two genres that each harbor a deeply rooted concern, if not an outright obsession with, the past.

With the vengeance V exacts on his former camp guards, and with the methods he uses to mold Evey, V is another of the genre's heroes who harbor this fixation, despite his vision of himself as a revolutionary. In this respect, drawn from the comic book page, and recalling the 1980s supermen and the 1970s vigilantes, V is like Batman, Spider-Man, X-Men, and The Punisher, like Van Helsing and Neo and Robocop, like Riggs, Rambo, and the Road Warrior, and like Kersey and Callahan, and others we have seen. Singular in his appearance, in his abilities, in his weaponry, but dual in nature, the action hero belongs to mythic traditions greater than himself, but can never truly belong to those he protects. Possessing these gifts and shouldering these burdens, he stands at the center of a beleaguered, but high-concept world and rights its tilt with the force of his vigilantism. He is the gunslinger, and fighting evil in the night, whether a literal or figurative night, is the thing that makes his day.

Conclusion
Sifting Through the Rubble

Arnold Schwarzenegger is the War on Terror.
—Home Video Commercial for Collateral Damage
(2002)

On August 9, 2002, two films opened across North America. One was Clint Eastwood's *Blood Work*. While less an action film than a thriller, *Blood Work* begins like a 1970s Eastwood film, introducing Eastwood's grizzled FBI investigator, Terry McCaleb, in a scene photographed by Tom Stern in the style of *Dirty Harry* and other 1970s entries. Similarly, the final showdown finds a killer pursuing McCaleb through the bowels of a rusting freighter: a sort of *Magnum Force 2002*. The other film was *XXX*, director Rob Cohen's follow-up to his surprise hit *The Fast and the Furious*. The title character of *XXX* is an extreme sportsman (Vin Diesel), recruited to become a secret agent. Presumably for the benefit of younger audiences, the film distends the James Bond framework with sensory overload. Noise, pyrotechnics, music, breakneck editing, and stunt work that captures the absurdity of the Bond films but not their wit: this and more add up to the undifferentiated mass of stimuli that is *XXX*. It is a rush that manages to drag, made in a style that is the antithesis of the more staid filmmaking technique utilized in *Dirty Harry* and others and recalled in *Blood Work*.

Similarly, July 2003 saw the release of Twentieth Century Fox's *The League of Extraordinary Gentlemen*, an adaptation of the Alan Moore comic book and special effects showcase from *Blade* director Stephen Norrington, making his first PG-13-rated film. A week later, Columbia Pictures opened the R-rated *Bad Boys II*, reuniting Will Smith and Martin Lawrence as Miami narcotics cops, for another go-around clearly influenced by the action cinema and television of the 1980s. In fact, *Bad Boys II* is Michael Bay's sequel to his directorial debut, *Bad Boys*, which seemed anachronistic when released in 1995.

Finally, April 2, 2004 saw two PG-13-rated action films open: the comic book adaptation *Hellboy*, the first non-R-rated feature from *Blade II* director Guillermo del Toro; and *Walking Tall*, starring The Rock in a remake of the

1973 film that, like the same year's rerelease Billy Jack, combined savvy marketing and grassroots support to help cement the modern vigilante as an American movie character type. Two weeks after the releases of Hellboy and Walking Tall, Lions Gate opened The Punisher, combining the trend of comic book adaptations with an overt nostalgia for the action filmmaking of the 1970s and 1980s.

The above pairings each represent both ends of what has been a more than thirty-five-year-long evolution, an evolution in which the action film has never meant one single, stable entity. At times bifurcating into different, overlapping trends, the genre has evolved into and out of different models and stylistic vogues, as all established movie genres have. The action film has progressed from being a genre of only slightly unreal heroes in a gritty world to one of supermen in an ordinary world to one of common men in a more spectacle-driven world, to one where the heroes and their environs both manifest the spectacular. Concurrently, the action film's political complexion has also changed. The genre's stewards have had to take up the domestic crises of the 1970s, Reagan's reinvigoration of Cold War anxieties in the 1980s, and the end of the Cold War and the rise of political correctness in the early 1990s. Along the way, these filmmakers have expanded their America-centric hero into a somewhat more global one.

Indeed, for well over the first decade of the action film's evolution, the genre's very name was also shifting. Terms such as "action," "actioner," "action-adventure," and others had been thrown about since before Dirty Harry, but without signifying any single, coherent genre. Conversely, even after the action genre had been established, its nomenclature would continue to evolve. This is best seen in how one trade publication categorized one franchise's various entries: Daily Variety called Dirty Harry a "Police Melodrama," Magnum Force a "Police Crime Melodrama," The Enforcer a "Crime Melodrama," and Sudden Impact a "Police Actioner." Only 1988's The Dead Pool, the last in the series and the first to be released in the action-friendly summer months, was given the designation "Action."[1] Another snapshot of the genre's evolution may also be glimpsed in the art direction of the Death Wish series. Whereas in the original 1974 film, Paul Kersey stands in front of a Newsweek advertisement blaring the word "Vigilantism," in 1987's Death Wish 4: The Crackdown, he chases a drug dealer through a fairground, past a large sign reading "Amusements."

The Dirty Harry and Death Wish franchises are fitting illustrations, as the genre's recent output suggests a curious trend that has emerged alongside Hollywood's family-friendlier action fare: a nostalgia for the 1970s and 1980s, and with it, a return to the vigilantism of yore. Remakes of *Shaft* (2000), *Get Carter* (2000), and *Assault on Precinct 13* (2004) all join *Walking Tall*. Additionally, recent years have seen a proposed sequel to *Taxi Driver*, a proposed remake of *Deathrace 2000* to be directed by Paul W. S. Anderson, and a planned but stalled remake of *Billy Jack*, at one time to have starred Keanu Reeves. (According to *Billy Jack* star, co-writer, and director Tom Laughlin, "People are lost today, and they always tell me we need another Billy Jack, who stood for moral and spiritual values and psychic truths." [2])

This nostalgia is also evident in two films drawn from television shows: *S.W.A.T.*, based on ABC's 1975–1976 series, and *Miami Vice* (2006), director Michael Mann's adaptation of his landmark 1980s television program. (Both films star Colin Farrell.) Also looking backward is the recent work of Sylvester Stallone and Michael Bay. Stallone may have been trying to recapture his glory from 1985, which saw both *Rambo: First Blood Part II* and *Rocky IV*, by planning to follow the Christmas 2006 release of *Rocky Balboa* (the sixth in the series) with *Rambo IV: Pearl of the Cobra*. Meanwhile, Bay, once a paragon of contemporary film style, has become focused on revisiting properties from the 1970s and 1980s. As of this writing, he is in production *Transformers*, a feature film based on the 1980s cartoon and toy line and slated to open just days after the release of the currently titled *Live Free or Die Hard*, which will mark the return of the *Die Hard* franchise to move screens after a twelve-year hiatus. Moreover, Bay's recent producing credits include the remakes of 1974's *The Texas Chainsaw Massacre*, 1979's *The Amityville Horror*, and 1986's *The Hitcher*, as well as a proposed *Friday the 13th* movie. To some, this might represent a niche; to others, a case of arrested development.

The Warriors has also capitalized on this trend, with a planned remake currently to be directed by Tony Scott, the original film's heavily advertised special edition DVD, and a recent video game tie-in, which was well-received by the video game industry and by the public. Similar games include a *Dirty Harry* title, being developed by The Collective, Inc. and Warner Bros. Interactive and planned to feature the voice of Clint Eastwood, and a game based on Brian De Palma's *Scarface* (1983), featuring the voice of co-star Steven Bauer. Also in the works was a *Taxi Driver* game, cancelled after several months of development by publisher Majesco. These video games follow *The Godfather* and *James Bond 007: From Russia with Love* spin-off games, for which original cast members, including Marlon Brando, James Caan, Robert Duvall, Sean Connery, and others, have recorded new dialogue.

Meanwhile, audiences have seen a rash of recent films that put a particularly fine point on vigilantism and vengeance. Such films include the Vin Diesel vehicle *A Man Apart* (2004), Tony Scott's *Man on Fire* (2004, based on a novel that had been adapted once before in 1987), John Singleton's *Four Brothers* (2005), and the comic book–based films *The Punisher*, *Batman Begins*, and *V for Vendetta*. Additionally, Steven E. de Souza has written a new adaptation of *The Phantom* comic strip, and "abandon[ed] the previous purple-spandex, retro-campy live and animated versions." Instead, de Souza has crafted "something closer to the more ominous vigilante of the thirties comic strip, who would often leave the jungle for gritty, urban *noir*-esque storylines."[3] De Souza's grittier, back-to-basics approach is consistent with *Batman Begins* and also the currently in-production *Casino Royale*, by all accounts a lower-tech James Bond film based on the novel that introduced the character and saw him earn his license to kill.

De Souza submitted his draft of *The Phantom* in April 2003. Six months later, however, production companies Hyde Park and Crusader Entertainment hired Olympic gold medalist-turned-screenwriter Mel Stewart to modernize the script and equip its hero with all manner of technology and high-concept gear.[4] If this version is produced, it is likely that The Phantom will recall Inspector Callahan less than he will Inspector Gadget. Still, as a property lending itself to both vigilante-nostalgia and lighter-hearted superheroism, *The Phantom* represents a snapshot of a period in the genre's history during which these two trends co-exist.

We can make at least one generalization about the genre's evolution, however: given the industry's advances in technology, the showman's constant drive to best what has been done before, and how quickly audiences can become inured toward last season's thrill-making technique, the action film has evolved along a trajectory of excess. And the fact that there is no single stylistic, ideological, or even narrative definition of the action film highlights that the genre's commitment to excess is its only constant. In 1971, Harry Callahan asks Scorpio, "Have I fired six shots, or only five?" In 1990, John McClane escapes more than that number of hand grenades. In a single stunt.

But beneath the stylistic techniques, the narrative tropes, and the cultural resonances, what we are dealing with in the action film is an aesthetic of killing people. Confronting the fact that the genre is a fundamentally violent one can have a funny way of raising issues about the people who enjoy it: if the movie industry can count on a "mainstream" audience to support these pictures, is this audience necessarily uniform? Heterogeneous but sharing some common ground? Or divided and deriving different pleasures from the same material?

Just as there is no one trend of action movie that typifies the genre, there is no one American identity that explains the genre's resonance. It is true that there are many American identities, but also true that there are relatively fewer American myths. And more than any other viable genre from the "New Hollywood" of the 1960s and 1970s on, the action film perpetuates these myths' fundamental tropes. The myths underpinning the American action film are also the ones on which much American history has been founded. These are what we share.

And to think: these questions only address issues of identity within the United States. As for the rest of the planet, it is well-known that American action films are successful outside our borders, sometimes even more than they are within them. In the mid-1980s, a film's foreign box office could be expected to equal 40 to 50 percent of its domestic gross; *Commando*, however, earned $40 million overseas, more than matching the $35 million it made domestically (despite receiving a high censorship rating in many countries and being outright banned in Norway and Sweden).[5] An even stronger performer, *Rambo: First Blood Part II* made $160 million in foreign markets, surpassing its $150 million take in America, where "Rambomania" was said to be everywhere. And although *Cobra*, Stallone's follow-up to *Rambo*, would fail in the United States, it would gross more than $90 million internationally and become one of the year's most successful exports for Warner Bros.[6] Similarly, as the *Los Angeles Herald Examiner* reports, the domestic disappointment *Rambo III* earned only $28 million in U.S. rentals, compared to $19 million in Japan alone. The same summer's Arnold Schwarzenegger vehicle *Red Heat* followed a similar pattern.[7]

Likewise, Schwarzenegger's later hits at the U.S. box office would go on to gross even more overseas. These include *Terminator 2* ($285.2 million overseas versus $204.8 million domestically) and *True Lies* ($218 million overseas; $146 million stateside).[8] The healthy foreign box office of the latter film is significant, given its cartoonish depiction of Arab villains.

Charting the increasing popularity of a franchise can be even more illuminating. While the foreign gross of Warner's *Lethal Weapon 2* trailed its domestic take by earning $80 million overseas and $147.2 million in the United States, the overseas receipts for the franchise's next installment edged out its domestic ones: *Lethal Weapon 3* earned $175 million internationally and $144.7 million stateside.[9] Interestingly, the sequels grossed roughly the same amount at the U.S. box office, but overseas, *Lethal Weapon 3*'s performance would improve on its predecessor's by over 100 percent. Seeming to pick up where this example leaves off, the domestic and international grosses of *Die Hard 2* were roughly equivalent ($117.5 million in the United States; $120.2 million overseas), but while the next installment, *Die Hard with a Vengeance* underperformed in the United States by just sneaking past the $100 million mark, overseas, it earned $254 million, becoming the world's second-highest grossing film of 1995 (after Disney/Pixar's *Toy Story*).[10]

Similarly, we have already seen how *War of the Worlds* proved to be something of a domestic disappointment relative to its strong foreign performance, as well as how the film's marketing and publicity was tailored to various segments of a global audience. And while the opening of Tom Cruise's follow-up, *Mission: Impossible III* also underwhelmed at the domestic box office, the film "showed considerably more muscle overseas" (especially in the Asian markets where Cruise has always been exceptionally popular) with a foreign opening weekend gross of $70.3 million.[11] An even better example would be *Independence Day*'s astounding $300 million gross that, with foreign receipts, swelled to three quarters of a billion dollars.[12] In 2003, *The Matrix Reloaded* made $450 million at the foreign box office, as compared not only to the $280 million the film made domestically, but also to the total, worldwide gross of $456 million earned by its predecessor, the first in the series. In November of the same year, Warner Bros. released *The Matrix Revolutions* in eighty countries simultaneously, rather than open the film in America first and abroad later, as has been standard Hollywood practice. This, more than any pairing of box office results, offers an image of how increasingly globalized our movies have become—as commodities to be sure, but also as cultural phenomena.

Ironically, this "day-and-date" distribution of major tentpoles may, to some extent, mitigate one of the greatest pressures placed on action filmmakers and marketers: delivering a huge opening weekend. These films are consistently expected to open as the number one movie in America, to pull in record-setting grosses (*some* record, *any* record); failure not only loses the studio millions of dollars in potential revenue over that three- or four-day window, but also depresses income from future revenue streams, including the foreign box office. But by opening in many international markets at once, the baggage that attends a poor domestic debut does not have as much of a chance to poison the film's reception overseas.

Stateside, the opening weekend is crucial to the film's long-term performance. Hollywood can reliably predict that a summer action movie's total domestic box office will equal only three times what the film earns in its first weekend (as opposed to a drama or romantic comedy that can earn five to six times its opening weekend gross, as these more adult-oriented movies often take longer finding their audiences). Therefore, as the opening weekend represents a disproportionate share of an action film's domestic revenue, studios spend more money on these first few days to ensure not only an extra few million dollars here, but also tens of millions over the lifespan of the property.

This lifespan includes the stateside and foreign box office, of course, but also such downstream revenue sources as network and syndicated broadcasts. In this sphere, many deals are structured such that the film's sale price is tied to its gross crossing certain thresholds. Another source of revenue affected by a film's opening weekend is the all-important DVD market. Here, a studio's immediate concern is how many units retailers will order, how high a return rate it will see should the title sit on the shelves a little too long, and even the quality of the shelf space the retailer will assign it.

A smash opening weekend generally means a studio can look forward to strong box office returns and future boons in these markets and others. On the other hand, a lackluster opening not only restricts such windfalls, but also compounds the movie's bad fortune by triggering a reallocation of resources. Seeking to staunch its losses, a studio will slash the marketing budgets it had dedicated for other windows—including international and home video releases. Thus, a weak performer is given even less of a chance to redeem itself by connecting with other, untapped audiences, because the resources to reach them are withheld.

Multiplexes intensify this pressure. Appearing on multiple screens every half hour, movies exhaust their supply of moviegoers more quickly. And given how quickly word of mouth can now travel over email, cell phones, and text messaging, a film's fate can be sealed not just with its first weekend, but with its opening night. When films open around the world on later dates, this word of mouth follows it, for good or ill. Hollywood's increasing reliance on worldwide day-and-date openings and on international premieres, as seen in the case of *War of the Worlds*, could therefore be seen as an attempt to reduce risk (to what extent that is possible) while maximizing opening grosses—and the bragging rights that come with them—as well as positioning its products as global events.

Of course, while action films typically fare well in the international market, they also generate their share of controversy. We have seen how some foreign Muslims responded to *The Siege*; likewise, the Russian press protested *Rambo*, just as the Munich press decried *Missing in Action*. In fact, the German newspaper *TAZ* not only called on the public to boycott the film but also suggested the use of the same tactics that had forced UIP (then the European distributor for Paramount, Universal, and MGM/UA) to withdraw *Red Dawn* from several theaters in Berlin, Dusseldorf, and Dortmund: namely, threats by demonstrators and attacks with acid.[13]

But as the numbers and distribution patterns indicate, American action movies find millions of foreign fans, such as the Balinese man Michael Bay recalls meeting, a man who lived in a hut and loved *The Rock*.[14] There are still more striking—and more political—examples. According to *Newsweek*, the Hollywood films Leonid Brezhnev most often borrowed from the state's film agency included *Dirty Harry, Magnum Force,* and *Taxi Driver*.[15] More recently, many residents of U.S.-controlled Baghdad who still had electricity reportedly sought diversion in watching American films on home video. Among the more popular titles were action films starring Wesley Snipes, Jean-Claude Van Damme, and Sylvester Stallone. One merchant said that his top performers included *Ticker* (2001) in which Steven Seagal's character searches San Francisco for a bomb, and *The Patriot* (2000), not an action film per se, but a movie in which Mel Gibson's Revolutionary War militia soldier uses guerrilla tactics against the occupying British.[16] More disquieting, however, is a Reuters news item from summer 1985, the summer of *Rambo*. The story, published in the *Los Angeles Times*, claims that "Rambo, an all-American killer extolled by President Reagan, has also captivated the gunmen of West Beirut." As the article maintains, throngs of militiamen, "like the ones who guarded U.S. hostages during the Beirut airport hijacking" attended *Rambo: First Blood Part II* at Beirut's Estral cinema. In fact, according to the Estral's projectionist, "Mostly it's the fighters and the gunmen who come to see the film." The article also says that members of the film's Muslim audience claimed to identify with the title character, including "his fighting prowess." One seventeen-year-old, a self-described mechanic and fighter, is quoted as saying, "A person who sacrifices himself for his country like that deserves much."[17]

Clearly, the world does not always embrace America's action mythology wholesale. (Neither the Iraqi merchant nor the *Variety* article in which he is quoted indicates just whom his customers were rooting for.) Aspects of a movie may be altered to make it more palatable to one territory or another: thus, in some German versions of *Die Hard*, dubbed dialogue has made the German terrorists British. In the Middle East, videotapes of *Rambo* featured French and Arabic subtitles that change the film's setting from modern-day Vietnam to the Philippines of 1943; Rambo has no longer made a name for himself in-country, but at Guadalcanal instead. Curiously, the subtitles, which excise all references to Vietnam and the Soviet Union, were not written by a legitimate distributor, but by video pirates.[18] Nonetheless, their efforts recall a practice common in Hollywood of the silent era: the altering of title cards and other content to tailor films to the sensibilities of particular foreign markets.[19]

More than any other contemporary genre, the action film is the face of Hollywood as seen by the world. But for the purposes of this study, the more pressing and less often explored question pertains not to foreign audiences being "worked on" by America, but the influence of foreign filmmakers on this American form. *Newsweek's* Howard Fineman speaks to this issue while reviewing *Air Force One*, part of the glut of summer 1997's action- and adventure-themed releases. He writes, "it may say something about the state of America—or Hollywood—that it took a Japanese studio (Sony) and a German-born director (Petersen) to bring to the screen a creature that we Americans can barely imagine: a president as hero."[20] Though Fineman is correct, he refers mainly to Americans' often-cynical view of politicians rather than see in *Air Force One* what has always been true of the genre. Yes, these films are a Hollywood projection of American-ness to the world; at the same time, however, they are also a venue for foreign voices to tell Americans who we are. Paul W. S. Anderson, Jack Cardiff, George Cosmatos, Jan de Bont, Roland Emmerich, Menahem Golan, Yorum Globus, Renny Harlin, Mario Kassar, Ang Lee, Wolfgang Petersen, Arnold Schwarzenegger, Tony Scott, Andrew Vajna, Jean-Claude Van Damme, Paul Verhoeven, Simon West, Michael Winner, John Woo, and others all belong to an international community that helps author American movies, and with them, American identity.

Then come the thorny facts that many filmmakers raised outside the United States grew up on our movies and that having later succeeded in Hollywood, they would be imitated by the native and the foreign-born alike. Regarding the stunt work in Woo's *Mission: Impossible II*, David Ansen writes, "Strange: here is Mr. Woo imitating the two white brothers who directed 'The Matrix' who were imitating the Hong Kong action style at which Woo was once peerless."[21] A chart of American film's influence on non-American filmmakers, and vice versa, can quickly double, triple, and quadruple back on itself. The web of nationality and influence soon loses its center.

Sooner or later, anyone spending serious time with the action film comes to an opposition still more fundamental than those of the foreign versus the domestic, or a mainstream audience versus minority ones. It is fantasy versus reality. Like all mythology, the movies have often been a vehicle for America to process its crises. Of course, a little hope and a little release are never all bad, but there is a deep fallacy here: not that the good guy always wins, or that we are always the good guy, but that a crisis—criminal, terrorist, or otherwise—is something self-contained. A culture such as ours, so immersed in entertainment, is primed to underpin its current events with a sense of narrative, and a narrative's drive toward resolution. Sequels aside, John McClane's War on Terror ends by the closing credits; ours has no credits. This point is articulated by The Siege, one of the few pre–September 11 action films to approximate an honest look at the threat Muslim extremists posed to the United States. When an Arab terrorist is described as being the last terrorist cell, he exclaims, "There will never be a last cell!" But even The Siege succumbs to classic structure: with this man shot dead, and the Army driven out of Brooklyn, the borough's residents cheer, greeting a sunny day and what promises to be an even brighter tomorrow.

Of course, this contradiction is more apparent in the aftermath of September 11. Images of the World Trade Center's destruction triggered astonished responses, including the often heard "It was like a movie"—the only referent many of us had for the sight. And as the genre was by then long-ensconced in the model of the white capitalist terrorist, where was our mythology when we had to confront an enemy that fought not from greed, but from belief, and because of that belief, seemed able to reproduce faster than it could be purged? But the occasional failure of myth does not mean we suspend our drive toward it. As reported in the trade publication Video Business, the two weeks after September 11 saw significant increases in video rentals of The Siege, Under Siege, Independence Day, and Die Hard (as well as sales of titles based on the work of Nostradamus).[22] Along with the spike in rentals, Home Media Retailing publisher Don Rosenberg claims that during the same two weeks, sales of The Siege—a movie largely ignored at the box office—tripled; meanwhile, sales of True Lies that had begun spiking the week of September 2, continued to boom through the week of September 16.[23]

Since before the terrorist attacks in New York and Washington, D.C., the action genre has been embroiled in the question of whether violent movies beget violence in our schools, workplaces, and neighborhoods. I have not occupied myself with that important, though quite separate, question in this study, but as a fan of the genre (even when it fails to merit any fandom), I will say this much: of course violence on screen influences violence in the real world; there is simply too much of the former not to affect the violently predisposed. But to me at least, it is equally obvious that only a culture already obsessed with violence could create a movie genre as violent as the action film out of other, violent influences, and sustain it. I say this much because I feel it would be irresponsible to spend a few hundred pages charting a genre that factors so prominently in this controversy, only to ignore the existence of the question.

This returns us to the action film's violence and excessiveness. These facets of the genre—including the controversies it triggers—make us finally ask what separates the violent movie we condemn from the violent one we cheer. Both draw from the same myths, and neither is likely to be concerned with *meaning*—at least not in any meaningful sense. Even at the genre's most self aware, the action film has no *Unforgiven*. With the arguable exception of a few films such as *Blood Work*, *Cop Land* (1997), and *Dark Blue* (2002), the action movie has tended to favor parody over interrogation, self-deprecation over self-reflection. (I stress "arguable" as these films are, to varying extents, dramas, as well as examples of the more broadly defined "thriller," which encompasses some action movies.) Therefore, the action genre's *The Man Who Shot Liberty Valance* would more likely be *The Man Who Said Something Cool Before Shooting Liberty Valance*. A rash of such films appeared in the early-to-mid 1990s, including *The Hard Way*, *The Last Boy Scout*, *Lethal Weapon 3*, *Eraser*, *The Long Kiss Goodnight*, and the apotheosis of self-parody for both the genre and for Hollywood as a whole, *Last Action Hero*. Indeed, when the film and television industries lampoon themselves, as in Frank Oz's *Bowfinger* (1999), the finale of Robert Altman's *The Player* (1992), Joel Silver's short-lived but acclaimed sitcom *Action* (1999), or with *The Simpsons*'s Rainer Wolfcastle character (a parody of Arnold Schwarzenegger), they are using the action film's inherent ridiculousness as an emblem of their own.

A more recent and outrageous example may be found in *Team America: World Police* (2004), from Trey Parker and Matt Stone, co-creators of *South Park*. The film, both a genre parody and a political satire (released less than three weeks before the 2004 election), pits Delta Force–like commandos against Islamic terrorists—all played by puppets. *Team America*, a $30 million production, owes much to filmmaking vogues and scenarios of the 1980s, especially with sequences such as a training montage set to a hard-driving pop song. More than anything, *Team America* resembles films such as *The Delta Force*, *Death Before Dishonor*, and one that seemed anachronistic even while in theaters, summer 1990's *Navy SEALS*. In fact, there is an all too strange similarity between Fred Dryer's line in *Death Before Dishonor*, "Tell your terrorist friends this: *don't get us mad*" and the *Team America* song lyric, "Terrorists, your game is through / 'cause now you have to answer to / America—*fuck yeah!*"

Though *Team America* targets an outdated model of action movie, such spoofing reveals much about how the genre has taken root in our imagination. Film and genre historian Jeanine Basinger has written that, "no one film ever appears that is quintessentially the genre," but instead, a number of films with shared qualities "emerge, blend, and become one film in memory" (emphasis original).[24] This remembered, hypothetical film is the one often lampooned by a genre's satirists. Here, in their parody of a filmmaking style that is roughly fifteen years out of date, Parker and Stone spoof our collective sense of what the action movie fundamentally is. (Many of their jokes would not work otherwise, as they are not referencing specific scenes or specific films.) It would seem then, that this definitive action movie that current audiences imagine is a product of the 1980s. This was the decade in which action movies reveled in supermen and in fears of the *other*, and in which the genre's conventions crystallized after the formative years of the 1970s and before the self-conscious ones of the 1990s. Though part of a continuum spanning thirty-five years (as of this writing), the 1980s emerge as the action film's classical era or golden age.

But beneath the genre's self-awareness, the action film is ultimately reducible to images of violence and spectacle. Therefore, what all good action movies must first share is that they are well-crafted. This does not only mean that the CGI is properly rendered and composited and has a sense of mass. It also means that the filmmakers must balance ferocity and finesse. The better directors working in the genre use restraint to make room for later intensity. Lesser directors use technique to bludgeon the audience and, with it, the fun—the fun of movies that, as these critically maligned filmmakers can so defensively point out, are made chiefly as entertainment. Much as *The Incredibles* posits, "when everyone is super, no one will be," Anthony Lane writes, in his review of *Con Air*, "There is nothing so boring in life, let alone in cinema, as the boredom of being excited all the time."[25]

Unfortunately, it is usually this more aggressive style of filmmaking that factors so prominently in discussions of action film aesthetics. Throughout this study, I have addressed the genre's stylistic devices, including editing, special effects, art direction, color, composition and camera movement, sound, and other considerations that should inform the discussion of any film genre. Despite the action film's popularity and role in representing Hollywood to the world, the genre has been widely disregarded because of its perceived politics and storytelling standards and virtually ignored for its aesthetics. But the action film has earned the right to be discussed in the same terms as those used to qualify other more established genres. In fact, it may have a privileged claim on these terms, as it is more dependent on raw images than are genres commonly regarded as more sophisticated and dialogue-driven, such as political and courtroom dramas, thrillers, and the romantic and screwball strains of comedy. In this regard, the action genre (especially its more special effects-driven entries) is contemporary Hollywood's closest approximation to the "Cinema of Attractions" that marked the earliest days of motion pictures, when films depicted simple, physical actions, rather than tell stories. The medium was a visual one before it was a narrative one.

So is the difference between the action movies we like and the ones we loathe a matter of craftsmanship? Yes, largely. Is it that they tweak conventions rather than grind them into clichés? To a certain extent, naturally. Is it that the action hinges on a "good script" with "good characters"? To be sure, but while quality writing for quality actors is widely espoused, it is seldom realized. In any event, whether lean (*Dirty Harry, First Blood*), complex (*Die Hard, Air Force One*), or something so clever that you cannot decide which (*Robocop, Speed*), quality screenplays hold the most promise for well-made films, action or otherwise.

The well-written, well-performed, well-crafted action movie offers its audience something more vital than excitement. It offers a sense that the characters are actually experiencing what the filmmakers stage. This is where many of the ironic action movies of the 1990s, and the more current CG extravaganzas fail: their hip sensibility and overwrought effects often come at the expense of the characters' emotional investment in what is happening to them. And if they have no investment, how can we? The films that *do* make real their heroes' emotional and physical experiences are charged with a sense of spontaneity. These films make conventions seem organic; they enact the genre's rituals without making them feel obligatory. They impart to the audience a sliver of what the hero experiences by going to the limits of himself. Most fundamentally, they demonstrate that stories about killing can be, at the same time, stories about being fully alive.

Notes

Introduction (1–8)

1. Patrick Goldstein, "'Wanted'—A Taut Thriller With Gore," *Los Angeles Times*, January 16, 1987, part VI, p. 6.

2. Duane Byrge, "Wanted Dead or Alive," *The Hollywood Reporter*, January 12, 1987, p. 92.

3. New World Pictures, "*Wanted Dead or Alive* Production Notes," 1987, p. 2.

4. For those interested in the etymology of Hollywood slang, Steven E. de Souza claims that the term was in use as early as the 1950s, at American International Pictures where Lawrence Gordon worked. In time, Gordon would become one of the industry's leading producers and executives, as well as mentor to Silver. Through the 1980s and 1990s, "the wham-o theory" would come to be called "the whammy theory."

Prelude (9–22)

1. As early as 1973, *Walking Tall* tweaks the archetype of the vigilante. Rather than depicting a big-city cop-turned-vigilante, *Walking Tall*, based on a true story, follows a vigilante-turned-cop punishing corruption and vice in his hometown.

2. Whitney Williams, "Film Review: Billy Jack," *Daily Variety*, April 29, 1971, p. 3; no attribution, "Billy Jack," *Box Office Showmandiser*, May 17, 1971, p. 11.

3. Richard Slotkin, *Gunfighter Nation: The Myth of the Frontier in Twentieth Century America*. New York: HarperCollins, 1992, p. 14.

4. Warner Bros., Billy Jack Column Items, no page number. (Billy Jack Production File, Margaret Herrick Library of the Academy of Motion Picture Arts and Sciences [hereafter, MHL, AMPAS].)

5. *Ibid.*, MAT 411-A, no page number.

6. Ralph Kaminsky, "'Billy Jack' Closing On $1 Mil Mark in First Week's Run," *The Hollywood Reporter*, May 16, 1973, p. 10.

7. Richard Albarino, "'Billy Jack' Hits Reissue Jackpot," *Variety*, November 7, 1973, p. 1.

8. *Ibid.*, p. 63.

9. "Black-Owned Ad Agency on 'Shaft' Credited for B.O. Boom, 80% Black," *Variety*, July 28, 1971, p. 5.

10. *Ibid.*, p. 5.

11. Thomas Cripps, *Black Film as Genre*. Bloomington: Indiana University Press, 1978, p. 50.

12. MGM, "Just a Guy Who Can't Say No," "Multi-Talented Parks," *Shaft* Pressbook, 1971, no page number. (*Shaft* Production File, MHL, AMPAS.) Prior to becoming a film director (*Shaft* was his sophomore effort), Parks was a celebrated photographer for *Life*.

13. Mark Reid, *Redefining Black Film*. Berkeley: University of California Press, 1993, p. 84.

14. *Ibid.*, p. 84–85.

15. For more on this, particularly *noir*'s linkage of homosexuality to scenes of physical torture, see James Naremore, *More Than Night: Film Noir in its Contexts*. Berkeley: University of California Press, 1998.

16. Naremore, p. 243.

17. *Ibid.*, p. 245.

18. Mike Phillips, "Chic and Beyond," *Sight and Sound*, August 1996. p. 25.

19. Naremore, p. 243.

20. Richard Combs, "Shaft," *Films and Filming*, April 1972, p. 52.

21. A. D. Murphy, "Shaft," *Daily Variety*, June 9, 1971, p. 8.

22. *Playboy*, October 1971, p. 52, 50.

23. Combs, p. 52.

24. Craig Fisher, "'Shaft' Looks Very Good: Special, General Audiences," *The Hollywood Reporter*, June 10, 1971, p. 3.

25. John C. Mahoney, "'Shaft' Playing at New Fox Theater," *Los Angeles Times*, June 25, 1971, part VI, p. 8.

26. MGM Publicity Dept., *Shaft* Production Notes, 1971, no page number.

27. *Ibid.*

28. Todd Berliner, "The Genre Film as Booby Trap: 1970s Genre Bending and *The French Connection*," *Cinema Journal* 40, no. 3, Spring 2001, pp. 25–46.

29. *Ibid.*, pp. 32, 30.

30. Robe, "The French Connection," *Daily Variety*, October 6, 1971, p. 2; Stephen Farber, "A Cops and Crooks Movie That Doesn't Cop Out . . ." *New York Times*, November 21, 1971, section 2, p. D15; Winfred Blevins, "'Connection:' Hard Boiled, Fast-Moving," *Los Angeles Herald Examiner*, November 4, 1971, p. B6; Jay Cocks, "Chasing Frog 1," *Time*, November 1, 1971, p. 109.

31. *Coogan's Bluff* marks Siegel's first collaboration with Clint Eastwood, in which the star plays an Arizona sheriff bent on apprehending a fugitive in New York City. The film is a clash between the law enforcement styles of the modern city and of a Western hero. As a police procedural, *Coogan's Bluff* is not hybridized with the Western so much as it is cross-referenced with it.

32. Robert Bazell and Leo Standora, "The French Connection Again: Nab Ex-Drug Agent in Sale of Heroin," *New York Post*, February 5, 1974, pp. 1, 4. Over time, almost all the "French Connection" heroin would be among the enormous amount of heroin and cocaine that disappeared from police custody in the early 1960s and early 1970s.

33. William Friedkin, William Friedkin Collection, box 8, folder 14, MHL, AMPAS. This document was later published as "Anatomy of a Chase" in the March–April 1972 issue of *Action*.

34. Frank Neill, Director of Publicity, 20th Century Fox Studio, Beverly Hills, Calif.;

"Biography of William Friedkin," June 18, 1971 (William Friedkin Collection, box 8, folder 14, MHL, AMPAS).

35. See among others, the Fox Home Entertainment DVD of *The French Connection*. Additionally, *Films and Filming*'s review calls the film "a resuscitation of the semi-documentary." (Gordon Gow, "The French Connection," *Films and Filming*, March 1972, p. 50.)

36. American Film Institute, "William Friedkin," *Dialogue on Film*, February–March 1974, p. 7, quoted in Thomas D. Clagett, *William Friedkin: Films of Obsession, Aberration, and Reality*. Jefferson, N.C.: McFarland and Co., 1990, p. 90. Interestingly, in Friedkin's AFI seminar (the transcript of which constitutes this issue of *Dialogue on Film*), Friedkin heatedly argues that movies should be less about contemplation than about provoking a visceral reaction in the audience. While acknowledging that filmmaking can serve social or educational needs, Friedkin also says, "I believe to the end, Pauline Kael notwithstanding . . . that the major reasons to make a film are to move people emotionally, to move them either to laughter, tears, or fear" (p. 27). It is for this reason that Friedkin offers an unlikely choice for the best movie of 1973: "To me, the best film I saw this year, me, [the one] I would give an Academy Award to [is] *Magnum Force*." Of the film, the first sequel to *Dirty Harry*, Friedkin claims, "It's the best picture I've seen this year. I mean, I was really involved in it" (p.28).

37. Berliner, p. 43.

Chapter 1: "The Law's Crazy" (23–59)

1. A. D. Murphy, "Dirty Harry," *Daily Variety*, December 22, 1971, p. 3.

2. Warner Bros., Press Releases, November 16, 1970 and December 12, 1970. (*Dirty Harry* Production File, MHL, AMPAS.)

3. Terrence Malick, John Milius, and H. J. Fink, *Dirty Harry* (draft not specified), November 17, 1970.

4. Eric Patterson, "Every Which Way But Lucid: The Critique of Authority in Clint Eastwood's Police Movies," *Journal of Popular Film and Television*, Fall 1982, p. 93.

5. *Ibid.*, p. 94.

6. Pauline Kael, "Saint Cop," *New Yorker*, January 15, 1972, p. 80.

7. *Ibid.*, p. 78.

8. Richard Combs, "8 Degrees of Separation: A Look at the Quiet Side of Dirty Harry and the New Wave Aspirations of Don Siegel," *Film Comment*, July–August 2002, p. 53.

9. Patterson, p. 96.

10. A. D. Murphy, "Dirty Harry," *Daily Variety*, December 22, 1971, p. 3.

11. Malick, Milius, and Fink, pp. 13, 110.

12. Kael, p. 79.

13. Rikke Schubart, "Passion and Acceleration: Generic Change in the Action Film," *Violence and American Cinema*, J. David Slocum, ed., New York: Routledge, 2001, p. 192.

14. Schubart, p. 193.

15. Vincent Canby, "Will Duke Survive 'McQ'?" *New York Times*, March 10, 1974, section 2, p. D5.

16. Warner Bros., *McQ* Pressbook, Program, 1974. (*McQ* Production File, MHL, AMPAS.)

17. Pauline Kael, "Nicholson's High," *New Yorker*, February 11, 1974, p. 96.

18. David Sutton, "John Wayne is 'McQ,'" *Motor Trend*, March 1974, pp. 54–56.

19. John H. Dorr, "Movie Review: Brannigan," *The Hollywood Reporter*, March 18, 1975, p. 6; A. D. Murphy, "Film Review: Brannigan," *Daily Variety*, March 18, 1975, p. 3.

20. This conversion also plays out overseas, in *Death Before Dishonor* (1987). After an American embassy in a fictional Middle Eastern country is attacked, Ambassador Virgil Morgan (Paul Winfield) chides the film's hero, U.S. Marine Gunnery Sergeant Joe "Gunny" Burns (Fred Dryer) for trying to intervene. Later, however, following the bombing of the embassy, Ambassador Morgan, blood-splattered and dirt-smeared, adopts a different attitude. "Sergeant, we have to get all of our people out of here," he tells Burns. "All these innocent people. What kind of savages would do this? What kind of sava—?... We can't wait, we have to get our people out of here.... So much blood everywhere. Why?" The question is not rhetorical; Morgan is genuinely asking, and deferring to, Burns. The filmmakers cut to Burns, who replies, "Maybe because it's so cheap here." The filmmakers then cut back to a silent Morgan, to show him processing this reflection.

21. Stanley Kauffmann, "The World's Most Popular Actor," *The New Republic*, August 10, 1974, p. 33.

22. Frank Rich, "Death Wish," *New Times*, August 23, 1974, page number omitted. (*Death Wish* Production File, MHL, AMPAS.)

23. John H. Dorr, "'Death Wish,'" *The Hollywood Reporter*, July 19, 1974, p. 7.

24. Anthony Burton, *Urban Terrorism: Theory, Practice, and Response*. London: Leo Cooper, Ltd., 1975, pp. 235–236.

25. Warner Bros., *Magnum Force* Pressbook, 1973, no page numbers. (*Magnum Force* Production File, MHL, AMPAS.)

26. Bridget Byrne, "Massive Firepower Perils Eastwood in 'Gauntlet,'" *Los Angeles Herald Examiner*, December 21, 1977, p. B6.

27. A. D. Murphy, "Black Sunday," *Daily Variety*, March 25, 1977, p. 3.

28. Arthur Knight, "Movie Reviews: Black Sunday," *The Hollywood Reporter*, March 25, 1977, p. 3.

29. "Lehman to Script Paramount's 'Sunday,'" *Daily Variety*, April 29, 1975, p. 1.

30. Christopher Sharrett, "The American Apocalypse: Scorsese's Taxi Driver," *Persistence of Vision*, Summer 1984, p. 56.

31. *Ibid.*, p. 56.

32. "Phillips Brings 'Taxi' Overseas," *The Hollywood Reporter*, May 11, 1976, pp. 26, 40.

33. A. D. Murphy, "Film Review: Taxi Driver," *Daily Variety*, February 4, 1976, p. 3.

34. Richard Corliss, "Movies: New York, New York," *New Times*, February 20, 1976, p. 58.

35. Arthur Knight, "Movie Review: *Taxi Driver*," *The Hollywood Reporter*, February 4, 1976, pp. 3, 10.

36. Sharrett, p. 57.

37. Richard Cuskelly, "Film Review: *Taxi Driver*—A Life on the Edge," *Los Angeles Herald Examiner*, February 22, 1976, p. E5.

38. David Boyd, "Prisoner of the Night," *Film Heritage*, Winter 1976–1977, p. 25

39. Sharrett, p. 61.

40. J. Hoberman, "Stand Up and Jeer," *Village Voice*, August 20, 1979, p. 50.

41. Ron Pennington, "Movie Review: *The Warriors*," *The Hollywood Reporter*, February 12, 1979, p. 4.

42. Jessie Berrett, "Rogue Cops and Bad Lieutenants," *Village Voice*, August 14, 2001, p. 130.

43. Pauline Kael, "Rumbling," *New Yorker*, March 5, 1979, p. 108. Hill's use of neon in The Warriors anticipates his use of it to frame Nick Nolte in his action-comedy *48 HRS.* (1982).

44. David Denby, "The Gangs All Here," *New York*, March 5, 1979, p. 104.

45. *Ibid.*

46. Paramount Pictures Corp., *The Warriors* Production Notes, 1979, p. 10.

47. Denby, p. 104.

48. Michael Sragow, "Presenting the New Wave Visigoths," *Los Angeles Herald Examiner*, February 13, 1979, p. B4.

49. *Variety*, May 5, 1982, p. 13.

Chapter 2: Automatons (60–95)

1. Richard Slotkin, *Gunfighter Nation: The Myth of the Frontier in Twentieth-Century America*. New York: HarperCollins, 1992, pp. 11–12.

2. Army Archerd, "Just for Variety," *Daily Variety*, February 1, 1980, p. 3.

3. Peter Rainer, "Stallone Stalks Terrorism," *Los Angeles Herald Examiner*, April 10, 1981, p. D20.

4. Todd McCarthy, "Hauer Moves to the 'Attack' in American Film Debut," *Daily Variety*, January 14, 1980, p. 12. In 1987, Hauer would star in *Wanted Dead or Alive*, as a bounty hunter tracking a terrorist—essentially an inversion of *Nighthawks*.

5. J. Harwood, "Film Reviews: *Nighthawks*," *Daily Variety*, April 6, 1981, p. 3.

6. The same strategy was used in print ads for *Nighthawks*'s October 16, 1983 television premiere. The viewer stares into a gun muzzle. Under Stallone's last name appears the line "In the biggest fight of his career." By then, three *Rocky* films had been released, as had *F.I.S.T.* (1978), *Victory* (1981), and *First Blood* (1982). (*TV Guide*, October 15, 1983, p. A72.)

7. Sheila Benson, "Life After Vietnam," *Los Angeles Times*, October 22, 1982, part VI, p. 12.

8. The special effects technician in charge of this stunt did not fare as well as the

character. At the Aculpuco location, Cliff Wenger, Jr., fell more than thirty feet to his death following the explosion. (Associated Press, "Special-Effects Man Dies," *Los Angeles Times*, December 1, 1984, part V, p. 9.)

9. *Variety*, October 14, 1981, pp. 74–75.

10. Yvonne Tasker, *Spectacular Bodies: Gender, Genre, and the Action Cinema*. London: Routledge, 1993, p. 78.

11. Pat H. Broeske, "Blood, Sweat, Dust," *Los Angeles Times Calendar*, October 11, 1987, p. 6; Richard Zoglin, "An Outbreak of Rambomania," *Time*, June 24, 1985, p. 73.

12. Broeske, p. 26.

13. Michael Wilmington, "Superhero Muscles: '*Rambo III*' Regenerates the Myth Machine," *Los Angeles Times*, May 25, 1988, part VI, p. 1.

14. Warner Bros., "Feature: Stallone's 'Cobra' is Film Noir of the '80s," 1986, p. 1. (*Cobra* Production File, MHL, AMPAS.)

15. Vincent Canby, "Inside 'Cobra' May Dwell a Pussycat," *New York Times*, June 1, 1986, section 2, p. H21.

16. Canby, p. H32.

17. Warner Bros., "Feature: Sylvester Stallone Drives Car As Unique as the Character He Portrays," 1986, p. 1. (*Cobra* Production File, MHL, AMPAS.)

18. William J. Palmer, *The Films of the Eighties: A Social History*. Carbondale, Ill.: Southern Illinois University Press, 1993, p. ix.

19. J. Hoberman, "Film: Planet of the Apes," *Village Voice*, June 10, 1986, p. 52.

20. *Ibid*.

21. Warner Bros., "Feature: Stallone Writes Extraordinary Weapons into 'Cobra' Script," 1986, p.1 (*Cobra* Production File, MHL, AMPAS.)

22. *Ibid*., p. 2.

23. *Ibid*., p. 2.

24. *Ibid*., p.1.

25. James Gibson, *Warrior Dreams: Violence and Manhood in Post-Vietnam America*. New York: Hill and Wang, 1994, p. 85.

26. The Beretta would become such an icon for the genre, it would even find its way into the hands of James Bond. In one of the most iconic shots from *License to Kill* (1989), Agent 007 (Timothy Dalton) wrenches back on the barrel of a Beretta, rather than his signature Walther PPK, before setting off to pursue a South American drug kingpin (Robert Davi, a supporting player in many of the era's action films). Of course, the plot of *License to Kill* resembles a 1980s action film more than it does an entry in the James Bond series: Bond goes rogue to avenge himself on the drug lord who attacks and leaves for dead his old friend (and sometimes partner), Felix Leiter.

27. Duane Byrge, "Film Review: 'Cobra,'" *The Hollywood Reporter*, May 27, 1986, p. 3.

28. Tasker, p. 124.

29. Gibson, p. 80.

30. "Drop it!" clearly sounds like it had been recorded later and added to the sound-

track. A possible implication of this is that prior to its addition, Cobra's knifing and then shooting the gunman was perceived as being too extreme; the line would have been added to suggest that Cobra was still in danger and, therefore, justified in following the knife with gunshots. The dialogue is not part of the final draft of the screenplay. (See Sylvester Stallone, *Cobra* Final Script, October 21, 1985 [with revisions through December 24, 1985], p. 9.)

31. Interview with Jackson DeGovia, July 27, 2003.

32. Gibson, p. 113.

33. *Ibid.*, pp. 112–113.

34. Tasker, p. 81.

35. *Ibid.*, p. 172.

36. *Ibid.*, p. 1.

37. Rikke Schubart, "Passion and Acceleration: Generic Change in the Action Film," *Violence and American Cinema*, J. David Slocum, ed. New York: Routledge, 2001, p. 192.

38. *Ibid.*, p. 193.

39. Michael Hirschorn, "The Most Important Film of the 80s," *Esquire*, September 1990, p. 118.

40. Charles Champlin, "Rewards of Reassurance: Big Votes, Large Grosses," *Los Angeles Times*, November 8, 1984, part VI, p. 1.

41. *Ibid.*

42. Marjorie Bilbow, "The Terminator," *Screen International*, December 22, 1984, p. 34.

43. Janet Maslin, "Monster Mash," *New York Times*, October 26, 1984, p. C19.

44. Kirk Ellis, "'Terminator' Tailor-Made Film to Put Schwarzenegger on Top," *The Hollywood Reporter*, October 26, 1984, pp. 3, 8.

45. Iain Johnstone, "The Mean Machine," *The Sunday Times* (London), January 13, 1985, p. 38.

46. Interview with Steven E. de Souza, August 1, 2003.

47. Richard Sparks, "Masculinity and Heroism in the Hollywood 'Blockbuster': The Culture Industry and Contemporary Images of Crime and Law Enforcement," *British Journal of Criminology*, vol. 36, no. 3, Special Issue, 1996, p. 357.

48. Twentieth Century Fox Film Corp., *Commando* Production Information, 1985, p. 9.

49. *Ibid.*, p. 8.

50. Interview with Steven E. de Souza, August 1, 2003.

51. Carolco Films, Inc., "The Rambo III Knife," *Rambo III* Production Notes, 1988, p. 47.

52. Twentieth Century Fox Film Corp., Press Release: "'Commando' Clothing Invading Department Stores," ca. September 1985, p. 1. (*Commando* Production File, MHL, AMPAS.)

53. *Ibid.*

54. *Ibid.*, p. 2.

55. *Long Beach Press-Telegram*, November 6, 1986, page number omitted. (*Commando* Production File, MHL, AMPAS.)

56. Coleco, Rambo action figure I.D. card, 1986.

57. John Voland, "Outtakes: The Rambo Report: Goin' for the Kids," *Los Angeles Times Calendar*, July 21, 1985, p. 26.

58. Paul Attanasio, "Beef Encounter: Schwarzenegger's Brutal 'Commando,'" *Washington Post*, October 4, 1985, p. E11.

59. Ibid.

60. Interview with Steven E. de Souza, August 1, 2003. De Souza made this remark five days before Schwarzenegger announced his candidacy for the governorship of California.

61. Twentieth Century Fox Film Corp., *Predator* Production Information, 1987, pp. 8, 9.

62. Ibid., pp. 9–10.

63. Martin A. Grove, "Hollywood Report," *The Hollywood Reporter*, February 27, 1987, p.8.

64. Twentieth Century Fox Film Corp., *Predator* Production Information, 1987, pp. 4–5.

65. Widely held to be the first film to cost over $100 million, *Terminator 2* trades much of the original's *film noir*–derived style, for a cooler, more polished hue. This is not surprising, as the *noir* aesthetic has often been a refuge for filmmakers striving for style on a restrictive budget. As comprehensive editions of the film have been issued on multiple laserdiscs and DVDs, there is little need to discuss its special effects in detail here. This brief note will do: According to *Terminator 2*'s publicity, Cameron turned to four sources to produce the film's 150 visual effects shots. Stan Winston, who created the Terminator in the first film, returned to create animatronic and special make-up effects; Industrial Light & Magic produced the computer-generated imagery; and Fantasy II Film Effects and 4-Ward Productions created miniature effects and opticals. (Tri-Star Pictures, *Terminator 2: Judgment Day* Production Information, 1991, p. 9.)

66. Jack Matthews, "Ultimately This Movie Is, on a Realistic Level, Just a Movie," *Los Angeles Times Calendar*, July 14, 1991, p. 22.

67. Caryn James, "A Warmer, Fuzzier Arnold," *New York Times*, July 14, 1991, section 2, p. 15.

Chapter 3: Enter the Fists (96–124)

1. B. J. Franklin, "How Chuck Gets His Films Kicks," *Screen International*, September 19, 1981, p. 35.

2. Fred Rappaport, "Violence Just for Kicks in 'Forced Vengeance,'" *Los Angeles Herald Examiner*, August 13, 1982, p. D20.

3. Todd McCarthy, "Film Review: 'Forced Vengeance,'" *Variety*, July 28, 1982, p. 20.

4. Janet Maslin, "Screen: Norris in 'Missing in Action,'" *New York Times*, November 17, 1984, p. 11.

5. David Chute, "Blood and Schlock: 'The Force' Is Not With Us," *Los Angeles Herald Examiner*, February 14, 1986, p. D8.

6. *Ibid.*

7. See Janet Maslin, "At the Movies: Cannon's Delta Force: An Act III Surprise," *New York Times*, February 14, 1986, p. C8.

8. Cannon Films, Inc., *The Delta Force*, Production Notes, 1986, p. 3.

9. Warner Bros., *Above the Law* Production Information, 1988, p. 9.; Patrick Goldstein, "Steven Seagal Gets a Shot at Stardom," *Los Angeles Times Calendar*, February 14, 1988, p. 5.

10. Goldstein, p. 5.

11. Ned Zeman, "Seagal Under Siege," *Vanity Fair*, October 2002, p. 239.

12. Vincent Canby, "'Above the Law,' a Detective's Battle," *New York Times*, April 4, 1988, p. C26.

13. Michael Wilmington, "'Above the Law' Not Above Lots of Violence," *Los Angeles Times*, April 8, 1988, part VI, p. 14.

14. See Cannon Films, Inc., "About the Players," *Kickboxer* Production Information, 1989, p. 2; Tri-Star Pictures, *Universal Soldier: The Return* Production Information, 1999, p. 9; and other studio biographies.

15. Mark Adams, "Kickboxer," *Variety*, August 30, 1989, p. 28.

16. Lawrence Grobel, "Playboy Interview: Jean-Claude Van Damme," *Playboy*, January 1995, p. 55. During this phase of Van Damme's career, he did not work with as many first time directors as he implies. Of the six films he headlined between 1988's *Bloodsport* and 1991's *Double Impact*, only *Kickboxer* (1989) and *Lionheart* (1990) were directed by first-time directors, and *Kickboxer* had two co-directors, only one of whom was a first-timer.

17. Cannon Films, Inc., *Bloodsport* Production Information, 1988, p. 1.

18. John Johnson, "Ninja Hero or Master Fake?" *Los Angeles Times* (Valley Edition), May 1, 1988, part II, pp. 4, 10.

19. *Ibid.*, pp. 4, 10.

20. *Ibid.*, p. 4.

21. Steve Pond, "The Kicking Man," *Us*, September 1991, p. 68.

22. Warner Bros., *Lethal Weapon* Production Information, 1987, p. 7.

23. According to Donner, who claims to idolize Westerns, "I tried to make it more like an old-fashioned western. . . . When I read this, I did a lot of research on the good old John Wayne films. In the fight at the end, between Mel Gibson and Gary Busey, John Wayne fans will recognize some punches right out of 'Red River.'" (Nina Darnton, "At the Movies," *New York Times*, April 3, 1987, p. C8.)

24. Warner Bros., *Lethal Weapon* Production Information, 1987, pp. 7–8.

25. Steven Schiff, "Mel Gibson—The Heartthrob Factor," *Vanity Fair*, July 1989, p. 128.

26. Christopher Ames, "Restoring the Black Man's Lethal Weapon: Race and Sexuality in Contemporary Cop Films," *Journal of Popular Film and Television*, Fall 1992, p. 52.

27. David Robb, "NAACP Gives Image Awards to 'Weapon,' Cites Danny Glover," *Variety*, December 23, 1987, p. 2.

28. Ames, p. 58. Also from 1988 is *Alien Nation*, in which James Caan and Mandy Patinkin portray the mismatched partners. The dynamic between the two fits the pattern Ames describes, if one sees the biological *otherness* of Patinkin's "Sam Francisco" as a more literal surrogate for race.

Chapter 4: Into the Jungle, Out of the Wasteland (125–158)

1. Michael Ventura, "Is 'The Road Warrior' The Last Fantasy?" *L.A. Weekly*, June 4–10, 1982, p. 20.

2. *Ibid.*

3. Warner Bros., *Mad Max Beyond Thunderdome* Production Information, 1985, p.10.

4. Warner Bros., *The Road Warrior* Production Information, 1982, p. 2.

5. Sheila Benson, "Action on a Full Tank in 'Warrior,'" *Los Angeles Times*, May 20, 1982, part VI, p. 1.

6. Andrew Sarris, "Of Heroes and Anti-Heroes," *Village Voice*, August 24, 1982, p. 43.

7. Mick Broderick, "Heroic Apocalypse: *Mad Max*, Mythology, and the Millennium," *Crisis Cinema: The Apocalyptic Idea in Postmodern Narrative*. Christopher Sharret, ed. Washington, D.C.: Maisonneuve Press, 1993, p. 252.

8. Cannon Films, Inc., *Cyborg* Production Information, 1989, p. 6.

9. Curiously, the film's Production Notes reveal that the plague followed a nuclear war that was waged seventy years earlier, but the film itself makes no such reference. (Columbia Pictures, "Creating Another World in 'Spacehunter,'" *Spacehunter: Adventures in the Forbidden Zone* Production Information, 1983, p. 1.)

10. Columbia Pictures, "Creating Another World in 'Spacehunter,'" *Spacehunter: Adventures in the Forbidden Zone* Production Information, 1983, p. 6.

11. Michael Ventura, "Uncommon Valor," *L.A. Weekly*, December 23–29, 1983, p. 75.

12. Elizabeth G. Traube, "Redeeming Images: The Wild Man Comes Home," *Persistence of Vision*, Summer 1986, p. 71.

13. *Ibid.*, p. 91.

14. *Monthly Film Bulletin* 54, no. 642, July 1987, pp. 209–210.

15. Catherine V. Scott, "Bound for Glory: The Hostage Crisis as Captivity Narrative in Iran," *International Studies Quarterly* 44, 2000, p. 177.

16. *Ibid.*, p. 179.

17. Teri Ritzer, "Par Promo Slogan Assists 'Uncommon' Box-Office Sleeper," *The Hollywood Reporter*, January 23, 1984, p. 28.

18. United Press International, "Private Raid on Laos Reported," *New York Times*, February 1, 1983, p. A2.

19. Paramount Pictures Corp., "Uncommon Valor Background Notes," 1983, p. 12.

20. Army Archerd, "Just for Variety," *Daily Variety*, June 17, 1983, p. 2.

21. Traube, p. 83.

22. The *Death Wish* franchise similarly exploits archaic weaponry. In the final sequence of *Death Wish 3* (1985), vigilante Paul Kersey uses a .30 caliber Browning machine gun from the Korean War against the gang members who have reduced the film's housing projects to lawless ruins. "Shoots some nice big holes in the sons-of-bitches," says the friend who gives Kersey the gun. The film also makes pointed reference to several other weapons, including the same antitank rocket launcher Harry Callahan uses in *The Enforcer*, and a .475 Wildey Magnum, which looks almost exactly like the .44 Automag used by Callahan in 1983's *Sudden Impact*. Kersey, extolling the virtues of the Wildey Magnum, explains the difference between his gun and Callahan's classic .44 Magnum: "a .44 Magnum is a pistol cartridge. A .475 Wildey Magnum is a shorter version of the African big game cartridge. Makes a real mess." (Incidentally, the .44 Magnum had been good enough for John Eastland, the vigilante of *The Exterminator*.) It is worth noting that as *Death Wish 3* progresses, the more violence Kersey lets loose, the more messianic he becomes to the community. Residents cheer him from their windows and ultimately form their own army, which, in the final sequence, plays a supporting role to Kersey's vigilante action.

23. Teri Ritzer, "Elias, Paramount Lauded for 'Uncommon' Viet Vet Homage," *The Hollywood Reporter*, December 27, 1983, p. 3.

24. Cannon Films, Inc., *Missing in Action 2: The Beginning* Production Notes, 1985, p. 5.

25. Dewey Gram, "The Politics of Machismo," *The Sunday Times* (London), July 7, 1985, p. 39.

26. Michael Ventura, "Missing in Action," *L.A. Weekly*, November 23–29, 1984, p. 79.

27. Stanley Kauffmann, "Now, About Rambo . . . ," *The New Republic*, July 1, 1985, p. 16.

28. Frank Sweeney, "What Mean Expendable? Myth, Ideology, and Meaning in *First Blood* and *Rambo*." *Journal of American Culture*, Fall 1999, pp. 63–64.

29. David Denby, "Blood Simple," *New York*, June 3, 1985, p. 72.

30. Douglas Kellner, "Films, Politics, and Ideology: Reflections on Hollywood Film in the Age of Reagan," *Velvet Light Trap*, Spring 1991, p. 12.

31. Richard Zoglin, "An Outbreak of Rambomania," *Time*, June 24, 1985, p. 72.

32. Scott, p. 180.

33. Sweeney, p. 65.

34. Carolco Films, Inc., "The Rambo III Knife," *Rambo III* Production Notes, 1988, pp. 47, 48. This echoes the comments of gun manufacturer J. Wildey Moore in Cannon's publicity material for *Death Wish 3*. Moore describes himself as "simply a traditionalist. Guns were the world's first-ever mass production industry and, as far as America is concerned, Connecticut is where they've always been made since the revolution of 1776. That's where Remington and Winchester and Colt set up shop. I'm just the latest in a long line." (The Cannon Group, Inc. *Death Wish 3* Production Notes, 1985, p. 5.)

35. Carolco Films, Inc., "Rambo's Bow," *Rambo III* Production Notes, 1988, pp. 48–49.

36. Andrew Cockburn, "Gun Crazy." *American Film*, December 1985, p. 51.

37. Ibid.

38. United Artists, Red Dawn Production Information, 1984, p. 2.

39. Interview with Jackson DeGovia, September 22, 2003.

40. United Artists, Red Dawn Production Information, 1984, p. 2.

41. David Denby, "The Nicaraguans Are Coming!" New York, August 20, 1984, p. 90.

42. David Chute, "Yankee Guerillas vs. Russkies in 'Red Dawn,'" Los Angeles Herald Examiner, August 10, 1984, p. D30.

43. Luke Y. Thompson, "Red Dawn," New Times (Los Angeles), Feb. 7, 2002, p. 40.

44. Ginger Varney, "Red Dawn," L.A. Weekly, August 10–16, 1984, p. 86.

45. Jan Cherubin, "A 'Red (White and Blue) Dawn,'" Los Angeles Herald Examiner, August 15, 1984, p. C1.

46. Ibid.

47. Interview with Jackson DeGovia, September 22, 2003.

48. Ibid.

49. Ibid.

50. J. Hoberman, "The Fascist Guns in the West," American Film, March 1986, pp. 45–46.

51. Ibid., p. 46.

52. J. Hoberman, "Getting Offensive: John Milius Sees Black and White," Village Voice, August 21, 1984, p. 54.

53. A fourth installment of the Mad Max series, Mad Max Fury Road was scheduled for release in summer 2004, with a budget of $104,000,000. This would have been the first Mad Max movie in nineteen years. Less than a week before the film's start date, however, production was suspended, offices were closed, and the sets were put into storage.

54. Cannon Films, Inc., Braddock: Missing in Action III Production Notes, 1988. p. 2.

55. Warner Bros., Mad Max Beyond Thunderdome Production Information, 1985, p. 4. The location for "The Crack in the Earth" was the Blue Mountains of New South Wales.

56. Ibid., p. 10. Fardon discovered this earthier, more organic solution after several failed experiments with artificial pigments.

57. Ibid., p. 9.

58. Marjorie Bilbow, "Mad Max Beyond Thunderdome," Screen International, September 28, 1985, p. 54.

59. Warner Bros., Mad Max Beyond Thunderdome Production Information, 1985, p. 12.

60. F. X. Feeney, "Roadie to the Max," L.A. Weekly, August 9, 1985, p. 49–50.

61. Ibid., p. 50.

Chapter 5: Blowing Up All Those Familiar Places (159–189)

1. Roderick Thorp, "Letter to the Editor," Creative Screenwriting, Fall 1996, p. 111.

2. Ibid.

3. 1,276 to be exact. By way of comparison, on Tuesday, July 3, 1990, Die Hard 2 was released on 1,828 screens for "previews;" jumped to 2,378 on Wednesday, July 4; and

settled in on 2,507 screens for its first weekend. (Joseph McBride, "'Die Hard 2' Lands at No. 1; 'Thunder' Shifts Into Second," *Daily Variety*, July 9, 1990, p. 46.)

4. Twentieth Century Fox Film Corp., *Die Hard* Audio/Visual Press Kit, 1988.

5. Todd McCarthy, "Film Reviews: Die Hard," *Daily Variety*, July 11, 1988, p. 26.

6. David Edelstein, "Dynamite Tonight," *Village Voice*, July 26, 1988, p. 57.

7. Twentieth Century Fox Film Corp., *Die Hard* Production Information, 1988, p. 40.

8. Interview with Jackson DeGovia, September 5, 2000.

9. In de Souza's second revised draft of the script, the Western's influence on the scene is even more overt. When McClane shoots Eddie, de Souza specifies an angle from behind McClane's widespread legs. "Eddie takes a gunshot, drops just like on 'Gunsmoke.'" (Jeb Stuart and Steven E. de Souza, *Die Hard*, Second Revised Draft, October 2, 1987, pp. 108–108A.)

10. Martin A. Grove, "Fox's 'Hard' Paces Summer Actioners," *The Hollywood Reporter*, August 9, 1988, p. 14.

11. Interview with Steven E. de Souza, January 2, 2004.

12. *Ibid.*

13. Ben Brantley, "A Lot of Blasts and Flames, But No Warmth," *New York Times*, June 16, 1996, p. H18.

14. Interview with Steven E. de Souza, August 1, 2003.

15. John H. Richardson, "In the Works," *Premiere*, September 1990, p. 27.

16. Jeffrey Wells, "'Die Hard 3' Blown Out of the Water by 'Siege,'" *Los Angeles Times*, November 1, 1992, p. 20.

17. Warner Bros., *Under Siege* Production Information, 1992, p. 3.

18. *Ibid.*, p. 4.

19. Duane Byrge, "Passenger 57," *The Hollywood Reporter*, November 6, 1992, p. 6.

20. Lisa Kennedy, "Reel to Reel," *Village Voice*, November 17, 1992, p. 102.

21. Beth Laski, "Fox High on 'Speed,'" *Variety*, June 20, 1994, p. 14.

22. Martin A. Grove, "'Decision' Maintains Altitude for WB, Silver," *The Hollywood Reporter*, March 27, 1996, p. 10.

23. Warner Bros., *Executive Decision* Production Information, 1996, p. 4.

24. Todd McCarthy, "Film Review: The Rock," *Daily Variety*, June 3, 1996, p. 2.

25. Peter Travers, "Bad Boys on Alcatraz," *Rolling Stone*, June 27, 1996, p. 62.

26. On the other end of the spectrum from *Lethal Weapon*, and more in keeping with *The Rock*, are *Total Recall* and *The Long Kiss Goodnight*. Both films feature train station shootouts that obliterate bystanders. In Paul Verhoeven's *Total Recall*, after crossfire kills a bystander, Quaid (Arnold Schwarzenegger) uses the man's body as a shield, subjecting the body to even further damage—after the bystander's blood has sprayed the camera lens. Furthering his getaway, Quaid then hurls the corpse at the villains. As if this were not enough, Verhoeven even cuts to an insert of the body being trampled. While this is a prime illustration of my point about the treatment of extras, the gruesomeness of this scene is mitigated—if only slightly—by the fact that Verhoe-

ven's use of gore is almost always inflected by a subversive, even comic book–like sense of humor. It may be difficult to isolate, perhaps, but it is certainly more sly and self-mocking than the tone of the depot raid in *The Rock*.

27. Janet Maslin, "Break Into Alcatraz? Why Not?" *New York Times*, June 7, 1996, p. C1.

28. Darrel L. Hope, "Upon This Rock . . ." *Venice*, June 1996, p. 33.

29. David Hochman, "Is Michael Bay the Devil?," *Entertainment Weekly*, July 19, 1998, p. 42.

30. Interview with Richard Francis-Bruce, September 17, 2003.

31. *Ibid.*

32. *Ibid.*

33. Joe Morgenstern, "Film: 'The Rock' and 'The Phantom,'" *Wall Street Journal*, June 7, 1996, p. A10.

34. Joe Morgenstern, "Film: Crash Landings," *Wall Street Journal*, June 6, 1997, p. A12.

35. Buena Vista Pictures Distribution, *Con Air* Production Information, 1997, p. 13.

36. Trevor Johnston, "Air Force One," *Time Out* (London), September 10, 1997, p. 79.

37. Several months after *Air Force One*'s release, the film's production company, Beacon Communications, responded to pressure from the Kazakhstani government and issued a press release acknowledging that the film had given the county a "bad rap," in the words of *The Hollywood Reporter*. According to the trade paper, "Beacon's Tom Bliss added, 'Kazakhstan is one of the most stable, democratic, and pro-Western of the former Soviet republics.'" (Stephen Galloway, "To Russia (Whoops! Kazakhstan) With Love," *The Hollywood Reporter*, November 20, 1997, p. 6.)

38. David Denby, "Commando in Chief," *New York*, August 4, 1997, p. 55.

39. Buena Vista International, *Air Force One* Production Information, 1997, pp. 5, 6.

40. This notion of gamesmanship characterizes some of this trend's most successful entries. *Speed*'s Jack Traven calls his contest with bomber Howard Payne "a game;" *Die Hard*, the progenitor of *Speed* and *Air Force One*, is likened to a "cat-and-mouse" game by Twentieth Century Fox publicists and to a video game by Steven E. de Souza; and there is also Simon (Jeremy Irons), the mad bomber/master thief of *Die Hard with a Vengeance*, who engages McClane in a literal game—one of "Simon Says." But the best articulation of this idea might come from—of all people—Steven Seagal, who describes *Under Siege* as being "like a chess game" where "there is a finite arena in which everything is played out; if you move one way, there are only so many ways your opponent can respond." (Twentieth Century Fox Film Corp., *Die Hard* Production Information, 1988, p. 2; interview with Steven E. de Souza, September 20, 2000; Warner Bros., *Under Siege* Production Information, 1992, p. 2.)

Chapter 6: Unmitigated Disasters (190–243)

1. Stephen Keane, *Disaster Movies: The Cinema of Catastrophe*, London: Wallflower Press, 2001, p. 6.

2. Following James Cameron's *The Abyss* (1989) and *Terminator 2* (1991), Steven Spiel-

berg's *Jurassic Park* (1993) is often held up as an early triumph for CGI. That same summer also saw Renny Harlin's *Cliffhanger*, an action movie in the *Die Hard* vein, for which Richard Edlund's Boss Studios, a leader in photochemical special effects, performed some of its earliest digital work. According to Edlund, his initial proposal called for 70 percent of the film's composites to be created optically, while the remaining 30 percent would be rendered digitally. "But between our bid . . . [and] the time we finished *Cliffhanger*, our composite ratio was exactly the opposite of what we'd proposed," Edlund says. "That's how quickly digital technology came into play." (Mark Cotta Vaz, "Boss Film Studios: End of an Era," *Cinefex* No. 73, March, 1998, p. 152.)

3. David Ansen, "Pick Your Disaster," *Newsweek*, February 17, 1997, p. 66. Ansen does not seem to appreciate the cyclical nature of the disaster film the way Keane does, nor does he seem to appreciate that this resurgence is part of an overall mid-1990s nostalgia for previously popular forms. During these years, Hollywood revived not only the disaster film, but also horror, the love story, and even the urban corruption dramas of the 1970s ("the Sidney Lumet genre," if you will), as well as a spate of older television programs, which were adapted to the big screen.

4. Interview with Jackson DeGovia, September 22, 2003.

5. Todd McCarthy, "Film Review: Independence Day," *Daily Variety*, July 1, 1996, p. 2.

6. "Summer Slate," *The Hollywood Reporter*, May 31, 1996, p. S11. To research the F-18 dogfights, the filmmakers sought the cooperation of the Israeli Defense Forces, which agreed to lend Fox training and promotional films depicting battles and maneuvers. (David Lipkin, "Israel Army Makes Fox's 'Day'," *The Hollywood Reporter*, August 15, 1995, p. I13.)

7. "Summer Slate," *The Hollywood Reporter*, May 31, 1996, p. S8.

8. James Wolcott, "Reborn on the Fourth of July," *New Yorker*, July 15, 1996, p. 80.

9. Steven Mikulan, "The Ray Guns of August," *L.A. Weekly*, July 19, 1996, p. 40.

10. Twentieth Century Fox Film Corp., *Independence Day* Production Information, 1996, p. 8.

11. See David Skal, *Screams of Reason: Mad Science and Popular Culture*, New York: W.W. Norton & Co., 1998, especially pp. 25–26, 206–209, and 215.

12. Duane Byrge, "'Independence' Days: $95 Mil," *The Hollywood Reporter*, July 8, 1996, p. 1 (inset).

13. Maria L. La Ganga, "Dole on Research Mission to the Movies," *Los Angeles Times*, July 30, 1996, p. A19. Endorsing *Independence Day* may well have purchased Dole political capital of a kind Clinton did not need. As La Ganga notes, the Republican candidate had previously alienated the Hollywood community with a speech he made in Los Angeles wherein he deemed popular culture "one of the greatest threats to American family values."

14. Patrick Goldstein, "Bring on the Debris," *Los Angeles Times Calendar*, May 12, 1996, p. 6.

15. Geoff King, "Spectacular Narratives: *Twister, Independence Day*, and Frontier Mythology in Contemporary Hollywood," *Journal of American Culture*, Spring 1999, p. 27.

16. Dan Cox, "'Scout's' Harris Set for Sly Pic," *Daily Variety*, August 24, 1995, p. 5; Colin Brown, "Daylight," *Screen International*, December 20, 1996, p. 26.

17. John Calhoun, "Disaster Italian Style," *TCI*, February, 1997, p. 41.

18. Universal Pictures, *Daylight* Production Information, 1996, p. 10. The set was built at Rome's Cinecitta Studios, where *Cliffhanger* had been shot from 1992 to 1993.

19. Universal Pictures, *Dante's Peak* Production Information, 1997, pp. 10–11.

20. Ibid., pp. 5, 11.

21. Twentieth Century Fox Film Corp., *Volcano* Production Notes, 1997, p. 5.

22. Ibid., p. 6.

23. Interview with Jackson DeGovia, September 22, 2003.

24. Twentieth Century Fox Film Corp., *The Siege* Production Notes, 1998, p. 4.

25. Peter Rainer, "Siege Mentality," *New York*, November 16, 1998, p. 62.

26. Julian E. Barnes, "Protesters Say a New Movie Likens Islam to Terrorism," *New York Times*, November 7, 1998, p. B3.

27. Bryan Pearson, "Bomb Threats Halt 'Siege,'" *Daily Variety*, January 14, 1999, p. 44. In an earlier edition, *Daily Variety* speculated that the August 1998 bombing of a South Africa Planet Hollywood franchise might have been motivated by the restaurant's symbolizing the West and by controversy surrounding *The Siege*, as Willis was a part owner of the chain. (Paul Karon, "H'wood on Alert," *Daily Variety*, August 26, 1998, pp. 1, 19.)

28. Interview with Peter Schindler, October 17, 2003.

29. Ibid.

30. Twentieth Century Fox Film Corp., *The Siege* Production Notes, 1998, p. 3; interview with Peter Schindler, October 17, 2003.

31. Interview with Peter Schindler, October 17, 2003.

32. See among others, National Commission on Terrorist Attacks, "The 9/11 Commission Report: Final Report of the National Commission on Terrorist Attacks Upon the United States (Authorized Edition)," New York: W.W. Norton, 2004, especially pp. 160–167, 226, 273–274, and 519.

33. Ryan Murphy, "Godzilla, Call Your Agent," *Los Angeles Times*, October 29, 1992, pp. F1, F10.

34. Interview with Robert Fried, February 22, 2006.

35. "TriStar adds 'Godzilla' to Slate," *Variety*, November 2, 1992, p.7.

36. Rex Weiner, "De Bont Helms New 'Godzilla,'" *Daily Variety*, July 8, 1994, p. 19; "Unwanted Import," *Los Angeles Times*, April 25, 1994, p. D1.

37. Interview with Robert Fried, February 22, 2006.

38. Donna Parker, "Monstrous Deal for De Bont: New 'Godzilla,'" *The Hollywood Reporter*," June 28, 1994, pp. 1, 57.

39. Dan Cox, "De Bont vs. Godzilla," *Daily Variety*, December 6, 1994, pp. 1, 33.

40. Michael J. Payne, "Godzilla: Man's Beast Friend," *Boxoffice*, October, 1997, p. 20.

41. Peter Travers, "Deconstructing Godzilla," *Rolling Stone*, June 25, 1998, p. 100.

42. David Denby, "Nobody Beats the Liz," *New York*, June 1, 1998, p. 96.

43. Anita M. Busch, "Bell Buoys Lizard," *Daily Variety*, May 16, 1997, p. 1.

44. Claudia Eller and James Bates, "Attack of the Killer Franchise," *Los Angeles Times*, November 7, 1997, p. D4.

45. Monica Roman, "Monster Promo for Sony," *Daily Variety*, February 10, 1998, p. 31.

46. Bruce Orwall, "Film Producers Play Cat and Mouse Game with Giant Lizard," *Wall Street Journal*, March 27, 1998, pp. A1, A8. Devlin would not identify the company, but people "familiar with the situation" did. A Fruit of the Loom spokeswoman declined to comment.

47. Monica Roman, "Monster Promo for Sony," *Daily Variety*, February 10, 1998, p. 31.

48. Peter Bart, "Scary Monsters," *GQ*, June 1998, p. 116.

49. Andrew Hindes, "Sony's Reptile Roars into Openings Record," *Daily Variety* May 14, 1998, p. 1

50. Dan Cox, "Gargantuan Release for 'Godzilla,'" *Variety*, April 13, 1998, p. 3.

51. Roger Cels, "Godzilla: Relatively Thin Lizard," *The Hollywood Reporter*, May 27, 1998, p. 4. TriStar's ad boasting the film's gross of $74,261,418 appears on the flipside, in a two-page spread (pp. 2–3).

52. Jeffrey Daniels, "Carmike Bitten by Weak Lizard," *The Hollywood Reporter*, May 29, 1998, pp. 1, 36.

53. Marla Matzer, "Toy Maker Feels Crush of 'Godzilla' in 3rd Quarter," *Los Angeles Times*, September 25, 1998, p. D1.

54. Interview with Robert Fried, February 22, 2006.

55. Lisa Bannon, "Summer Blues for Big-Budget Movies," *Wall Street Journal*, September 4, 1998, p. W14.

56. Interview with Robert Fried, February 22, 2006.

57. Chris Petrikin, "Five Scribes Get Pic Credit," *Daily Variety*, June 8, 1998, p. 5.

58. Todd McCarthy, "Noisy 'Armageddon' Plays 'Con' Game," *Variety*, June 19, 1998, p. 38.

59. Dennis Lim, "Film: Armageddon," *Village Voice*, July 7, 1998, p. 117.

60. Interview with Mark Goldblatt, October 7, 2003.

61. *Ibid.*

62. Bruce Orwall, "Here is How Disney Tries to Put the 'Event' Into the Event Film," *Wall Street Journal*, June 30, 1998, p. A1.

63. Interview with Oren Aviv, March 2, 2006.

64. Touchstone Pictures, *Armageddon* Production Information, 1998, p. 20.

65. Michael Bay, "Letter to the Editor," *Rolling Stone*, February 18, 1999, p. 10.

66. David Ansen and Corie Brown, "Demolition Man," *Newsweek*, July 6, 1998, p. 65.

67. Kent Jones, "Bay Watch," *Film Comment*, July–August, 2001, p. 29; David Hochman, "Is Michael Bay the Devil?," *Entertainment Weekly*, July 19, 1998, p. 42.

68. Joe Morgenstern, "'Film: Cosmic Crashes; Comic Cons," *Wall Street Journal*, July 1, 1998, p. A16.

69. Orwall, p. A6.

70. Ibid., p. A1.

71. Paramount Pictures, Press Release, 2003 (*The Core* Production File, MHL, AMPAS).

72. Mark Olsen, "Sci-fi, Yes, but Science Too," *Los Angeles Times*, March 28, 2003, p. D12.

73. Interview with John Rogers, February 27, 2006.

74. Ibid.

75. Joe Fordham, "Inner Space," *Cinefex*, July 2003, p. 27

76. Ibid., p. 33

77. Ibid., pp. 18, 31.

78. Todd McCarthy, "Timing is a 'Core' Issue for 'Actioner," *Variety*, March 24, 2003, p. 25.

79. Marc Graser and Dave McNary, "F/X Par's 'Core' Issue," *Daily Variety*, October 2, 2002, p. 3; Lorenza Munoz, "Paramount Cuts Trailer's Shuttle Scene," *Los Angeles Times*, February 4, 2003, p. D2.

80. Interview with John Rogers, February 27, 2006.

81. Cathy Dunkley and Tim Swanson, "Amiel Drives to 'Core,'" *Daily Variety*, September 21, 2001, p. 3.

82. Andrew C. Revkin, "When Manhattan Freezes Over," *New York Times*, May 23, 2004, p. AR22.

83. Tad Friend, "The Pictures: Wicked Again," *New Yorker*, May 24, 2004, p. 36.

84. Andrew C. Revkin, "NASA Curbs Comments on Ice Age Disaster Movie," *New York Times*, April 25, 2004, p. N16.

85. Ibid.

86. John Lippman, "Hollywood Report," *Wall Street Journal*, April 23, 2004, p. W6.

87. Gabriel Snyder, "Activists Plan to Make 'Day' Eye of the Storm," *Daily Variety*, May 24, 2004, p. 26

88. Ibid.

89. Gabriel Snyder, "Will Political Heat Fuel Boffo B.O. for 'Day'?" *Daily Variety*, April 28, 2004, p. 9.

90. Daniel Frankel, "The Day After Tomorrow," *Daily Variety*, January 11, 2005, p. A3. Karen Goulekas, Visual Effects Supervisor, "*The Day After Tomorrow*," 2004 (*The Day After Tomorrow* Production File, MHL, AMPAS).

91. Tad Friend, "The Pictures: Wicked Again," *New Yorker*, May 24, 2004, p. 36.

92. Twentieth Century Fox Film Corp. *The Day After Tomorrow* Production Information, 2004, p. 8.

93. Rachel Abramowitz, "Scared Silly," *Los Angeles Times*, May 8, 2005, p. E26.

94. Randy Dutra, Personal Appearance, "Hollywood Master Storytellers," Los Angeles, February 16, 2005.

95. Scott Foundas, "Starfire and Brimstone," *L.A. Weekly*, July 1, 2005, p. 76.

96. Abramowitz, p. E27.

97. Interview with Joanna Johnston, March 7, 2006.

98. *Ibid.*

99. Pablo Helman, Visual Effects Supervisor, "War of the Worlds," *War of the Worlds* Visual Effects Press Kit, 2005, p. 1. (*War of the Worlds* Production File, MHL, AMPAS.)

100. "Hollywood Soundtrack" *Variety*, August 27, 1986, p. 20.

101. Dennis Muren, Senior Visual Effects Supervisor, "War of the Worlds," *War of the Worlds* Visual Effects Press Kit, 2005, p. 1. (*War of the Worlds* Production File, MHL, AMPAS.)

102. Dennis Muren, Personal Appearance, "Hollywood Master Storytellers," Los Angeles, February 16, 2005.

103. Abramowitz, p. E27.

104. Nicole Sperling, "No July Fourth Par-Fox Battle as 'Four' Shift," *The Hollywood Reporter*, February 8, 2005, pp. 1, 88.

105. Gabriel Snyder, "Invaders Mint Mega Moolah," *Daily Variety*, July 5, 2005, p. 1; Rachel Abramowitz and John Horn, "Post-9/11 Anxieties Influence Spate of Films," *Los Angeles Times*, June 29, 2005, p. E1.

106. Ben Fritz, "Par's 'Mission': Impossible?," *Daily Variety*, May 8, 2006, p. 1.

107. "Clips: 'Wages of 'War,'" *The Hollywood Reporter*, August 2–8, 2005, p. 5.

108. "Trendspotting," *Screen International*, December 17, 2004, p. 53

109. Mark Schilling, "The Importance of Being Eastern," *Screen International*, June 24, 2005, p. 6.

110. *Ibid.*

111. Robert Mitchell, "War of the Worlds' Mission Impossible," *Screen International*, March 18, 2005, p. 4.

Chapter 7: Tomorrow's Heroes Today (244–285)

1. Christopher Probst, "Welcome to the Machine," *American Cinematographer*, April 1999, p. 33.

2. *Ibid.*

3. *Ibid.*, p. 70. Another of Manex's projects underscores the increasing conflation of visual effects and art direction in contemporary Hollywood films: the (literally) painterly landscapes of *What Dreams May Come* (1998) earned an Academy Award for Visual Effects; the same imagery earned production designer Eugenio Zanetti an Academy Award nomination and the Art Directors Guild Award for Excellence in Production Design.

4. Probst, p. 34.

5. Paramount Pictures, Inc. *Face/Off* Production Information, 1997, p. 9.

6. Kim Newman, "Rubber Reality," *Sight and Sound*, June, 1999, p. 9.

7. Orion Pictures Corp., *Robocop* Production Information, 1987, p. 2.

8. Jack Matthews, "The Marketing of a Mechanical Hero," *Los Angeles Times*, July 21, 1987, part VI, p. 1.

9. David Edelstein, "Heavy Metal," *Village Voice*, July 21, 1987, p. 58; J. Galbraith, "Film Review: Robocop," *Daily Variety*, July 8, 1987, p. 3.

10. Pauline Kael, "Siblings and Cyborgs," *New Yorker*, August 10, 1987, p. 72.

11. Interview with William Sandell, November 4, 2003.

12. Duane Byrge, "'Robocop'," *The Hollywood Reporter*, July 8, 1987, p. 37.

13. Interview with William Sandell, November 4, 2003.

14. *Ibid.*

15. Edelstein, p. 58.

16. Hank Werba, "De Laurentiis Back in Italy for 2 Features; May Coproduce Them with Cinecitta Studios," *Variety*, April 4, 1984, p. 7; Rod Granger, "De Laurentiis Preps '85's Summer Slate," *The Hollywood Reporter*, October 12, 1984, p. 28; "DEG Six-Pack Boasts Lynch's Next Pic, Plus Variety of Genres," *Variety*, May 6, 1987, p. 14.

17. Interview with William Sandell, November 4, 2003.

18. David Denby, "Jaw," *New York*, June 18, 1990, p. 68.

19. Donald Chase, "A Hard Man is Good to Film," *Entertainment Weekly*, June 8, 1990, p. 36.

20. Interview with William Sandell, November 4, 2003.

21. Nancy Griffin, "Mars Needs Arnold," *Premiere*, June 1990, p. 74.

22. James Wolcott, "Blood Test," *New Yorker*, August 23, 1993, pp. 64–65.

23. Richard Corliss, "One Dumb Summer," *Time*, June 30, 1997, p. 66.

24. Bernard Weinraub, "Ballets with Bullets," *New York Times*, February 22, 1996, p. C4.

25. Paramount Pictures, Inc., *Face/Off* Production Information, 1997, p. 8.

26. Amy Wu, "Wooing Hollywood," *Wall Street Journal*, August 6, 1997, p. A12; Weinraub, p. C4.

27. Andy Klein, "Hurray for Holly-Woo," *New Times* (Los Angeles), June 16, 1997, p. 74.

28. *Ibid.*

29. Josh Chetywind, "Once-Apathetic Studios Face Music of 'Face/Off,'" *The Hollywood Reporter*, June 30, 1997, p. 5. Ironically, after *Face/Off* had migrated from Warner Bros. to Paramount, the project's new studio very nearly made the film with *Demolition Man* director Marco Brambilla. (See Paul F. Young, "Brambilla 'Faces' Par Pic Pact," *Daily Variety*, April 27, 1995, p.1.)

30. These monitors are established showing footage of a deer. This could well be a reference to a film, directed by one of Woo's idols, Sam Peckinpah's *The Getaway* (1972), which opens with a deer outside the prison from which Steve McQueen will soon be released.

31. Chris Petrikin, "Par Digs Up Rights to Tomb Raider," *Daily Variety*, March 18, 1998, p. 5.

32. In 2002, Creative Artists Agency added the star of the bestselling Eidos Inter-

active game franchise to its list of clients in the hopes of brokering Lara Croft tie-ins with sports, apparel, consumer products, publishing, and a television series. (See Marc Graser, "H'wood's New Big Game Hunt," *Variety*, April 1, 2002, p. 13.)

33. Michael Fleming, "Dish: CD-Rom Books Deals," *Daily Variety*, August 15, 1994, p. 4.

34. John Gaudiosi, "Studio-to-Studio March of 'Doom' Film May End," *The Hollywood Reporter*, September 1, 2004, p. 6.

35. John Gaudiosi, "See More 'Evil': Sequel Planned," *The Hollywood Reporter*, March 7, 2002, p. 48.

36. Adam Dawtrey, "Euro 'Evil' Triumphs Around the Globe," *Variety*, July 29, 2002, p. 13.

37. Dave Kehr, "Into the Depths for a Thriller," *New York Times*, March 15, 2002, p. E29.

38. John Gaudiosi, "Anderson Presages 'Doom 3' Day," *The Hollywood Reporter*, March 21, 2005, p. 8; Michael Fleming and Ian Mohr, "Dimension Does Dracula," *Daily Variety*, November 8, 2005, p. 1.

39. Dark Horse's affinity for this "match up" format is not limited to *Aliens vs. Predator*. The company has also pit the Predator against Judge Dredd (1997), Tarzan (1996), and twice against Batman (1991–1992, 1994). The Aliens have also faced Judge Dredd (2003) and Batman (1997), as well as Superman (1995, 2002), and perhaps most ho-hummingly, Green Lantern (2000). For his part, Superman also battled the Terminator (2000), which had previously fought Robocop (1992) and which would fight both the Aliens and Predators (2000), both of which had fought Batman, who had once teamed up with Tarzan (1999), who would later join forces with Superman (2001–2002).

40. Jeffrey Wells, "Now, if Oliver Stone Can Find Roddy McDowall's Killer . . ." *Los Angeles Times Calendar*, October 24, 1993, p. 21.

41. Dennis Harvey, "Alien vs. Predator," *Daily Variety*, August 16, 2004, p. 14. The Motion Picture Association of America rated *Alien vs. Predator* PG-13 for "violence, language, horror images, slime, and gore."

42. John Horn, "Universal Takes a Risk with 'Riddick'," *Los Angeles Times*, June 14, 2004, p. E6.

43. Michael Fleming, "Diesel to Drive 'Riddick,'" *Daily Variety*, September 26, 2001, pp. 1, 13.

44. Michael Fleming, "Helmer Twohy Swings on U, Radar's 'Pitch'," *Daily Variety*, June 6, 2002, p. 50.

45. See David Rooney, "The Chronicles of Riddick," *Variety*, June 14, 2004, p. 36; Michael Rechtshaffen, "'Chronicles of Riddick,'" *The Hollywood Reporter*, June 11, 2004, p. 59; Manhola Dargis, "Planet of Lost Opportunity," *Los Angeles Times*, June 10, 2004, p. E4; Jessica Winter, "'The Chronicles of Riddick,'" *Time Out* (London), August 25, 2004, page number omitted.

46. Jody Duncan, "Man Made Monsters," *Cinefex*, July 2004, p.106.

47. Ibid.

48. Douglas Bankston, "Monster Hunter," American Cinematographer, May 2004, p. 38.

49. Duncan, p. 117.

50. Ibid., p. 123.

51. Ibid., p. 124.

52. Josef Adalain and Michael Fleming, "NBC's Monster Mash," Daily Varity, September 16, 2003, p. 1.

53. Gail Schiller, "Monster Marketing Mash for 'Van Helsing,'" The Hollywood Reporter, April 21, 2004, pp. 1, 8.

54. Gail Schiller, "NBA to Feature Reel Highlights," The Hollywood Reporter, April 20, 2004, pp. 4, 99.

55. Interview with Graham Leggat, February 26, 2006.

56. Jonathan Romney, "Everywhere and Nowhere," Sight and Sound, July 2003, p. 24.

Chapter 8: Excelsior! (286–331)

1. John Evan Frook and Kathleen O'Steen, "Fox X's Out Bidding Foes," Daily Variety, June 29, 1993, p. 20. Marvel sold the X-Men to Fox instead of rival studio Columbia Pictures, which Daily Variety reports had been "one of the most aggressive suitors for the property," and expected to secure the rights (Frook, p. 1.). Even though X-Men was to be put on Fox's "development fast track," nothing would come of the project until nearly the decade's end.

2. Andy Marx, "'Crow' Flies with Computer Aid," Variety, May 9, 1994, p. 202.

3. Crowvision, Inc., "From Print to Film: How The Crow Came to Fly," ca. 1994, p. 2. (The Crow Production File, MHL, AMPAS.)

4. Ibid., pp. 3–4.

5. Terrence Rafferty, "Superhero," New Yorker, May 23, 1994, pp. 93, 94.

6. David Denby, "Bird-Brained," New York, May 23, 1994, p. 72.

7. Rafferty, p. 93.

8. Denby, p. 72.

9. Peter Rainer, "'The Crow' Flies with Grim Glee," Los Angeles Times, May 11, 1994, pp. F1–F4.

10. Marc Graser, "Seven F/X Houses Will Share 'X-Men' Duties," Daily Variety, December 8, 1999, p. 5.

11. Ella Taylor, "Gods and Monsters," L.A. Weekly, June 20, 2003, p. 42.

12. Universal Pictures, Hulk Production Information, 2003, pp. 23–24.

13. Ron Magid, "Climbing the Walls," American Cinematographer, June 2002, p. 48.

14. Universal Pictures, Hulk Production Information, 2003, p. 28.

15. Jonathan Bing, "A Tangled Web," Variety, May 20, 2002, p. 5.

16. Michael A. Hiltzik, "Untangling the Web," Los Angeles Times Magazine, March 24, 2002, p. 35.

17. Bing, p. 5.

18. Meredith Amdur and Dade Hayes, "Not So Jolly Green Giant?," *Daily Variety*, June 24, 2003, p. 1.

19. Chris Patrikin, "U Has 'Hulk' Take a Seat," *Daily Variety*, March 2, 1998, p. 38.

20. Gina McIntyre, "'X-Men' to Rescue of Comic Pics," *The Hollywood Reporter*, July 20, 2000, p. 1.

21. *Ibid.*, p. 29.

22. Chris Gardner, "Punisher Pair," *The Hollywood Reporter*, March 29, 2004, p. 17.

23. *The Punisher* was still in post-production as of the writing of the first edition of *Action Speaks Louder*. At the time, my discussion of the film was based on early cuts of individual scenes. I have since revised that analysis based on the film's theatrical cut. Though excised from that version, I have elected to retain the *Rambo* reference.

24. David M. Halbfinger, "A Film Offers Buckets of Blood in White, Yellow, and Red," *New York Times*, March 31, 2005, p. B7.

25. Ken Tucker, "Rough Justice," *New York*, April 4, 2005, p. 69.

26. Anthony Lane, "Feelings," *New Yorker*, April 11, 2005, p. 86.

27. Michael Fleming, "'Batman' Captures Director," *Daily Variety*, January 28, 2002, pp. 1, 26.

28. Caryn James, "Cosmic Struggles of Cultural Proportions." *New York Times*, June 17, 2004. pp. B1, B8.

29. Interview with Oren Aviv, March 2, 2006.

30. *Ibid.*

31. *Ibid.*

32. John Gaudiosi, "'Incredibles' Flaunts its Game Appeal," *The Hollywood Reporter*, May 12, 2004, p. 40.

33. The ESRB's game ratings may be found at http://www.esrb.org/esrbratings_guide.asp and its symbols at http://www.esrb.org/esrbratings_guide.asp#sym.

34. R. Kinsey Lowe, "'V' is Popular in Size XXL," *Los Angeles Times*, March 20, 2006, p. E9. Adapting the grim, dystopian tale, the Wachowski brothers wrote their first draft of the screenplay in the mid-1990s, "long before Iraq and George Bush," as *Vanity Fair* notes. (Michael Wolff, "R for Revolution," *Vanity Fair*, February 2006, p. 104.)

35. J. Hoberman, "Anarchy in the U.K.," *The Village Voice*, March 15–21, 2006, p. 26.

36. *Ibid.*

37. Pamela McClintock, "WB's 'V' Veering to Later Date," *Daily Variety*, August 19, 2005, p. 2.

38. Although *V for Vendetta* debuted as the number one movie in America, its $26.1 million opening weekend was considered "solid," but also "a bit softer than many had hoped." (Ben Fritz, "Masked Man's Mixed Message," *Daily Variety*, March 20, 2006, p. 1.)

39. Matt Singer, "Pulp Friction," *Village Voice*, March 15, 2006, p. 28.

40. Warner Bros., *V for Vendetta* Production Information, 2006, p. 15.

41. Alan Moore, "Behind the Painted Smile," *V for Vendetta*, New York: DC Comics, 1988, p. 269.

Conclusion (332–344)

1. A. D. Murphy, "Dirty Harry," *Daily Variety*, December 22, 1971, p. 3; A. D. Murphy, "The Enforcer," *Daily Variety*, December 12, 1973, p. 2; A. D. Murphy, "The Enforcer," *Daily Variety*, December 22, 1976, p. 3; Todd McCarthy, "Sudden Impact," *Daily Variety*, December 6, 1983, p. 3; J. Harwood, "The Dead Pool," *Daily Variety*, July 13, 1988, p. 3.

2. Michael Fleming, "'Billy Jack' on Way Back," *Daily Variety*, March 5, 2002, p. 1.; Michael Fleming, "Dish: Billy Jack's Back," *Daily Variety*, April 9, 2002, p. 34.

3. Personal correspondence with Steven E. de Souza, March 10, 2006.

4. *Ibid.*; Chris Gardner, "Stewart Swims with 'Phantom'," *The Hollywood Reporter*, October 27, 2003, pp. 3, 15.

5. Hilary Roberts, "Commando Takes World By Storm," *Screen International*, May 3, 1986, p. 6.

6. Hilary Roberts, "Warner Bros. Breaks All-Time Billings Record," *Screen International*, December 13, 1986, p. 9.

7. Richard Natale, "Film's Foreign Affair," *Los Angeles Herald Examiner*, February 19, 1989, p. E1.

8. Leonard Klady, "Foreign B.O. Beckons," *Variety*, August 28, 1995, p. 79.

9. *Ibid.*

10. *Ibid.*; Hy Holinger, "Int'l Vs. Domestic B.O. Now a 50–50 Proposition," *The Hollywood Reporter*, November 9, 1996, p. 10.

11. Ben Fritz, "Par's 'Mission': Impossible?," *Daily Variety*, May 8, 2006, p. 1.

12. "Box Office Chart," *Variety*, December 23, 1996–January 5, 1997, p. 13.

13. Billy Kocian, "International News in Brief (Germany)," *The Hollywood Reporter*, March 19, 1985, p. 16.

14. David Hochman, "Is Michael Bay the Devil?," *Entertainment Weekly*, July 19, 1998, p. 42.

15. Ned Zemen and Kendall Hamilton, "Periscope: War & Peace," *Newsweek*, June 15, 1992, p. 8.

16. Brian Cochrane, "'Patriot' Games," *Variety*, April 14, 2003, p. 4.

17. Reuters, "'Rambo' Going Great Guns With Beirut Militiamen," *Los Angeles Times*, July 24, 1985, part VI, p. 5.

18. Mounir B. Abboud, "Pirated 'Rambo' Tapes Tell A Different Tale: WWII Replaces 'Nam," *Variety*, November 27, 1985, p. 156.

19. See Ruth Vasey, *The World According to Hollywood: 1918–1939*, Madison: University of Wisconsin Press, 1997 (particularly chapter 6).

20. Howard Fineman, "Last Action President," *Newsweek*, July 21, 1997, p. 67.

21. David Ansen, "Muffled Mission," *Newsweek*, June 5, 2000, p. 69.

22. Paul Sweeting with Scott Hettrick, "Grilled Swordfish a la Big Blue," *Video Business*, October 1, 2001, p. 37; Jennifer Netherby, "Video Vigor in Tough Times," *Video Journal*, September 24, 2001, pp. 1, 47. As Netherby reports, the week ending September 16, 2001 saw an overall increase in VHS and DVD rentals of 29.7 percent compared to the

same timeframe in 2000. Among the most popular categories rented were "comedies and terrorist tales."

23. Interview with Don Rosenberg, March 13, 2006.

24. Jeanine Basinger, *The World War II Combat Film: Anatomy of a Genre*, Middletown: Wesleyan University Press, 2003, p. 17.

25. Anthony Lane, "Winging It," *New Yorker*, June 9, 1997, p. 108.

Index

Page numbers in **bold** represent illustrations.

Gordon, Lawrence, 58, 160, 161, 165, 168, 169, 270, 345n

Guns. See Weapons

Hackman, Gene, 20, 133, 201

Haig, Alexander, 147

Hamilton, Linda, 78, 91, 203

Hard Target, 261

Hard to Kill, 109, **110,** 170

Hard Way, The, 77, 119, 342

Harlin, Renny, 166, 167, 340, 359n

Hauer, Rutger, 1, 61, 64, 349n

Hawks, Howard, 52

Hellboy, 332, 333

Hensleigh, Jonathan, 305–306, 307, 308

Hero and the Terror, 161

High Noon, 25–26, 34, 164, 165, 185, 194, 208, 254

Hill, Walter, 55, 56, 57, 58, 349n

Hindenburg, The, 190

Home video/DVD, 160, 267, 275, 276, 283, 284, 285, 287, 325, 332, 334, 338, 339–340, 341, 352n, 368–369n

Hooks, Kevin, 171

Hool, Lance, 101, 139

Hopkins, Stephen, 208

Horror films, x, xi, 5, 66, 127, 148, 239, 270, 273, 274, 280, 283–284, 288, 302, 334, 359n; and/in action films, 49, 53, 54, 55, 66, 85, 87, 90, 251, 267–268, 271, 275, 280; franchises, 127, 148, 274, 302

Hulk, 290, 295–296, 297, 298, 302–305, 316; comic book, 295, 320; unproduced version, 305

Incredibles, The, 314, 323–326, **327,** 328

Independence Day, 190, 191, 193–198, **195,** 201, 202, 215, 221–222, 225, 230, 231, 232, 234, 239, 243, 337, 341, 359n

Industrial settings, 1, 61–62, 76, 85–87, **86,** 91, 150, 163, 165, 169–170, 253, 262

Invasion U.S.A., 100, 102–104, 105, 304

Jackie Chan's First Strike, 261

Jackman, Hugh, 271, 279–280, **282,** 293

James Bond, 6, 97, 167, 179, 265, 280, 326, 332, 334, 335, 350n

Jovovich, Milla, 271

Judge Dredd, 132, 287; comic book character of, 365n

Kassar, Mario, 66, 340

Kickboxer, 111, 112, 114, 115, **117,** 353n

Kirby, Jack, 293, 295, 320

Kotcheff, Ted, 64, 133–134, 135

Lara Croft: Tomb Raider, 265– 266, 267; series/sequel to, 265, 266. See also Tomb Raider

Last Action Hero, 95, 119, 261, 342

Last Boy Scout, The, 119, 168, 342

Laughlin, Tom, 9, 11, 14, 334

League of Extraordinary Gentlemen, The, 332

Lee, Ang, 302, 303, 320, 340

Lee, Brandon, 287–288

Lee, Bruce, 96, 287

Lee, Stan, 293, 295, 320

Lester, Mark L., 81, 85, 90

Lethal Weapon, 1, 42, 63, 66, 72, 116, 118–119, **120,** 121, 122–123, 158, 180, 357n; character of "Martin Riggs," 116, 122, 123, 169, 306; series, 76, 77, 97, 119, 122, 159, 283

Lethal Weapon 2, 118, 121, 122, 123, 286, 336

Lethal Weapon 3, 122, 336, 342

Lethal Weapon 4, 261

Let's Get Harry, 133, 135

Li, Jet, 261

POW/MIA films, 6, 100–102, 125, 128, 131, 132–139, 140–144, 150–152, 154, 199, 307. *See also* Vietnam; *specific titles*

Predator, 1, 75, 81, 82, 83, 87–90, 92, 136, 161, 176, 182, 259, 274, 275, 277; series, 272, 273, 275. See also *Alien vs. Predator*

Predator 2, 131, 274, 275

Production design. *See* Art direction/ production design

Proyas, Alex, 287, 288, 306, 320

Punisher, The, 41, 287, 305–308, 314, 322, 325, 330, 333, 335, 367n; 1989 version, 287

Pyun, Albert, 114, 287

Race/ethnicity, 2, 7, 9, 10, 11, 14–15, 16, 17–19, 37, 46, 56, 58, 63–64, 80, 87, 88, 104, 112–113, 119, 121, 123, 136, 150, 166, 173, 196, 198, 208, 213, 322, 336, 343, 354n; surrogates for, 26, 29, 74, 78, 104, 354n. *See also* "Man Who Knows Indians, The"; Western, the, conventions and themes of

Raimi, Sam, 247, 297, 298, 299, 301, 302, 320

Rambo: character of, 64, 67, 73, 82 101, 102, 105, 118, 148, 165, 247, 308, 330, 367n; merchandising of, 84; series, 61, 72, 82, 89, 136, 158, 161, 270; weapons of, 65, 84, 128, 143–144. See also *First Blood; Rambo: First Blood Part II; Rambo III; Rambo IV*

Rambo: First Blood Part II, 1, 6, 41, 61, 64, 65–67, 69, 81, 82, 84, 105, 125, 137, 138, 139–140, **141**, 142–144, 146, 158, 159, 169, 202, 218, 277, 292, 334, 336, 338, 339–340

Rambo III, 64, 67–69, 83, 84, 161, 213, 336

Rambo IV, 65, 334

Reagan, Ronald, 60–61, 65, 71, 77, 78, 79, 93, 95, 125, 132, 138, 144, 147, 185, 192, 250, 333, 339

Red Dawn, 76, 134, 136, 144–150, **149**, 161, 238, 238–239, 339

Red Heat, 91, 119, 161, 336

Reeves, Keanu, 173, **175**, 245, 246, **249, 334**

Replacement Killers, The, 261

Resident Evil, 268, 270–272, 278, 280; game franchise, 268; series, 265

Ricochet, 32

Rio Bravo, 52, 72

Road Warrior, The, 78, 85, 125, 126–130, 151, 155–156, 158, 295; character of, 330; costumes of, 126–127; and depictions of technology, 126, 128, 136, 142; landscape of, 126, 144, 245; and mythic traditions, 128, 129–130, 131. See also *Mad Max Beyond Thunderdome*; Postapocalyptic films

Robocop, 1, 41, 44, 76, 79, 131, 244, 250–257, **255**, 258, 259, 260, 261, 278, 290, 309, 321, 344; character of, 247, 271, 280, 330, 365n; franchise, 135, 287

Robocop 2, 182

Rock, The (Dwayne Johnson), 267, **269**, 332

Rock, The, 116, 119, 160, 167, 171, 178–182, 183, 184, 186, 188, 220, 222, 223, 306, 324, 339, 357n, 358n

Rocky: films, 61, 65, 67, 82, 144, 334, 349n; character of, 73, 82

Rodriguez, Robert, 308, 309, 310, 311, 312, 320

Rogers, John, xiii, 226–227, 228, 296

Roth, Joe, 165, 176, 221, 224, 225

Roundtree, Richard, 14, 15, 16, 18, 97

Rumble in the Bronx, 261

About the Author

Eric Lichtenfeld has worked in many areas of the film industry, and his articles have appeared in film publications including *The Scenographer*, *Film Score Monthly*, and *Trace*, the journal of the Art Directors Guild. He has contributed features and commentaries to special edition DVDs of such films as *Predator*, *Die Hard*, and *Speed*, and has taught film studies at Loyola Marymount University.